The Color of Social Policy

Edited by King E. Davis & Tricia B. Bent-Goodley

With a foreword by the Honorable L. Douglas Wilder

Council on Social Work Education
Alexandria, VA

In the same series

Advancing Social Work Education

Confronting Oppression, Restoring Justice: From Policy Analysis to Social Action (2004), by Katherine van Wormer

Education for Multicultural Social Work Practice: Critical Viewpoints and Future Directions

Diversity Education for Social Justice: Mastering Teaching Skills (2003), by Dorothy Van Soest & Betty Garcia

Ethics Education in Social Work (2001), by Frederic G. Reamer

Copyright © 2004 Council on Social Work Education

All rights reserved. No part of this book may be reproduced or transmitted in any manner whatsoever without the prior written permission of the publisher.

Council on Social Work Education
1725 Duke Street, Suite 500
Alexandria, VA 22314-3457

Library of Congress Cataloging-in-Publication Data

The color of social policy / edited by King Davis and Tricia B. Bent-Goodley.
    p. cm. — (Advancing social work education)
Includes bibliographical references and index.
  ISBN 0-87293-111-0
  1. United States—Social policy. 2. Social service and race relations—United States.
3. Discrimination—Government policy—United States. 4. Minorities—Government policy—
United States. I. Davis, King E. II. Bent-Goodley, Tricia B. III. Series.
  HN65.C612 2004
  361.6'1'0973—dc22
                        2004001977

Printed in the United States of America

CONTENTS

Foreword

The multiple debates, televised presentations, and state-level primaries that form a major part of the events leading to a national presidential election reflect a crying need for more extensive public discussion on the differential impact of social policies on the American population—particularly people of color and the poor. Past, current, and proposed social polices raise numerous questions about their impact: How will changes in Social Security, Medicare, Temporary Assistance to Needy Families, Medicaid, State Children Health Insurance Programs, national health care, immigration, the minimum wage, court sentencing, child welfare, mental health, or education affect these groups? What have been the outcomes to date of these and related policies on various segments of the American population? What is the responsibility of government to determine, prevent, and reduce the adverse impact of its social polices? At the state and local level, anachronistic patterns of thought and approaches to policy making continue to lead us away from viable policy solutions that can meet the needs of our citizens. The results of federal, state, and local policies have often been disastrous—decreased interest in voting, massive loss of jobs, increased poverty, scores of uninsured citizens, increased health care costs, homelessness, unfair court sentencing, untreated illness, substandard housing, and a pervasive loss of hope. There is a clear need for new leadership but also a better understanding of what policies are needed for all Americans to live on an equal floor of opportunity and to have an equal stake in the country.

Professors King Davis and Tricia Bent-Goodley and their colleagues have skillfully entered the controversial public policy debate through the publication of this edited work. In this book, they raise questions concerning a wide range of policies and their impact on four historically disenfranchised groups—Africans, American Indians, Asians, and Latinos. In addition, their analyses give us important information about the history, values, concepts, and hypotheses that have found their way into the formulation of polices, with devastating effects on communities of color. The authors challenge the view that the dismal socioeconomic status of these populations is self-imposed. The authors also offer us viable prescriptions for changes in public policy.

These authors make clear that public policies are the mechanisms that bind, direct, as well as separate, the various populations and social classes in the United States. They show how policies are designed to underscore the fact that we are a nation guided by laws and not the whims, narrow values, or economic interests of a few men or a single social class. That is the promise and unique character of the America that I have worked to ensure throughout my 30-year-long career in public office. Our policies determine the distribution of and access to vital societal resources and to numerous opportunities that determine life chances and quality of life. Our policies are also instrumental in structuring the relationships between people within a society, as well as the relationship of the individual to society's array of institutions. Our written instruments of democracy promise fairness and equality to all citizens. However, some of the most intense debates historically have come about when race, gender, and social class characteristics have been included in the creation and implementation of our public policies and openly discriminate against some of our citizens. Although this discrimination was a reflection of widely held American values, it clearly contradicted the promises of the Constitution and the Bill of Rights. Once these personal characteristics became the focus of public policy, disenfranchised and dispossessed populations were forced to rely on the outcomes of legal suits brought before federal and state courts, wherever possible, to address their grievances. A key example of the interaction between these complex issues and legal strategies is found in America's long-standing policy of "separate but equal" public education. The resulting 1954 *Brown v. Board of Education of Topeka, Kansas* lawsuit and its eventual decision is an excellent example of the complex issues that are involved when social policy is used to disenfranchise people of color, or any population for that matter.

It has been close to 50 years since the momentous *Brown* decision was rendered by the Supreme Court. The factors that precipitated the 1954 *Brown* suit and the policy lessons we learned must be kept clearly in mind as we celebrate its 50th anniversary. This decision was an effort to eliminate federal and state policies that maintained racially segregated and unequal schools. The values, practices, and policies that gave rise to the *Brown* suit have an extensive history. Unquestionably, there has been much good since *Brown v. Board of Education of Topeka*. This is no time for cynicism or despair. But we need to keep the history of this legal decision in context.

When the First Continental Congress met in Philadelphia in 1774, it established as one of its goals "to wholly discontinue the slave trade" (First Continental Congress, 2004). But in codifying the laws of the new nation in 1787, the framers of the Constitution did not abolish slavery; they did an about face and wrote slavery into the law, declaring that each slave, for purposes of taxation and representation, would count as three-fifths of a person. In 1867, 2 years after the Civil War, Pennsylvania Congressman Thaddeus Stevens and Senator Charles Sumner of Massachusetts sought the seizure of slave holders' property and redistribution of the land to slaves as compensation for generations of unjust treatment (Stevens, 1867). It became known as "40 acres and a mule." Had this effort at reparations via redistribution of property succeeded, this would have been a true "reconstruction of the South." However, by 1877, the North pulled out its troops, and Reconstruction—which had already proven weak in many parts of the Deep South—collapsed.

Nowhere was the sharing of second-class citizenship based on adverse public policy more prominently displayed than by the dismal educational opportunities provided to people of color: African Americans, Native Americans, Chinese Americans, Japanese Americans, and Mexican Americans. The history of the nation, portrayed in the early colonization and subsequent legalization of slavery and displacement is replete with instances of making certain that those who were forced to live their lives in bondage, immigrants from certain countries, indigenous Native Americans, and Mexicans should never have the enlightening of their minds with formal education. Though this practice was eventually corrected by the federal courts in response to suits brought by African Americans, the problem of inferior quality of education and second-class citizenship still existed for decades.

In my home state of Virginia, it was a crime—and many other states had similar laws—for anyone to formally teach and educate Africans (Knight, 1953). Even after the Civil War and the period of Reconstruction, the "Black Codes," among other policies and practices, continued the suppression of acquiring equal access to education (Knight & Hall, 1951). Some years later in response to discriminatory education policies, the NAACP brought a suit called *Davis v. County School Board of Prince Edward County, Virginia* (1952). At the time of the filing of that suit, there was already litigation pending in Clarendon County, South Carolina. There were also two other cases in Kansas known as *Brown v. Board of Education of Topeka, Kansas*. All of these cases addressed the central policy of separate but equal education. That doctrine emanated from the U. S. Supreme Court case of *Plessy v. Ferguson* decided in 1898 (1896). This decision affirmed the separation of facilities such as schools, libraries, hospitals, and other tax-supported places of public accommodation. The Supreme Court consolidated these cases, which all came under the aegis and controlling legal authority of *Brown v. Board of Education of Topeka*. The decision of the court was rendered May 17, 1954. We are now 50 years since that historic decision and many are assessing where we, as a nation, have come. The authors in this book look far beyond the *Brown v. Board of Education* decision and include critical analyses of similar effects within the welfare, health, criminal justice, and mental health systems.

What has happened since the *Brown* decision and in related social welfare systems is what the authors of this new book analyze and evaluate. Their treatment of these issues fills a major gap in the social science literature. Federal and state government sanctions of the injustices of slavery, segregation, and racial hegemony are long past. However, the authors acknowledge that the effects of these policies are still being felt today in the lives of families and children and in the communities where they live. They outline for us the evolutionary changes that are needed to bring about the overdue promises of our Constitution—guaranteed to all citizens. They note that we can affect the direction of change by being clear in our vision and unified in how we want that evolution to occur. It will not happen by chance. There is no mathmatical progression that automatically comes about. These authors analyze and evaluate what has happened and what set of policies are needed to create and sustain social change. There are hard questions to be asked as to whether we have seen improvement in life chances and quality of life. A century and a quarter after slavery, a huge color chasm remains.

There has been and there is a color divide in this nation that reflects itself in our social policies and governmental practices. How we deal with that is the true question. The most visible signs of discrimination toward people of color ended in this country almost 140 years ago. The authors of this book conclude that the negative effects of public policy on people of color remain and await our efforts. However long it takes and whatever else must be done, we must continue to close the color divide. It is up to us, and the time for it to happen has always been the same. . . *it is now.*

L. Douglas Wilder, JD
Governor, Commonwealth of Virginia, 1990–1994

References

Brown v. Board of Education of Topeka, Kansas, 347 U.S. 483. (1954).

Davis v. County School Board of Prince Edward County. C. A. No. 1333 (E. D. Va. Decided March 7, 1952).

First Continental Congress. (2004). Articles of incorporation 1779. Retrieved January 30, 2004, from http://www.yale.edu/lawweb/avalon/contcong/10-20-74.htm

Knight, E. W. (1953). *A documentary history of education in the South before 1860*. Chapel Hill, NC: University of North Carolina Press.

Knight, E. W., & Hall, C. L. (1951). *Readings in American education history*. New York: Appleton.

Plessy v. Ferguson, 163 U.S. 537 (1896).

Stevens, T. (1867). The 1867 Slave Reparation Bill. H.R. 29, Sec. 4. U.S. House of Representatives.

Preface

Social policy plays a causative role in the development and maintenance of specific socioeconomic disparities that weaken the life chances and quality of life of people of color. However, the interdependent roles (causative, preventive, restorative, and rehabilitative) of social policy, in determining the life chances of people of color are not discussed frequently in social work literature or given adequate prominence in the curriculum. Even when the history of social welfare is presented, the role of these groups is often ignored or insufficiently represented. Rarely are complex social policy issues, theoretical perspectives, or change strategies—as viewed by social work scholars of color—found in the literature. Yet, social work scholars of color do offer differing perspectives of social policy, the impact of policy on people of color, and the resourcefulness of these populations to respond to injustice (Carlton-LaNey, 2001; DeHaymes, Kilty, & Segal, 2000; Schiele, 2000; Segal & Kilty, 1998).

In the title and content of their text on social policy analysis, Popple and Leighninger (1998) propose that the social work profession is historically and currently grounded, at least philosophically, in social welfare policy. More specifically, Jansson (1994) concludes that social work practice and education, more than other disciplines, must recognize the extent to which its identity, competency, professional status, and societal sanction are dependent on the intent, processes, content, and outcomes of American social policy. Popple and Leighninger's (1998) and Jansson's (1994) perspective that social policy is instrumental in creating and maintaining social work identity is supported by a number of other social work scholars. However, other authors (DiNitto, 2000; Ginsberg, 1998; Jansson, 1994) also conclude that the profession has not fulfilled the social policy opportunities and obligations inherent in its historical development and its current social justice ethos and mission. Schiele (2000) concludes that social work has failed to follow a more defined social policy path because of the nation's Eurocentric orientation, in which capitalistic demands for low-wage labor are congruent with the Protestant value of individual responsibility. Popple and Leighninger (2000) propose that social work's strategic choice to pursue a micro-practice, grounded in Freudian and Jungian theories that were congruent with the Protestant emphasis on individual responsibility, eliminated the need for social activism and greater involvement in policy practice.

The tenor and content of this somewhat philosophical argument about social policy in the literature raises several fundamental concerns that influenced our thinking about both the need for this book as well as decisions about its eventual structure, content, and writers. The first of these concerns centers around the question of whether the minimal involvement of social work as a discipline in social policy has resulted in a systemic loss of opportunity to change the status quo to the detriment of its clients and its own inveterate quest for an acceptable professional identity. The effort to maintain the status quo is reflected not only through social policy but also in such by-products as the maldistribution of wealth, access, and opportunities; oppression;

discrimination; and poverty (Conley, 1999). The need to increase the diversity of voices in the social policy arena is critical to addressing these issues.

Social workers are often perceived as those persons who enforce social policy as opposed to serving as advocates to change policies that negatively affect their clients. It is critical for the profession to take the lead in ensuring the rights and well being of those who often feel they have no voice. Distinctly positioned to digest the perspectives of the oppressed, social workers have a unique role in the policy process. Social workers can engage in grassroots mobilization through established client networks. Working in communities, social workers are at the pulse of cutting-edge issues and see the daily impact of long-term problems. Providing clinical services, social workers have first hand knowledge of how social policy influences the lives of individuals. People of color, and all groups, can be better served when social workers harness their power to create social change. It is the voices of people of color that often go unnoticed because of a lack of representation and a lack of perceived commonality of issues. Educating social workers to be more aware of the complexity of social policy in the lives of people of color and motivating them to make a difference can change negative perceptions of the social work profession and make a difference in the lives of those most vulnerable to the policy process. Beyond the profession's code of ethics and educational requirements by the Council on Social Work Education, social work educators should be motivated to present diverse policy perspectives and explore the inequity within the social policy arena if they are truly concerned about social and economic justice. In addition to the diverse perspectives on social policy represented in this book, the references in each chapter provide additional resources for expanding how social work students are educated.

Layout of the Book

We chose to focus on select topics as a beginning effort toward building the literature in this area. In that sense, the topic areas are not an exhaustive list but a beginning dialogue. It is our hope that this book will provide the impetus for additional publications in this area and enhanced action to address policy issues. Some topics, such as HIV and substance abuse, are critical to the well being of people of color but are not designated as separate chapters in this book. Acknowledging the significance of these and other issues, it is our hope that this book will serve as a catalyst for an increased dialogue among scholars and additional publications.

This book includes the ideas of seasoned and newly established scholars in an effort to represent a range of perspectives. An effort was also made to include scholars from diverse racial and ethnic backgrounds. This endeavor proved to be difficult despite contacting professional organizations of color and using listservs from social work organizations. In many ways, it speaks to the challenges of bringing diverse racial and ethnic groups together. Simultaneously, this publication bears witness to the commonality of social policy issues among people of color and the need to bring these groups together toward true collective empowerment.

The first part of the book presents discussions of topic areas reflected among diverse groups of color. The analysis represented in Part One attempts to assemble the commonality among people of color and illustrate the similar ways in which social policy affects these populations. Part Two provides case analyses that build on these broad areas by offering a series of narrow policy illustrations. This second part focuses on specific racial and ethnic populations' experiences with different policy areas. The seminal role of social policy in causing, maintaining, and expanding a plethora of disparities raises additional questions about the definition of social justice—a cardinal value in social work education—and the integrative strategies for including people of color in the process of policy development and change. We address these important issues in Part Three.

Chapters one and two provide a historical and a contemporary perspective of social policy, focusing on the unique experiences and circumstances of people of color. These chapters allow the reader to link key historical policy views to current policy issues and problems for each group of color, while highlighting the commonalities among the groups. Chapter three discusses the experiences of children of color in the child welfare system. Examining child welfare policy and its impact on children of color, this chapter provides the reader with clear implications of contemporary child welfare policy issues for social workers. Chapter four analyzes a range of policy issues connected to domestic violence among people of color as opposed to focusing on domestic violence as a criminal justice issue. The author offers both differences and similarities among groups of color warranting social advocacy and change. Chapter five explores the impact of Social Security reform on people of color, stressing the ways in which people of color are particularly vulnerable to changes in this area of social policy. The author provides illustrations for future action. Chapter six begins with an exaggerated vignette of a family's long-term interaction with the criminal justice system. The chapter explores critical criminal justice issues that include the different experiences of women, men, and youth. Chapter seven summarizes and examines the major findings of the Surgeon General's report on the linkages among ethnicity, race, and culture.

The second section of the book provides analyses of different policy issues related to particular groups of color. Chapter eight analyzes two key policies that have influenced the life chances of the Native American population. Chapter nine focuses on the health care challenges, barriers, and suggested change efforts for Latinos. The chapter includes a focus on Mexican Americans and indigenous health care solutions for this population. Chapter ten provides a much-needed analysis of the diverse experiences within the Pacific Islander population, as well as the discriminatory treatment experienced by Pacific Islander youth. Chapter eleven examines the impact of welfare reform on African Americans from a familial and community perspective. Connecting the historical experiences to the contemporary realities, this chapter illuminates the need for progressive family policy and a renewed sense of justice for poor families.

The final section of the book urges readers to examine the social justice implications of the inequity within the social policy arena and presents a charge for individual and social action. In chapter twelve, Barbara Solomon proposes that future social services must find a balance of perspectives and approaches to meet the needs of a diverse population of Americans. Chapter thirteen offers suggestions on how people of color can work together toward social change. Presenting common issues for concern and challenges to working together, this chapter provides organizing principles and motivations to unite against inequity and oppression. In the final chapter, the author seeks to link social work's historical interest in social justice to the level of interest in social policy.

Conclusion

We set out to raise and examine many of the issues that surround social policy, social work, and disparities from the standpoint of populations of color. Their perspectives on social policy are often discordant with the Anglo voices that represent the mainstream of intellectual thought on social policy. We believe that by presenting this focus on social policy and its effects, social work practice will be stronger, less inclined toward bifurcation in its methods, and more likely to move closer to the fulfillment of its historical policy roots and promise. Our intent was for social work educators and practitioners to incorporate more social policy emphasis in general in their work and more on the need to advocate for equity in policy processes and outcomes. For the groups of color represented in this book, social policy is a veritable key to life that should not be marked by a *laissez faire* approach from a profession grounded in and distinguished by its opportunities and obligations to change social policy.

King E. Davis

Tricia B. Bent-Goodley

References

Carlton-LaNey, I. B. (Ed.). (2001). *African American leadership: An empowerment tradition in social welfare history.* Washington, DC: NASW Press.

Conley, D. (1999). *Being black, living in the red: Race, wealth, and social policy in America.* Berkeley, CA: University of California Press.

DeHaymes, M. V., Kilty, K. M., & Segal, E. (Eds.). (2000). *Latino poverty in the new century: Inequities, challenges, and barriers.* New York: Haworth Press.

DiNitto, D. M. (2000). *Social welfare: Politics and public policy* (5th ed.). Boston: Allyn & Bacon.

Ginsberg, L. (1998). *Understanding social problems, policies, and programs.* Charleston, SC: University of South Carolina Press.

Jansson, B. S. (1994). *Social policy: From theory to policy practice* (2nd ed.). Pacific Grove, California: Brooks/Cole.

Popple, P. R., & Leighninger, L. (1998). *The policy-based profession: An introduction to social welfare policy for social workers.* Boston: Allyn & Bacon.

Schiele, J. H. (2000). *Human services and the Afrocentric paradigm.* New York: Haworth Press.

Segal, E. A., & Kilty, K. M. (Eds.). (1998). *Pressing issues of inequality and American Indian communities.* New York: Haworth Press.

Acknowledgements

We would like to thank the Council on Social Work Education (CSWE) Publications and Media Commission for supporting this book, particularly Ruth McRoy, and the reviewers who provided invaluable feedback. The CSWE editorial staff were extraordinarily professional, supportive, and highly detailed with the publication of the book. We thank them, particularly Michael Monti, Vic Fanney, and John Cooney. We appreciate the cooperation of each contributing author in making the book strong and diverse in scope.

From King Davis

Successful completion of an edited book is truly a most collaborative effort. In some ways the process reminds me of what occurs in an orchestra when the performance requires and reflects the contributions of so many individual artists over an extended period to make it work successfully. I am particularly grateful to my coeditor, Tricia Bent-Goodley, for her ability to persevere with and focus on this effort while going through the birth of her two sons and preparing for tenure. Other individuals also helped at varying points along the way. I appreciate the continuous support from Barbara White, dean of the School of Social Work at the University of Texas at Austin; Toni Johnson of the University of Tennessee at Memphis, who was very helpful while completing her dissertation at Austin; Rita Takahashi, University of San Francisco, for her assistance in reading and commenting on numerous changes in our first chapter; Kim Faris and Tara Earl, doctoral students at Austin who helped tremendously with the extensive bibliographies; Lynda Frost of the Hogg Foundation for Mental Health for her assistance in locating vintage legal citations; and Allison Supancic and Ellen Moutous-Lee, Hogg Regional Foundation Library, for their assistance. I am deeply indebted to David Gil of Brandeis University for his willingness to share his intellectual perspectives on the importance of social policy over many years.

From Tricia Bent-Goodley

I thank the Creator for allowing our voices to be heard through this medium and for giving each of us the opportunity to share our diverse messages. I would like to thank my mentors who continue to motivate me to strive for excellence—Iris Carlton-LaNey, Alma Jones Norment, and Carol Spigner. I am eternally grateful to King Davis for asking me to share in this adventure. He provides a model, both professionally and personally, that I cherish daily. I am grateful to my friends and family for understanding the solitude required to produce scholarship. Thanks to my close friend, Lauren Francis, for her feedback on a number of these chapters. My mother is the reason I am able to do all that I do. I continue to marvel at how my children motivate me in ways that only they can. Many thanks to my husband for believing in me and always pushing me forward. Loving you warms my heart and invigorates my spirit.

PART ONE. Topic Areas

— Indigenous Tribal Populations and Africans in America

— Mexicans, Chinese, and Japanese in America

— Child Welfare

— Policy Implications of Domestic Violence

— Social Security Reform

— Racial Disparities in the Criminal Justice System

— Mental Health Policy

Chapter One

The Color of Social Policy: Oppression of Indigenous Tribal Populations and Africans in America

King E. Davis and Ethleen Iron Cloud-Two Dogs

The majority of current and past social problems are the results of current and prior public policies. — David Gil

American public policies have historically created, maintained, and exacerbated socioeconomic inequality along racial, ethnic, and social class lines. The major effect of hundreds of interlocking public policies has been to deny certain groups access—not only to a livable share of the nation's abundant wealth, but also to the political power to change the circumstances of their lives. This approach to American public policy has created antagonistic, hostile, hyphenated, and competitive American groups separated from each other not just by color but by life chances: how they are born, their condition at birth, whether they or their mothers survive the birth, whether their parents have an opportunity to learn, where they live, whether they work, what they eat, and the time and circumstances in which they die. The promise of American democracy, this magnificent ideal, has been harmed by such narrowly constructed policies.

It is important for social work educators and students to use this historical context to increase our understanding of the significance of color in the formulation and implementation of contemporary American public policies and services. Social work is increasingly viewed as a policy-based profession (Popple & Leighninger, 2000) with an ethical mandate to change the underlying conditions that lead to and sustain social inequity (National Association of Social Workers, 1996). The policy history covered in this chapter helps social work to place current societal tension in context. This context illustrates the historical failure of key social institutions to provide equal protection and access to all American citizens. Two parallel hypotheses guide this chapter's discussion of the color of American social policy. First, it is hypothesized that there is a causal connection between the current lower socioeconomic status of populations of color and the presence of these historical themes and strategies in public policy. Second, as there are decreases in the presence of these strategies in public policy, the socioeconomic status and condition of populations of color improves and starts to approximate that of their fellow citizens.

The substantive progress that has occurred in the socioeconomic fortunes of many oppressed populations in the past decade can be attributed to changes in the content of public policy. Clearly, social work education must address public policy as a major vehicle for bringing about change in the condition of people of color.

In this first chapter, the focus is on two populations of color: indigenous tribal nations and Africans in America. Latinos (Mexicans) and Asians (Chinese and Japanese) in America are discussed in the second chapter.[1] The order of presentation is based on the degree and frequency of policy development associated with each group between 1600 and 1900. The greatest number of public policies were drafted and implemented to govern interactions between British Americans and indigenous tribal populations (Vaughan & Rosen, 1997). Numerous policies were crafted following the importation of Africans into colonial America. Until the end of the Mexican American War in 1848, American public policy contained few references to the Mexican population. American public policy focused on the Chinese population in the second half of the 19th century and then toward the Japanese once severe restrictions were placed on the immigration of the Chinese. For each group discussed in this and the second chapter, the intent is to provide an overview of the history of relevant public policy and then examine a more contemporary judicial or legislative case that juxtaposes some of the core historical policy issues and principles related to the Naturalization Act of 1790. The major assumption made in these two chapters and the historical approach taken herein is that there is a causative linkage between the policy formulation process and the current dilemmas faced by people of color in the United States. Furthermore, it is assumed that the long-term effectiveness of social work interventions with these populations is dependent on the extent to which the interventions change both the traditional policy making processes as well as the content of American policies.

The Naturalization Act of 1790: The Key to American Policy Toward People of Color

The colonization of the North America continent by European explorers after their accidental "discovery" of the land in the 15th century and the subsequent competition between colonial powers to find a permanent labor class raised a series of complex issues (ethical, legal, psychological, political, spiritual, and economic). These issues would lead eventually to armed conflict and the post–Revolutionary War formulation of public policies that favored the victorious Ameri-

---

[1]The terms America's Indians, Africans in America, Asians in America, and Mexicans in America are used throughout the chapter as an accurate way to portray the absence of legal and social standing, citizenship, naturalization, and voting rights of the majority of these populations until well into the 20th century. This characterization is based on the Supreme Court's decision in *Scott v. Sanford* (1856). In that decision, the Supreme Court found that persons "of the African race, whose ancestors were brought to this country and sold as slaves, is not a citizen within the meaning of the Constitution of the United States." Furthermore, the Court found that, "When the constitution was adopted, they were not regarded in any of the states as members of the community which constituted the states, and were not numbered among its people or citizens" (*Scott v. Sanford*, 1856, p. 1). Based on the Court's decision, the legal way to describe these populations prior to the extension of citizenship was as Africans, Chinese, Indians, Japanese, or Mexicans in America. Once citizenship and its requisite rights were obtained, these legally descriptive labels could be eliminated. In some instances, groups (Africans) lacked citizenship in any country.

cans. Post-war British-American policies were based on an admixture of strict Christian/Protestant religious dogma, keen economic interests in accumulating wealth, remnants of the Elizabethan Poor Laws, an emerging nationalistic ideology (grounded in notions of racial superiority), and individualistic legal precepts (private property) that had fermented in British society for centuries (Balz, 1998). The extent of this lineal thinking is reflected in the writings of John Jay (Rossiter, 1999) in the *Federalist Papers*, the intellectual precursor of the Constitution and subsequent public policies in the United States:

> With equal pleasure I have taken notice that Providence has been pleased to give this one connected country to one united people—a people descended from the same ancestors, speaking the same language, professing the same religion, attached to the same principles of government, very similar in their manners and customs, and who by their joint counsels, arms and efforts, fighting side by side throughout a long and bloody war have nobly established general liberty and independence. This country and this people seem to have been made for each other. (p.6)

In John Jay's worldview, limited consideration needed to have been given in British American thought or documents to the culture, existing laws, economic interests or safety of indigenous tribal populations in the creation of these emerging American public policies or the nascent republic (Bothwell, 2002). Additionally, there was no room for compromise or adoption of the policies from any of the indigenous tribal populations since European colonialists judged their policies, language, governance, values, religions, and indeed whole civilizations (but not their assets and resources), as inferior (Berkhofer, 1979). The British-American conceptualization of indigenous tribal populations as inferior and the strong belief that Christian providence yielded Europeans a religious and national manifest to conquer and convert tribal members to Christianity led to long-term struggles (racial, legal, economic, psychological, and political). These struggles continue into the 21st century (*Cobell v. Babbitt*, 1999; Guinier & Torres, 2002). The focus of many of these struggles is the aftermath of hundreds of adverse British-American policies on the quality of life of indigenous tribal nations, other people of color, and their cultures and assets. The intellectual basis of these contemporary policy disparities is discussed in this chapter, while the remaining chapters in this book outline and discuss the disparities in child welfare, Social Security, corrections, health, public welfare, and mental health that confront social work.

A major proportion of the earliest British-American policies toward indigenous tribal nations were based on the disingenuous "Doctrine of Discovery in the 16th century that gave legal title to the newly discovered lands to the discovering nation" (EchoHawk, 1999, p.1), with minimal recognition in British law or religion of the rights of the indigenous inhabitants (McAuliffe, 2001). Although states and individuals sought to use this same doctrine to acquire valuable tribal land, the Supreme Court held that only the federal government had the power to render as invalid real property claims by indigenous tribes (McAuliff, 2001).

Dominance and control of this new arable land and its vast natural resources was seen by the Europeans as requiring policies that would structure competition and distribution of private and public ownership rights (Berkofer, 1979; McAuliff, 2001). Part of the overt interest in acquiring real property was its long-term potential for increasing wealth and political power. However, the covert interest was survival (Davis, 2003). Since only landholders were considered worthy of citizenship, voting, and holding public office, the demand for real estate, by whatever means, was intoxicating. However, successful competition for economic and political dominance could not be accomplished by any European nation without creating a semblance of balance between Europe's quest for dominance and the rights of the indigenous tribal populations that had occupied the arable land and held natural claim to its resources centuries before European expansion. A significant issue that influenced the strategies and policies created was the different perspectives, values, and symbolism attached to land and minerals by the Europeans and the indigenous populations.

John Jay's 1789 perspective in the *Federalist Papers* (Rossiter, 1999) confirms that the balance sought, and deemed providential in origin, favored the newly emerging federal government and citizens of the American republic at the considerable long-term expense of the indigenous nations and their tribal populations. British-American public policies converted once free and independent tribal populations to wards dependent on federal government policies by 1910 (Bothwell, 2002).

The seminal issue that confronted the Continental Congress in 1787 was to develop the legislative parameters that defined American citizenship. Separation from Britain and its dominant social institutions not only required a new form of government but also a clear set of prerequisites for participation in America's emerging social, political, educational, and economic institutions (Foner, 2001; Joshi, 1999; Naturalization Act, 1790; Randall, 2002b; Ziegler, 1958). The definition of American identity was inextricably tied to the tripartite concepts of citizenship, voting rights, and private property. Power to declare American citizenship was delegated to the federal government, but state governments retained the power to decide the prerequisites for the right to vote in elections and to own property. The power retained by the states and the broad way that it was interpreted allowed states to neutralize the intent of congressional amendments to the Constitution that were seen as philosophically antagonistic to the states. Those groups that lacked recognition as citizens, voters, or property owners were unable to control their own economic destiny or share in constitutional guarantees, rights, or privileges. The bulk of indigenous tribal populations and the Africans and Mexicans in America were prevented by state governments from participation in the basic social, political, and economic institutions of America that would determine their current and future socioeconomic status. The Chinese and Japanese would be subject to the same restrictions in the 19th century. As a result, each of these groups and their descendents inherited a higher-than-expected risk of poverty and related problems caused by a lack of access to wealth-producing social institutions in a capital-based society (Conley, 1999). Works by Anderson (1994), Conley (1999), and Sherraden (1991) suggest that these restrictions on wealth and asset accumulation have long-term implications for populations of color. Sherraden (1991) proposes an asset-focused strategy as a means of reducing poverty in the 21st century in these groups.

Efforts to define the legislative parameters of citizenship and voting rights were reflected in a series of naturalization acts passed by the Continental Congress and reinforced by decisions of the U.S. Supreme Court. The first of these acts was passed in 1790, with subsequent acts passed, repealing or amending each previous one, in 1795 and in 1798. The first of the naturalization acts (1790) restricted the privilege of citizenship to free Whites (Foner, 2001). Foner notes that this race-based prerequisite resulted not only in a denial of citizenship to indigenous tribal members and Africans in America but also restricted citizenship for White immigrants up through 1870. By 1795, the United States Congress repealed the 1790 act. However, the new law (Naturalization Act, 1795) greatly reinforced the nexus between race, free status, and the privileges of citizenship. Only free White men could become citizens of the United States with the right to vote in federal elections. The newly passed (1795) version of the naturalization act consisted of four related sections that specified the eligibility prerequisites for a person (alien) to become a citizen of the United States. The first two sections of the act outlined the prerequisites as these applied to adults, while the third section outlined the conditions under which minors could become naturalized citizens.

The naturalization acts passed in 1790 and 1795 were constructed on a number of philosophical principles and concepts that reinforced the distribution and concentration of political and economic power by race within the society at that time. However, a second principle in the 1795 act connected citizenship, even for Whites, to status as a free or enslaved person. A third principle was reflected in the requirement that the applicant must make a declaration renouncing any prior allegiance to a foreign power or government, followed by a similar declaration of allegiance to the United States Constitution and related laws. The final principle articulated in the acts was the demand that the applicant yield any official titles or connections to nobility. The 1795 act also placed an emphasis on the length of residency of the individual in the United States and the specific states in which the petition for citizenship was made.

In 1798, the Naturalization Act of 1795 was repealed and replaced by a new statute (Naturalization Act, 1798). However, the newer act did not change the fundamental racial principles and assumptions of either of the two priora acts. The 1798 act did, however, increase the number of years of residency required to qualify for citizenship from 5 to 14 and ensured that no one could acquire citizenship if at the time of application the United States was at war with their country of origin.

Implementation of the Naturalization Act of 1798 not only reflected the racial views held relative to citizenship but also the racially narrow and gender-dominated process of how public policy was formulated in the United States. What was clear in the declaration of naturalization was that the content of public policy was resolutely dependent on the race and gender of the policymaker. In 1798, no persons of color or women were permitted to participate in developing public policy. African men were not given the federal right to vote until 1870 and women of all races were not permitted voting rights at the federal level until 1920. The long-term monopolization of the legislative process by a single race and gender raises exceptionally pointed questions about the fundamental flaws in U.S. democracy, as well as the contradictions between its basic principles and the process of implementation at the state and judicial levels for populations of color. What was so important in this public policy was its direct use and justification of race, gender, and social class as the basis for determining access to vital societal institutions. The naturalization acts clearly established these principles as the basis of America's most cherished public policies and also gave rise to a monopolizing political process that guaranteed that a single socioeconomic class and a single gender would continue to determine the content and direction of public policy throughout the 20th century.

The complex interplay of values, principles, and philosophies in the various naturalization acts caused and exacerbated fractious relationships between Europeans and the indigenous tribal populations in America. They became the morally questionable templates for future policies to structure relationships and respond to disputes between European and African, Asian, and Mexican populations throughout most of the 20th century. A number of overlapping themes (points of tension) and status-maintaining strategies, connected to the naturalization acts, were at the center of conflict and routinely included in subsequent American policies. These themes and strategies established an environment of racial, gender, and class privilege as key ideas in much of American public policy from the 18th to the 21st century.

American Public Policy Toward Indigenous Tribal Populations

While the British Crown controlled the content of many laws in the American colonies, colonial governments sought to control local issues related to indigenous tribes: enslavement, war, Christian conversion, intermarriage, citizenship, holding of political office, voting rights, prosecution for crimes, protection under the law, and the establishment of reservations (Joshi, 1999; Randall, 2002a; Vaughan & Rosen, 1997). Vaughan and Rosen (1997) identify by state or colony the hundreds of policies created in the British colonial period between 1607 and 1789.

Before the formulation of the American Constitution, relations between indigenous tribal populations and the British colonies were constrained by a series of treaties and agreements that focused on land, trade, and the control of violence. McLemore and Romo (1998) note that by the end of the 17th century, colonial policies provided just three narrow options for the indigenous tribal populations: give up rights of ownership to their lands; assimilate as much of British culture as possible and remain under colonial control; or, if neither of these two options were satisfactory, be "annihilated or forcibly removed to reservations" (see chapter eight in this volume).

Later policies granted citizenship rights to indigenous tribal members, but enumerable other policy issues were marked by continued acrimonious conflicts. These conflicts were over definitions of the concept of sovereignty, acceptable levels of economic development rights, payments from the federal government for land illegally taken, the role of the Bureau of Indian Affairs, and the failure of the U.S. government to carry out treaties and agreements or provide adequate stewardship of financial annuities set aside for the benefit of indigenous tribal populations. By the close of the 20th century, many of these policy conflicts remained unresolved but on the dockets in federal or state courts (Brown & LaCounte, 2002). One of the major legal cases, *Cobell v. Babbitt* (1999), is based on these longstanding issues.

Contemporary and Historical Policy and Legal Issues for Indigenous Tribal Nations

Indigenous tribal populations and European colonists held vastly different spiritual perspectives and values regarding public policy, wealth, ownership, law, and governance. Many of these differences were reflected in disputes over ownership, sale, transfer of, and payment for real property. In tribal governance, real property was used collectively by the tribal nation, whereas in European law, value was placed on individual ownership and private utilization (Berkhofer, 1979). Property in indigenous tribal nations remained in the tribe and passed from one generation to another, whereas in European culture, property could be bought and sold as a means of increasing individual wealth. European nations used a variety of quasi-legal concepts and strategies to obtain land from tribal nations that did not recognize or sanction European laws or their underlying values. Since indigenous tribes did not build fixed structures on land, European settlers concluded that the former were not making proper use of the land or enhancing its value. Europeans used such reasoning to legally challenge continued ownership of land by indigenous tribes (Cronon, 1983). The compensation provided for land was generally far less than the value perceived by the purchaser. At the beginning of the 21st century, disputes continue over real property, and these disputes have resulted in numerous lawsuits brought against individuals, tribes, states, and the federal government. Many of these lawsuits were started in an attempt to settle disputes over land ownership that were initiated more than 200 years before their filing (Blakemore, 2002; *Cobell v. Babbitt*, 1999; EchoHawk, 1999; National Indian Law Library, 2002; Randall, 2002a).

The intellectual basis of much of the public case law extends to the Non-Intercourse Act of 1809. This act and related federal policies stipulated that land belonging to indigenous tribal governments could not be obtained through purchase or trade by any individual, group, or state government without the explicit sanction of the federal government (Getches, 1998). At least one major Supreme Court ruling upheld the constitutionality of the ideas within the Non-Intercourse Act (McAuliffe, 2001). Despite the act's stipulations for protecting tribal lands from encroachment, such lands continued to be appropriated by individuals, states, and the federal government itself up to the 20th century.

In their recent lawsuits, indigenous tribal nations claim that state and federal governments acted in violation of previous federal laws, treaties, and agreements. The tribes sought the return of their lands, compensation for the loss of land, and in some instances, damages. A key dilemma for the tribes, and for subsequent populations of color, is the requirement to present their cases against the federal and state governments in federal and state courts from which they had been excluded for centuries. Indigenous populations also had no opportunity to influence the laws that governed such courts or the process that resulted in the appointment of judges.

McAuliffe (2001) indicates that the United States government and the Supreme Court have not provided adequate guidance on these very complex real property cases, starting with *Fletcher v. Peck* (1810). In this case, a suit was brought against a state legislature that decided to withdraw support for a land grant. The plaintiff's argument rested on the "doctrine of discovery"—the assumption that European settlement on a piece of land invalidated any claims by the tribes. Although the court ruled in favor of the tribe's claim, the suit illuminated clearly the complexity of real property law. With *Johnson v. McIntosh* in 1823 (McAuliffe, 2001), the court clarified its 1810 ruling in *Fletcher v. Peck*. In a related case in 1823, the court clarified its ruling in *Fletcher v. Peck* (1810) by decreeing that only the federal government had the power to exercise the "doctrine of discovery" leading to the extinction of tribal claims on real property (McAuliffe, 2001). The court also indicated that under the "doctrine of discovery" concept, the indigenous tribes should be viewed as wards of the United States. Afterwards, the United States was seen by the courts as holding a trust relationship with the tribes.

The legal definition and parameters of the trust relationship referred to by the courts was included in the General Allotment Act/Dawes Act (1887). This act gave the United States government broad fiduciary power and responsibility to hold allotted lands and any fees or income generated from leases of the land or its mineral rights in federal trust accounts on behalf of tribal nations or members. Under the Dawes Act, all monies collected and held in the trust accounts could be invested by the federal government without consultation with the tribes. The income and interest gained were to have been accounted for by the Departments of the Treasury and Interior. The intent of Congress in establishing the trust policy was to generate income that would eventually revert to the tribal nations and individuals for their welfare and development. The specifics of this reversion process (timetables and processes) were not spelled out clearly in the Dawes Act.

A number of legal cases have challenged both the fundamental principle of the trust relationship as well as the extent to which the United States had honored its fiduciary obligations to properly manage the income and interests of the tribes from 1887 to 1980 (*Cobell v. Babbitt*, 1999; Getches, 1998). One key consideration was the relationship between the alleged mismanagement of the trust funds and the deteriorating socioeconomic condition of the tribes. The cases before the courts alleged that hundreds of millions of dollars were owed to tribes whose members lived in abject poverty. A recent case addressing this issue is *Cobell v. Babbitt* (1999).

Cobell v. Babbitt

Passage of the Indian Claims Act in 1946 seems to have increased the interest in using litigation as the major strategy for challenging earlier public policies on ownership and compensation for real property and quality of life issues for indigenous tribal populations. New York, Maine, Rhode Island, and Connecticut became the major targets of suits to regain real property. These suits were brought by the Oneida, Cayuga, Narragansett, and Seneca Nations (Getches, 1998). In most instances, the claims filed by these nations have been upheld by the courts, although disagreements continue over the amount of compensation to be awarded. Numerous other cases also remain active in state and federal courts and in the Supreme Court (Brown & LaCounte, 2002). However, one class action case appears to encompass many of the historical policy issues related to real property, compensation, government responsibility, and the quality of life of indigenous tribal populations.

Cobell v. Babbitt is a class action suit filed in the Federal District Court for the District of Columbia in 1996 by Elouise Cobell, a member of the Blackfeet Nation. The class she represents includes between 300,000 and 500,000 members of indigenous tribes. The suit charges the United States government with gross mismanagement of funds held in trust since passage of the Dawes Act in 1887. The defendants in the suit are the Secretary of the Interior and the Secretary of the Treasury. The members of the class allege that the defendants did not keep adequate records of deposits into their accounts, did not invest funds wisely, and failed to provide any regular accounting of the status of the trust (McAulliffe, 2001). Because of the absence of oversight and adequate record keeping, the plaintiffs alleged that it is not possible to determine how much money should be in the trust accounts or how funds had been disbursed over the years. Some estimates of the balance in the trust accounts place the total in excess of $500 million, while others project a total of more than $20 billion.

In a historic ruling, the Federal District Court for the District of Columbia found in favor of Cobell and the members of the class action suit. In his ruling and findings of fact, Judge Lamberth ascribed the causes of the trust mismanagement to a series of interlocking federal actions (relocation, allotment, and reservation) that took place over several centuries. According to Judge Lamberth (*Cobell v. Babbitt*, 1999), these federal policy actions and others were designed to carry out the intent of the United States Congress to force tribes from their land and deprive the tribes' "ancestors of their native lands and rid the nation of their tribal identity" (p. 5). The judge concluded that the clear intent of many government policies (the Indian Removal Act of 1830) was to eradicate the culture of the tribes, leading to the elimination of the indigenous peoples with whom the United States was in conflict. Judge Lamberth found that the United States had severely violated its fiduciary responsibility to manage the trust accounts for individual members of numerous tribes. The judge ordered that the case remain open while efforts are made to reach a reasonable settlement of issues that have been a part of the policies of the United States toward America's Indians since the colonization of North America by European explorers in the 15th century.

Native Americans were the first non-European population to be subjected to British laws in America, and no reference was made to the maintenance or integration of existing, but unwritten, policies under which indigenous cultures had operated for centuries. Nor were provisions made for inclusion of Native American representation in the decision making process as voting citizens or as elected members of state or federal legislative bodies. By law, Native Americans could not occupy seats in the American judiciary or in Congress. Existing tribal governments were not given an opportunity to negotiate the policy provisions of the emerging United States government. Relationships between the colonies and the indigenous population were formalized through an extensive series of acts, ordinances, deeds, and articles of agreement, but principally through hundreds of treaties signed between 1600 and 1999 (Randall, 2002a). Most of these legal instruments centered on the transfer of land and ownership of resources from the indigenous population to the federal government.

American Public Policy Toward Africans

It was not until 1862 that the first meeting to discuss public policy toward Africans in the United States was held between an American president and Africans in America (Aptheker, 1968; Bennett, 1962). In the 143 years prior to this historic meeting, hundreds of public policies had been promulgated to govern every aspect of the lives of Africans in the United States, albeit without their involvement. The harshness of American public policy, and its underlying philosophy of racial superiority, had supplied Africans in America with numerous reasons for complaints, concerns, and grievances that were easily ignored by each of the three branches of the federal government. However, the basis of the government's consistent response was simple. Under the 1790 Naturalization Act and subsequent judicial decisions, Africans were not citizens, could not vote or hold elective office, did not have access to the courts to petition their grievances, and were considered as real property. Although many of their petitions for access to constitutional guarantees had been placed before state legislatures for decades, most of these petitions had been caught in the cauldron of states' rights legislation that denied Africans in America access to the courts (Vaughan & Rosen, 1997). Slavery, the Naturalization Act of 1790, and subsequent court rulings rendered Africans in America as a class without citizenship or identity in any country.

The prospective list of grievances by Africans in America could have easily overwhelmed Abraham Lincoln's presidency. However, the singular agenda item for the unprecedented public policy meeting in 1862 was to hear and debate Lincoln's speech in which he proposed the African population in America, both slave and free, should agree to emigrate to Africa or South America (Sandburg, 1939). To President Lincoln, out-migration of all Africans in the United States (a prospective policy for which he set aside $100,000) was viewed as the optimal public policy to mitigate the national chaos and bring immediate closure to a civil war between those factions of White men who supported policies that offered full freedom and citizenship for enslaved Africans and those who saw the discontinuance of slavery as the premier challenge to the sanctity of states' rights ideology. Congressional passage of a national policy requiring out-migration of all Africans in America might have served to save Lincoln's weakened presidency, his vision for a unified White America, and perhaps his life. However, passage without economic compensation for the loss of real property to southerners would have precipitated equally divisive legal and political challenges. The southern economy was dependent on the uncompensated labor of Africans in America, while the middle states gained from selling and buying slaves (Franklin, 1957).

In the 150 years before and the 140 years after this historic meeting between Abraham Lincoln and Africans in America, it was clear that public policy was the most powerful vehicle in determining whether enslaved Africans in America would be free and what would be the post-slavery parameters of that freedom. The bitter political and social context of the nation determined the narrow parameters for this first meeting between Africans in America and President

Lincoln. The regional division and bitterness over the future of slavery and the rights of states—the bookends of American policy—transfixed the focus of President Lincoln and forced his search for a permanent policy solution that would solve the most intense internal struggle in America's short history as a republic.

The ensuing philosophical and economic debate over slavery, citizenship, states' rights, voting, and integration raised a variety of policy questions of content and merit similar to those raised when America faced a policy dilemma about the future of indigenous tribal populations. However, unlike the tenor of claims by indigenous tribal populations that American policy caused them the loss of real property, culture, and life, Africans in America based many of their claims on the fact that American policy caused them to be viewed and treated as real property: real property that could be bought, sold, rented, leased, and auctioned in the American marketplace. The corresponding dilemma for Africans in America was that the conditions under which they were brought and held in the United States denied them any economic portfolio or access to assets or inheritance from their countries of origin.

From the time that Africans were introduced to American public policy, three major issues were significant in their tense relationship with Euro-Americans: freedom from slavery, citizenship and voting, and integration into mainstream American social and economic institutions. These three issues have formed the conceptual basis of most public policies and legal cases brought by this group up through the year 2000.

Parenthetically, while public policy was vitally important to the health and economic vitality of people of color, it was in the realm of public policy formulation and participation in elective office that Africans in America were permitted only minimal involvement by state governments, although the Constitution guarantees these rights. The socioeconomic destiny of Africans in America, and indeed the entire populace, was in the hands of a small number of wealthy White men who were uncertain about who they were and unsure about how to resolve the inherent contradictions and incongruities between the eloquence of their written instruments of democracy and the reality of the undemocratic oppression, exploitation, and enslavement of people of color and the treatment of women (Deloria, 1969; Hagan, 1961; Jordan, 1968). Creating a series of state and federal policies, supported by Supreme Court decisions, that tied economic and political rights to land-owning citizens, while simultaneously denying people of color citizenship or property rights, provided a temporary, albeit disingenuous, solution (Non-Intercourse Act of 1809). Randall (2002b) provides a valuable list of examples of public policies by critical themes and chronological periods that helps illuminate the condition of Africans in America from the beginning of the 18th century to the end of the 20th.

As a result of unconstitutional restrictions on access to and participation in voting and elective office, Africans in America have had very limited opportunities, compared to White men, to protect their own interests and rights by either creating policy (via elective office) or by sanctioning those who made policy for them (via voting). Upper-income White males have effectively used public policy to create and maintain their dominance and a monopoly American political and economic institutions since the founding of the republic.

Between 1619 and 1866, Africans in America were not permitted by state statutes and policies to own or purchase real property, sign legal contracts, receive wages, invest, maintain bank savings accounts, or receive or give inheritances. State policies did not allow Africans in America to accumulate any of the economic assets that determine wealth: houses, land, minerals, savings, crops, animals, wagons, or personal possessions (Conley, 1999). In 1865, soon after the end of the public policies that sanctioned slavery and denied African Americans access to the economy, they collectively owned less than 0.5% of the national wealth; by 1990, their share of the national purse was only 1% (Conley, 1999).

Contemporary Policy and Legal Issues for Africans in America

The reaction to the multiple questions of citizenship, property rights, voting, elective office, education, and economic participation for Africans in America from 1776 to the end of the 20th century became a series of bitter public policies and court decisions that reflected the inherent contradiction between the freedoms promised to all by the writers of the American Constitution and the omnipresent barriers erected at the state and local levels that allowed the continued abrogation of the rights, economic opportunities, and safety of Africans in America. At one end of these contentious issues was passage of the Naturalization Act of 1790 and issuance of the 1863 Emancipation Proclamation, officially ending slavery. At the other end is *Brown v. Board of Education* (1954), which eliminated the legal foundation of segregation, and a recent class action suit (*Farmer-Paellmann v. FleetBoston et al.*, 2002) that raises the issues of compensation and reparations for unpaid labor and racial discrimination. Each of these cases addressed the long-term pattern of discrimination based on race supported by state governments. Recent comments by Trent Lott (Toner, 2002) reminded the American population of how the rights of African Americans were denied through public policy throughout the South (Gettleman, 2002; Toner, 2002).

Some of the most significant public policies that denied access to Africans in America and to other populations of color were the series of decisions and interpretations labeled "states' rights." States' rights was a doctrine that was based on interpretations of the 10th Amendment to the Constitution (United States Congress, 1787). In this amendment, "The powers not delegated to the United States by the Constitution, nor prohibited by it to the states, are reserved to the states respectively, or to the people" (1787). State governments and courts interpreted this amendment as though states had all the remaining rights that are not articulated in the Constitution but also have all rights that are not explicitly denied them by the Constitution. As such, the federal government was viewed as having relatively limited Constitutional powers, while states were seen as constitutionally sovereign in numerous areas of daily life and commerce. Based on these interpretations, the federal government had limited or no control over public education, public safety, marriage, divorce, inheritance, health care, welfare, property, business, loans, travel, local taxes, public order, or whether states could discriminate in any of these or other areas by race, color, or gender. Throughout the South, people of color were the subject of varying forms of economic discrimination based in great measure on the power of the doctrine of states' rights and a weakened federal government that had limited power to protect them or enforce their constitutional rights.

The concept and practices under states' rights were reinforced by the Supreme Court's 1856 decision in *Scott v. Sandford* (Ziegler, 1958). The Supreme Court denied that Africans in America were citizens by confirming the views held in the Naturalization Act of 1790 that only Whites could acquire citizenship. Of equal importance, the Court concluded that Africans in America did not have "rights or privileges" that should be respected by Whites. Rather than having any rights to own property or seek economic profit, the Supreme Court decreed in its decision that Africans in America were property [real] to be controlled, "bought and sold, and treated as an ordinary article of merchandise and traffic, whenever a profit could be made by it" (Ziegler, 1958, p.37).

The second major decision by the Supreme Court that lessened the economic access of Africans in America and reinforced the doctrine of states' rights in the United States was rendered in *Plessy v. Ferguson* in 1896. The significance of the *Plessy* decision is in its conclusion that separate facilities for citizens by race and color are in fact constitutional as long as they are equal. The *Plessy* decision was consistent with the doctrine of states' rights and permitted almost all public and private facilities, public schools, restaurants, stores, public offices, public bathrooms, colleges, neighborhoods, medical offices, and state hospitals to be segregated by race under the guise they were equal. Along with states' rights, the *Plessy* decision become the conceptual basis of racial segregation in U.S. policies and practices until it was overturned by the *Brown v. Topeka Board of Education* decision (1954). The *Brown* decision tilted the long-term racial assumptions and rationalizations that undergird many of America's public policies. However, the impact of the *Brown* decision did not compensate for decades of denied opportunities. The *Brown* decision helped to identify that governmental policies contribute to actual monetary as well as civil rights losses. The issue of whether groups of color should be allowed to recover their losses through reparations continues to be the focus of intense debate.

Farmer-Paellman v. FleetBoston Financial Corporation, Aetna Inc.

In President Lincoln's preliminary draft of the Emancipation Proclamation (Lincoln, 1862) there was recognition that termination of slavery would cause severe economic losses of real property and future earnings for slave owners. Lincoln obviously had considered compensating the owners and perhaps the states for whatever economic shortfalls or losses might accompany compliance with a federal mandate to end the immoral practice of holding and trading in slaves. In his final draft of the proclamation, Lincoln also gave recognition to the need for federal military assistance to protect slaves from threatened retaliatory violence. Part of the brutish response to the end of slavery was psychological, but a major part was also the fear of economic collapse from the loss of real property and income invested in forced, uncompensated African labor (Barnett, 1991). Lincoln and the Congress also seemed to recognize the tremendous dislocation that would befall the newly enfranchised Africans in America. In response, the Congress passed legislation establishing the Freedman's Bureau. However, the mission of the bureau was more as a social welfare service organization than as a vehicle for economic and political development of a group that lacked assets.

In the final versions of the Emancipation Proclamation, Lincoln (Lincoln, 1863) did not refer to compensation of the Africans in America for their damages, losses, or for the length of time they toiled as uncompensated labor. Lincoln did not publicly consider reparations for the losses suffered by enslaved Africans in America or the losses by European slave owners. The document remained silent on the issue of reparations.

Although the federal government did not immediately consider reparations, Africans in America and a group of reformers had made these requests for many years—but without response. In 1867, Thaddeus Stevens of Pennsylvania introduced a Reparations Bill (H.R. 29, 1867) for the African slaves in the United States (Stevens, 1867). Stevens sought to finance his call for reparations from the sale of land that constituted the 10 states that had fought against the United States. Stevens reasoned that this property should be seized as belonging to the "enemy" and, as such, should be forfeited to the federal government. Once the land had been seized, Stevens proposed that it should be allotted in 40-acre plots to former slaves. In addition, Stevens proposed that a pool of finances be raised and invested and the interest used to compensate citizens in the Confederate states who remained loyal to the United States. In his presentation to the

House of Representatives, Stevens supported his proposed legislation based on long years of uncompensated labor.

During the Civil Rights Movement of the 1960s, a number of proposals were made in support of reparations (BlackStar Press, 1970). None of the early proposals for reparations to Africans in America for enslavement received serious consideration in the press or the general community or resulted in legislation (Bittker, 1973). However, in 1997, Congressman John Conyers introduced legislation to establish a commission (similar to a proposal by Stevens in 1867) to study the issue of reparations. Conyers's request to establish a study commission on the issue of reparations has died in conference committee each time for the past 11 years (*Farmer-Paellmann v. FleetBoston et al.*, 2002). However, reparations and forms of compensation have been engaged in by the United States and other nations for damages and losses incurred by the Jews, Japanese, and Native Americans (Murchison Center, 2002; National Coalition of Blacks for Reparations in America, 2002).

In March 2002, Deadria Farmer-Paellman filed a class action suit (*Farmer-Paellman v. FleetBoston Financial*, 2002) against a number of specific American companies seeking relief for herself and a class of close to 8 million African Americans and their descendents. The suit was filed in the United States District Court for the Eastern District of New York. This suit represents the first class action suit in which the plaintiff identifies and calculates the degree of monetary loss as well as specific defendants (corporations, universities, churches, organizations) who are alleged to have profited from the uncompensated labor of enslaved Africans. *Farmer-Paellmann* claims that the corporations listed in the suit, as well as others unnamed, "conspired with slave traders, with each other and other entities and institutions" to illegally deprive Africans in America of wages, quality of life, participation in government, equal protection under the law, and economic and educational opportunities. The defendants are alleged to have knowingly profited from these deprivations. The basis of the class action suit is five charges against the defendants: conspiracy, failure to provide an accounting, human rights violations, conversion of the value of labor into profits, and unjust enrichment.

Farmer-Paellman's class action suit provides a detailed historical chronology of the contributions made by enslaved Africans to the development of an infrastructure for the United States, specific states, cities, and organizations. Using a variety of findings from research studies, the class action petition charges that the enslaved Africans in America were treated inhumanely and that such treatment contributed to their early deaths.

Farmer-Paellmann's suit alleges that slave labor was a primary factor in the successful growth of the American economy and that such uncompensated labor equaled between $40 million and $1.4 trillion. The suit proposes that in addition to the monetary losses incurred, Africans in America suffered the loss of their culture and history as African people. When federal law required the official termination of slavery, the class action suit alleges that other informal, but nonetheless *de facto* policies (Black Codes, segregation, peonage, discrimination, sharecropping), continued a form of servitude and racial barriers that resulted in identifiable economic and civil losses for the class. Farmer-Paellmann cites specific cases of quasi-slavery that continued unabated into the 1950s as evidence of her claims. In the final sections of the suit, Farmer-Paellmann makes an effort to show that many of the current disparities in college graduation rates, child welfare, education, health care, literacy, prison sentences, death penalties, life expectancy, income, and mental health care are correlated to slavery and the informal policies that replaced it.

The class action suit seeks to force the corporations to reveal through discovery their profits from slavery and to provide an unspecified level of restitution, compensation, and punitive damages to the plaintiff and the members of the class.

The Farmer-Paellmann suit raises and examines a number of the critical policy issues, concepts, principles, and practices that have marked the governmental and proprietary response to Africans in America. The essence of the suit is in many respects the outgrowth of concepts reflected in earlier polices. One of the issues raised indirectly in the suit borders on the interface between the concepts of humanity as applied to this population and the related concept of citizenship. The multiple naturalization acts specifically delimited citizenship by race, while Justice Taney in the *Dred Scott* decision (*Scott v. Sanford*, 1856) questioned the humanness of Africans. These and related concepts pervaded early American public policies in the public and private sectors and then found their way into the various informal mechanisms created in the wake of the end of slavery. Many of these policies openly denied citizenship, equal protection, the opportunity to participate in elective office, voting rights, the ability to use the courts to address grievances, and the ability to accumulate and use wealth. In addition, these and other policies were supported through the passage of statutes by the federal and state governments and in the form of judicial decisions that reinforced adverse policy actions toward Africans in America. The long history of policy abrogation seems to support the idea that Africans in America have incurred a significant degree of monetary losses for which specific compensation has not been provided by government or the private sector. Perhaps of equal importance, the long history as outlined in this class action suit rests on the content of public policy and the racial measures that mark its formulation and implementation in the United States.

Conclusion

Quality of life in the United States, at least since the colonial period, bears a distinct relationship to the content, focus, and equality of public policy. Where public policy is based on racial, class, or gender monopolies, access to the most vital needs-meeting institutions within a society are compromised for some groups. Concomitantly, the risks for such excluded or stereotyped groups increase substantially. The contemporary nature of these increased risks is seen most vividly in the *Cobell v. Babbitt* federal class action suit. Although indigenous tribal populations held claim to vast land and mineral wealth for centuries, American public policies all but eliminated their ability to use their wealth to meet their ongoing basic needs. Cobell alleged in her suit that thousands of Native Americans lived in abject poverty when federal policies failed to yield them interest on their investments held in trust.

A similar set of conclusions can be reached about the long-term condition of Africans in America. However, unlike the Native American population, Africans in America were involuntarily brought to the United States but without real assets and without access to capital or inheritance. The inveterate American position on slavery did not permit this population to receive compensation for its labor or participate in the economy to acquire or hold assets. The economic losses associated with slavery are chronicled in the *Farmer-Paellman v. FleetBoston* class action suit filed in 2002. In addition, the dilemmas of acquiring wealth in a society in which policies limit access is described by Conley (1999). He indicates that at the end of slavery, African Americans owned less than 0.5% of the wealth in the United States, and by 1990 their ownership of America's wealth had only increased to 1%.

The long-term barriers to wealth accumulation by both indigenous tribal populations and African Americans greatly increased their risk of economic dependency well into the 20th century. Disportionately high rates of poverty, disease, crime, substance abuse, and related problems are seen as the byproducts of exclusions supported by public policy.

Gil (1973), Sherraden (1991), and Conley (1999) proposed that most of our current social problems have their origins in prior policies that have a deleterious effect on lower social classes and people of color. If that is the case, <u>social work services cannot meet the needs of its contemporary clients without a change</u> both in the content of public policy <u>and in the process that creates adverse policies.</u>

The next chapter in this volume looks at the impact of public policy on Mexican, Chinese, and Japanese populations.

References

Anderson, C. (1994). *Black labor, white wealth: The search for power and economic justice*. Edgewood, MD: Duncan and Duncan.

Aptheker, H. (1968). A documentary history of the Negro people in the United States (6th ed.). New York: Citadel Press.

Balz, D. (1998, January 19). The state of the union: Focused on policy, speech is a brief return to normalcy. *The Washington Post*, p. A19.

Barnett, J. W. (1991). *A history of the Church of Saint Andrew*. Collierville, TN: Saint Andrew's Episcopal Church.

Bennett, L. (1962). *Before the Mayflower*. Chicago: Johnson Publications.

Berkhofer, J. (1979). *The White Man's Indian*. New York: Vintage Books.

Bittker, B. L. (1973). *The case for Black reparations*. New York: Vintage Books.

BlackStar Press. (1970). *The political thought of James Forman*. Detroit: Black Star Press.

Blakemore, E. (2002). Native American struggles in reclaiming their land. Retrieved August 28, 2002, from http://academic.udayton.edu/race/02rights/s98blak2.htm

Bothwell, A. P. X. (2002). We live on their land. *Annual Survey of International and Comparative Law, 6 ,* 175–209.

Brown and LaCounte, LLC. (2002). *United States Supreme Court decisions*. Retrieved October 1, 2002, from http:// www.brownlacounte.com/cases.html

Brown v. Board of Education of Topeka, 347 U.S. 483 (1954).

Cobell v. Babbit, No.96-1285 (D.C. October 14, 1999).

Conley, D. (1999). *Being Black, living in the red: Race, wealth, and social policy in America*. New York: Columbia University Press.

Cronon, W. (1983). *Changes in the land: Indians, colonists, and the ecology of New England*. New York: Hill and Wang.

Davis, K. (2003). Expanding the theoretical understanding of oppression. Alexandria, VA: Council on Social Work Education.

Dawes Act or General Allotment Act. Ch. 818, 25 Stat. 392 (1888).

Deloria, V. (1969). *Custer died for your sins: An Indian manifesto*. New York: Avon Books.

EchoHawk, L. (1999). Justice for Native Americans requires returning to our constitutional origins. In V. Deloria & D. E. Wilkins (Eds.), *Treaties and constitutional tribulations*. Austin: University of Texas Press.

Farmer-Paellman v. FleetBoston Financial Corp., C.A. No. 1:02-1862 (E. D. N.Y. filed March 26, 2002).

Foner, E. (2001). *Race in America: From the Naturalization Act of 1790 to the Civil War*. NY: Columbia University Board of Trustees.

Franklin, J. H. (1957). *From slavery to freedom*. New York: Alfred A. Knopf.

Franklin, J. H. (1961). *Reconstruction after the Civil War*. Chicago: University of Chicago Press.

Franklin, J. H. (1993). The Emancipation Proclamation. *Prologue, 25*(2), 1–6.

Getches, D. H. (1998). *Cases and materials on federal Indian law* (4th ed.). West Group.

Gettleman, J. (2002, December 22). The nation: Southern liberals had Lott moments, too. *The New York Times*, Week in Review Desk, p. 7.

Gil, D. (1973). *Unraveling social policy*. Cambridge, MA: Schenkman Press.

Guinier, L., & Torres, G. (2002). The miner's canary: Enlisting race, resisting power, transforming democracy. Cambridge, MA: Harvard University Press.

Hagan, W. T. (1961). *American Indians*. Chicago: University of Chicago Press.

Jordan, W. D. (1968). *White over Black: American attitudes toward the Negro, 1550–1812*. Chapel Hill: University of North Carolina Press.

Joshi, S. T. (1999). *Documents of American prejudice*. New York: Basic Books.

Lincoln, A. (1862). *Preliminary Emancipation Proclamation*.

Lincoln, A. (1863). *The Emancipation Proclamation*.

McAuliffe, B. E. (2001). Forcing action: Seeking to "clean up" the Indian Trust Fund: Cobell v. Babbitt, 30 F Supp.2d 24 (D.D.C. 1998). *Southern Illinois University Law Journal, 25*, 647–661.

McLemore, S. D., & Romo, H. D. (1998). *Racial and ethnic relations in America*. Boston: Allyn & Bacon.

Murchison Center. (2000). *Reparations history*. Retrieved October 5, 2002, from http://www.murchisoncenter.org/reparations/history.htm

National Association of Social Workers. (1999). *Code of ethics*. Washington, DC: Author.

National Coalition of Blacks for Reparations in America. (2002). *History of reparation payments*. Retrieved October 5, 2002, from http://ncobra.com/documents/history.htm

National Indian Law Library. *Indian Law Cases before the Supreme Court 1988-1998*. Retrieved August 30, 2002, from http://narf.or/nill/sctdecade.htm

Naturalization Act. Ch.3, 1 Stat.103 (1790).

Naturalization Act. Ch. 20, 1 Stat. 414 (1795).

Naturalization Act. Ch. 54, 1 Stat.566 (1798).

Non-Intercourse Act. Ch. 24, 2 Stat. 528 (1809).

Plessy v. Ferguson, 163 U.S. 537 (1896).

Popple, P. R., & Leighninger, L. (2000). *The policy-based profession: An introduction to social welfare policy analysis for social workers*. Boston: Allyn & Bacon.

Porter, R. B. (1999). The demise of the Ongwehoweh—Part 1. *Harvard BlackLetter Law Journal, 15*, 107–183.

Randall, V. R. (2002a). *American Indians: Laws and policies*. Retrieved September 10, 2002, from http://academic.udayton/race/93justice/nalaws.htm

Randall, V. R. (2002b). *African Americans: Laws and policies*. Retrieved September 10, 2002, from http://academic.udayton.edu/race/03justice/aalaws.htm

Removal of the Indians West of the Mississippi Act, Ch. 148, 4 Stat. 411 (1830).

Rossiter, C. (1999). *The Federalist papers*. New York: New American Library

Sandburg, C. (1939). *Lincoln, the war years*. New York: Harcourt Trade.

Schaefer, R. T. (1990). *Ethnic and racial groups*. NY: Harper Collins.

Schefler, C. (2002). *U.S. theft of Mexican territory*. Retrieved September 10, 2002, from http://academic.udayton.edu/race/02rights/guadalu3.htm

Scott v. Sanford, 60 U.S. 393 (1856).

Sherraden, M. (1991). *Assets and the poor: A new direction for social policy*. New York: Armonk.

Stevens, T. (1867). Reparations bill for the African slaves in the United States, H.R. 29, 40th Cong. Retrieved December 9, 2003, from http://directblackaction.com/rep_bills/hr29_1867.txt

Toner, R. (2002, Dec. 15). Ugly echoes: A sanitized past comes back to haunt Trent Lott—and America. *The New York Times*. Section 4., p.1.

Toro, L. A.(1995). Chicanos as a racialized minority. *Texas Tech Law Review, 15*(26), 1219–1252.

U.S. Constitution, Amend. X (1787).

Vaughan, A., & Rosen, D. A. (1997). *Early American Indian documents: Treaties and laws, 1607–1789*. Washington, DC: University Press of America.

Ziegler, B. M. (1958). *Desegregation and the Supreme Court*. Boston: D. C. Heath and Co.

Chapter Two

The Color of Social Policy: Mexicans, Chinese, and Japanese in America

King E. Davis, Eunjeong Kim, and Josie Romero

American Public Policy Toward Mexican Americans

To a significant extent, the Mexican population in America (Chicanos) shares a common historical burden with other groups of color in their interaction with the United States (Acuna, 1981; Randall, 2002c). Policies created by an Anglo majority restricted their rights and opportunities to participate or share fully in the social, political, educational, and economic systems (benefits) of the country for centuries (Luhman & Gilman, 1980; Schaefer, 1990). The cumulative effects of such limited access to needs-meeting institutions increased the risks for the disproportionately high incidence of poverty, low accumulation of wealth, limited political participation, lower educational achievement, and lower life quality in this population that we see at the start of the 21st century (DeHaymes, Kilty, & Segal, 2000). However, in several key areas, the Mexican American population's historical experience with public policies differs markedly from that of other groups of color in the United States. These differences are most notable in that Chicanos can be considered as both an immigrant and an indigenous population; Mexico shares a border with the United States and there is continued conflict over rates of immigration, population growth, and employment with the host country (Toro, 1995).

The Mexican population evolved from a mixture of Spanish, Indian, and African bloodlines and cultures. Features of these three cultures (singularly and in combination) remain visible parts of Mexican society, language, and its population (Schaefer, 1990). In its 200-year occupation of Mexican territory (1600–1822), Spain explored and colonized major portions of the western United States and enslaved its indigenous tribal populations and introduced African slaves as laborers (Randall, 2002b). Prior to colonization by Spain, the indigenous tribal populations laid historical claim to almost all of the land in the western United States from what is now Mexico to California (McWilliams, 1968). The tribal populations and Spanish colonists anticipated they would be able to maintain their identity, land, freedom, and lifestyles from being overwhelmed by the British after winning their freedom from Spain in 1822. However, racial and cultural admixture and dominance by Spain not only brought about a new nation but also a racially hybrid population with a history that distinguished it from other groups of color dominated by the British in the United States (Acuna, 1981; Moquin & Van Doren, 1971; Toro,

1995). Under British rule, tribal populations were eventually segregated on reservations. Intermixture across racial lines was clandestine and considered illegal in most instances (Vaughan & Rosen, 1997). The dominance and control of the western states by Spain introduced the Spanish language and Catholicism to the indigenous tribes—characteristics that would set them further apart from the eastern United States, where English language and the Anglican religion were viewed as superior and revered as marks of high culture (Toro, 1995).

It had been Spain's intent to increase its national wealth through the acquisition of gold rather than follow the exact path of Britain and its monopolistic investments in and dependency on slave trading and agriculture. Although Spain also participated in slavery, its reliance on gold mining was a slow process that taxed the patience of the monarchy, particularly when coupled with an increased spirit of revolution in the population in Mexico. Spain eventually was unsuccessful, financially, militarily, and politically in the "New World." Mexico had little to fear from a disinterested Spain after 1822. However, conflict between the newly emerged nation of Mexico and the United States over the policy of "Manifest Destiny" subsequently led to war in 1846–1848 (Randall, 2002a; Toro, 1995). Under this policy, the United States proclaimed a right to own and control all lands from the Atlantic to the Pacific—as though they were a divine right for former citizens of Britain. Victory by the United States over an ill-equipped Mexican army led to a marked change in policies that affected Mexicans and the remaining indigenous tribal populations and their claims to vast lands and minerals in the western United States. The end of the war in 1848 pushed the boundaries of the United States further south to the Rio Grande, leaving the Mexican population still in "New Mexico" vulnerable to rule by the United States. The end of the war between Mexico and the United States raised anew multiple questions about citizenship, voting, and racial privilege that were originally addressed in the Naturalization Act of 1790 and the Federalist Papers (Rossiter, 1999; Toro, 1995). Was the right of citizenship to be extended to the Mexican population that remained in New Mexico? Would this population have the right to maintain ownership of land that they had held under Mexican law? Would they have the right to immigrate freely across the new border into the United States? Which nation's laws would govern the resolution of disputes over land ownership? How would Mexicans who choose to stay in the United States be protected from encroachment by settlers? Would land in New Mexico be included in the estates of the population at their death or would it revert to the United States? Each of these questions was addressed, albeit without finality and clarity, by the Treaty of Hidalgo.

The Treaty of Guadalupe Hidalgo, 1848

The Treaty of Guadalupe Hidalgo was not developed as a public law by the American legislature (Haynes, 2001; Randall, 2002c). However, it is a critical historical document that established the parameters of relationships and policy obligations between the United States and Mexico after their war over territory in what is now the southwestern United States. More specifically, the Hidalgo treaty included responsibilities and obligations by the United States to the Mexican citizens who remained in the conquered territory. Some of the issues about citizenship, voting, and ownership of land raised in the treaty are also at the center of controversy between the United States and other Spanish-speaking nations (Puerto Rico, Cuba, and Panama) at the start of the 21st century. Although the Treaty of Guadalupe Hidalgo was signed in 1848, many Mexican families contended in 2002 that the United States failed to meet its obligations to ensure that their property rights were inviolate (Ferry, 2000; Haynes, 2001; Schefler, 2002). Several of these families have brought suit against the United States based on their claims of a loss of rights to historic lands. To date, none of the suits have been successful.

The Treaty of Guadalupe Hidalgo was agreed to on February 2, 1848, and proclaimed as final on July 4, 1848. The treaty consists of 23 articles as well as an end document titled the Protocol of Queretaro (Randall, 2002c). The protocol is a statement that explains the amendments and substitute language changes in articles 9 and 10 that were made by the United States.

The first four articles in the Treaty of Guadalupe Hidalgo outline the steps taken to end the war between Mexico and the United States. These articles include specific agreements, rules, and timetables for withdrawing soldiers, eliminating blockades, and removing military equipment. Most of these conditional agreements applied to the United States, because its military had moved considerable equipment to Mexican territory in support of U.S. troops. Articles 8–10 outline the procedures and timetables for maintenance and disposition of real property and agreements related to citizenship rights and the obligations of the United States to provide protection to those populations that chose to remain in the territory. Five provisions within these articles are helpful in understanding how the United States engaged this population and the potential sources of conflict as recently as 2002:

a. Persons who decide to stay in the territory ceded to the United States or who eventually decide to leave will retain ownership of their property;

b. Individuals in the territory will have up to one year to elect whether they want to become citizens of the United States; citizenship in the United States will occur automatically after the one-year period expires for any Mexican citizen who remains in the territory;

c. Citizenship for Mexicans will include all rights under the Constitution of the United States;

d. Property of every kind that belongs to Mexicans shall be inviolate and can be transferred to heirs in perpetuity; and

e. Mexicans will be free to practice their religion without restriction.

The initial language of articles 9 and 10 was amended by the United States Congress. The language that appears in the treaty as shown here is less specific about the extent of citizenship rights and the freedom to practice Catholicism. The original article 10 was also more specific about the ownership of land by Mexicans and how their claims to their existing homeland would be ratified in accord with American policy. The changes in these two articles were outlined and agreed to in the Protocol of Queretaro by representatives of both nations.

As noted, allegations continue to be made that the United States did not honor the 10 articles that comprise the Treaty of Hidalgo (Randall, 2002b). Although the focus of most of the disputes has been the loss of land ownership, intense dispute also centers around the right of Mexican citizens to immigrate freely into the United States. The various policies created by the United States to curb the immigration of Mexicans and the way these policies have been enforced by the border patrol have become major points of conflict.

The Immigration Acts of the United States

Mexico is the only nation of color with whom the United States shares a common border. From 1848 forward, the right of Mexicans to move freely back and forth across that border as immigrants has not been consistently enforced. The right to free immigration from Mexico has depended in great measure on the need of the United States for low-income and low-skilled labor. As the need for labor increased, strict attention to the enforcement of immigration rules dissipated. When the need for labor declined, allegations have been made (Randall, 2002b) that the United States created policies that result in a virtual closing of the border and deportation of individuals who have been in the United States for many years. The dispute over previous and current immigration rules and preferences (and the harshness of their enforcement) is the seminal public policy issue between Mexican Americans and the United States in the 21st century. U.S. immigration policies have remnants of the Treaty of Hidalgo as well as the Naturalization Act of 1790.

Previous immigration policies have variously banned or given preference to persons based on race, ethnicity, gender, health status, personal behavior, criminal record, occupation, country of origin, or marital status. However, the reliance on personal characteristics and the utilization of these characteristics as the basis of quotas started in 1906. The immigration policy of 1906 established English literacy as a standard prerequisite for admission. By 1917, immigration policy specifically banned all Asians from admission to the United States. This ban went considerably further than the Chinese Exclusion Act of 1824. In 1921, the restrictiveness of immigration policy shifted toward the establishment of specific quotas based on country of origin. Because of a rise in racial and nationalistic concerns, American political leaders sought to ensure that the dominance of Whites from Northern Europe was not altered by an open policy on immigration. The 1921 quota system restricted immigration to 3% of the population in the United States per country of origin as shown in the census for 1920. No restrictive quotas were applied to persons from Northern Europe or the Western Hemisphere, including Mexico. Asians, particularly Japanese, were banned.

However, by 1924 the Johnson-Reed Immigration Act was passed with the intent of maintaining and increasing the historical racial characteristics of the United States that favored Northern Europeans. To accomplish its goal, the act specifically banned immigrants who were not eligible for citizenship—curtailing Japanese immigrants entirely. In addition, the language of the Johnson-Reed Act (1924) included these restrictions:

1. The number of immigrants per country will be determined by calculating 2% of their total number in the United States population based on the census of 1890;
2. A minimum number of immigrants will be allowed from nations that are not preferred (Southern Europe, Africa)
3. A global total of immigrants will be determined and not exceeded;
4. A consular system will be established and given responsibility for screening all applicants for admission; and
5. A series of formal procedures will be established to guide the consular system in determining eligibility for admission as an immigrant.

Congress expressed concern about finding ways to curb illegal entry into the United States from countries along its northern and southern borders. The southern border was seen as the major source of low-wage and low-skilled labor that at times competed with White American laborers and at other times was sought out by White American farmers who were unable to secure other laborers at below-market wages. To manage its ambivalent policy about illegal immigrants, the United States established the Border Patrol as part of the Johnson-Reed Act of 1924. The ambivalence of the United States about illegal Mexican immigrants is reflected in the uneven and fluctuating manner in which immigration policy has been enforced between 1924 and 2000. The key determinant in enforcement seems to be the extent to which the American labor market demands a major source of below-market wage labor. As the demand increases, enforcement of immigration policy weakens and when demand subsides or when opposition to open immigration increases, so does the effort to enforce immigration policy. The major target of these inconsistent policies enforced by the Border Patrol has been the Mexican population.

These earlier policies, most notably the Immigration Act of 1924, established strict racial quotas. The Johnson-Reed Immigration Act of 1924 gave 82% of the annual immigration slots to Eastern and Northern Europeans, while Southern Europeans were given 14% of the annual slots (Ogletree, 1999). Populations from nations considered racially, socially, or economically undesirable in American immigration policy shared the remaining 4% of the annual slots. This strict observance of a nationalistic and racial quota system was not repealed until 1965. The recent proposal President Bush to increase the ease of Mexican immigration by (Laidlaw, 2001) appears to break precedent with most prior policies established over the past 180 years, including the 1965 amendments.

Many of these earlier policies on immigration reflected the ambivalence in the United States toward immigrants generally and, more specifically, its xenophobia toward people of color. At best, American immigration policy has been inconsistent, biased, and unevenly applied. But, at its worse, the basis of much of the policy has been racist. Congressional Representative Mel Watt of North Carolina concluded that "immigrant law and immigrant policy reflect the confusion and dishonest and racial attitudes and class attitudes we have in this country in other domestic areas, and I have found that same kind of irrational class-based race-based kind of thinking in our immigration policies" (Ogletree, 1999, p. 2).The thinking that undergirds American policy towards immigrants has been a combination of what Ogletree (1999) terms wealth-based criteria and xenophobia. The wealth-based criteria sought to distinguish between acceptable and unacceptable immigrants based on their socioeconomic risks: level of income, overall assets, education, literacy, and marketable skills. Ostensibly, the emphasis on wealth in the policies was to reduce the risk that the person would require general relief or other public assistance supported by local and state revenues. Yet a stated principle and value of American democracy and its Judao-Christian ethos has been its willingness to accept immigrants without concern for their poverty (Chan, 1994; Chang, 1997; Hing, 1998).

Contemporary Policies and Legal Issues for Mexican Populations in America

Near the end of his first 6 months as President of the United States, George W. Bush proposed a radical departure from American immigration policy established at the beginning of the 20th century (Laidlaw, 2001). Many of the earlier policies focused on restricting immigration by race, ethnicity, geographical origin, gender, martial status, and occupation. Obviously, many of these areas contradicted 19th-century amendments to the Constitution and were more congruent with the narrow nationalistic values expressed in the Naturalization Act of 1790.

Within the past 2 decades, the emphasis in American immigration policy has been on enforcement of restrictions on the heretofore unimpeded flow of Mexican citizens across the U.S. border. Thousands of illegal immigrants have risked traversing the Rio Grande to enter the United States and penetrate an American labor force that welcomed their willingness to work for below-market wages. As the pressure to stop the flow has increased, many Mexicans in the United States live in fear that they will be detected and then deported. Bush proposed to provide amnesty and citizenship to more than 3 million low-income Mexican immigrants who entered the United States in violation of existing immigration law (Laidlaw, 2001). Bush's proposal, considered by some as largely a strategy to increase his support among Spanish-speaking populations prior to the next presidential race, drew criticism from other members of his party, notably former Senator Phil Gramm. Gramm believed that the change proposed in existing policy would reinforce illegal immigration overall to the United States and would increase rather than decrease the influx of Mexicans to border states like Texas, which he represented until his retirement from the U.S. Senate in January of 2003 (Laidlaw, 2001).

Although Bush's proposal may be based on increasing his chances of re-election, the proposal does appear to deviate significantly from the emphasis of previous immigration policies that severely affected the access Mexicans and other groups of color had to the United States throughout the 19th and 20th centuries. The Naturalization Act of 1790 established a precedent by the United States to control the racial and ethnic characteristics of its population through federal control of immigration and citizenship and state government control of voting. Prior to the Treaty of Guadalupe Hidalgo in 1848 (Randall, 2002b), the United States did not have any national interests that would have led to the development of polices to govern their relationships with the Mexican people. The Hidalgo treaty, developed as the instrument to end the war between the two nations, established the need for social policies. The United States had a long history of developing and using treaties in their relations with indigenous populations. American treaties had been an effective tool in acquiring land and suppressing conflict with indigenous tribal nations. The use of treaties established strong precedents that favored and supported the economic, political, and national interests of the United States. With the application of a treaty to determine the parameters for ending the war, Mexicans became only the second group in American history whose interface with the United States was codified in such a legal instrument.

The Treaty of Guadalupe Hidalgo and the way that it was implemented established the moral template for future relationships and legal precedents for policies between the United States and Puerto Rico, Cuba, Panama, and other countries in Central and South America (Haynes, 2001). Various Latino populations have made effective use of the courts over the past 100 years to challenge the fairness and constitutionality of American public policy (Klein, 2002). One of the earliest cases filed was *Botiller v. Dominguez* (1887/1889) filed in the California Supreme Court (Klein, 2002). In 1889, Botiller brought an action before the California courts in which he challenged the right of settlers to claim land under various homestead acts that he owned. Botiller held claim to the land based on its prior status as a part of Mexico. Under the Hidalgo treaty, Botiller should have been protected from such land seizure. Although his petition had been supported by the California courts, the Supreme Court dismissed his claim because it found that he did not follow the policies that required he present his land grant claims within the period allotted. The failure of the Supreme Court to uphold the claims by Botiller was significant because of the prior obligations contained in Hidalgo. In close to 30% of the claims cases brought before the California courts citing Hidalgo guarantees, the courts denied the claims (Klein, 2002), while close to 75% of similar claims in New Mexico were thrown out by the courts.

A second case (*Minturn v. Brower*, 1864) brought similar charges that land guaranteed under the Treaty of Guadalupe Hidalgo had been forfeited because the owner failed to register the land within a time prescribed by current policies (Klein, 2002). However, the courts found in favor of the owner and protected the land as part of the provisions under the Hidalgo treaty.

Recent Advocacy and Legislative Actions in Response to the Treaty of Hidalgo

Increased interest on the part of Mexican families in recovering lost land rights under the Hidalgo treaty have taken two related paths between 1997 and 2000. First, a number of families have sought judicial relief for claims that the United States did not protect their land as promised under the Hidalgo treaty (Ferry, 2000; Haynes, 2001). These families allege that their historic lands were taken away under a series of illegal actions supported in part by policies promulgated by the United States but favoring White settlers. To date these claims have not received judicial support (Ferry, 2000). These families have also sought to have the United States Congress investigate and document their claims. The congressional efforts by Mexican Americans have been more successful but remain incomplete.

On September 24, 1997, former Representative Bill Redmond of New Mexico introduced House Resolution 2538 to establish a presidential commission to determine the validity of certain land claims arising out of the Treaty of Guadalup-Hidalgo. The title of the resolution was "Guadalupe Hidalgo Treaty Claims Bill" (1998). The intent of the bill was to restore lands back to the Mexican families who are descendants of the original land owners who were made numerous promises in the treaty. The original H.R. 2538 was revised four times in the House until 1998. The 1998 version passed the House and included provisions to establish the presidential commission, acknowledge the history of the acquisition, identify the need to attend to the specific elements in the treaty that had not been fully implemented, and invite eligible descendants to submit land claims. The bill also required that any claims be submitted within a 5-year period following its enactment. H.R. 2438 required that all testimony, hearings, and debate take place within the state of New Mexico. In a direct response to opponents of the bill, a provision was included to exempt from recovery any lands not held by the federal government.

In February 2000, a companion bill (S. 2155) was introduced in the U.S. Senate. The bill was titled "The Fair Deal for Northern New Mexico of 1998." This bill sought "to provide for the development of remedies to resolve unmet community land grant claims in New Mexico" ("Fair Deal for Northern New Mexico, 1998, p. 105). The Senate version was designed to provide monetary restitution to settle the economic losses incurred by descendants and included in their claims. Debate in the Senate focused on the obligation of the federal government to determine an equitable remedy for the errors in implementation of the original treaty.

The Senate made a second effort to resolve the Hidalgo treaty dispute in 2000 by passing a new bill (S. 2022, Fair Deal for Northern New Mexico, 2000). As in the earlier Senate resolution, this newer bill sought to find remedies that would satisfy the numerous claims that are pending. Of importance, this Senate bill cites a number of research studies that provides data that support many of the claims. The Senate bill also required that the Government Accounting Office (GAO) conduct a study of the issues related to the Hidalgo treaty claims and provide an assessment to the Congress. The timetable for completion of the GAO report requires that it be submitted to the president in July 2003.

Each of the actions considered by Mexican families is similar to the actions taken in the past several decades by indigenous tribal nations. The first step in these efforts has been to document the losses or abrogation of rights through a commission or committee. These findings have in general become the basis of congressional action or lawsuits. To date, the efforts of Mexican American groups to document their losses, present their claims either to the Congress or the courts, or find satisfaction for their claims have not been highly successful. No specific legal challenge to the losses associated with the Treaty of Hidalgo has been successful.

American Public Policy Toward Asians

The relationship between two groups of Asian populations—Chinese and Japanese—in America and American public policy is based on the perception of and interaction between multiple forces that have been present from the mid-1800s. Some of these forces include restrictions on immigration, economic development opportunities, land ownership, competition over skilled jobs, and such constitutional issues as citizenship, voting rights, and equal protection under the law (Segal, 2002). Although these issues differ outwardly to some extent from those presented by other populations of color, the resulting policy dilemmas, implementation processes, and outcomes are very similar. Segal (2002) suggests that the disparities in rates of poverty, poor health, joblessness, and absence of wealth are related to restrictive public policies on populations of color from the colonial period to the 21st century. She concludes that the Asian population has not been exempt from these outcomes. However, the societal manifestation of such social problems in the form of demand for government assistance may be less evident.

Many of the Chinese immigrants who came to the United States in the mid-1800s shared a basic characteristic with the early European settlers who colonized the country and established its basic public policies (Wong, 1995). Europeans and Chinese were often voluntary immigrants to the United States, lured at least in part by what appeared to be open opportunities for skilled work, ownership of land, and business opportunities. Although the flow of Chinese immigrants to the United States was relatively slow in the mid-1800s, the discovery of gold in California greatly increased both the pace and the overall number of men who emigrated (Wong, 1995). However, in numerous other areas, the differences between the immigration experiences and the post-immigration experiences were striking. Daniels (1995) concludes that:

> The immigration of Asians to the United States has differed significantly from the immigration of Europeans. Immigration from Asia has involved the United States in disputes with Asian governments about persecutions, legal and extralegal, encountered here by Asian [i]mmigrants. The diplomatic aspects of Asian immigration have thus been far more important and complex, and have held far graver consequences, than have the diplomatic aspects of European immigration. (p.67)

The experiences of Asian and European immigrants also differed in the roles they were allowed to play and the extent of participation they were allowed in the creation and implementation of public policy. Obviously, in the 200 years that Europeans had settled the country, their policies represented the context in which the cultural traditions brought by the Chinese and Japanese immigrants were to be judged. The Chinese and Japanese in America had no role in the creation of these early public policies or the set of values or philosophical assumptions that formed their conceptual base.

Chinese men were the first group of Asians who were permitted to immigrate to the United States. Wong (1995) notes that this wave of Asian immigration started after 1840, although there are some references to the presence of Chinese immigrants as early as 1795 (Segal, 2002). Prior to that time, the number of Chinese immigrants in the United States was well below 100. However, economic conditions in China and in the United States resulted in a reduction of demand for labor in China while substantially increasing demand for skilled labor, professionals, and merchants in the United States (TaKaki, 1989). The American practice of meeting its labor demand through uncompensated slave labor had not been an acceptable policy in the western states as the United States expanded. The demand for labor was followed by increased immigration of Chinese immigrants.

In the earliest years of Chinese immigration, the ability to fill the intense demand for labor in the western states masked an insidious form of racism against their presence in these states. However, as the number of Chinese and then Japanese men in the population increased, and as the demand for labor decreased, White laborers pushed for and eventually obtained severely restrictive labor policies, constructed on old assumptions about the importance of maintaining racial and cultural purity and privilege. These surface issues masked the inveterate Euro-American concerns about competition and scarcity (Davis, 2003) and the "threats" represented by populations of color.

Contemporary Policy and Legal Issues for Asians in America

The racial animus openly expressed toward Chinese immigrants to the United States was projected onto each new wave of Asian immigrants (Randall, 2002a). Following the restrictions on the number of Chinese immigrants based on the 1882 Exclusion Act, Japanese laborers were sought as replacements. This population grew rapidly and soon experienced a similar racial backlash from organized White labor in California. Efforts to curb the immigration and naturalization of Japanese populations became highly visible, organized, and received considerable support from the California legislature and attorney general. Efforts to establish federal laws based on the false sense of economic threat posed by the Japanese resulted in federal and state legislation to either completely bar their entry into the United States or severely restrict their acquisition of land, business opportunities, and access to education. Many of the most severe discriminatory measures against the Japanese were passed at the state level and supported locally by White citizens. Constitutional barriers against the Japanese were intensified with the declaration of war after Japan bombed Pearl Harbor. The rise in racial hysteria and the successful efforts by organized labor to curtail Japanese inroads into the labor force resulted in federal policy designed to intern the entire population. President Roosevelt was urged by the California congressional delegation to adopt a policy, of questionable constitutional merit, that would give the military power to confine any individual or group deemed a potential internal danger to the nation. At the time that successful pressure was exerted on the president, German, Italian, and Japanese populations in the United States were viewed as potential targets of the emerging federal policy. President Roosevelt issued Executive Order 9066 that created both a means and an end with remarkable similarity to the Indian Removal Act of 1824 and its precipitous implementation that resulted in the deaths of hundreds of indigenous people.

Executive Order 9066 was issued on February 19, 1942 (Executive Order No. 9066, 1942). The publicized intent of the order was "to establish a process that would help insure that the United States would be successful in the conduct of its war effort." The president proposed that the ability of the nation to win at war was threatened by the potential for collusion and cooperation with the enemy and that espionage and sabotage by persons living near military installations in the United States represented a threat. Executive Order 9066 (1942) allowed the Secretary of War and military commanders to identify or designate any geographic area of the country as a restricted military area. The Secretary of War was given the discretion to develop and impose any restriction on any individual or group that was viewed as an internal threat to the United States. However, the executive order and the powers delegated to the Secretary of War violated due process rights ostensibly guaranteed to all citizens under the Constitution.

Congress passed legislation (Violations of Military Orders Act, 1942) reinforcing the executive order. This public law indicated that failure to comply with Executive Order 9066 would be a crime punishable by a fine and imprisonment. The Supreme Court issued supportive rulings on the constitutionality of the executive order and the legislation. Executive Order 9066 was not enforced *en masse* against either the German or the Italian populations in the United States. Although consideration was given to its enforcement eith these populations, the policy was never carried out.

Implementation of the executive order resulted in the forced displacement of the majority of the 126,000 Japanese immigrants and citizens living in the United States. The population was moved to concentration or internment camps in several states, where many remained until 1946. In addition to psychological and spiritual losses, the Japanese suffered major uncompensated losses of real property.

With the implementation of Executive Order 9066, the United States had reestablished its earlier pattern of responding to irrational racial fears and xenophobia at the state and local level by violating the civil rights guaranteed in the U.S. Constitution to citizens of color. Federal officials, including the president of the United States, were unwilling to control the unlawful behavior of White citizens by offering protection to the Japanese. Under the guise of "internal threats," it allowed egregious abrogation of the constitutional rights of its citizens. The executive order also reinforced the states' rights policy of segregating populations of color into geographically isolated areas.

Based on the urging of Senator Daniel Inouye of Hawaii, the United States Congress authorized development of a commission to study the constitutionality of the forced internment and relocation of Japanese Americans under Roosevelt's Executive Order 9066 (see Commission on Wartime Relocation, 1980). Jimmy Carter, President of the United States, signed the commission into law (PL 96-317) in 1980 and gave the commission a 3-year period in which to complete its review and recommendations. Nine members were appointed to the commission and its official title was the Commission on Wartime Relocation and Internment of Civilians.

In 1983, the commission issued its report (Commission on Wartime Relocation and Internment, 1983) and concluded that Presidential Executive Order 9066 had violated the rights of the Japanese population, citizens and permanent residents, in the United States by ordering they be relocated and interned. The commission also concluded that the United States did not have any evidentiary basis for its actions against Japanese citizens or permanent residents, although several Supreme Court decisions (*Minoru Yasui v. United States*, 1943; *Ex Parte Mitsuye Endo*, 1944; *Hirabayarni v. U.S.*, 1975; *Korematasu v. U.S.*, 1944) supported the order and the process of implementation as constitutional. To the contrary, the commission found that the factors leading to the executive order to intern Japanese citizens were based on racial prejudice, discrimination, hysteria, and a failure in national leadership. In the footnotes to the commission's report were indications that pressure from labor organizations that wanted to displace Japanese workers and farmers had been instrumental in developing strong anti-Japanese sentiment. The commission also identified that the losses of real and personal property associated with relocation and internment totaled close to $1 billion.

In response to the commission's report, the United States passed the Civil Liberties Act of 1988. The purpose of the Civil Liberties Act was to provide a remediation plan to compensate the Japanese population for its losses associated with relocation and internment. The Civil Liberties Act sought the achievement of four related goals:

1. To acknowledge the fundamental injustice of the evacuation, relocation, and internment of citizens and permanent resident aliens of Japanese ancestry during World War II;
2. To apologize on behalf of the people of the United States for the evacuation, internment, and relocations of such citizens and permanent residing aliens;
3. To provide for a public education fund to finance efforts to inform the public about internment so as to prevent the recurrence of any similar event; and
4. To make restitution to those individuals of Japanese ancestry who were interned.

The United States Congress issued an apology in 1988 and a presidential apology was issued in 1993.

The Congress authorized that a sum of $1.25 billion be established to find, identify, and compensate the persons who were evacuated, relocated, and interned. A total of $20,000 per person was authorized by Congress as payment. Congress also authorized a sum of $12,000 per person for the Aleuts who were also relocated during World War II. The final requirement of

Congress was that all documents associated with evacuation, relocation, and internment of American citizens during World War II be maintained by the archivist of the United States.

By 1999, close to 82,000 individuals of Japanese ancestry had been identified as eligible for compensation. In February 1999, the federal office responsible for administration of this public law was closed with 1,400 cases outstanding.

Korematsu v. United States, *1944 and 1984*

The two cases in which Toyasaburo Korematsu is the plaintiff are based on a number of the constitutional and human rights issues brought about by public policy in the United States dating back to the 1700s (Randall, 2002c). These issues include citizenship, voting, freedom from unlawful search and seizure, and equal protection under the Constitution. In the original case in 1944 (*Korematsu v. U.S.*, 1944), the plaintiff pleaded for relief from the Supreme Court after his prior appeals had been denied. Toyasaburo Korematsu, a citizen of the United States, was charged and convicted in Federal District Court and subsequently imprisoned for violating Civilian Exclusion Order #34. It was alleged that Korematsu had knowingly and voluntarily violated the order of General Dewitt, commander in charge of implementing Executive Order 9066. As part of his attempts to carry out the executive order, General Dewitt issued a number of proclamations and exclusion orders, which required that Korematsu abandon his home in San Leandro, California. Because Korematsu remained in his home area rather than follow the order, he was charged with violating the law and thus was subject to a fine and imprisonment. After being jailed, Korematsu appealed his conviction to the Supreme Court. Korematsu's appeal of his sentence rested on several legal grounds as argued by his attorneys. His appeal consisted of the following points:

1. The exclusion order was an unconstitutional delegation of power;
2. The exclusion order went beyond the war powers of Congress, the military and the president;
3. Application of the order was confined to citizens and permanent residents of Japanese ancestry and amounted to discrimination based solely on race in violation of the constitution;
4. At the time the exclusion order was developed, the threat of an invasion by Japan of the West Coast had disappeared.

The Supreme Court denied the appeal. Justice Black wrote the majority opinion rejecting the four points raised by Korematsu's appeal and upholding the sentence. The majority opinion was based on the finding that the military and Congress had sufficient military reasons to carry out the exclusion orders since an unknown proportion of the Japanese population in the United States at the time represented a threat of sabotage and espionage. Since the military could not determine which members of the population represented that threat, the court found that it was justified in detaining the entire population. Justice Black and the court majority rejected the argument put forth by Korematsu that the basis of the relocation order and its subsequent actions were evidence of racial discrimination, prejudice, and hostility toward Japanese citizens. The court found the language used by the plaintiff to describe relocation as racial segregation to be objectionable. In its ruling, the court declared that segregation was a necessary public policy because of the multiple threats of invasion against the United States.

Justices Roberts, Murphy, and Jackson dissented from the majority opinion. They based their dissent on their findings and interpretation of fact of the original Executive Order 9066 and the subsequent evacuation orders promulgated by General Dewitt. The three justices found that these orders were unconstitutional. Furthermore, the three justices raised the following key issues in reaching their minority opinion:

1. Korematsu was convicted solely on his Japanese ancestry and what Justice Roberts termed "legitimization of racism." The case hinged on the rights of a citizen to disobey an unconstitutional standard;

2. The decision was based on an assumption of racial guilt rather than military necessity. Justice Murphy indicated that the commanding general's own report confirmed this finding where the general stated "All individuals of Japanese descent are 'subversive' and belong to 'an enemy race'" (*Korematsu v. United States*, 1944, p. 326); and

3. The military order was not supported by evidence of a danger either by the population or by the actions of the plaintiff and as such violated constitutional guarantees afforded citizens of the United States.

In testimony presented to the court, it was noted that many anti-Japanese labor groups had sought to expel them from California because they offered competition to White farmers and laborers. In addition, comments from General Dewitt raised additional questions about the objectivity of his orders. In testimony before the House Naval Affairs Subcommittee to Investigate Congested Areas, he stated,

> I don't want any of them [persons of Japanese ancestry] here. They are a dangerous element. There is no way to determine their loyalty. The west coast contains too many vital installations essential to the defense of the country to allow any Japanese on this coast. The danger of the Japanese was, and is now—if they are permitted to come back—espionage and sabotage. It makes no difference whether he is an American citizen, he is still Japanese. American citizenship does not necessarily determine loyalty. But we must worry about the Japanese all the time until he is wiped off the map. (House Naval Affairs Subcommittee, 1944, p. 739)

General DeWitt's own statements supported the court's findings that racism against the Japanese was the primary factor that led to their unconstitutional and inhumane internment.

In 1984, the Korematsu conviction was overturned in the U.S. District Court in San Francisco based on evidence submitted by attorneys for Korematsu that the government had withheld information highly pertinent to the case. Judge Patel indicated that government attorneys had suppressed evidence from the Office of Naval Intelligence, Federal Bureau of Investigation, Federal Communications Commission, and Army Intelligence that fundamentally contradicted the claims of military necessity on which the case was argued. In fact, it was noted that efforts by attorneys for the Justice Department to provide information to the Supreme Court that would have contradicted the claims of military necessity were suppressed. Judge Patel concluded that the decision to convict Korematsu was based on "unsubstantiated facts, distortions, and representations of at least one military commander, whose view were seriously infected by racism" (*Korematsu v. United States*, 1984, p. 1409).

Conclusion

Monopoly of public policy by one population segment creates a series of societal standards and cultural expectations based on a single set of characteristics and worldviews. More importantly, such a monopoly also conveys benefit and privilege to a few. Mexicans, Chinese, and Japanese people were summarily excluded from participation in creating and modifying public policy for significant portions of American history. As a result, they have had to invest their meager resources and energies in a variety of costly strategies (legal suits, protest, advocacy, and empowerment) to shift the nation's policies even marginally away from gross monopolization and White male privilege. However, such advocacy has come at a price. The efforts to force the nation towards introspection of the discrepancies in its democratic creed and its ethos of equality have often been met with massive resistance, scapegoating, state-sanctioned violence, and "blame the victim theorizing" about the causes of inequality and the persistence of poverty (Conley, 1999; Diamond, 1997; Gil, 1973; Hodge, Struckmann, & Trost, 1975; Neuwirth, 1968; Yette, 1971). It really comes as no surprise that economic and political policy is at the heart of poverty.

Concomitant with these assertions is the proposal that major improvements in the life circumstances of Americans of color in the past half century and in the future are inextricably tied to passage and implementation of a series of legislatively contested social policies. But there have been few policies that address the underlying issues of economic inequality borne of prior policies. A central dilemma that derives from the linkage between American policy and people of color is to determine what to do about the cumulative impact of 250 years of adverse public policies on the socioeconomic condition of people of color and their decedents and how long it will take to fully overcome these disparate conditions borne of American public policy (Cavalli-Sforza & Cavalli-Sforza, 1995; Conley, 1999; Davis, 1976; King, 1967; Robinson, 2000; Sherraden, 1991). Part of the ongoing debate between conservative and liberal policymakers and factions in the United States centers around the issue of what constitutes acceptable "affirmative action," defined here as a recognition of the need for comprehensive economic policies that attempt to repair the cumulative economic effects of previous policies inimical to people of color, women, and low-income Whites. The seminal question for each of these groups is whether social, political, legal, and economic justice is obtained merely by removing or replacing written policy barriers in the latter half of the 20th century without consideration of how to redress the cumulative harm of hundreds of years of oppressive, monopolistic, and illegal practices emanating from these policies. After many years of rejection, the Japanese population obtained reparations from the federal government for their documented losses. The amount of the compensation did not equal their actual losses and could be considered as more symbolic. In addition, the Japanese received a formal apology from President Clinton for the mistreatment they were afforded in the 1940s. Other populations of color have not received compensation for their losses as seen in recent law suits that seek recovery. The United States experienced the aftermath of such policy dilemmas when it passed the Reconstruction Act in 1867 (Franklin, 1961), the Johnson-Reed Immigration Act of 1924, and the Supreme Court decision in *Brown v. Board of Education*, which were stronger in their written form than their implementation (Bell, 1992; Feagin & Feagin, 1978; Franklin, 1961; Moreland, 1970; Nelson, 1999; Scott, 1997; Steinhorn & Diggs-Brown, 1999; Turner, Singleton, & Musick, 1986; Yette, 1971).

Several related conclusions can be drawn from these perspectives on the history of American public policies. People do not voluntarily choose to ignore their biologically inherent needs for food, shelter, health, clean water, procreation, or safety. However, there is clear evidence of continued disproportionality in unmet needs by class, race, color, and gender that threaten the sanctity of life and its quality. There does appear to be a causal connection between public policies and current social, political, and economic conditions of people of color and society as a whole. Participation by people of color and women in all phases of policymaking remains limited and inadequate.

The retrospective review taken in this and the previous chapter shows clearly that some changes in policy and practice take a century. The gradient of socioeconomic change is both steep and incremental. But it is not clear how long it takes for a once-enslaved, disenfranchised, interned, conquered, or oppressed population to reach parity without supportive policies. Many critical questions face the field of social work regarding public policy: What is the long-term price of failing to ensure that people are literate or safe or that men and women have an opportunity to feed, house, and care for their children and each other? What is the long-term price of oppression? What is the long-term price of misdiagnosis or bias in health and mental health care? What is the price of cultural incompetence? What will these families have to transmit to their children to prepare them for the next millennia? These are critical questions that are on the agenda of social work.

The question is where do we go now in the history of the republic? Is there a way to go, a clear policy path to follow? Is there a consistent way to harness the extraordinary promise of democracy for all Americans? It seems possible that within a 10-year period this nation can be in a very different place racially and economically if we base future public policy and strategies on what we learned in the 20th century. Whereas public policy is designed ostensibly to solve and prevent social ills by facilitating resources and access, for people of color public policy creates and helps to sustain not just inequality but the disquieting sense that inequality for people of color is as acceptable a public policy in the United States at the beginning of the 21st century as it was at the beginning of the previous century.

References

Acuna, R. (1981). *Occupied America: A history of Chicanos* (2nd ed.). New York: Harper and Row.

Bell, D. (1992). Faces at the bottom of the well: The permanence of racism. Boston: Basic Books.

Botiller v. Dominguez, Rev'd, 130 U.S. 238 (1889).

Brown v. Board of Education, 347 U.S. 483 (1954).

Cavalli-Sforza, L. L., & Cavalli-Sforza, F. (1995). *The great human diasporas: The history of diversity and evolution*. Milano, Italy: Addison-Wesley.

Chan, S. (1994). *Entry denied*. Philadelphia: Temple University Press.

Chang, C. (1997). Immigrants under the new welfare law: A call for uniformity, a call for justice. *UCLA Law Review, 45*(1), 205–280.

Chinese Exclusion Act, ch. 126, 22 Stat.58 (1882).

Civil Liberties Act, ch. 50, 102 Stat. 903 (1988).

Commission on Wartime Relocation and Interment of Citizens Act, 94 Stat. 964 (1880).

Commission on Wartime Relocation and Interment of Citizens. (1983). *Personal justice denied: Report of the Commission on Wartime Relocation of Civilians*. Washington, DC: U.S. Government Publications Office.

Conley, D. (1999). *Being Black, living in the red: Race, wealth, and social policy in America*. New York: Columbia University Press.

Daniels, R., & Kitano, H. L. (1995). *Asian Americans: Emerging minorities* (2nd ed.). Ingleside Cliffs, NJ: Prentice Hall.

Davis, F. G. (1976). *The economics of Black community development*. Washington, DC: University Press of America.

Davis, K. (2003). *Expanding the theoretical understanding of oppression*. Alexandria, VA: Council on Social Work Education.

Dawes General Allotment Act, ch. 818, 25 Stat. 392 (1887).

DeHaymes, M. V., Kilty, K. M., & Segal, E. (Eds.). (2000). *Latino poverty in the new century: Inequities, challenges, and barriers*. New York: Haworth Press.

Diamond, J. (1997). *Guns, germs and steel: The fates of human societies*. New York: Norton.

Executive Order No. 9066 3 CFR 1–19 (1942).

Ex Parte Mitsuye Endo, 323 U.S. 283 (1944).

Fair Deal for Northern New Mexico, S. 2155, 105th Cong. (1998).

Fair Deal for Northern New Mexico, S. 2022, 106th Cong. (2000).

Feagin, J. R., & Feagin, C. B. (1978). *Discrimination American style: Institutional racism and sexism.* Englewood Cliffs, NJ: Prentice Hall.

Ferry, B. (2000). *Homesteaders sue over ancestral land.* Retrieved March 27, 2000, from http://www/hcn.org

Franklin, J. H. (1961). *Reconstruction after the Civil War.* Chicago: University of Chicago Press.

Gil, D. (1973). *Unraveling social policy.* Cambridge, MA: Schenkman Press.

Guadalupe Treaty Claims Bill, H.R. 2538, 105th Cong. (1998).

Haynes, J. M. (2001). The forgotten promises of the Treaty of Guadalupe Hidalgo. *St. Mary's Law School Review on Minority Issues, 3,* 231–264.

Hing, B. O. (1998). Don't give me your tired, your poor: Conflicted immigrant stories and welfare reform. *Harvard Law Review, 33,* 159–161.

Hirabayashi v. U.S., 320 U.S. 81 (1943).

Hodge, J. L., Struckmann, D. K., & Trost, L. D. (1975). *Cultural bases of racism and group oppression.* Berkeley, CA: Two Riders Press.

House Naval Affairs Subcommittee (1944). Committee to Investigate Congested Areas. 78th Congress, 1st Session, Part 3, 739–740. Washington, DC: U.S. House of Representatives.

Johnson-Reed Act of 1924. An act to limit the migration of aliens into the United States. Pub. L. 68-185. Retrieved Jan. 4, 2004, from http://www.washington.edu.uwired/outreach/cspn/curaaw/aawdoc02.html.

King, M. L. (1967). *Where do we go from here? Chaos or community.* New York: Bantam.

Klein, C. A. (2002). *Federal legislation and court cases.* Retrieved Nov. 3, 2002, from http://academic.udayton.edu/race/02rights/guadalu6.htm.

Korematsu v. United States (1944, October Term). *Cases argued and decided in the Supreme Court of the United States* (Book 90, Lawyer's Edition). Rochester, NY: Lawyers' Cooperative Publishing.

Korematsu v. United States, 584 F. Supp.(N.D. Cal. 1984).

Korematsu v. United States (1983, November 10). Transcript from proceedings (November 10, 1983). San Francisco.

Laidlaw, S. (2001, July 16). Bush weighs residency for Mexicans. *Associated Press Wire Service,* 1–2.

Luhman, R., & Gilman, S. (1980). *Race and ethnic relations: The social and political experience of minority groups.* Belmont, CA: Wadsworth.

McWilliams, C. (1968). *North from Mexico: The Spanish-speaking people of the United States.* New York: Greenwood Press.

Minturn v. Brower, 24 Cal. 644(1864).

Moquin, W., & Van Doren, C. (Eds.). (1971). *A documentary history of the Mexican Americans.* New York: Bantam.

Moreland, L. B. (1970). *White racism and the law.* Columbus, OH: Merrill.

Naturalization Act of 1790, ch. 3, 1 Stat.103, 104 (1790).

Naturalization Act of 1795, ch. 20, 1 Stat.414 (1795).

Naturalization Act of 1798, ch. 54, 1 Stat. 566 (1798).

Nelson, S. R. (1999). *Iron confederacies: Southern railways, Klan violence, & reconstruction.* Chapel Hill, NC: University of North Carolina Press.

Neuwirth, G. (1968). A Weberian outline of a theory of community: Its application to the Dark Ghetto. *British Journal of Sociology, 20,* 148–163.

Non-Intercourse Act of 1809, Ch. 24, 2 Stat. 528 (1809).

Ogletree, C. J. (1999). *America's schizophrenic immigration policy: Race, class and reason.* Boston: Harvard University Criminal Justice Institute.

Randall, V. R. (2002a). *Race, racism and the law: Asian Pacific Americans.* Retrieved Nov. 18, 2002, from http://academic.udayton.edu/race/03justice/aspilaws.htm.

Randall, V. R. (2002b). *Treaty of Guadalupe Hidalgo.* Retrieved Nov. 18, 2002, from http://academic.udayton.edu/race/02rights/guadalu.htm

Randall, V. R. (2002c). *Hispanic/Latino Americans: Laws and policies.* Retrieved December 30, 2003, from http://academic.udayton.edu/race/03justice/hispaws01.htm

Reconstruction Act of 1867, Ch. CLIII, (1867), Retrieved Jan. 1, 2004, from http://www.ncrepublic.org/recon1/html

Removal of the Indians West of the Mississippi Act, Ch. 148, 4 Stat. 411 (1830).

Robinson, R. (2000). *The debt: What America owes to Blacks.* New York: Dutton Press.

Rossiter, C. (1999). *The Federalist Papers.* New York: New American Library.

Schaefer, R. T. (1990). *Ethnic and racial groups.* New York: Harper Collins.

Schefler, C. (2002). *U.S. theft of Mexican territory.* Retrieved Nov. 11, 2002, from http://academic.udayton.edu/race/02rights/guadalu3.htm

Scott, D. M. (1997). *Social policy and the image of the damaged Black psyche 1880–1996.* Chapel Hill: University of North Carolina Press.

Segal, U. A. (2002). *A framework for immigration—Asians in the United States.* New York: Columbia University Press.

Sherraden, M. (1991). *Assets and the poor: A new direction for social policy.* New York: Armonk.

Steinhorn, L., & Diggs-Brown, B. (1999). *By the color of our skin: The illusion of integration and the reality of race.* New York: Penguin Group.

TaKaki, R. (1989). *Strangers from a different shore: A history of Asian Americans.* Boston: Little, Brown.

Toro, L. A.(1995). Chicanos as a racialized minority. *Texas Tech Law Review, 15,* 1219–1252.

Turner, J. H., Singleton, R., & Musick, D. (1986). *Oppression: A socio-history of Black–White relations in America.* Chicago: Nelson-Hall.

Snyder Act of 1921, ch. 115, 42 Stat. 208 (1921).

U. S. Constitution. Amend. X. (1787).

Vaughan, A., & Rosen, D. A. (1997). *Early American Indian documents: Treaties and laws, 1607–1789.* Washington, DC: University Press of America.

Violations of Military Orders Act of 1942, Pub. L. No. 77-503, ch. 18, 56 Stat. 173 (1942).

Wong, M. G. (1995). Post-1965 Asian immigrations: Where do they come from, where are they now, and where are they going? In F. Ng (Ed.), *The history and immigration of Asian Americans* (pp. 150–167). New York: Garland.

Yasui v. U.S. 320 U.S. 115 (1943).

Yette, S. F. (1971). *The choice: The issue of Black survival in America.* New York: Putnam.

Chapter Three

The Color of Child Welfare

Ruth McRoy

Each year a disproportionately high number of children of color are removed from their families and placed into the nation's child welfare system. African Americans represent only 12.9% of the nation's population and African American children represent 15% of the total U.S. child population (U.S. Census Bureau, 2001). However, according to the Administration for Children and Families (2001), 38% of children in the foster care population are African American, 17% are Hispanic, 37% are White ,1% Asian, 2% American Indian, 3% are unknown, and 2% are two or more races. According to Morton (1993), "overrepresentation in foster care is a polite way of saying that our child protection system more frequently separates African American children from their birth families, and keeps them separated, than it does White children" (p. 1). What is most disturbing about these statistics is that child welfare professionals have been aware of the disproportionate representation for years. Some suggest that this overrepresentation of African American children is to be expected because they are overrepresented among the poor, the population most likely to be served by public child welfare. However, Garland, Ellis-MacLeod, Landsverk, Ganger, and Johnson (1998) found that race/ethnicity is a factor in determining placement of African American children and not simply a confounder related to socioeconomic factors. This chapter will explore these and other factors that may lead to the overrepresentation of African American children in the foster care system as an example of the differential impact of child welfare policies on populations of color. A historical overview of the impact of child welfare policies and practices on African American families and children will be provided. Specific policies including the Adoption and Safe Families Act of 1997 (ASFA), Multiethnic Placement Act (1994), and Interethnic Provisions (1994), as well as research findings and recent court rulings that demonstrate this pattern of racial inequities in the provision of child welfare services will be explored and implications for social work education and practice will be given. (Throughout this chapter, the terms "Black" and "African American" will be used interchangeably due to variations that occur in the literature.)

From Underrepresentation to Overrepresentation: Historical Background of Child Welfare Services to African American Children

Historically, child welfare service provision in this country was based upon English traditions and values that tended to link poverty with personal inadequacy. Therefore assistance to the poor has been based upon the philosophy that the "superior" (non poor) know what is best for the "inferior" (poor) (Billingsley & Giovannoni, 1972). In early colonial times, poor children were cared for primarily through indenture and the almshouse. Until 1865, since slavery was considered the major child welfare system for African American children in this country, Black children's needs tended to be overlooked or denied (Billingsley & Giovannoni, 1972). In today's terms, Black children were either not represented or underrepresented in child welfare services provision. For example, in the early 19th century when orphanages were established to rescue children from the deplorable conditions of almshouses, Black children were typically excluded. Therefore, the only option for poor Black orphans was the almshouse until the Society of Friends (a religious group advocating the abolition of slavery) founded the first Black orphanage, the Philadelphia Association for the Care of Colored Children. Similar associations were founded in other cities to care for orphaned Black children. However, many Black orphans continued to be sent to almshouses because of the limited number of orphanages that would accept them.

Toward the second half of the century, soon after the end of slavery, White children were moved out of the indenture system and orphanages into free foster homes. Under this arrangement, dependent children were placed in foster homes and expected to work for the family until the child reached adulthood. The child worked for his keep, yet was free to leave as no money was paid to the foster family. Children in free foster homes primarily were relocated from the cities to farms thousands of miles away through a "placing out" system originally founded by Charles Loring Brace and Martin Van Arsdale (Bremmer, 1983).

In 1909 at the first White House Conference on Children, concerns were raised about the practice of breaking up families and removing children for reasons of poverty alone. Until then, needy families had voluntarily surrendered their children to Children's Aid Societies or to orphanages, hoping that they would have more opportunities than the birth family could provide. In 1909 "an estimated 170,000 children were living in out-of-home care (approximately 95,000 in orphanages and institutions for the developmentally disabled; 50,000 in foster care; and 25,000 in juvenile correctional facilities)" (Curtis, Dale, & Kendall, 1999, p. 4). In response, the first statewide mothers' pension law was enacted in Illinois in 1911 and by 1920, 40 states had passed similar legislation (Pelton, 1989). Under these laws, field investigators could judge which mothers were "inefficient" or "immoral" and which were truly deserving of aid (Pelton, 1989). By 1920, mothers' pension programs were administered through juvenile courts in many states, which in many locales were the same courts responsible for removing children from their homes due to neglect.

For Black children during this same time period, a different picture emerges. Extensive poverty followed the Civil War and emancipation, leaving many African American children, along with children of immigrant groups, in great need. The short-lived and under-funded Freedmen's Bureau helped for a time in providing direct relief to poor Black children with their families. Black self-help efforts through orphanages, day care, and services for poor children offered through churches, social organizations, and schools developed to respond to the needs of Black children. Organizations like the National Urban League, founded in 1910, began to advocate for equitable distribution of child welfare services for African American children. However, in 1923 in most northern states, the majority of child welfare institutions admitted White children only.

During the first half of the 20th century, foster boarding homes were established in which foster parents were paid to care for children. Through this shift from institutional care to boarding homes, gradually Black children were offered the option of foster family care and were less likely to live in institutions. Most of these foster placements were with Black families. At that time, racial exclusion was much more characteristic of private agencies than public agencies. However, as public agencies opened their doors to Black children, the number of private Black-owned institutions declined (Billingsley & Giovannoni, 1972).

At the 1930 White House Conference on Children, Ira De A. Reid of the Urban League called attention to the discrimination that existed against Black parents in income maintenance programs, medical care, services to unwed mothers, and day care services. He noted that mothers' pension programs in some states denied benefits to Blacks and that discrimination in day care facilities limited access for Black children and presented obstacles for Black mothers seeking to work. Similarly, services and housing for Black unwed mothers were often not available and there was a lack of medical and health services for Black children and adults (Billingsley & Giovannoni, 1972).

By 1935, mothers' pension laws had been adopted in 46 states and in that year the Aid to Dependent Children (ADC) program was established as Title IV-A to the Social Security Act. However, because in the early years states provided a 50–50 match to the federal government in providing public assistance, states had discretion in determining who was eligible to receive these benefits. Some states adopted "home suitability clauses," "substitute father rules," "man-in-the-house rules" and "illegitimate child clauses" (Piven & Cloward, 1971). These policies were established to weed out "immoral" homes (often defined as homes in which men other than biological fathers were in the home, mothers had children born out of wedlock, or the worker believed a man was living in the home) from being eligible for receipt of benefits. Such policies until 1959 served to rule out the majority of African American families living in the South from receiving any public welfare benefits for reasons such as having a child outside of marriage.

Following Mississippi's lead in removing many children from the welfare rolls for these reasons, in 1959 Florida removed 14,000 children (over 90% African American) and in 1960, Louisiana removed 23,000 children from receiving benefits. Referred to as the "Louisiana Incident," this state not only declared many African American clients ineligible for ADC benefits but subsequently labeled their children as "neglected" since their parents did not have the financial resources to support them. However, despite the children having been labeled as neglected, families generally received no follow-up services to aid these children.

In an attempt to rectify this situation, then Secretary of Health, Education and Welfare Arthur Flemming in 1961 ruled that social services as well as cash payments should be provided to parents or other relatives caring for children. Flemming called attention to the fact that home eligibility requirements were unfair as food, clothing, and shelter were being denied to many African American children because of the behavioral conduct of a relative with whom the child lived, while allowing the child to remain in that same environment. The Flemming Rule became law with the passage of P.L. 87-31 in 1962, which called for services to be provided to families as well as provided federal financial assistance to states to facilitate the removal of children from neglectful or abusive parents. In 1962, ADC officially became Aid to Families with Dependent Children; the 1962 social services amendments further emphasized follow-up services for families charged with neglect and made open-ended funds available for out-of-home placement. Unfortunately, however, although the Flemming Rule was designed to protect the rights of children, the mandated services often led to more weakening of family systems. Often culturally insensitive service providers quickly removed children from what they judged to be "undesirable family situations" and placed them in foster care. For example, in 1963, 81% of children in out-of-home care were there because their parents were unmarried or because they came from "broken homes" (Lawrence-Webb, 1997). The majority of these children were children of color, primarily African American and Indian.

However, as Black children became increasingly represented among the foster care population, they were not gaining equal access to services while in care. For example in 1959, Maas and Engler reported that many Black children in foster care were in need of adoption, but were less likely to be adopted. Similarly, a few years later Jeter (1963) also found that Black children were remaining in foster care for longer periods of time than White children, and adoption was not being offered on an equitable basis. Jeter also identified ongoing discrimination in service provision, noting that Black children were primarily being served by public agencies and private voluntary agencies were primarily serving White children.

Private adoption agencies had been established initially in the 1920s and were designed to assist White couples seeking healthy White infants placed for adoption by unmarried mothers. According to Morgernstern (1971), " until the 1960s, official agency adoptions had been considered a White middle-class affair" (p. 68). Historically, dependent African American children have been cared for within the family through a system of informal adoption by members of the African American extended family (Hill, 1997) since they were excluded from consideration by most adoption agencies.

In the early 1960s, the growing use of contraceptives, liberalized abortion laws, and increased social acceptability of unwed parenthood reduced the supply of healthy White infants available for adoption (McRoy & Zurcher, 1983). By 1971, the number of White children accepted for adoption had decreased from 9,672 in 1969 to 5,983 (Child Welfare League of America [CWLA], 1972).

The reduction in the number of White children available for adoption led many private agencies to focus on placing Black infants for adoption. Private agencies that had previously discouraged or even denied the relinquishment of Black infants were open to accepting them. In fact, they began to encourage the placement of Black infants through transracial adoptions with the large supply of waiting White families. In keeping with this trend, the CWLA changed its earlier race-matching policy in 1968 to the following: "In most communities there are families who have the capacity to adopt a child whose racial background is different from their own. Such couples should be encouraged to consider such a child" (CWLA, 1968, p. 34). In 1968, 35% of Black children who were adopted were placed in White homes, and in 1971 approximately 2,500 Black children were placed transracially (Simon, 1984). The majority of these children were African American or racially mixed infants.

In 1972, the National Association of Black Social Workers (NABSW) challenged this practice and passed a resolution that stated:

Black children belong physically and psychologically and culturally in Black families where they receive the total sense of themselves and develop a sound projection of their future. Only a Black family can transmit the emotional and sensitive subtleties of perceptions and reactions essential for a Black child's survival in a racist society. (pp. 2–3)

Moreover, the NABSW cautioned that many Black families interested in adoption were being disqualified because of the stringent adoption criteria established by White adoption agencies. Responding to the NABSW concerns, the Child Welfare League reversed its policy encouraging transracial adoptions, and in 1973 indicated that "inracial placements were preferable because children placed in adoptive families with similar racial characteristics could become integrated more easily into the average family group and community." The league encouraged agencies to consider all resources for African American children, including registering children on adoption exchanges, before seeking a transracial placement. In 1975, only 831 transracial adoptions occurred (Day, 1979).

Similarly, after a great deal of concern about American Indian children being removed from their tribes and reservations and placed in boarding schools as well as with White foster or adoptive families, American Indian leaders successfully moved toward the passage of the Indian Child Welfare Act of 1978 (P.L. 95-608). This legislation specified priority for placing Indian children in extended families or with Indian foster or adoptive families in the same tribe or another tribe before considering placement off the reservation or with White adoptive families.

In the meantime, attention was being placed on the growth in the number of children in foster care due to abuse and neglect. In 1974, the Child Abuse Prevention and Treatment Act (CAPTA) was passed, which provided funds to states for the prevention and treatment of child abuse and neglect (See National Center on Child Abuse and Neglect [NCCAN], 1996). It also required states seeking such funds to pass laws mandating the reporting of child abuse and neglect. Increased reporting led to more investigations and removals of children in care. By 1977, more than 502,000 children were in the out-of-home care system (Curtis, 1999) and children were remaining in care for an average of 2.4 years.

Concerned about finding permanency for the growing number of "special needs" children (older children, children with disabilities, children of color) growing up in foster care, the first federal legislation specifically dealing with adoption, Public Law 95-266, the Adoption Opportunities Act of 1978, was passed by Congress (Courtney, 1999). It was designed to eliminate barriers to the adoption of special needs children. Funding was provided for post-adoption services and specialized adoption programs for children of color.

Two years later, Congress passed the Adoption Assistance and Child Welfare Act of 1980 (P.L. 96-272) also in response to the growing number of children lingering in foster care. This legislation required that a written case plan be developed for each child and administrative or court reviews at least every 6 months "to determine the continuing necessity for and appropriateness of the placement…and to project a likely date by which the child might be returned to the home or placed for adoption or legal guardianship" (Adoption Assistance and Child Welfare Act of 1980, p. 511). Agencies were also required to show the court that "reasonable efforts" had been made to maintain the child in his or her own home (Harrison & Johnson, 1994). This law established the desirability of permanence for children and prioritized child welfare services outcomes as follows: (1) family preservation, (2) family reunification, (3) adoption, and (4) foster care. Additionally, the legislation mandated that states implement a statewide information system and inventory of children in care.

This act was initially effective in reducing the number of children in institutions and increasing the number of children reunified or adopted and decreasing time in foster care. By 1982 the number of children in care was reduced significantly; however, a disproportionately large number of children in the out-of-home care system continued to be African American. For example in 1982, of the 262,000 children in foster care, 52% were Anglo, 34% were African American, and 6.7% were Hispanic. In 1983, Mech analyzed the U.S. Office of Civil Rights 1980 Youth Referral Survey of 301,943 children and found that prevalence rates for out-of-home placement per 1,000 were highest for African American children (9.5), followed by Native

Americans (8.8), Caucasians (3.1), Latinos (3), and Asian Americans (2). Similarly, an analysis of the impact of the 1980 Adoption and Assistance and Child Welfare Act on states' child welfare services between 1985–1988 revealed that prevention efforts were lower in states that had higher proportions of children living below the poverty level (Altstein & McRoy, 2000; Newlin, 1997).

The effects of the law were short lived, as it was never fully funded as proposed (Harrison & Johnson, 1994, p. 146; Pelton, 1991). In a short period of time, the number of children in care began rising again and many of these were recycled through the system due to failed reunification efforts or disruptions (Harrison & Johnson, 1994, p. 146; Pelton, 1991).

Another attempt at addressing the issue occurred in 1993 with the passage of the Family Preservation and Support Services Program (Omnibus Budget Reconciliation Act of 1993). This legislation required states to establish an integrated continuum of services for families at risk or in crisis, including reunification or permanency planning, preplacement/preventive services, follow-up services, respite care, and parent skills training (Newlin, 1997).

However, the overrepresentation of African American children has continued. According to statistics provided by the American Public Welfare Association, in 1992 approximately 429,000 children were in foster care (McKenzie, 1993), a 63% increase from 1982. By 1993, 38% of the children in out-of-home care were Anglo, 46% were African American, 14% were Hispanic, and 2% other (Native Americans, Asian, and Asian Pacific) (Williams, 1997). Of this number, only about 15% to 20% of these children had adoption plans (McKenzie, 1993).

By 1994, there were an estimated 462,000 children living outside of their homes (MacDonald, 1994) and in 1995 the number had risen to an estimated 486,000 (see Table 1.). Between 1990 and 1996, although the child population grew only 7.6%, the population of children referred for abuse and neglect investigation rose by 16.7% from 2.5 million to more than 3 million children (Petit et al., 1999, p. 7). Protective services staff conducted about 1.6 million investigations of these reports and substantiated reports were made on more than 970,000 children (U.S. Department of Health and Human Services [DHHS], 1999). In 1996, 16% of children who were identified as being victims of child abuse and neglect were removed from their homes and placed into foster care.

In 1997, the federal government again became involved in addressing the problem of children in foster care through passage of the Adoption and Safe Families Act of 1997 (P.L. 105-89). This law called for DHHS to set annual adoption targets for each state. States would receive per-child bonuses for placements made beyond their annual target. In addition, the legislation required states to set up a permanency placement plan for a child after 12 months, instead of 18 months as under prior policies. The law reauthorized and provided more funding for the family support and family preservation programs and changed the name of this program to "Promot-

Table 1. Number of Children in Foster Care, 1982–2001

1982	262,000		1996	500,000
1986	280,000		1999	567,000
1990	400,000		2000	552,000
1994	468,000		2001	542,000
1995	494,000			

Sources: Congressional Research Service Report for Congress (1997); National Adoption Information Clearinghouse (1998); Administration for Children and Families (2003).

ing Safe and Stable Families." Concurrent planning was mandated to "identify, recruit, process and approve a qualified family for an adoption" while filing a termination of parental rights petition for workers to simultaneously plan for more than one outcome (Altstein & McRoy, 2000).

By 1998, approximately 520,000 children were in foster care (Administration for Children and Families, 1998). In New York, California, Michigan, and Illinois African American children are more likely to stay in care longer than other groups (CWLA, 2001). According to the October 2000 Adoption and Foster Care Analysis and Reporting System data, in September 1999, 567,000 children were in foster care. Some reductions occurred in the foster care population at the beginning of 2000 and by September 2001, 542,000 children were in care. The average age of the children in care is 10.1 years. About 60% are children of color. In some urban areas like New York and Detroit, about 80–90% of the children in care are African American (McRoy, 1994). In North Carolina, although Blacks make up approximately 27% of the population age 19 and under across the state, almost 50% of the 11,000 children in out-of-home care are African American (Children's Services Practice Notes, 2001). About 77% of the children in the District of Columbia are African American, yet 97% of the children in out-of-home foster care are African American. Goerge, Wulczyn, and Harden (1994) analyzed prevalence rates in California, Illinois, Michigan, New York, and Texas and reported that the proportion of African American children in out-of-home care ranged from 3 times as high to more than 10 times as high as the proportion of Anglo children (See Courtney et al., 1996). Of the 126,000 of these 542,000 children in care who have a goal of adoption, 34% are White, 45% are Black, 12% are Hispanic, 2% are American Indian, 0% are Asian/Pacific Islander, 4% are unknown/unable to determine, and 2% are two or more races (ACF, 2003).

Another factor often not discussed related to the growth in the number of children in care, is the funding mechanism for foster care. Reimbursement to states for foster care payments and adoption-assistance programs are open-ended and dependent on the number of children placed in out-of-home care and the cost of their care. Since funding for these programs is dependent on the number of children in care, there is a fiscal incentive for placements in out-of-home care. Preventive services, like family preservation, typically have fixed funding streams. Between 1981 and 1985, federal funding for foster care maintenance and administration increased from $309 million to more than $3 billion (Courtney, 1999, p. 130). Funding for these programs continues to increase yet funding for family support and investigations has not risen at the same rate (Courtney, 1998).

Experiences of Children in Foster Care

Children in foster care are three to six times more likely than children not in care to have emotional, behavioral, and developmental problems, including conduct disorders, depression, difficulties in school, and impaired social relationships. Some experts estimate that about 30% of the children in foster care have marked or severe emotional problems. According to a U.S. General Accounting Office (GAO) study (1995), 58% of young children in foster care had serious health problems and 62% had been subject to prenatal drug exposure, placing them at significant risk for numerous health problems. Children entering care, according to the CWLA (Simms, Freundlich, Battistelli, & Kaufman, 1999), should:

> have access to a range of services, including the collection of evidence that abuse and or neglect has occurred; an assessment for any significant urgent health care needs or restric-

tions on the type of placement, assessment of their health, dental, developmental and mental health care needs. (p. 173)

The educational needs of children in care can be substantial. Many have limited education and job skills, perform poorly in school compared to children who are not in foster care, lag behind in their education by at least 1 year, and have lower educational attainment than the general population. Each year 20,000 youth "age out" of foster care and must make the transition to self-sufficiency. Studies of youth who aged out of foster care, have revealed "an increased likelihood of early parenting and instability in relationships, higher arrest rates, lower high school graduation rates and lower school performance, greater likelihood of health and mental health problems, experiencing homelessness, substance abuse and unemployment" (Casey Family Programs, 2001, p. 9).

The Link Between Poverty, Child Maltreatment, and Out-of-Home Placement

Although child maltreatment was for years viewed as the result of parental psychopathology and often intergenerational psychopathology, recent research has demonstrated that child maltreatment is a result of multiple risk factors outweighing protective factors. According to Wells and Tracy (1996):

> these risk factors include child factors such as handicapping condition; parent factors such as aggressive personality; marital factors such as domestic violence; family factors such as presence of a chaotic family system, social isolation, and unemployment; neighborhood factors such as a geographic area containing a concentration of impoverished people; and cultural factors such as norms promoting the use of violence. (p. 673)

Moreover, the child's age and developmental stage also play an important role is assessing risk and protective factors.

An increase in poverty and substance abuse have been identified as factors influencing the growth of maltreatment (Wells & Tracy, 1996). Although poverty does not cause maltreatment, "the effects of poverty appear to interact with other risk factors such as unrealistic expectations, depression, isolation, substance abuse and domestic violence to increase the likelihood of maltreatment" (English, 1998, p. 47). According to Garbarino, Kostelny, and Dubrow (1991), child abuse in the poorest neighborhoods is four times the rate in more affluent areas. As a result of these allegations, many of these children are placed in out-of-home care. Lindsey (1991) noted that for all age groups, parental income level is the best predictor of children being removed from their biological families and placed in foster care. It is no surprise then that the majority of children in foster care come from single-parent, low-income households (Lindsey, 1991; Pelton, 1989).

Sedlak and Broadhurst (1996) reported that "the incidence of abuse and neglect is approximately 22 times higher among families with incomes less than $15,000 per year than among families with incomes of more than $30,000 per year" (Courtney, 1998, p. 95). It is also important to note that physicians and other service providers may be more likely to attribute an injury to abuse in cases of children in lower income homes and attribute the same injury to an accident in families of higher income (Newberger, Reed, Daniel, Hyde, & Kotelchuck, 1977; O'Toole, Turbett, & Nalpeka, 1983). These differential attributions and labeling biases against low-income families may account for some of the relationships that have been found between poverty and abuse.

Neglect is often a product of poverty and, as populations of color are disproportionately poor, children of color are disproportionately placed in out-of-home care for reasons of neglect.

According to Pelton (1989), there is a strong relationship between child abuse and neglect and poverty. Although some suggest that because poor people are more susceptible to public scrutiny—as many are receiving assistance—and are more likely to be reported, this may be a factor. However, Wolock and Horowitz (1979) found in their study that many families involved in child abuse and neglect were living in crowded, dilapidated households and often had no food. Many such families live in neighborhoods with high crime rates and insecure apartments with many health and safety hazards, such as lack of heating and poor wiring. In addition, child care is not readily available and to provide for their families, some parents may end up taking chances with neighbors watching their children or leaving them unattended while they shop or look for a job. As families adapt to the isolation, impoverished conditions, and stressful environment, children are sometimes left unattended or victimized by strangers and non-relatives. Once reported, these children are often removed from the home and placed in care for reasons of abuse and neglect (Pelton, 1989). However, according to Pelton (1989), in reality:

> the reason for placement is that the family, frequently due to poverty, does not have the resources to offset the impact of situational or personal problems which themselves are often caused by poverty, and the agencies have failed to provide the needed supports, such as baby sitting, homemaking, day care, financial assistance, and housing assistance. (pp. 52–53)

As more and more children live in single-parent families (triple the rate in 1960), the number of poor families has increased (Pelton, 1989). Lindsey (1991) noted that most of the children in foster care come from single-parent households. As the poverty rate for children in female-headed households is 46.1% compared to 9.7% in all other family types (Children's Defense Fund, 2000), it is no surprise that these families would be more vulnerable. Single mothers rarely get child support and low wages make it very difficult to get good child care.

According to a recent Better Homes Fund and University of Massachusetts Medical Center study, 9 out of 10 low-income single mothers had experienced family violence either as children or as adults (Children's Defense Fund, 2000, p. 7). Lindsey (1991) found that adequacy of income (more than reason for referral) is the crucial determinant in deciding on child removal and placement in foster care (p. 278). Once a child is removed, parents receiving assistance often have the financial assistance and other services reduced by the amount attributable to the child. Thus, lowering the income of a parent whose low income may have led to the decision to remove actually results in a greater likelihood of the child remaining in care and reduces the chance of family reunification (Lindsey, 1991, p. 280).

Implications for African American Children Among Children in Care

If children coming into the system are primarily removed due to child maltreatment by parents, are African American families more likely to neglect or abuse their children than other groups? To examine the reasons for disproportionate representation of African American children in foster care, we must look first at some of the correlates of out-of-home placement. Many factors, including poverty, substance abuse, and homelessness, compounded by racism, have been cited to explain the differential admissions to and treatment of children of color in the nation's child welfare system. Courtney (1999) suggests that the child welfare system is a *"de facto* poverty program" since the government is basically taking over child rearing responsibilities from poor parents. As African American children are disproportionately poor, they are more likely to be removed from their homes and placed in care.

According to the Children's Defense Fund (1999), although child poverty fell in the 1940s through the 1960s, rates have been rising since the 1970s. In the 1970s, 15.7% of American children were poor, in the 1980s, 20.5% of children were poor, and in the 1990s, 21% of American children were poor. In 1998, 13.5 million children were poor (nearly one in five). Although the poverty threshold was $13,003 for a three-person family in 1998, the average poor family made less than $9,000 a year in cash income. Although three out of five poor children in America are White, the poverty rates for Black and Hispanic children are more than twice the White child poverty rate. Black children similarly are more likely to be extremely poor (48.3% live below half the poverty line) (Children's Defense Fund, 1999, p. 5).

Although Blacks represent only about 12.9% of the population, they continue to be disproportionately poor (U.S. Census Bureau, 2000). In 1999, 23.6% (8.4 million) of African Americans were poor and nearly one half of all poor Blacks are less than 18 years old. Although the poverty rate for African Americans is the lowest ever measured by the Census Bureau, it is still much higher than for Whites (7.7% or 14.9 million people; U.S. Census Bureau, 2000).

The median annual income for African Americans is $27,910, compared to $51,205 for Asian and Pacific Islanders, $44,366 for Whites, and $30,735 for Hispanics (U.S. Census Bureau, 2000). Sixty-seven percent of Black female householders with no spouse present make less than $25,000 a year and 43% of Black male householders with no spouse present make less than $25,000 a year. Forty-one percent of Black families maintained by women with no spouse present are in poverty.

In 1992, African Americans represented about 12.4% of the nation's population but about 37.2% of AFDC recipients that year, while Whites represented about three fourths of the U.S. population and 38.9% of AFDC recipients (U.S. House Committee on Ways and Means, 1994). With the reduction in cash aid benefits for families through the passage of the Personal Responsibility and Work Opportunity Reconciliation Act of 1996 (P.L. 104-193), other benefits such as food stamps, welfare, and disability assistance for children with mental health and emotional disorders, along with the new policies requiring stricter work requirements and time limits have been predicted to increase the number of children entering out-of-home care (Simms et al., 1999).

Further, TANF legislation will have a disproportionate impact on the African American population in several ways: (1) potential increase in the number of African American families who are poor due to a 5-year time limit for cash aid; (2) increased pressure to work will increase family stress due to limited affordable child care options; and (3) decreased income may increase likelihood of child neglect and maltreatment and decrease the chance of family reunification of children already in the system (Burnam & Melamid, 2000).

The Links Between Substance Abuse, Child Maltreatment, Criminal Justice, Welfare Reform, and Foster Care

In 1995, about 1 million children were found to be substantiated victims of child abuse and neglect and at least 50% had chemically involved caregivers (CWLA, 1997). In that same year more than 80% of states reported that substance abuse is one of the top two conditions reported by maltreating families. Alcohol and drug abuse are factors in the placement of more than 75% of the children who are entering care.

There are approximately 1.3 million parents today with problem levels of illicit drug use and even more alcoholic parents who are raising children under the age of 18. Recent studies have shown a strong relationship between child maltreatment and parental substance abuse cases (DHHS, 1999, p. 50). According to the 1993 Study of Child Maltreatment in Alcohol Abusing Families (DHHS, 1993), parental substance abuse was one of the presenting problems for 42% of the children who were victims of abuse and neglect. In 77% of these cases, alcohol was the problem substance and cocaine was the problem substance in 23%. Typically, these cases involved younger children and 46% involved physical neglect. The authors found that alcohol- and drug-related cases were more likely to result in foster care placement than other cases (DHHS, 1999, p. 43).

Imprisonment of parents is another factor leading more children into the child welfare system. In the United States in 2000, about 1.5 million children had at least one parent in prison. More than half of these children were less than 10 years of age. About 89% of imprisoned parents were in state prisons and half of these parents were African American, one fifth were Hispanic, and about one fourth were White (U.S. Dept. of Justice, 2000).

Drug and alcohol abuse and addiction are implicated in the incarceration of 80%—1.4 million—of the 1.7 million men and women in prison today. Among the 1.4 million substance-involved inmates are parents of 2.4 million children, many of them minors. This has far-reaching implications for the economic frailty of families and their children. For example, Title 1, Section 115 of the Personal Responsibility Act denies eligibility for temporary state assistance to individuals who are convicted of a federal or state felony for possession, use, or distribution of a controlled or illicit substance. Worse yet, the individual's family is penalized because the amount of assistance a family might receive is reduced by the amount that would have been otherwise available to the family member who is convicted of the felony. Since African Americans are more likely to be convicted of drug-related crimes, fewer will be eligible for benefits (Schiele, 1998). Penalizing the whole family for alleged criminal activity of one member is not only unfair but guarantees that many more African Americans will experience economic insecurity. Moreover, since parental alcohol and drug use are factors in the placement of the majority of families involved in the system, it is likely that more children will enter the child welfare system.

The length of parents' sentences also differentially affects the outcomes for African American children in the child welfare system. Genty (1998) noted that:

> although 60% of women sentenced to state prison in 1991 received maximum sentences of 5 years, women actually served an average of 15 months in state prisons (range—less than 1 year to 7 years depending on the offense and race of the offender). Men served an average of 21 to 23 months (ranging from less than 1 year to 9 years depending on the offense and race of the offender). (pp. 547)

African American men and women typically served more time than Whites for the same offense (U.S. Department of Justice, 1995).

Thus African American children are likely to be separated longer than White children from their parents due to the longer incarceration of their parents. Some may be placed in foster care and others may be in the care of relatives while the parent is imprisoned. According to the Adoption and Safe Families Act of 1997 discussed earlier, termination proceedings must begin whenever a child has been in care for 15 of the past 22 months. This will have a disproportionately negative impact on Black children and parents, since it is unlikely that their parents will be able to resume parental responsibilities for at least 15 months if incarcerated. However, exceptions to the rule can occur if the child is being cared for by a relative or a compelling reason can be given for not terminating the parental rights. In addition, the state will have to prove that the parent is "unfit."

Another factor that can affect outcomes for African American children concerns whether the child and incarcerated parent can keep in touch and maintain a parent–child attachment. Unfortunately, visitation between children and parents is problematic, as prisons are often located in rural areas and often are not accessible by public transportation (Genty, 1998). One survey reported that fewer than 20% of incarcerated parents saw their children as often as once a month and half never saw their children while incarcerated (Snell, 1994).

Discussion and Analysis of Specific Child Welfare Services Policies and Practices

Besides social policies, which have differentially affected African American children in the child welfare system, differential child welfare services provision may also lead to longer stays for African American children. Although the majority of children in the system are children of color, a study conducted by the National Child Welfare Training Center found that 78% of the workers are White and 80% of supervisors are White and the majority have not received training in service provision to African Americans (Courtney, 1996; McRoy, Oglesby, & Grape, 1997; Vinokur-Kaplan & Hartman, 1986).

Some suggest that the lack of culturally competent child protective services workers may lead them to fail to understand cultural differences and variations in child rearing (Leashore, Chipungu, & Everett, 1991; Stehno, 1982). For example, in one state, 1 in 20 African American infants born in 1 year were placed in out-of-home care, while 1 in 100 White infants were removed from their families (McRoy et al., 1997; Morton, 1993).

Courtney et al. (1996) reviewed much of the literature on disparities in services provision and found research accounts of inequities from child maltreatment reporting, child welfare service provision, kinship care, family preservation services, exit rates and length of care, placement stability, and adoption. Although a few studies he reported did not find an association with race, the majority did. He also found that the majority of racial differences reported were between African Americans and Anglos rather than other groups.

Eckenrode, Powers, Doris, Munsch, and Bolger (1988) reported study findings which suggested that child maltreatment reports are much more likely to be substantiated for African American and Latino children than for Anglo children. Although some studies have found no racial differences in allegations of sexual abuse by race or ethnicity (NCCAN, 1981, 1988), others (Cappelleri, Eckenrode, & Powers, 1993; Jones & McCurdy, 1992) found that Anglo children were more likely to experience sexual abuse (as compared to neglect) than African American children. Using hypothetical vignettes of cases of sexual abuse, Zellman (1992) found that survey participants were more likely to believe that the law required a report to be made when children of color were described in the vignettes than when Anglo children were described.

Several researchers have examined the impact of ethnicity on service provision. Close (1983) and Stehno (1990) found African American children in care are more likely to remain in care longer, be less likely to have visitation with their families, and have fewer contacts with workers. Olsen (1982) found that Anglo and Asian American families had the greatest chance for receiving recommendations for services and Native American families had the least chance for service recommendations. African American and Latino children were least likely to have plans for contact with their families. Similarly, Fein, Maluccio, and Kluger (1990) found in their study of 779 children who had been in out-of-home care in Connecticut for at least 2 years in 1985 that Anglo children and foster families received more services and support than children and foster families of color.

Barth, Berry, Carson, Goodfield, and Feinberg (1986) reported that in their study of 101 physically abused children in California that African American children were more likely experience permanent out-of-home placement as compared to Anglo children. Goerge (1990) found that over an 8-year period, African American children in Cook County remained in care for a median of 54 months, while the median length of stay for all other children was 18 months. Goerge et al. (1994) found significant differences in median duration in care for African Americans and Whites. In California the rate was 30.8 months for African Americans compared to 13.6 months for Anglos. In Illinois, African Americans had a median duration of 36.5 months compared to 6.6 months for Anglos. In Michigan, African Americans remained in care 17.5 months, while Anglos had a median duration of 11.2 months. In Texas, although the duration of care was not as great, there was a difference of 7.3 months for Anglos and 9 months for African Americans. McMurtry and Young Lie (1992) studied 775 children in Arizona and found that African American children spent an average of 3 or more years in out-of-home care, while Anglo and Latino children spent an average of 2.5 years and other children of color 2 years.

Courtney (1994) found that in California, African American children placed in kinship care went home at about half the rate of similarly placed Anglo children. Courtney (1995) also found that African American children have significantly higher reentry rates into foster care than all other children, even after controlling for the child's age, health problems, placement history, and AFDC eligibility. Finally, Courtney et al. (1996) reported that African American children are also less likely to be adopted than Anglo or Latino children.

Barth (1997) reported in his longitudinal study of 3,873 children who were less than 6 years of age upon entry into care that age and race had substantial direct effects on outcomes:

> Controlling for age, African American children were considerably less likely to be adopted than Anglo or Latino children. The estimated adopted/remained in care odds-ratio was more than five times as great for Caucasian children as for African American children. (p. 296)

Also, the odds of African American children being reunified from non-kinship foster care were one fourth those of Anglo children in care.

Similarly, once legally free for adoption, African American children are also more likely to wait longer for adoptive placements. Unfortunately, many agencies have been reluctant to either establish or use specialized minority adoption programs (McKenzie, 1993), although the North American Council on Adoptable Children (NACAC) has reported that minority specializing agencies have been successful in placing 94% of their African American children inracially, while only 51% of traditional agencies place African American children inracially (NACAC, 1993).

A glimpse at federal laws and programs in family preservation, kinship care, and adoption, designed to address the foster care crisis leads one to be hopeful that programs are in place that will reduce placements and facilitate permanence through adoption. However, a closer look reveals problems in implementation and service delivery relating to African American families and children.

Family Preservation

The growth in the number of children in the foster care system, as well as concern about the children without specific "permanency plans" who were remaining in care far too long, influenced the passage of the Adoption Assistance and Child Welfare Act of 1980 (P.L. 96-272) discussed earlier. This act called for states to develop programs aimed at preventing foster care placements. The law required the following order of placement considerations: reunification with the child's family, adoption, guardianship, and long-term foster care (Barth & Berry, 1987). Moreover, the act called for agencies to provide evidence that they have made "reasonable efforts" to maintain a child in his or her own home. In cases in which placement was made, court or administrative reviews were required every 6 months to "determine the continuing necessity for and appropriateness of the placement, and to project a likely date by which the child might be returned home or placed in legal guardianship or adoption" (Adoption Asssistance and Child Welfare Act of 1980, p. 511; Harrison & Johnson, 1994). Although this law stimulated the development of a number of family support programs, reduced the time children were in placement, increased adoptions and reunifications, and led to a reduction in the number of children in out-of-home care from more than 500,000 in 1977 to 286,000 in 1985, it was never adequately funded and not fully implemented (Harrison & Johnson, 1994).

In the late 1980s factors such as the growing incidence of AIDS, teen parenthood, poverty, and parental substance abuse and violence all contributed to the rise of children in care. In 1993, the Family Preservation and Support Services Program was established, which set aside $1 billion in funding over 5 years for family support services. Family preservation was again emphasized through ASFA (discussed earlier), in which family support and family preservation were reauthorized through a program called "Promoting Safe and Stable Families."

However, Hollingsworth (2000) cautions that the Adoption and Safe Families Act (P.L. 105-89) tends to "dilute the requirement of reasonable efforts to avoid a child's removal or reunification with his or her biological parent and also allows for a worker to simultaneously work towards adoption and reunification" (p. 183). The call for more family preservation services is somewhat compromised through ASFA, which gives states financial incentives to increase adoptions.

In practice, one of the most important decision points in child welfare services is the decision to remove a child or provide services that may enable the child to remain in the home. Lindsey (1991) found that income was the most influential factor in determining whether a child will be referred for placement. Because the family often receives fewer services and is no longer eligible for income assistance once the child has been removed, the system itself is restricting the likelihood of family reunification. Similarly, the 1996 *Third National Incidence Study of Child Abuse and Neglect* (Sedlak & Broadhurst, 1996) reported that children from families with an annual income under $15,000 were at least 22 times more likely to experience maltreatment, almost 56 times more likely to be educationally neglected, and 22 times more likely to be seriously injured than children from families whose incomes were greater than $30,000. Since African American families are disproportionately poor, they may be disproportionately affected by this factor.

Close (1983), the NABSW (1992), the National Black Child Development Institute (1989), Pinderhughes (1991), Stehno (1990), Morisey (1990), and Denby, Curtis, and Alford (1998) all have found that even though family preservation services have been emphasized in the law and may serve to reduce the number of children in care, African American children and their families are often not receiving these services. Morisey (1990), Schuerman, Rzepnicki, Littell, and Budde (1992), and Rossi (1992) noted that workers often do not view African American families as "treatable" and often do not believe they would benefit from services and therefore do not refer these families for services. Hodges (1991) similarly found that racist attitudes and lack of understanding about ethnic family issues contribute to placement decisions. Denby and

Alford (1995) reported that workers did not consider targeting services to African American clients because of their concern that this would be considered a type of affirmative action process. Even if services are provided, it is likely that they will be temporary and often not sufficient to permanently raise these families out of poverty, the condition that led them to be involved in the child welfare system in the first place.

Kinship Care

As might be expected, along with the increase in the number of children needing foster placements, there was an increased need for foster families to care for these children. Unfortunately, however, the number of available foster families has been decreasing. In 1984, there were approximately 147,000 foster parents, but by 1990, there were only about 100,000 (National Commission on Foster Family Care, 1991). Although figures on foster parents of color are not available, it is unlikely that there has ever been an adequate supply of foster parents of color because of the economic need for women of color to work outside the home, strict licensing regulations, and limited recruitment of people of color for foster parenting (Stehno, 1990).

Several factors account for the decline in the number of foster parents, including the need for more dual earner households, increased geographic mobility of families, the increase in single parent households and divorce, and the cost of child rearing, as well as the types of presenting problems many of the children in care exhibit (Berrick, 1998). Responding to the strain on the foster care system, along with an increasing societal belief that children fare better in their own families, some child welfare professionals have begun seeking placements with extended family members.

The philosophical shift toward considering relatives as an option actually began in 1978 with the passage of the Indian Child Welfare Act, which listed relatives at the top of the hierarchy of preferred placements for Indian children. A year later in 1979, the U.S. Supreme Court in *Miller v. Youakim* ruled that kin must be given an equal opportunity to qualify for foster parent status and be eligible for federal foster care benefits (Altstein & McRoy, 2000). Moreover, the Adoption Assistance and Child Welfare Act of 1980 (P.L. 96-272) called for children to be placed in the least restrictive environment possible, and in most cases this meant relatives if at all possible. By 1990, more than half of the total foster care population in New York City was placed with relatives (Walker, Zangrillo, & Smith, 1994). Out-of-home placement with relatives of children who are in the custody of state and local child welfare agencies is now referred to as kinship care (Scannapieco, Hegar, & McAlpine, 1997, p. 480).

In 1996, the Personal Responsibility and Work Opportunity Reconciliation Act required that states "consider giving preference to an adult relative over a non-related caregiver" as long as the "relative caregiver meets all the relevant state child protection standards" (Leos-Urbel, Bess, & Geen, 2000). Further, the Adoption and Safe Families Act of 1997 called for a panel to study kinship care and also included mention of the "kinship exemption," which stipulated that the time limit clauses regarding termination of parental rights do not apply to kinship care (Bartholet, 1999).

In 2002, about 2. 3 million children in the United States were living in some type of kinship arrangement without a parent present (Geen, 2003). Of this number, approximately 131,000 children are in kinship foster care, representing 24% of all foster children (Geen, 2003).

Studies of kinship care in cities such as Baltimore, MD, Berkeley, CA, Los Angeles, Philadelphia, and in the states of Illinois, Michigan, and New York all revealed that the majority (most well over 80%) of children in kinship care are African American (Benedict, Zuravin, & Stallings,

1996; Berrick, Barth, & Needell, 1994; Dubowitz, Feigelman, & Zuravin, 1993; Iglehart, 1994; Ingram, 1996; Link, 1996; Mayor's Commission for the Foster Care of Children, 1993; Mills & Usher, 1996; Testa, Shook, Cohen, & Woods, 1996; Thornton, 1991). In most of these families, children are typically living with a grandmother or another female relative.

Most studies suggest that the majority of kinship care providers make less than $10,000 per year (Dubowitz et al., 1993; Mayor's Commission for the Foster Care of Children, 1993). Thornton (1991) found that 45% of caregivers had incomes of less than $5,000 per year. Several researchers have found that less than half of kinship caregivers had completed high school (Berrick et al., 1994; Dubowitz et al., 1993; Testa et al., 1996; Thornton, 1991). These placements have been heralded as being more stable than other placements, yet children in kinship care arrangements are less likely to be adopted than children in non-kinship care. Kin providers, although often eligible for services, are less likely to receive training, respite care, counseling, tutoring, or assessments for children in their care than non-kin care providers (Berrick et al., 1994; Chipungu, Everett, Verduik, & Jones (1998); Ehrle et al., 2001).

Gleeson, O'Donnell, and Bonecutter (1997) found that caseworkers providing services to kinship caregivers rarely involve members of the kinship network in the planning and decision making for children, and they also found a low rate of achievement of permanency plans for children in kinship care.

Noting that the majority of kin care providers are African American and are less likely to receive the same level of funding as well as services as foster care providers, Scannapieco and Hegar (1999) asked, "Is kinship foster care the newest way for society to leave minority, especially African American children, to the care of their own willing but poorly resourced extended families and communities?" (pp. 8–9). Similarly, Harden, Clark, and McGuire (1997) noted that there exists a "two-tiered, racially segregated system of foster care," which is evident in that non-kin foster parents are reimbursed at a higher rate than both public and private kin caregivers (p. 8).

Differential payment for providers may change, as the implementation guidelines for ASFA mandated that "relatives must meet the same licensing/approval standards as non-relative foster family homes" if states are to receive federal funds toward placement with a relative (DHHS, 2000). However, it is yet unclear how service provisions will change for these families.

Adoption

The most permanent placement option for children in the system is adoption. Although agencies staffed primarily by White female professionals have had much success in placing White infants for adoption and some success in placing White older children for adoption, historically public and private agencies have had limited success in finding adoptive families for African American children (McRoy et al., 1997). For example Barth (1997) found that even after age was controlled, African American children were significantly less likely to be adopted than White children. An African American infant had nearly the same likelihood of being adopted as a White 3- to 5-year-old.

Several researchers have examined factors that may have influenced the shortage of prospective adoptive resources for children of color. In 1990, Rodriguez and Meyer reported the findings of their research on adoptive applicants of color from five large cities and found that agency policies, lack of sufficient and trained staff members of color, and some attitudes within communities of color were obstacles to recruiting families for older children of color. Among the practices successful in placing these children were: personalized presentations of children, culturally sensitized staff, use of adoption subsidies, single parents, foster adoptions, and community education. The North American Council on Adoptable Children also found obstacles to adoptions of children of color to include agency fees, inflexible standards as well as institutional/systemic racism, and lack of staff members of color (McRoy et al., 1997; NACAC, 1991). A 1990–1991 survey of adoption agencies revealed that 83% of agencies were aware of barriers that discouraged or prevented families of color from adopting (Gilles & Kroll, 1991). Minority-specializing programs (such as the Institute for Black Parenting in Los Angeles, Homes for Black Children in Detroit, Black Adoption Program and Services in Kansas City, One Church One Child, have been found to be successful in recruiting and successfully placing African American children (NACAC, 1991). However, most agencies have not developed such specialized recruitment and placement programs and therefore have not been very successful in placing African American children.

Instead of accepting responsibility for not placing African American children, some agencies have often blamed African American families for their failure to adopt children, whereas in reality most are being screened out of the process. In a National Urban League study of 800 African American families who applied to adopt, only two were approved for adoption. However, the national average for approval is 10% (Altstein & McRoy, 2000; National Transracial Adoption, 1985). Moreover, the CWLA has acknowledged that African American families can be found for infants, preschoolers, and school-age African American children (Sullivan, 1994). In fact, Mason and Williams (1985) found that when family composition, income and age are controlled, African American families actually adopt at four times the rate of White families.

Discounting the availability of African American adoptive families, some believe African American children remain in the system because transracial adoptions have been discouraged through position statements by the NABSW, as well as state laws and policies which sought to match children and families racially (Simon, Altstein, & Melli, 1994). Influenced by these attitudes and numerous lawsuits by White foster families who were being denied or discouraged from adopting African American infants and young children in their care (e.g., *Burich v. Cuyahoga Cty. Dept. of Children & Family Servs.*, 1994; *Tallman v. Tabor*, 1994), Senator Howard M. Metzenbaum proposed the Multiethnic Placement Act. This was signed into law by President Clinton in 1994 (P.L. 103-382) in an attempt to "do something to help children who were being denied the opportunity to be part of a stable and caring family, when a same race family was not available" (Bussiere, 1995) and therefore reduce the length of time children wait to be adopted. The law mandated that an agency receiving federal funds should not: (a) categorically deny to any person the opportunity to become an adoptive or a foster parent, solely on the basis of race, color, or national origin of the adoptive or foster parent, or the child, involved; or (b) delay or deny the placement of a child for adoption or into foster care or otherwise discriminate in making a placement decision, solely on the basis of the race, color or national origin of the adoptive or foster parent, or the child involved (Multiethnic Placement Act, 1994). The original act allowed consideration of the racial background of the child and capacity of parents to meet the child's needs. It also required states to undertake recruitment efforts to seek families that reflected the children in care.

This law was strengthened in January 1997 as section 1808, "Removal of Barriers to Interethnic Adoption," of P.L. 104-188, the Small Business Job Protection Act of 1996. According to these amendments, states cannot:

- deny to any person the opportunity to become an adoptive or foster parent on the basis of race, color or national origin of the person; or

- delay or deny the placement of a child for adoption or foster care on the basis of race, color or national origin of the adoptive or foster parent or child involved.

This amendment removed language that allowed routine consideration of race and instead stated that if race were used in making a decision, the agency would have to prove to the courts that this was justified by a "compelling government interest and was necessary to the best interest of the child" (Interethnic Placement Act Amendments of 1996). Significant monetary penalties were added as a deterrent to the violation of the amended act. The recruitment provision of the original law was strengthened to call for child welfare services to provide for the diligent recruitment of potential foster and adoptive families that reflect the ethnic and racial diversity of children in the state for whom foster and adoptive homes are needed.

What is most interesting about the original act and the amendment that was designed to end discriminatory placement activities, is that despite claims to the contrary, it seemed in reality to apply primarily to the placement of one group—children of color. Race-matching has always been standard practice for White children and families. Rarely are White children placed transracially with families of color (Brooks, Bussiere, Barth, & Patterson, 1997; Freundlich, 2000). The rationale often given for continuing to place White children with White families has been based on the large supply of White families and the limited supply of White children (McRoy et al., 1997). Moreover, the federal government acted on placement practices that seemed to discriminate against White families, yet has been silent for years on placement practices which have tended to discriminate against African American families.

The reality is that this law will probably help a small number of White families adopt foster children of color who have been in their homes since infancy. However, as transracial adoptions only account for about 1% of all adoptions (Stolley, 1993), it is unlikely that transracial adoptions will have an impact on reducing the number of older children of color in the child welfare system. Further, the majority of families seeking to adopt transracially are seeking infants and young children.

Instead, it is more likely that this act will become an even greater barrier for African American families since racial matching can no longer be considered a priority in adoptive placements. In Texas, workers can lose their jobs if they delay or deny a placement for the purposes of racial matching (McRoy et al., 1997). Due to these federal and state laws, some workers may be reluctant to advocate for African American families seeking to adopt African American children and thus create further barriers to African American adoptions. Moreover, having to fight for the right to be considered a viable option for an African American child may tend to discourage some African American families from considering adoption.

Implications for Social Work Practice and Education

In the child welfare system, the majority of families are poor and of color, and the majority of workers are White and have had limited preparation and skills in working with culturally diverse populations. Pinderhughes (1997) describes the current child welfare system as follows:

> Driven by deficit thinking, and using American middle-class norms as a marker for family assessment, the systems of delivery that have created mutual mistrust between families are plagued by rigidity and limited options, along with a crisis and "protection and removal" philosophy. (p. 20)

Although the child welfare literature contains numerous references to cultural diversity and many child welfare professionals advocate for an understanding of ethnic differences, many child welfare services programs and policies reflect values and attitudes more consistent with majority culture (Jenson & Whittaker, 1989; McGowan & Meezan, 1983; Siegel, 1994; Weissman, Epstein, & Savage, 1983). Social workers must now be willing to acknowledge that existing policies and practices often are not addressing the needs of African American children and families. It is clear that existing service models are working for Anglo families but not for African American families.

Cultural competency training is no longer an option—it must be a requirement to work in this system. Social service staff must be assessed to determine their level of competency and to help them focus on increased self-awareness of attitudes and pre-conceptions about African American populations. Specific course work on social work practice with African American families and children is needed if workers are going to be prepared to join families and work closely with them demonstrating respect and valuing their strengths. As historically African American extended family members have been involved in child rearing, they can be a wonderful resource in finding ways in which they can either provide kinship care, support family caregivers in meeting the needs of the child, or participate in making plans for children (Gleeson et al., 1997). In addition to gaining a better understanding of practice with this population, workers need to participate in undoing–racism training so they can be better able to identify vestiges of racism and to help empower families as well as agencies to change the status quo and make a difference in outcomes for children. They must also participate in training that emphasizes cross-cultural practice (Pinderhughes, 1989).

Since there is an apparent shortage of African American child welfare workers, and since the availability of staff members of color seems to enhance service delivery with clients of color (McRoy et al., 1997), public and private agencies must seek staff of color. For them to be successful in hiring staff, social work education programs must begin to actively recruit more African American students into graduate school. Many social work programs have received IV-E grants from the federal government through state agencies to provide stipends for students planning to return to work in child welfare. Priority should be placed on recruiting African American students for these stipends and all students in these programs should be trained in culturally competent service provision.

Most child welfare services for African American families seem to be focused on African American women and children. Too often service providers as well as policy makers tend to ignore African American men. As stated earlier in this paper, the majority of children in the system come from single-parent, mostly mother-headed families. Yet this does not necessarily mean that African American men are not involved at all in the lives of their children. Many fathers, grandfathers, uncles, brothers, friends, and neighbors are very involved and workers must not be patronizing to, nor fail to recognize the significance of their roles in the family. Permanency planning must include fathers, paternal relatives, and others who have an important role in the lives of children (Leashore, 1997).

Many of our existing service models are not working, and every aspect of child welfare policies as well as practices need to be assessed and most likely revamped to effectively address the needs of all children in the system. To improve services to African American families, efforts should be made to explore the use of Africentric models that incorporate African American cultural strengths. Moreover, since family preservation services often are not targeted toward African American clients, we need to not only target existing programs toward this population, we must develop culturally based models of family preservation (Stehno, 1990). Through successful family preservation efforts, fewer children will enter the child welfare system.

Child welfare services providers need to adopt specific performance indicators in which agencies can assess the work of staff in moving children to permanence. Workers must be expected to visit families and children on a regular basis, keep up-to-date service plans, and develop more systematic strategies for placement decision making. Additional funding is needed to hire more trained staff, reduce caseloads, provide mandatory training, develop updated computerized tracking systems, develop better communication among workers within the agency, and specifically target the placement of children. As soon as financial incentives were in place through ASFA for the placement of children in adoption, agencies found that they were more successful in making placements.

Despite the various policies that have been passed to promote permanency for children, only limited federal efforts have been designed to respond to the needs of children and families of color. The Indian Child Welfare Act (P.L. 95-608) was specifically designed to reduce the number of Native American children entering foster care and being placed away from their culture and tribes into White families. However, while this policy made the criteria for placement more stringent, it was "inadequately funded and unevenly implemented" (Pecora, Kinney, Mitchell, & Tolley, 1990, p. 344). The Multiethnic Placement Act and the Interethnic provisions were designed to remove barriers to interethnic adoption, and supposedly facilitate the adoption of children of color, especially, African American children. However, in reality, it perhaps has had more of an impact on protecting the rights of White foster parents than in making more adoption opportunities available for the older African American children remaining in the child welfare system.

Additional policies are needed which are designed to actually promote birth family permanence and the security of children in their own families of origin by addressing concrete needs such as food, child care, housing, and substance abuse treatment, as well as offering parenting classes and clinical services. Such services will reduce the number of children for whom adoption planning will be needed.

Conclusion

Many social problems are facing our children and families today, including poverty, exposure to violence, inadequate health care, high rates of abuse and neglect, parental substance abuse, deteriorating neighborhoods, deteriorating educational opportunities, and family and community breakdown (Harrison & Johnson, 1994; National Commission on Children, 1991). All of these factors are implicated in the growing number of children in the child welfare system. It is time that we acknowledge that the overrepresentation of African American children in the system has been affected by racism and racial inequities in the child welfare practice and policy arena, economic system, criminal justice system, legal system, and welfare system, as well as society a whole.

Despite the disparate treatment that has occurred for years, only recently has litigation been filed that addresses these concerns. Children's Rights of New York has filed suits on the basis of civil rights violations specifically aimed at reforming the nation's child welfare system. Under Title VI of the Civil Rights Act of 1964, any state program or activity that receives federal financial assistance is prohibited from excluding from participation, denying benefits to or subjecting to discrimination, any persons on the basis of race, color, or national origin. Title VI applies to the administration and provision of child welfare services. Moreover, the U.S. Department of Health and Human Services has issued regulations, pursuant to Title VI, that prohibit any state programs or activities that receive federal financial assistance from using criteria or methods of administration that have the effect of subjecting individuals to discrimination because of their race, color, or national origin, or have the effect of defeating or substantially impairing the accomplishment of the objectives of the programs with respect to individuals of a particular race, color, or national origin.

In five jurisdictions where Children's Rights has filed suit, child welfare funding has been increased by more than $1.6 billion. These lawsuits have led to better training for workers and foster parents; increases in services for parents, children, and foster parents; increased adoptions; better information systems; the establishment of standards; and regular monitoring and reporting of compliance (Impact, 2001).

A recent widely acclaimed settlement brought about by Children's Rights with the state of Tennessee on May 15, 2001, has led to specific remedies, including requirements like caseload limitations, time periods for case planning, and most importantly a required full examination by an independent evaluator of the racial disparities in the foster care system. It is expected that this will lead to recommendations for a comprehensive reform of the state-run child welfare system.

It is unfortunate that lawsuits have been needed to force states to remedy the racist practices which have led to the overrepresentation and disparate treatment of African American children in the child welfare system. However, placement in foster care is a symptom of a much bigger problem—the declining economic well-being of African American families in our society in the 21st century. We must continue to look at larger societal forces including racism and inequitable opportunities that put African American children at risk.

References

Administration for Children and Families, U.S. Department of Health and Human Services. (1998). Adoption and Foster Care Analysis and Reporting System. Retrieved May 23, 2001, from http://www.acf.dhhs.gov/programs/cb/publications/afcars/apr2001.htm

Administration for Children and Families, U.S. Department of Health and Human Services. (2001). Adoption and Foster Care Analysis and Reporting System. Retrieved Dec. 8, 2002, from http://www.acf.dhhs.gov/ programs/cb

Adoption Assistance and Child Welfare Act, 42 USC § 630–635 (1980)

Adoption Opportunities Act, 42 USC chapter 67, subchapter II (1978).

Altstein, H., & McRoy, R. G. (2000). *Does family preservation serve a child's best interests?* Washington, DC: Georgetown University Press.

Barth, R. (1997). Effects of age and race on the odds of adoption versus remaining in long-term out-of-home care. *Child Welfare, 76*, 285–308.

Barth, R. P., & Berry, M. (1987). Outcomes of child welfare services since permanency planning. *Social Service Review, 61*, 71–90.

Barth, R. P., Berry, M., Carson, M., Goodfield, R., & Feinberg, B. (1986). Contributors to disruption and dissolution of older child adoption. *Child Welfare, 65*, 359–371.

Bartholet, E. (1999). *Nobody's children: Abuse and neglect, foster drift, and the adoption alternative.* Boston: Beacon Press.

Benedict, M. I., Zuravin, S., & Stallings, R. (1996). Adult functioning of children who lived in kin versus nonkin family foster homes. *Child Welfare, 75*, 529–549.

Berrick, J. (1998). When children cannot remain home: Foster family care and kinship care. *The Future of Children, 8*, 72–87.

Berrick, J., Barth, R., & Needell, B. (1994). A comparison of kinship foster homes and foster family homes: Implications for kinship foster care as family preservation. *Children and Youth Services Review, 16*(1/2), 33–63.

Billingsley, A., & Giovannoni, J. M. (1972). *Children of the storm: Black children and American child welfare.* New York: Harcourt Brace Jovanovich.

Bremmer, R. H. (1983). Other people's children. *Journal of Social History, 16,* 83–103.

Brooks, D., Bussiere, A., Barth, R., & Patterson, G. (1997). *Adoption and race: Implementing the Multiethnic Placement Act of 1994 and the Interethnic Adoption Provisions.* San Francisco: The Stuart Foundation.

Burnam, A., & Melamid, E. (2000). Child protection and welfare reform. In J. Hosek & R. Levine (Eds.), *The new fiscal federalism and the social safety net: A view from California.* Retrieved July 6, 2001, from http://www.rand.org/publications/CF/CF123/burnam

Burich v. Cuyahoga Cty. Dept. of Children & Family Servs., 1994 U.S. App. Lexis 14943, 6th Cir.

Bussiere, A. *A Guide to the Multiethnic Placement Act of 1994.* National Resource Center on Legal and Court Issues. Washington, DC: American Bar Association

Cappelleri, J. C., Eckenrode, J., & Powers, J. L. (1993). The epidemiology of child abuse: Findings from the Second National Incidence and Prevalence Study of Child Abuse and Neglect. *American Journal of Public Health, 83,* 1622–1624.

Casey Family Programs. (2001). *Transition from foster care: A state-by state data base project.* Seattle, WA: Author.

Child Abuse Prevention and Treatment Act, 42 USC § 5101; 42 USC § 5116 (1974).

Child Welfare League of America. (1968). *Standards for adoption service.* New York: Author.

Child Welfare League of America. (1972). *Selected adoption data for 1969, 1970, 1971* [Special report]. New York: CWLA Research Center.

Child Welfare League of America. (1997). *Child abuse and neglect: A look at the states.* Washington, DC: CWLA Press.

Child Welfare League of America. (1998). *Family foster care fact sheet. Statistics package.* Retrieved February 4, 1999, from http://www.cwla.org

Children's Defense Fund. (1999). *The state of America's children.* Washington, DC: Author.

Children's Defense Fund. (2000). *The state of America's children.* Washington, DC: Author.

Children's Services Practice Notes. (2001, May). African American children in the child welfare system. *Children's Services Practice Notes, 6*(2). Retrieved October 15, 2003, from http://sswnt7.sowo.unc.edu/fcrp/Cspn/vol6_no2.htm

Chipungu, S., Everett, J., Verduik, M., & Jones, J. (1998). *Children placed in foster care with relatives: A multi-state study.* Washington, DC: U.S. Department of Health and Human Services, Administration for Children and Families.

Civil Rights Act, *6 U.S.C. § 601(1964).*

Close, M. (1983). Child welfare and people of color: Denial of equal access. *Social Work, 28,* 13–20.

Congressional Research Service Report for Congress (1997, January 15). *Foster care and adoption statistics: Summary.* Retrieved October 15, 2003, from http://web.archive.org/web/19981205063809/http://www.casanet.org/library/foster_care/fost.htm

Courtney, M. E. (1994). Factors associated with the reunification of foster children with their families. *Social Service Review, 68,* 82–108.

Courtney, M. E. (1995). Reentry to foster care of children returned to their families. *Social Service Review, 69,* 226–241.

Courtney, M. E. (1996). Kinship foster care and children's welfare: The California experience. *Focus, 17*(3), 42–48.

Courtney, M. E. (1998). The costs of child protection in the context of welfare reform. *The Future of Children, 8,* 88–103.

Courtney, M. E. (1999). Foster care and the costs of welfare reform. In P. Curtis, G. Dale, & J. Kendall (Eds.), *The foster care crisis: Translating research into policy and practice* (pp. 129–151). Lincoln, NE: University of Nebraska Press.

Courtney, M. E., Barth, R. P., Berrick, J. D., Brooks, D., Needell, B., & Park, L. (1996). Race and child welfare services: Past research and future directions. *Child Welfare, 75*, 99–137.

Curtis, P. (1999). Introduction: The chronic nature of the foster care crisis. In P. Curtis, G. Dale, & J. Kendall (Eds.), *The foster care crisis: Translating research into policy and practice* (pp. 1–16). Lincoln, NE: University of Nebraska Press.

Curtis, P., Dale, G., & Kendall, J. (Eds.). (1999). *The foster care crisis: Translating research into policy and practice*. Lincoln, NE: University of Nebraska Press.

Day, D. (1979). *The adoption of Black children*. Lexington, MA: Heath

Denby, R. W., & Alford, K. A. (1995, October 12–15). *Special populations and family preservation: Strengthening our commitment and meeting needs*. Paper presented at the National Association of Social Workers Meeting of the Profession, Philadelphia, PA.

Denby, R. W., Curtis, C. M., & Alford, K. A. (1998). Family preservation and special populations: The invisible target. *Families in Society, 79*(1), 3–14.

Dubowitz, H., Feigelman, S., & Zuravin, S. (1993). A profile of kinship care. *Child Welfare, 72*, 153–169.

Eckenrode, J., Powers, J., Doris, J., Munsch, J., & Bolger, N. (1988). Substantiation of child abuse and neglect reports. *Journal of Consulting and Clinical Psychology, 56*, 9–16.

Ehrle, J., Geen, R., & Clark, R. (2001). Children cared for by relatives: Who are they and how are they faring? *New federalism: National survey of America's families* (Series B, No. B-2). Washington, DC: Urban Institute.

English, D. J. (1998). The extent and consequences of child maltreatment. *The Future of Children, 8*, 39–53.

Fein, E., Maluccio, A., & Kluger, M. (1990). *No more partings. An examination of long-term foster care*. Washington, DC: Child Welfare League of America.

Flemming Rule of 1962, Public Law 87-31.

Freundlich. M. (2000). *The role of race, culture, and national origin in adoption*. Washington, DC: Child Welfare League of America.

Garbarino, J., Kostelny, K., & Dubrow, N. (1991). *No place to be a child: Growing up in a war zone*. Lexington, MA: Lexington Books.

Garland, A. F., Ellis-MacLeod, E., Landsverk, J. A., Ganger, W., & Johnson, I. (1998). Minority populations in the child welfare system: The visibility hypothesis reexamined. *American Journal of Orthopsychiatry, 68*(1), 142–146.

Geen, R. (2003). Kinship foster care: An ongoing yet largely uninformed debate. In R. Geen (Ed.), *Kinship Care*. Washington, DC: Urban Institute Press.

Genty, P. M. (1998). Permanency planning in the context of parental incarceration: Legal issues and recommendations. *Child Welfare, 77*, 543–559.

Gilles, T., & Kroll, J. (1991). *Barriers to same-race placement*. St. Paul, MN: North American Council on Adoptable Children.

Gleeson, J. P., O'Donnell, J., & Bonecutter, F. J. (1997). Understanding the complexity of practice in kinship foster care. *Child Welfare, 76*, 801–826.

Goerge, R. (1990). The reunification process in substitute care. *Social Service Review, 64*, 422–457.

Goerge, R. M., Wulczyn, F. H., & Harden, A. W. (1994). *Foster care dynamics 1983–1992, California, Illinois, Michigan, New York and Texas: A report from the Multistate Foster Care Data Archive*. Chicago: Chapin Hall Center for Children, University of Chicago.

Harden, A. W., Clark, R. L., & McGuire, K. (1997). *Informal and formal kinship care*. Chicago: Chapin Hall Center for Children.

Harrison, W. D., & Johnson, M. S. (1994). Child welfare policy in the United States. *Social Policy & Administration, 28*(2), 139–150.

Hill, R. B. (1997). *The strengths of African American families: Twenty-five years later.* Washington, DC: R & B Publishers.

Hodges, V. G. (1991). Providing culturally sensitive intensive family preservation services to ethnic minority families. In E. M. Tracy, D. A. Haappala, J. Kinney, & P. J. Pecora (Eds.), *Intensive family preservation services: An instructional sourcebook* (pp. 95–116). Cleveland, OH: Mandel School of Applied Social Sciences, Case Western Reserve University.

Hollingsworth, L. D. (2000). Adoption policy in the United States: A word of caution. *Social Work, 45*(2), 183–186.

Iglehart, A. (1994). Kinship foster care: Placement, service, and outcome issues. *Children and Youth Services Review, 16*(1-2), 107–122.

Impact. (2001, Summer). *Children's Rights Annual Newsletter*, p. 2.

Indian Child Welfare Act, 25 U.S.C. § 1901-1923 (1978).

Interethnic Placement Act Amendments of 1996, Pub. L. No. 104-188 (1996).

Ingram, C. (1996). Kinship care: Last resort to first choice. *Child Welfare, 75*, 550–566.

Interethnic Placement Act Amendments of 1996, Public Law No. 104-188.

Jenson, J. M., & Whittaker, J. K. (1989). Parental involvement in children's residential treatment: From preplacement to aftercare. In E. A. Balcerzak (Ed.), *Group care of children: Transitions toward the year 2000.* Washington, DC: Child Welfare League of America.

Jeter, H. R., (1963). *Children, problems and services in child welfare programs* (Children's Bureau Publication No. 403-1963). Washington, DC: U.S. Department of Health, Education and Welfare.

Jones, E. D., & McCurdy, K. (1992). The links between types of maltreatment and demographic characteristicsof children. *Child Abuse and Neglect, 16*, 201–214.

Lawrence-Webb, C. (1997). African American children in the modern child welfare system: A legacy of the Flemming Rule. *Child Welfare, 76*, 9–30.

Leashore, B. R. (1997). African American men, child welfare, and permanency planning. In G. R. Anderson, A. S. Ryan, & B. R. Leashore (Eds.), *The challenge of permanency planning in a multicultural society* (pp. 39–48). Boston: Haworth Press.

Leashore, B. R., Chipungu, S. S., & Everett, J. E. (1991). *Child welfare: An Africentric perspective.* New Brunswick, NJ: Rutgers University Press.

Leos-Urbel, J., Bess, R., & Geen, R. (2000). *State policies for assessing and supporting kinship foster parents.* Washington, DC: Urban Institute.

Lindsey, D. (1991). Factors affecting the foster care placement decision: An analysis of national survey data. *American Journal of Orthopsychiatry, 61*, 272–281.

Link, M. K. (1996). Permanency outcomes in kinship care: A study of children placed in kinship care in Erie County, New York. *Child Welfare, 75*, 509–528.

Maas, H. S., & Engler, R. E., Jr. (1959). *Children in need of parents.* New York: Columbia University Press.

MacDonald, H. (1994). The ideology of "family preservation." *The Public Interest, Spring*, 45–60.

Mason, J., & Williams, C. (1985). The adoption of minority children: Issues in developing law and policy. In E. C. Segal & M. Hardin (Eds.), *Adoption of children with special needs: Issues in law and policy* (pp. 81–93). Washington, DC : American Bar Association.

Mayor's Commission for the Foster Care of Children. (1993). *Family assets: Kinship foster care in New York City.* New York: Author.

McGowan, B., & Meezan, W. (1983). *Child welfare.* Itasca, IL: Peacock.

McKenzie, J. (1993). Adoption of children with special needs. *The Future of Children, 3*, 62–76.

McMurtry, S., & Young Lie, G. (1992). Differential exit rates of minority children in foster care. *Social Work Research and Abstracts, 28*, 42–48.

McRoy, R. G. (1994). Attachment and racial identity issues: Implications for child placement decision making. *Journal of Multicultural Social Work, 3,* 59–74.

McRoy, R. G., Oglesby, Z., & Grape H. (1997). Achieving same-race adoptive placements for African American children: Culturally sensitive practice approaches. *Child Welfare, 76,* 85–106.

McRoy, R., G., & Zurcher, L. (1983). *Transracial and inraacial adoptees: The adolescent years.* Springfield, IL: Thomas.

Mech, E. V. (1983). Out-of-home placement rates. *Social Service Review, 57,* 659–667

Miller v. Youakim. (1979). Supreme Court 440 U.S. 125.

Mills, C. S., & Usher, D. (1996). A kinship care case management approach. *Child Welfare, 75,* 600–618.

Morgernstern, J. (1971, September 13). The new face of adoption. *Newsweek,* pp. 67–72.

Morisey, P. G. (1990). Black children in foster care. In S. M. Logan, E. M. Freeman, & R. G. McRoy (Eds.), *Social work practice with Black families: A culturally specific perspective* (pp. 133–147). New York: Longman.

Morton, T. (1993). Ideas in action: The issue is race. *Child Welfare Institute Newsletter,* Spring, 1–2.

Multiethnic Placement Act, 42 U.S.C. § 5115a (1994).

National Adoption Information Clearinghouse. (1998). *Adoption statistics—A brief overview.* Retrieved November 9, 1998, from http://naic.acf.hhs.gov/index.cfm

National Association of Black Social Workers. (1972, April). *Position statement on transracial adoptions.* Presented at the National Association of Black Social Workers Conference, Nashville, TN.

National Association of Black Social Workers. (1992). *Preserving African American families: Research and action beyond the rhetoric.* Detroit, MI: Author.

National Black Child Development Institute. (1989). *Who will care when parents can't? A study of Black children in foster care.* Washington, DC: Author.

National Center on Child Abuse and Neglect. (1981). *Study findings: National study of incidence and severity of child abuse and neglect.* Washington, DC: U.S. Department of Health, Education, and Welfare.

National Center on Child Abuse and Neglect. (1988). *Study findings: Study of national incidence and prevalence of child abuse and neglect.* Washington, DC: Government Printing Office.

National Center on Child Abuse and Neglect. (1996). *Child abuse and neglect state statute series* [Vol. 1, Reporting Laws]. Washington, DC: U.S. Department of Health and Human Services.

National Commission on Children. (1991). *Beyond rhetoric: A new American agenda for children and families.* Washington, DC: Author.

National Commission on Foster Family Care (1991). *A blueprint for fostering infants, children, and youths in the 1990s.* Washington, DC: Child Welfare League of America.

Newberger, E., Reed, R., Daniel, J. H., Hyde, J., & Kotelchuck, M. (1977). Pediatric social illness: Toward an etiologic classification. *Pediatrics, 60,* 178–185.

Newlin, P. B. (1997). Family preservation: Where have we been? How can we as social workers continue to collaborate? In *Change and challenge: MCH social work make the difference.* Proceedings of the BiRegional Conference for Public Health Social Workers, June 11–14, 1995. Columbia, SC: College of Social Work, University of South Carolina.

North American Council on Adoptable Children. (1991). *Barriers to race placement.* St. Paul, MN: Author.

North American Council on Adoptable Children. (1993). *Transracial adoption position statement.* St. Paul, MN: Author.

Olsen, L. (1982). Predicting the permanency status of children in family foster care. *Social Work Research and Abstracts, 18*(1), 9–19.

Omnibus Budget Reconciliation Act of 1993, P.L. 103-66, 107 Stat. 31.

O'Toole, R., Turbett, P., & Nalpeka, C. (1983). Theories, professional knowledge, and diagnosis of child abuse. In D. Finkelhor, R. J. Gelles, G. T. Hotaling, & M. A. Straus (Eds.), *The dark side of families: Current family violence research* (pp. 349–362). Beverly Hills, CA: Sage.

Pecora, P. J., Kinney, K. M., Mitchell, L., & Tolley, G. (1990). Selecting an agency auspice for family preservation services. *Social Service Review, 64*, 288–307.

Pelton, L. H. (1989). *For reasons of poverty*. New York: Praeger.

Pelton, L. H. (1991). Beyond permanency planning: Restructuring the public child welfare system. *Social Work, 36*, 337–344.

Personal Responsibility and Work Opportunity Reconciliation Act of 1996, Public Law 104-193, 110 Stat. 2105.

Petit, M. R., Curtis, P. A., Woodruff, K., Arnold, L., Feagans, L., & Ang, J. (1999). *Child abuse and neglect: A look at the states*. Washington, DC: CWLA Press.

Pinderhughes, E. E. (1989). *Understanding race, ethnicity and power: Key to efficacy in clinical practice*. New York: Free Press.

Pinderhughes, E. E. (1991). The delivery of child welfare services to African American clients. *American Journal of Orthopsychiatry, 61*, 599–605.

Pinderhughes, E. E. (1997). Developing diversity competence in child welfare and permanency planning. In G. R. Anderson, A. S. Ryan, & B. R. Leashore (Eds.), *The challenge of permanency planning in a multicultural society* (pp. 19–38). Boston: Haworth Press.

Piven, F. F., & Cloward, R. A. (1971). *Regulating the poor*. New York: Random House.

Rodriguez, P., & Meyer, A. (1990). Minority adoptions and agency practices. *Social Work, 35*, 528–531.

Rossi, P. (1992). Assessing family preservation programs. *Children and Youth Services Review, 14*, 77–98.

Scannapieco, M., & Hegar, R. (1999). Kinship foster care in context. In R. Hegar & M. Scannapeico (Eds.), *Kinship foster care: Policy, practice, and research* (pp. 1–16). New York: Oxford University Press.

Scannapieco, M., Hegar, R. L., & McAlpine, C. (1997). Kinship care and traditional foster care: A comparison of characteristics and outcomes. *Families in Society, 78*, 480–488.

Schiele, J. H. (1998). The Personal Responsibility Act of 1996: The bitter and the sweet for African American families. *Families in Society, 79*, 424–432.

Schuerman, J., Rzepnicki, T. L., Littell, J. H., & Budde, S. (1992). Implementation issues. *Children and Youth Services Review, 14*, 193–206.

Sedlak, A. J., & Broadhurst, D. D. (1996). *Third national incidence study of child abuse and neglect, final report*. Washington, DC: U. S. Department of Health and Human Services.

Siegel, L. (1994). Cultural differences and their impact on practice in child welfare. *Journal of Multicultural Social Work, 3*(3), 87–96.

Simms, M., Freundlich, M., Battistelli, E., & Kaufman, N. D. (1999). Delivering health care and mental health care services to children in family foster care after welfare and health care reform. *Child Welfare, 78*, 166–183.

Simon, R. (1984). Adoption of Black children by White parents in the USA. In P. Bean (Ed.), *Adoption essays in social policy, law and sociology* (pp. 229–242). New York: Tavistock.

Simon, R., Altstein, H., & Melli, M. (1994). *The case for transracial adoption*. Washington, DC: American University Press.

Snell, T. L. (1994). *Special report: Women in prison*. Washington, DC: U.S. Department of Justice, Bureau of Justice Statistics.

Stehno, S. (1982). Differential treatment of minority children in service systems. *Social Work, 27*, 39–45.

Stehno, S. (1990). The elusive continuum of child welfare services: implications for minority children and youth. *Child Welfare, 69*, 551–562.

Stolley, K. (1993). Statistics on adoption in the United States. *The Future of Children, 3*, 26–43.

Sullivan, A. (1994). On transracial adoption. *Children's Voice, 3*(3), 4–6.

Title VI (Civil Rights Act), 42 U.S.C. § 2000d (1964).

Testa, M. F., Shook, K. L., Cohen, L. S., & Woods, M. G. (1996). Permanency planning options for children in formal kinship care. *Child Welfare, 75,* 451–470.

Thornton, J. L. (1991). Permanency planning for children in kinship foster homes. *Child Welfare, 70,* 593–601.

Transracial adoption controversy grows. (1985, October 3–4). *National Association of Social Workers News.*

U.S. Census Bureau. (2000). *Poverty rate lowest in 20 years, household income at record high, Census Bureau reports.* Retrieved Jan. 5, 2003, from http://www.census.gov/hhes/poverty/poverty00/pov00hi.html

U.S. Census Bureau. (2001). *The Black population: 2000.* Retrieved January 20, 2004 from http://www.census.gov/prod/2001pubs/c2kbr01-5

U.S. Department of Heath and Human Services, Children's Bureau. (1993). *Study of child maltreatment in alcohol abusing families.* Washington, DC: U.S. Government Printing Office.

U.S. Department of Health and Human Services. (1999). *Blending perspectives and building common ground: A report to Congress on substance abuse and child protection.* Washington, DC: U.S. Government Printing Office.

U.S. Department of Health and Human Services, Children's Bureau. (2000). *Report to Congress on kinship foster care.* Retrieved January 20, 2004, from http://aspe.hhs.gov/hsp/kinr2c00/full.pdf

U.S. Department of Health and Human Services, Administration for Children and Families. (2000). *HHS reports new child abuse and neglect statistics.* Press release April 10, 2000. Washington, DC: Author.

U.S. Department of Justice, Bureau of Justice Statistics. (2000). *Sourcebook of criminal justice statistics 2000.* Washington, DC: Author.

U.S. General Accounting Office. (1995). *Foster care: Health needs of many young children are unknown and unmet* (GAO/HEHS-95-114). Washington, DC: U.S. Government Printing Office.

U.S. House Committee on Ways and Means. (1994). *1993 Green book: Overview of federal entitlement programs.* Washington, DC: U.S. Government Printing Office.

Vinokur-Kaplan, D., & Hartman, A. L. (1986). A national profile of child welfare workers and supervisors. *Child Welfare, 65,* 323–335.

Walker, C. D., Zangrillo, P., & Smith, J. M. (1994). Parental drug abuse and African-American children in foster care. In R. Barth, J. D. Berrick, & N. Gilbert (Eds.), *Child welfare research review* (Vol. 1). New York: Columbia University Press.

Weissman, H. H., Epstein, I., & Savage, A. (1983). *Agency-based social work: Neglected aspects of clinical practice.* Philadelphia: Temple University Press.

Wells, K., & Tracy, E. (1996). Reorienting intensive family preservation services in relation to public child welfare practice. *Child Welfare, 75,* 667–692.

Williams, C. W. (1997). Personal reflections on permanency planning and cultural competency. In G. R. Anderson, A. S. Ryan, & B. R. Leashore (Eds.), *The challenge of permanency planning in a multicultural society* (pp. 9–18). Boston: Haworth Press.

Wolock, I., & Horowitz, B. (1979). Child maltreatment and material deprivation among AFDC recipient families. *Social Service Review, 53,* 175–194.

Zellman, G. L. (1992). The impact of case characteristics on child abuse reporting decisions. *Child Abuse and Neglect, 16*(1), 57–74.

Chapter Four

Policy Implications of Domestic Violence for People of Color

Tricia B. Bent-Goodley

Domestic violence is a problem for all groups, regardless of ethnicity, socioeconomic status, religion, or sexual orientation (Straus & Gelles, 1986). Some contend that domestic violence is more prevalent in communities of color (Asbury, 1999; Hampton & Yung, 1996; Rennison, 2001; Rennison & Welchans, 2000; Straus & Smith, 1990). Others consider domestic violence rates consistent across groups, particularly after controlling for sociodemographic status (Lee, Sanders, & Mechanic, 2002; Sorenson & Telles, 1991; Tjaden & Thoennes, 2000), because of the relatively few empirical studies of domestic violence in communities of color (Asbury, 1999; Chen & True, 1994; Hampton, Carrillo, & Kim, 1998; West, 1998). There is insufficient information to validate either assertion (Krishnan, Hilbert, VanLeeumen, & Kolia, 1997). The need for increased research and understanding of domestic violence within communities of color is imperative (Almeida, Woods, Font, & Messineo, 1992; Asbury, 1999; Hampton, Carrillo, & Kim, 1998; Neff, Holamon & Schulter, 1995). Adequate measures and inquiry both within and between groups of color are sorely needed (Krishnan et al., 1997; Sorenson, 1996; Tjaden & Thoennes, 2000).

Domestic violence continues to be largely hidden in Asian American communities but is acknowledged as a problem that needs to be addressed (Chen & True, 1994; Rimonte, 1989; Tjaden & Thoennes, 2000; Yoshihama, 2002). Only recently getting the necessary attention, American Indians are also affected by domestic violence (Bachman, 1992; Chester, Robin, Koss & Lopez, 1994; Fairchild, Fairchild, & Stoner, 1998; Kunitz & Levy, 2000; Tjaden & Thoennes, 2000; Walters & Simoni, 1999). Yet it has been stated that African Americans and American Indians/Alaska Natives experience domestic violence at greater levels than other ethnic groups (Rennison & Welchans, 2000; Straus & Smith, 1990; Tjaden & Thoennes, 2000).

While practice considerations are critical to effective service, the policy issues that perpetuate poor practice demand equal attention. Policy fuels practice options; it can be used to either exacerbate or resolve practice dilemmas. While social policy is not the sole cause of some of the practical dilemmas faced by communities of color, it must be considered if social workers are to address issues from a comprehensive perspective. Social policy that promotes equity allows for broader advocacy within communities, institutions, and the legal framework (Johnson & Sigler, 2000).

Domestic violence has been defined as "a pattern of assaultive and coercive behaviors including physical, sexual and psychological attacks, as well as economic coercion that adults or adolescents use against their intimate partners" (Schechter & Ganley, 1995, p.10). Findings from the National Violence Against Women Survey and the National Crime Victimization Survey found that 85% of survivors of intimate partner violence are women (Tjaden & Thoennes, 2000). One and a half million women report being a survivor of rape or physical abuse at the hands of a partner; 834,732 men report similar violence. Yet, the medical community reports treating an estimated 4.8 million people for injuries related to intimate partner violence, with estimated costs of $67 billion annually (Lee et al., 2002). Legal experts estimate that these numbers are ten times lower than actual domestic violence rates due to underreporting. This chapter will assess current policy issues specific to people of color and domestic violence and provide a culturally competent framework for analyzing domestic violence policy.

The Violence Against Women Act of 1994 (VAWA), signed as a part of the Violent Crime Control and Law Enforcement Act of 1994, was designed to send a message that society would not tolerate violence against women. The original act provided funds for training criminal justice personnel and judges; research on domestic violence; a national hotline; additional shelters; and protections for immigrants in cases of domestic violence, such as the ability to self-petition for immigration status and to suspend deportation until a hearing is provided. The VAWA of 1994 also established support for the mandatory arrest policy to be discussed later in this chapter. In essence, the act sought to provide holistic and better integrated domestic violence services (Johnson & Sigler, 2000). This legislation has been acknowledged for being cost-effective and socially conscious (Clark, Biddle, & Martin, 2002; Yodanis, Godenzi, & Stanko, 2000).

On October 28, 2000, VAWA (P.L. No. 106.386) was reauthorized and strengthened. The VAWA of 2000 increases appropriations to Indian tribal governments and gives tribal courts full civic jurisdiction to enforce orders of protection. This policy also provides a new grant program for transitional housing assistance for survivors. Arrests continue to be mandatory and there is a new emphasis on enforcing protection orders. The VAWA of 2000 corrected some provisions that limited protection for immigrants (Raj & Silverman, 2002). As a result of this act, spouses who have experienced partner violence can apply for protection both from abroad and within the United States if their spouse is a legal U.S. resident. Spouses that have experienced intimate partner violence can self-petition for citizenship within 2 years of a divorce. The abuser's citizenship status does not affect the self-petition of the abused partner. Finally, the definition of underserved populations is expanded to include race, ethnicity, and language barriers.

Despite these critical additions and clarity of focus, the needs of people of color remain largely unmet. To better understand these needs, a holistic method of analyzing domestic violence policy is needed. A comprehensive analysis of domestic violence policy will take into account: (1) access to and advocacy for safety and protection; (2) the nature of services and the model of service delivery; and (3) investment in long-term support and intervention (Owens-Manley, 1999). Access to domestic violence services must be universal and respond to policies that support the rights and safety of survivors of domestic violence. The nature of service models speaks to how providers deliver services and the quality of those services. Funding for such services as hotlines and shelters is included under this component. Long-term investment speaks to the need for more enduring, comprehensive services rather than concentrating on crisis intervention and short-term resolutions to what are often complex and persistent problems. These three criteria will be used to analyze themes presented in the literature on people of color and domestic violence.

Literature Review

While there is diversity between groups of color, there is also great heterogeneity within each group (Acevedo, 2000; Brice-Baker, 1994; Gibbs & Bankhead, 2001; Kaufman Kantor, Jasinski & Aldarondo, 1994; Oboler, 1998; Yoshihama, 2002). This chapter focuses on similar experiences among ethnic groups for the purpose of identifying a common agenda. This method is not intended to suggest that there is no diversity among these populations; however, the focus is instead on the similarities.

The primary issues related to accessibility of domestic violence services for people of color are geographic inaccessibility, enforcement of the mandatory arrest policy, and discriminatory treatment. These issues speak to limited access to safety and feelings of a lack of protection from officials. The inability to access domestic violence services within a reasonable distance has been acknowledged as a barrier for people of color, particularly African Americans (Bent-Goodley, in press; Pressman, 1994; Root, 1996; Sorenson, 1996; Torres, 1998; West, 1998; Williams & Becker, 1994). When services are not within the immediate community, transportation and financial constraints often make these services impractical to use. Moreover, some people of color may feel uncomfortable going into predominantly White communities to ask for help for domestic violence services or batterer's intervention (West, 1998; Williams & Becker, 1994). Although this problem has been identified, little has been done to create more geographically accessible services for people of color.

Mandatory arrest policy does not reinforce feelings of safety and protection for most people of color. In fact, it may even increase the likelihood of further domestic violence for some groups (Mills, 1998). "The Milwaukee, Wisconsin, domestic violence arrest experiment provides substantial evidence that arrest makes some kinds of people more frequently violent against their cohabitants"(Sherman et al., 1992, p. 139). Mandatory arrest has been found to increase domestic violence against women of color when the batterer is unemployed or has a criminal record (Mills, 1999; Sherman et al., 1992). Arguably, mandatory arrest policy actually disempowers women by taking away from her the choice to arrest and prosecute the case (Mills, 1998). Each of these considerations is important in shaping a policy that is implemented fairly and is reflective of the unique relationships of some communities with the police.

Women often fail to access domestic violence services because they lack confidence in law enforcement (Melton, 1999). Their perceptions of less protection within the criminal justice system discourage women of color from reporting domestic violence (Dennis, Key, Kirk, & Smith, 1995; Kupenda, 1998; Peterson-Lewis, Turner, & Adams, 1988; Rivera, 1998). While African American women have been found to contact the police more often than other ethnic groups (Tjaden & Thoennes, 2000), they often do not report domestic violence due to a fear that police will treat the abuser brutally or unfairly (Richie, 1996; West, 1998). Many Latinas are also uncomfortable about contacting the police for fear of not securing an officer who can speak Spanish and respect their culture (Torres, 1998). The lack of faith in and fear of law enforcement can actually perpetuate violence in the home by discouraging these women from seeing law enforcement as an option for help.

Discriminatory treatment is often a result of negative stereotyping. Services have been denied to women of color based on their ethnicity (Greene, 1994; Joseph, 1997; Kupenda, 1998; Loke, 1997; Rivera, 1998). African American women have been rejected from shelters for not sounding stressed enough (West, 1999). Shelter workers have been found to treat women of color differently due to cultural traditions and rituals (Loke, 1997; Sorenson, 1996; Torres, 1998b).

African American women and Latinas have felt that conflicts between definitions of child abuse and spanking serve as a deterrent to seeking shelter assistance (Rivera, 1998). When a service provider does not understand a group's customs and services offered to the client are constrained, then a discriminatory act has occurred.

Language barriers limit the accessibility of domestic violence services for people of color (Kanuha, 1994; Krishnan et al., 1997; Lee, 2000; Pressman, 1994; Rodriguez, Bauer, Florez-Ortiz, & Szkupinski-Quiroga, 1998; Root, 1996; Sorenson, 1996; Takagi, 1991). Family members, often the children, are asked to translate for domestic violence survivors in the absence of bilingual staff (Campbell & Campbell, 1996). Interpreters who translate for domestic violence survivors have been found to cover up abuse in order to not bring shame to the community (Abraham, 2000b). Recently, telephone companies have established translation services to meet this type of growing need. However, understanding language is more than understanding the words; it includes recognizing different cultural expressions and the ability to understand different dialects (Campbell & Campbell, 1996). Thus, it is not enough to hire someone who speaks the language; staff from the indigenous population should be sought who understand the nuances of the language and the culture of that community.

The child welfare system also demonstrates discriminatory treatment as it relates to domestic violence. Child removal rates in cases of domestic violence are greater among African Americans and American Indians than any other population or ethnicity (Edelman, 1989; Takagi, 1991), leading to the suggestion that there is racial profiling within the child welfare system. It is unclear if socioeconomic status is the predominate reason for this. Regardless, women of color have been found to hide domestic violence from child welfare workers in fear that their child will be removed (Bent-Goodley, in press). This situation does little to protect children or to keep women safe. Greater empirical information is needed in this area to determine the prevalence of the situation.

American Indians experience further discrimination in access to protection as a result of *Oliphant v. Suquamish Indian Tribe* (435 U.S. 191). This 1978 Supreme Court decision states that "tribal courts do not have criminal jurisdiction over non-Indians" (Reina, 2000, p. 47). This decision allows non–American Indians to essentially abuse American Indian women without consequence. Reina (2000) states that domestic violence rates among American Indians are "twice as high as the national average" and points out that "75% of intimate victimization . . . involved an offender of a different race" (p. 33). While VAWA of 2000 expands the ability of tribal courts to prosecute batterers, it does not address the inequity inherent in the *Oliphant* decision. This inequity warrants greater investigation and advocacy.

Cultural Considerations Affecting the Nature of Services to People of Color

The fragmentation of domestic violence services and lack of cultural competence are two critical issues related to the nature of service provision (Bohn, 1998; Carrillo & Gouband-Reyna, 1998; DeBruyn, Hymbaugh & Valdez, 1988; Loke, 1997; Nelson, McCoy, Stetter, & Vanderwagen, 1992; Norton & Manson, 1997; Tran & Des-Jardins, 2000; Yoshihama, 2002). Fragmentation speaks to the limited service integration of domestic violence services and lack of cultural competency that frames the poor way in which services are delivered.

Domestic violence services are often provided on a fragmented basis (Owens-Manley, 1999; Panzer, Phillip, & Hayward, 2000). While it is recognized that domestic violence is linked to other social ills, such as mental health challenges, it is difficult to find programs that provide multiple services. For instance, substance abuse has been heavily linked to domestic violence (Bachman, 1992; Kunitz, Levy, McCloskey, & Gabriel, 1998; Markward, Dozier, Hicks, & Markward, 2001; Nelson, McCoy, Stetter, & Vanderwagen, 1992; Norton & Manson, 1995; Perilla, Bakeman, & Norris, 1994); yet substance abuse services are often offered separately from domestic violence or batterer's intervention services. Thus clients are required to travel to multiple places at multiple times to receive services for issues knowingly connected. The fragmentation then serves as a barrier to obtaining the needed services and healing.

An additional example of fragmentation of services is related to the connection between HIV infection and domestic violence. Latinas and African American women are at a greater risk of contracting HIV due to a fear of asking an abusive partner to wear a condom (de la Vega, 1990; Kalichman, Williams, Cherry, Belcher, & Nachimson, 1998; Perilla, 1999; Wingood & DiClemente, 1997; Wyatt, Axelrod, Chin, Vargas Carmona, & Burns Loeb, 2000; Wyatt et al., 2002). Yet, HIV clinics rarely conduct domestic violence screenings and shelters often do not ask about HIV risk. Again, addressing only one component erodes the possibility of healing for the client and successful outcomes with regards to the intervention.

Cultural competence can be defined as "an ongoing process in which one continuously strives to achieve the ability to work effectively within the cultural context of the individual or community" (Campbell & Campbell, 1996, p. 457). Social workers must be cognizant of each ethnic group's cultural strengths and barriers to success (Gondolf, Fisher, Fullilove, & McFerron, 1988; Hernandez-Truyol, 1998). A lack of cultural competence, the inability to recognize cultural barriers and nuances, can render even the best-intentioned intervention and practitioner ineffective. While there are similarities across groups of color, such as the emphasis on keeping the family together (Ho, 1990; Lee, 2000; Perilla, 1999; Rivera, 1998; Torres, 1987; West, 1999; Yoshihama, 2002), each group has unique nuances that one must be aware of to be effective. Religion is a significant cultural strength for Latinos. Yet, religion has been used to preserve marriages, and women are expected to sustain the family unit (Acevedo, 2000; Perilla, 1999; Zambrano, 1985). Latinas have been found to seek assistance first from the church before going to formal resources such as shelters (Torres, 1987). Consequently, a knowledge of the role of religion as both a cultural strength and a barrier to ending violence is key to assisting the Latino population. In addition, addressing the between-group variations among Latinos is critical to determining effective protective factors (Aldarondo, Kantor, & Jasinski, 2002).

An additional example of the need to understand cultural competency relates to Asian Americans. The expectation that men dominate women can trap Asian American women in an abusive relationship (Abraham, 2000a; Ayyub, 2000; Chan & Leong, 1994; Chow, 1989; Loke, 1997; Norton & Manson, 1992; Purkayastha, 2000; Yoshihama, 2002). An Asian American woman's reputation can be ruined for reporting domestic violence; she may be considered a cultural traitor for publicly acknowledging what is still perceived as a private issue (Dasgupta, 2000; Ho, 1990; Loke, 1997). Worse, the extended kin of her husband can also abuse her without penalty, making her feel more isolated and hopeless (Abraham, 2000b). In describing some of the cultural issues facing Chinese women, Lee (2000) describes the three obediences: "Before marriage, a woman follows and obeys her father; after marriage, she follows and obeys her husband; after the death of her husband, she follows and obeys her son. The three obediences establish cultural ideas of unquestionable submission of women to men" (Lee, 2000, p. 220). Despite this pressure, Asian American women have demonstrated resistance to domestic violence (Mehrotra, 1999); still, many choose to endure the abuse rather than "dishonor" the family by reporting it.

The lack of understanding of cultural traditions similarly inhibits effective practice with American Indians (Bohn, 1998; DeBruyn, Humbaugh, & Valdez, 1988; Murray, 1998; Nelson et al., 1992; Norton & Manson, 1997). There has been a failure to use culturally appropriate tools to eradicate domestic violence among American Indians. It is rare, for instance, to provide domestic violence services in the home; most domestic violence interventions take place in an office setting. Yet conducting home visits has been found to be a particularly effective tool to engage American Indians (Norton & Manson, 1997). Another option is "Navajo Peacemaking," which incorporates spirituality, communalism, rituals, and family participation (Coker, 1999). American Indian women have been encouraged to reinforce these types of traditional tribal values of respect for women and children to challenge domestic violence (American Indian Women Against Domestic Violence, 1984). Without an understanding and appreciation of these cultural nuances, ineffective domestic violence services will continue to be offered to this population.

Racial loyalty is often a barrier to seeking domestic violence services for African American women. Racial loyalty is when an "African American woman withstands abuse and makes a conscious self-sacrifice for what she perceives as the greater good of the community, to her own physical, psychological, and spiritual demise" (Bent-Goodley, 2001, p. 323). After having been taught to place the needs of others before her own, she may feel obligated to withstand the abuse to not embarrass herself or the community (Barnes, 1999; West, 1999; Williams-Campbell, 1993). This notion of protecting the race and shielding the man is an important cultural consideration for those working with this population.

Investment in Long-Term Support

Domestic violence services cannot just focus on crisis and short-term intervention; nor can these services be limited to micro or mezzo levels of change. It is equally important to recognize how institutionalized racism affects communities of color. This history of oppression, reinforced by continued discrimination, connects these diverse groups. Domestic violence has been discussed as it relates to enslavement for African Americans (Dennis et al., 1995; Franklin, 2000; Hobbs, 1992; Karenga, 1993), colonization for Latinos and Asian Americans (Almeida & Dolan-Delvecchio, 1999; Carrillo & Gouband-Reyna, 1998), and stealing land and resources from American Indians (Kahn, 1982). These histories are critical to fully understanding the complexity of how to intervene in domestic violence with people of color and the centrality of a long-term view, as well as simply meeting the client where she or he presents (Bent-Goodley, 2001; DeVore & Schlesinger, 1996; Yoshihama, 2002).

This common history of oppression is reinforced for all of these groups by persistent discrimination and racism. African Americans and Latinos are more likely to experience racial profiling by law enforcement officers and be disproportionately incarcerated compared to other groups of color and White Americans (Gibbs & Bankhead, 2001). People of color are also more likely to be denied employment based on ethnicity (Barnes, 1999; Gibbs & Bankhead, 2001; Hacker, 1992). These macro issues affect interpersonal relationships in ways that require further inquiry.

Limited economic self-sufficiency is a key reason why women, particularly women of color, stay in domestic violence relationships (Campbell & Campbell, 1996). In fact, it has been found that "50% of homeless women and children became homeless after fleeing abuse" (Rennison & Welchans, 2000, p. 8). The inability to provide for children can reinforce a decision to stay in an abusive relationship.

The Personal Responsibility and Work Opportunity Reconciliation Act of 1996 (P.L. No. 104-193) (PRWORA) removed one economic safety net; welfare is no longer guaranteed as an option. Time limits force recipients off the welfare rolls after 5 years of support. Some survivors have been so traumatized by domestic violence that they may not be emotionally able to stay employed (Sable, Libbus, Huneke, & Anger, 1999). The Wellstone-Murray Family Violence Amendment (42 U.S.C. 602 [a][7]) of the PRWORA allows for referral services, residency waivers, and exemptions to the 5-year lifetime cap for domestic violence survivors. Though this amendment is important, it is certified in only 31 states and remains an option rather than an enforceable mandate (Sable et al., 1999). It is critical to empirically assess the length of time a domestic violence survivor needs to adequately recover from abuse to support her family. Five years may be insufficient.

Welfare reform poses additional challenges for immigrants. Immigrants are required to provide additional documentation of abuse, find a separate residence from the batterer, have a child who is also being abused, and be able to provide a connection between the abuse and need for public assistance (Loke, 1997; Orloff, 1999). Immigrants must also have entered the United States on or after August 22, 1996, to be considered for welfare assistance eligibility; undocumented immigrants do not qualify at all. In this situation, economic challenges become even more oppressive for this population of women.

Immigration status is a major concern for Asian American, Latino, African and Caribbean American women (Brice-Baker, 1994; Espenoza, 1999; Kaguyutan, Orloff, & Ashtari, 2001; Merchant, 2000; Pressman, 1994; Raj & Silverman, 2002; Sorenson, 1996). Immigration status can trap these women in an abusive relationship (Dasgupta, 2000). "In addition to the fears that all domestic violence victims face, battered immigrant women live with fears that are unique to their situation—fear of deportation, a general distrust of authorities, and language and cultural barriers" (Loke, 1997, p. 589). Needing to preserve their legal status and possibly having a limited command of English, many immigrant women continue to withstand abuse, feeling hopeless to stop the cycle (Kanuha, 1994; Takagi, 1991). Worse, acculturation to American society can cause disruption in the home (Campbell & Campbell, 1996; Lovell, Tran & Nguyen, 1987). In Haas, Dutton, and Orloff (2000), violence against Latinas increased if the woman was undocumented and married to a permanent resident or United States citizen. Asian American women born in United States are more likely to seek help than those that are not (Preisser, 1999).

A Culturally Competent Framework for Analyzing Domestic Violence Policy

The complexity of the issues confronting people of color vis-à-vis domestic violence policy is daunting. A culturally competent framework for analyzing domestic violence policy is provided to address the unique circumstances of people of color (Table 1).

Geographic Accessibility

Placing shelters in a community can be problematic in terms of the safety of the survivor and children. However, other types of domestic violence services that might allow women to stay within the community are desperately needed. Mental health services, intervention for batterers, and actual prevention activities can be provided in the community. These services are key to helping people of color who are experiencing or are at risk of domestic violence.

Programs outside of the community should be established with great deliberation, involving stakeholders as key decision makers and community support mechanisms built into the program. Shelters and other support networks should be located in similar communities to maintain a sense of comfort and familiarity for the woman. Recognizing the importance of extended family and community, there must also be an effort to better understand how to keep survivors safe while being community based. When it is not possible to locate shelters in the community, there should be an effort to bring the community to the shelter, which is to say the shelter represents a range of cultures—in staff, food, magazines, pictures, toys—so that the survivor and children can feel at home. These perceived small changes could make a significant difference in ensuring effective and appropriate services.

Fair and Equal Treatment Across Systems

The fair and equal treatment of people of color in the criminal justice and child welfare system is crucial to assisting them. While domestic violence is a crime, there remain many ways of addressing it. It is often within the culture that the greatest strength, and the best answers, can be found. By simply treating violence as a crime, one misses the necessity to acknowledge it and respond to it as an offense not just against the individual and the family, but also against the community.

Treating domestic violence as a crime means that people of color will continue to be treated disproportionately as criminals. The author is not advocating that batterers not be forced to face just penalties. However, a careful evaluation to substantiate whether policies such as the mandatory arrest policy actually keep survivors of color safe, or in fact pose an even greater threat to safety, is an important consideration.

The fear of engaging the child welfare system presents an additional policy dilemma (Bent-Goodley, in-press). If domestic violence poses a threat to a child and the survivor is unwilling to

Table 1. A Culturally Competent Framework for Analyzing Domestic Violence Policy

Access to Safety and Protection	Nature of Services	Investment in Long-Term Support
1. Are services geographically accessible or community-based?	1. Are services provided in a comprehensive and holistic fashion for survivors, children, and abusers?	1. Are services provided with consideration of the sociohistorical experiences of the population?
2. Is there fair and equal treatment across systems, particularly within the criminal justice, child welfare, domestic violence, and judicial arenas?	2. Does service delivery protect women from the effects of negative stereotyping?	2. Is there adequate support for direct supportive services, such as employment placement, job training, literacy development, and traditional housing?
		3. Do the services address the economic self-sufficiency of the women?

disengage the threat, then the child's safety must be the priority. However, when the child is not in grave danger and the survivor is willing to seek assistance, it may not be necessary to remove the child. Child welfare workers often remove children who have witnessed domestic violence because the workers have a negative perception of women who are abused (Fleck-Henderson, 2000; Jones & Gross, 2000). Moreover, those who are poor are more likely to have their children removed (Findlater & Kelly, 1999). Child welfare workers need to be trained on domestic violence, but sustainable services must be backed by mezzo level policies holding workers accountable for value-free assessments rather than assessments resulting from negative stereotyping. Suitable training tools have been designed for working with child protective service workers around domestic violence (Magen, Conroy, & Tufo, 2000; Schechter & Edleson, 1998). The agency policy must be clear—that bias will not be tolerated against domestic violence survivors regardless of ethnicity, class, or sexual orientation.

Confronting Negative Stereotypes

Stereotyping and denial of access to domestic violence services is simply inexcusable. To deny a woman access to safety based on negative stereotypes goes against social work values and ethics. Unfortunately, perceptions of women of color often fuel decisions about the kinds of services available to them. Domestic violence shelters and other services need systems to track worker responses, assess worker bias, and monitor outcomes of clients of color, linking evaluations and promotions to this information. When a worker demonstrates bias, no matter how subtle, the policy response should include immediate dismissal. Without such policy, there is no way to reinforce the need for cultural competence. The policy must set the tone for the action when individuals do not perform appropriately.

Holistic Domestic Violence Policy

Those shaping policy often give limited consideration to how social problems overlap. Clients often struggle with multiple complex issues. There needs to be a better way of serving such clients. A multi-dimensional program might include clinical services, substance abuse services, training in health care and parenting, and connecting clients with employment programs. Policies that support funding efforts which include a multidimensional framework would make it possible to actually assist the person more effectively. If funding continues to simply address the violence, the issues exacerbating the violence are ignored. A comprehensive approach that includes job training, child care, and protection in the workplace should be a part of domestic violence policy (Bent-Goodley, 2001; Sable et al., 1999).

Cultural Competence

Given an opportunity to respond to cultural competence issues, many domestic violence service providers continue to conduct business as usual (Williams & Becker, 1994). Policies, therefore, must be in place to force agencies to include bicultural and bilingual staff on direct services and administrative levels. Each community should be key to determining the funding or renewal of grants. This policy would require providers to know and be connected with the community as opposed to working in the community and then rushing to get out of the neighborhood at the close of business.

A commitment to providing culturally competent services means more than conducting a session, for example, on African dance. Cultural competence means that the ideas of the population are infused throughout an agency's programs, including implementation and evaluation.

Agencies must commit to providing such services in practice, not simply on paper. One way of supporting such policies is to create criteria and outcomes that evaluate employee and agency performance related to cultural competence.

The Sociohistorical Context

There is a need to better understanding how cultural oppression, discrimination, and sociohistorical events have affected people of color. Greater historical research is needed to fully understand and tackle the complexity of the problem. At the same time, while the history is critical, current discrimination is unrelenting and perhaps even more significant. Domestic violence advocates should speak resoundingly on behalf of policies that combat contemporary barriers to equality by promoting and initiating opportunities for fairness in employment, higher minimum wages, wealth development, greater opportunity for economic self-sufficiency, and safe, affordable housing.

Economic Self-Sufficiency

One mechanism to achieve economic self-sufficiency for some women is through public assistance. While the Wellstone-Murray Amendment provides an important buffer, more needs to be done to protect domestic violence survivors and offer more long-term support. For example, the high cost of housing, health, and child care could be key reasons a survivor returns home to an abuser. Providing such services beyond welfare to poor and middle-income women can provide greater options. Public assistance should be available to all of those attempting to flee a violent home, regardless of citizenship status. Fighting for equality in income for women that is comparable with men is an additional factor of concern for domestic violence advocates.

Conclusion

One department or state government cannot change the culture alone. This type of change takes place at multiple levels within families, organizations, communities, and across society at large. The message must be consistent—protecting survivors and children without bias and enhancing their sustenance and safety—is our collective priority.

People of color share many policy issues related to domestic violence. While there are unique histories and different cultural dynamics, both within and across these ethnic groups, there is also great commonality. Here, within this commonality, is the source of a mutually beneficial policy agenda. Respecting each group's unique differences, their collective strengths can be harnessed to ensure that domestic violence is eradicated within communities of color.

References

Abraham, M. (2000a). Isolation as a form of marital violence: The South Asian immigrant experience. *Journal of Social Distress and the Homeless, 9*, 221–236.

Abraham, M. (2000b). *Speaking the unspeakable: Marital violence among South Asian immigrants in the United States.* New Brunswick, NJ: Rutgers University Press.

Acevedo, M. J. (2000). Battered immigrant Mexican women's perspectives regarding abuse and help seeking. *Journal of Multicultural Social Work, 8*, 243–282.

Aldarondo, E., Kantor, G. K., & Jasinski, J. L. (2002). A risk marker analysis of wife assault in Latino families. *Violence Against Women, 8*, 429–454.

Almeida, R. V., & Dolan-Delvecchio, K. (1999). Addressing culture in batterer's intervention: The Asian Indian community as an illustrative example. *Violence Against Women, 5,* 654–683.

Almeida, R., Woods, R., Font, R., & Messineo, T. (1992). The cultural context model. *Journal of Feminist Family Therapy, 5,* 3–23.

American Indian Women Against Domestic Violence. (1984). *Position paper.* St. Paul, MN: Minnesota Coalition for Battered Women.

Asbury, J. (1999). What do we know now about spouse abuse and child sexual abuse in families of color in the United States? In R.L. Hampton (Ed.), *Family violence: Prevention and treatment* (2nd ed., pp. 148–167). Thousand Oaks, CA: Sage.

Ayyub, R. (2000). Domestic violence in the South Asian Muslim immigrant population in the United States. *Journal of Social Distress and the Homeless, 9,* 237–48.

Bachman, R. (1992). *Death and violence on the reservation: Homicide, family violence, and suicide in American Indian populations.* Westport, CT: Auburn House.

Barnes, S. Y. (1999). Theories of spouse abuse: Relevance to African Americans. *Issues in Mental Health Nursing, 20,* 357–71.

Bent-Goodley, T. B. (2001). Eradicating domestic violence in the African American community: A literature review and action agenda. *Trauma, Violence, and Abuse, 2,* 316–330.

Bent-Goodley, T. B. (in press). Perceptions of domestic violence: A dialogue with African American women. *Health and Social Work.*

Bohn, D. K. (1998). Clinical interventions with Native American battered women. In J.C. Campbell (Ed.), *Empowering survivors of abuse: Health care for battered women and their children* (pp. 241–258). Thousand Oaks, CA: Sage.

Brice-Baker, J. R. (1994). Domestic violence in African American and African-Caribbean families. *Journal of Social Distress and the Homeless, 3,* 23–38.

Campbell, J. C., & Campbell, D. W. (1996). Cultural competence in the care of abused women. *Journal of Nurse-Midwifery, 41,* 457–462.

Carrillo, R., & Goubaud-Reyna, R. (1998). Clinical treatment of Latino domestic violence offenders. In R. Carrillo & J. Tello (Eds.), *Family violence and men of color: Healing the wounded male spirit* (pp. 53–73). New York: Springer.

Chan, S., & Leong, C. W. (1994). Chinese families in transition: Cultural conflicts and adjustment problems. *Journal of Social Distress and the Homeless, 3,* 263–281.

Chen, S. A., & True, R. H. (1994). Asian/Pacific Island Americans. In L. D. Eron, J. H. Gontry, & J. P. Schleyel (Eds.), *Reason to hope: A psychological perspective on violence and youth* (pp. 145–162). Washington, DC: American Psychological Association.

Chester, B., Robin, R. W., Koss, M. P., & Lopez, J. (1994). Grandmother dishonored: Violence against women by male partners in American Indian communities. *Violence and Victims, 9,* 249–258.

Chow, E. N. (1989). The feminist movement: Where are all the Asian American women? In Asian Women United of California (Ed.), *Making waves: An anthology of writings by and about Asian American women* (pp. 362–376). Boston: Beacon Press.

Clark, K. A., Biddle, A. K., & Martin, S. L. (2002). A cost-benefit analysis of the Violence Against Women Act of 1994. *Violence Against Women, 9,* 417–428.

Coker, D. (1999). Enhancing autonomy for battered women: Lessons from Navajo Peacemaking. *UCLA Law Review, 47,* 1–11.

DeBruyn, L. M., Hymbaugh, K., & Valdez, N. (1988). Helping communities address suicide and violence: The special initiatives team of the Indian Health Service. *American Indian and Alaska Native Mental Health Research, 1,* 56–65.

Dennis, R. E., Key, L. J., Kirk, A. L., & Smith, A. (1995). Addressing domestic violence in the African American community. *Journal of Health Care for the Poor and Underserved, 6,* 284–93.

Devore, W., & Schlesinger, E. G. (1996). *Ethnic-sensitive social work practice* (4th ed.). Boston: Allyn & Bacon.

de la Vega, E. (1990). *Considerations for reaching the Latino population with sexuality and HIV/AIDS information and education.* New York: Sexuality Information and Education Council of the United States.

Dasgupta, S. D. (2000). Charting the course: An overview of domestic violence in the South Asian community in the United States. *Journal of Social Distress and the Homeless, 9,* 173–185.

Edelman, M. W. (1989). *Families in peril: An agenda for social change.* Cambridge, MA: Harvard University Press.

Espenoza, C. M. (1999). No relief for the weary: Violence Against Women Act relief denied for battered immigrants lost in the intersections. *Marquette Law Review, 83,* 163–220.

Fairchild, D. G., Fairchild, M. W., & Stoner, S. (1998). Prevalence of adult domestic violence among women seeking routine care in a Native American health care facility. *American Journal of Public Health, 88,* 1515–1517.

Findlater, J. E., & Kelly, S. (1999). Child protective services and domestic violence. In R. E. Behrman (Ed.), *The future of children: Domestic violence and children* (pp. 84–96). Los Angeles, CA: David and Lucile Packard Foundation.

Fleck-Henderson, A. (2000). Domestic violence in the child protective system: Seeing double. *Children and Youth Services Review, 22,* 333–354.

Franklin, D. L. (2000). *What's love got to do with it? Understanding and healing the rift between Black men and women.* New York: Simon and Schuster.

Gondolf, E. W., Fisher, E. R., Fullilove, R. E., & McFerron, R. (1988). Racial differences among shelter residents. *Journal of Family Violence, 3,* 39–51.

Greene, B. (1994). African American women. In L. Comas-Diaz & B. Greene (Eds.), *Women of color: Integrating ethnic and gender identities in psychotherapy* (pp. 10–29). New York: Guilford Press.

Haas, G. A., Dutton, M. A., & Orloff, L. E. (2000). Lifetime prevalence of violence against Latina immigrants: Legal and policy implications. *International Review of Victimology, 7,* 93–113.

Hacker, A. (1992). *Two nations: Black and white, separate, hostile, unequal.* New York: Macmillan.

Hampton, R. L., & Yung, B. R. (1996). Violence in communities of color: Where we were, where we are, and where we need to be. In R. L. Hampton, P. Jenkins, & T. P. Gullota (Eds.), *Preventing violence in America* (pp. 53–86). Thousand Oaks, CA: Sage.

Hampton, R., Carrillo, R., & Kim, J. (1998). Violence in communities of color. In R. Carrillo & J. Tello (Eds.), *Family violence and men of color: Healing the wounded male spirit* (pp. 1–30). New York: Springer.

Hernandez-Truyol, B. E. (1998). Building bridges: Latinas and Latinos at the crossroads. In R. Delgado & J. Stefancic (Eds.), *The Latino/a condition: A critical reader* (pp. 24–31). New York: NYU Press.

Ho, C. K. (1990). An analysis of domestic violence in Asian American communities: A multicultural approach to counseling. *Women and Therapy, 9,* 129–150.

Hobbs, S. H. (1992). Gender and racial stereotypes, family law, and the Black family: Harpo's blues. *International Review of Comparative Public Policy, 4,* 35–49.

Johnson, I. M., & Sigler, R. T. (2000). Public perceptions: The stability of the public's endorsements of the definition and criminalization of the abuse of women. *Journal of Criminal Justice, 28,* 165–179.

Jones, L. P., & Gross, E. (2000). Perceptions and practice with domestic violence among child protective service workers. *Children and Youth Services Review, 22,* 355–371.

Joseph, J. (1997). Woman battering: A comparative analysis of Black and White women. In G. K. Kantor & J. L. Jasinski (Eds.), *Out of darkness: Contemporary perspectives on family violence* (pp. 161–169). Thousand Oaks, CA: Sage.

Kaguyutan, J., Orloff, L., & Ashtari, N. (2001). The Violence Against Woman Act of 1994 and 2000: Immigration protections for battered immigrants. *Domestic Violence Report, 6,* 33–34, 46–47.

Kahn, M. W. (1982). Cultural clash and psychopathology in three aboriginal cultures. *Academic Psychology Bulletin, 4,* 553–561.

Kalichman, S. C., Williams, E. A., Cherry, C., Belcher, L., & Nachimson, D. (1998). Sexual coercion, domestic violence, and negotiating condom use among low-income African American women. *Journal of Women's Health, 7,* 371–378.

Kanuha, V. (1994). Women of color in battering relationships. In L. Comas-Diaz & B. Greene (Eds.), *Women of color: Integrating ethnic and gender identities in psychotherapy* (pp. 428–454). New York: Guilford Press.

Karenga, M. (1993). *Introduction to Black studies* (2nd ed.). California: University of Sankore Press.

Kaufman Kantor, G., Jasinski, J. L., & Aldarondo, E. (1994). Sociocultural status and incidence of marital violence in Hispanic families. *Violence and Victims, 9,* 207–22.

Krishnan, S. P., Hilbert, J. C., VanLeeuwen, D., & Kolia, R. (1997). Documenting domestic violence among ethnically diverse populations: Results from a preliminary study. *Family and Community Health, 20,* 32–48.

Kunitz, S. J., & Levy, J. E. (2000). *Drinking, conduct disorder, and social change: Navajo experiences.* New York: Oxford University Press.

Kunitz, S. J., Levy, J. E., McCloskey, J., & Gabriel, K. R. (1998). Alcohol dependence and domestic violence as sequelae of abuse and conduct disorder in childhood. *Child Abuse and Neglect, 22,* 1079–1091.

Kupenda, A. M. (1998). Law, life, and literature: A critical reflection of life and literature to illuminate how laws of domestic violence, race and class bind Black women based on Alice Walker's book *The Third Life of Grange Copeland. Howard Law Journal, 42,* 1–26.

Lee, M. Y. (2000). Understanding Chinese battered women in North America: A review of the literature and practice implications. *Journal of Multicultural Social Work, 8,* 215–241.

Lee, R. Y., Sanders, V. L. T., & Mechanic, M.B. (2002). Intimate partner violence and women of color: A call for innovations. *American Journal of Public Health, 92,* 530–535.

Loke, T. (1997). Trapped in domestic violence: The impact of United States immigration laws on battered immigrant women. *Boston University Public Interest Law Journal, 6,* 589–628.

Lovell, M. L., Tran, T., & Nguyen, C. D. (1987). Refugee women: Lives in transition. *International Social Work, 30,* 317–325.

Magen, R. H., Conroy, K., & Tufo, A. D. (2000). Domestic violence in child welfare preventative services: Results from an intake screening questionnaire. *Children and Youth Services Review, 22,* 251–274.

Markward, M., Dozier, C., Hooks, K., & Markward, N. (2001). Culture and the intergenerational transmissions of substance abuse, woman abuse and child abuse: A diathesis–stress perspective. *Child and Youth Services Review, 22,* 237–250.

Mehrotra, M. (1999). The social construction of wife abuse: Experiences of Asian women in the United States. *Violence Against Women, 5,* 619–640.

Melton, H. C. (1999). Police response to domestic violence. *Journal of Offender Rehabilitation, 29,* 1–21.

Merchant, M. (2000). A comparative study of agencies assisting domestic violence victims: Does the South Asian community have special needs? *Journal of Social Distress and the Homeless, 9,* 249–259.

Mills, L. G. (1999). Killing her softly: Intimate abuse and the violence of state interventions, *Harvard Law Review, 113,* 550–613.

Mills, L. G. (1998). Mandatory arrest and prosecution policies for domestic violence: A critical literature review and the case for more research to test victim empowerment approaches. *Criminal Justice and Behavior, 25,* 306–318.

Murray, V. H. (1998). A comparative survey of the historic civil, common, and American Indian tribal law responses to domestic violence. *Oklahoma City Law Review, 23,* 433–457.

Neff, J. A., Holamon, B., & Schulter, D. (1995). Spousal violence among Anglos, Blacks, and Mexican Americans: The role of demographic variables, psychosocial predictors and alcohol consumption. *Journal of Family Violence, 10,* 1–21.

Nelson, S. H., McCoy, G. F., Stetter, M., & Vanderwagen, W. C. (1992). An overview of mental health services for American Indian and Alaska natives in the 1990s. *Hospital and Community Psychiatry, 43,* 257–261.

Norton, I. M., & Manson, S. M. (1992). An association between domestic violence and depression among Southeast Asian refugee women. *Journal of Nervous and Mental Disease, 180,* 729–730.

Norton, I. M., & Manson, S. M. (1995). A silent minority: Battered American Indian women. *Journal of Family Violence, 10,* 307–318.

Norton, I. M., & Manson, S. M. (1997). Domestic violence intervention in an urban Indian health center. *Community Mental Health Journal, 33,* 331–37.

Oboler, S. (1998). Hispanics? That's what they call us. In R. Delgado & J. Stefancic (Eds.), *The Latino/a condition: A critical reader* (pp. 3–5). New York: NYU Press.

Owens-Manley, J. (1999). Battered women and their children: A public policy response. *Affilia, 14,* 439–459.

Orloff, L. E. (1999). Access to public benefits for battered immigrant women and children. *Journal of Poverty Law and Policy Clearinghouse Review, 33,* 237–256.

Panzer, P. G., Philip, M. B., & Hayward, R. A. (2000). Trends in domestic violence service and leadership: Implications for an integrated shelter model. *Administration & Policy in Mental Health, 27,* 339–352.

Perilla, J. L. (1999). Domestic violence as a human rights issue: The case of immigrant Latinos. *Hispanic Journal of Behavioral Sciences, 21,* 107–33.

Perilla, J. L., Bakeman, R., & Norris, F. H. (1994). Culture and domestic violence: The ecology of abused Latinas. *Violence and Victims, 9,* 325–39.

Peterson-Lewis, S., Turner, C. W., & Adams, A. M. (1988). Attributional processes in repeatedly abused women. In G. W. Russell (Ed.), *Violence in intimate relationships* (pp. 107–130). New York: Police Management Association.

Preisser, A. B. (1999). Domestic violence in South Asian communities in America: Advocacy and intervention. *Violence against Women, 5,* 684–99.

Pressman, B. (1994). Violence against women: Ramifications of gender, class, and race inequality. In M.P. Mirkin (Ed.), *Women in context: Toward a feminist reconstruction of psychotherapy* (pp. 352–389). New York: Guilford.

Purkayastha, B. (2000). Liminal lives: South Asian youth and domestic violence. *Journal of Social Distress and the Homeless, 9,* 201–219.

Raj, A., & Silverman, J. (2002). Violence against immigrant women: The roles of culture, context and the legal immigrant status on intimate partner violence. *Violence Against Women, 8,* 367–398.

Reina, E. (2000). Domestic violence in Indian country: A dilemma of justice. *Domestic Violence Report, 5,* 33, 47.

Rennison, C. M. (2001, October). Intimate partner violence and age of victim, 1993–1999. (NCJ Pub 187635). Washington, DC: Office of Justice Programs.

Rennison, C. M., & Welchans, S. (2000, May). *Intimate partner violence.* Washington, DC: U.S. Department of Justice, Bureau of Justice Statistics.

Richie, B. (1996). *Compelled to crime: The gender entrapment of battered black women.* New York: Routledge.

Rimonte, N. (1989). Domestic violence against Pacific Asians and Asian women. In United of California (Eds.), *Making waves* (pp. 327–337). Boston: Beacon Press.

Rivera, J. (1998). Domestic violence against Latinas by Latino males. In R. Delgado & J. Stefancic (Eds.), *The Latino/a condition: A critical reader* (pp. 501–507). New York: NYU Press.

Rodriguez, M. A., Bauer, H. M., Flores-Ortiz, Y., & Szkupinski-Quiraga, S. (1998). Factors affecting patient-physician communication for abused Latino and Asian immigrant women. *Journal of Family Practice, 47,* 309–311.

Root, M. P. (1996). Women of color and traumatic stress in domestic captivity: Gender and race as disempowering statuses. In A. J. Marcella, M. J. Friedman, D. G. Gerrity, & R. M. Scurfield (Eds.), *Ethno-cultural aspects of posttraumatic stress disorder: Issues, research, and clinical applications* (pp. 363–87). Washington, DC: American Psychological Association.

Sable, M. R., Libbus, M. K., Huneke, D., & Anger, K. (1999). Domestic violence among AFDC recipients: Implications for welfare-to-work programs. *Affilia, 14*, 199–217.

Schechter, S., & Edelson, J. L. (1998). Effective intervention in domestic violence and child maltreatment cases: Guidelines for policy and practice. Reno, NV: National Council of Juvenile and Family Court Judges.

Schechter, S., & Ganley, A. L. (1995). *Domestic violence: A national curriculum for family preservation practitioners.* San Francisco: Family Violence Prevention Fund.

Sherman, L. W., Schmidt, J. D., Rogan, D. P., Smith, D. A., Gartin, P. R., Cohn, E. G., et al. (1992). The variable effects of arrest on criminal careers: The Milwaukee domestic violence experiment. *Journal of Criminal Law and Criminology, 83*, 137–169.

Sorenson, S. B. (1996). Violence against women: Examining ethnic differences and commonalties. *Evaluation Review, 20*, 123–45.

Sorenson, S. B., & Telles, C. A. (1991). Self-reports of spousal violence in a Mexican American and non-Hispanic white population. *Violence and Victims, 6*, 3–15.

Straus, M. A., & Gelles, R. (1986). Societal change and change in family violence from 1975 to 1985 as revealed by two national surveys. *Journal of Marriage and the Family, 48*, 465–479.

Straus, M. A., & Smith, C. (1990). Violence in Hispanic families in the United States: Incidence rates and structural interpretations. In M. A. Straus & R. J Gelles (Eds.), *Physical violence in American families: Risk factors and adaptations to violence in 8,145 families* (pp. 341–368). New Brunswick, NJ: Transaction.

Takagi, T. (1991). Women of color and violence against women. In C. Moliner (Ed.), *National Network of Women's Funds and Foundations/Corporate Philanthropy Violence against Women Supplement* (pp. 51, 56). St. Paul, MN: National Network of Women's Fund and Foundations Corporate Philanthropy.

Taylor-Gibbs, J., & Bankhead, T. (2001). *Preserving privilege: California politics, propositions, and people of color.* Westport, CT: Praeger.

Tjaden, P., & Thoennes, N. (2000, July). *Extent, nature, and consequences of intimate partner violence: Findings from the national violence against women survey* (NCJ Publication No.181867). Washington, DC: U.S. Department of Justice, Office of Justice Programs.

Torres, S. (1998). Intervening with battered Hispanic pregnant women. In J. C. Campbell (Ed.), *Empowering survivors of abuse: Health care for battered women and their children* (pp. 259–270). Thousand Oaks, CA: Sage.

Torres, S. (1987). Hispanic American battered women: Why consider cultural differences? *Response, 10*, 20–21.

Tran, C., & Des-Jardins, K. (2000). Domestic violence in Vietnamese refugee and Korean immigrant communities. In J. L. Chin (Ed.), *Relationship among Asian American women* (pp. 71–96). Washington, DC: American Psychological Association.

Walters, K. L., & Simoni, J. M. (1999). Trauma, substance abuse, and HIV risk among urban American Indian women. *Cultural Diversity and Ethnic Minority Psychology, 5*, 236–248.

West, C. M. (1998). Lifting the "political gag order": Breaking the silence around partner violence in ethnic minority families. In J. L. Jasinski & L. M. Williams (Eds.), *Partner violence: A comprehensive review of 20 years of research* (pp. 184–209). Thousand Oaks, CA: Sage.

West, T. C. (1999). *Wounds of the spirit: Black women, violence and resistance ethics.* New York: New York University Press.

Williams, O., & Becker, R. L. (1994). Domestic partner abuse: The results of a national survey. *Violence and Victims, 9*, 287–96.

Williams-Campbell, D. (1993). Nursing care of African-American battered women: Afrocentric perspectives. *AWHONN's Clinical Issues, 4*, 407–415.

Wingood, G. M., & DiClemente, R. J. (1997). The effects of an abusive primary partner on the condom use and sexual negotiation practices of African-American women. *American Journal of Public Health, 87*, 1016–1018.

Wyatt, G. E., Axelrod, J., Chin, D., Vargas Carmona, J., & Burns Loeb, T. (2000). Examining patterns of vulnerability to domestic violence among African American women. *Violence against Women, 6*, 495–514.

Wyatt, G. E., Williams, J. K., Loeb, T., Carmona, J. V., Chin, D., & Presely, N. (2002). Does history of trauma contribute to HIV risk for women of color? Implications for prevention and policy. *American Journal of Public Health, 92*, 660–666.

Yodanis, C. L., Godenzi, A., & Stanko, E. A. (2000). The benefits of studying costs: A review of agenda for studies on the economic costs of violence against women. *Policy Studies, 21*, 263–276.

Yoshihama, M. (2002). Breaking the web of abuse and silence: Voices of battered women in Japan. *Social Work, 47*, 389–401.

Zambrano, M. M. (1985). *For the Latina in an abusive relationship*. Seattle, WA: Seal Press.

Chapter Five

Social Security Reform and People of Color: Implications of Barriers to Continuous Employment and Reentry Into the Labor Force

Namkee G. Choi

The 2000 Census data attested to the increasing racial and ethnic diversity in the United States, showing a population composed of approximately 12.3% Blacks, 12.5% Hispanics or Latinos (referred to as Hispanics hereafter), and 3.6% Asians (U.S. Census Bureau, 2001). The Census Bureau projects that these racial/ethnic populations will increase more rapidly in the future and that the number and share of elders of color age 65 and older will increase at a rate even faster than that of people of color as a whole. According to the population projections, by the year 2030 Black and Hispanic elders alone will make up more than 20% of the elderly U.S. population (U.S. Census Bureau, 1996). Despite their increasing number and share, the economic conditions of elders of color have not kept up with those of the majority, or White, elders. Although the U.S. Census Bureau reported that the 3-year average poverty rate from 1998 to 2000 among older persons was 10.1%, one of the lowest rates on record, elders of color had poverty rates in excess of 20% to 25%. Moreover, much larger fractions of them (e.g., 33.5% of Blacks and 31.8% of Hispanics in 1999) had incomes just above, but less than 125%, of the poverty line (U.S. Census Bureau, 2000, 2002)

The poverty rates among older persons in general have been declining steadily since the mid-1970s owing primarily to Social Security benefits. In the absence of Social Security benefits, the elderly poverty rate would have been close to 50% even in recent years (see Porter, Larin, & Primus, 1999). Social Security is the most important, and often the only, source of income for elders of color. In 2000, for example, 34% of Black married-couple elders and 45% of Hispanic married-couple elders, as compared to 25% of White married-couple elders, received 80% or more of their income from Social Security. In the case of unmarried persons, 61% of Black women and 62% of Hispanic women, as compared to 48% of White women; and 50% of Black men and 62% of Hispanic men, as compared to 38% of White men, received at least 80% of their income from Social Security. For 75% of all married and unmarried elderly units in the bottom quintile of income distribution, Social Security was the essential source of income, providing at least 90% (Grad, 2002).

Considering the overriding significance of Social Security as the retirement income source for low income elders, the current debate on Social Security reform should pay special attention to the potential consequences of various reform proposals for low-income elders of color. Of the reform proposals, issues pertinent to and the potential impact of the privatization proposals on low-income workers have been comprehensively discussed (Diamond, 1997; Ferrara, 1997; Friedland, 1996; Gramlich, 1997; Hieger & Shipman, 1997; Jones, 1996; Kijakazi, 1998; Mashaw & Marmor, 1996; Munnell, 1998; Niggle, 2000; Quinn & Mitchell, 1996; Schieber, 1996; Smeeding, 1999; Weller, 2000; Williamson, 1997; Williamson & Rix, 2000).

On the other hand, the potential consequences for low-income elders of the proposals related to increasing the eligible age for full benefits, extending the benefit-computation period, and improving the incentives for workers to extend their working careers have not been extensively evaluated. Starting from the year 2003, the Social Security full retirement age will be increased in gradual steps until it reaches age 67 in 2022. The 1996 Advisory Council on Social Security and other advisory bodies for Social Security reform proposed to increase further the eligibility age for full and reduced Social Security benefits. It has been reported that President Bush's Commission on Social Security is also reviewing raising the Social Security retirement age as a possible option to improve the financial integrity of the Social Security system, and the commission needs to be fully informed of potential consequences of reform on low-income, minority workers.

In this chapter, I address the potential impact of the proposal to raise the eligibility age for Social Security benefits on the future cohorts of elders of color by analyzing the association between individual strengths/constraints, social–structural opportunities and constraints, and economic need variables, and the likelihood of work versus non-work among the cohort of men and women born between 1931 and 1941. The analysis focuses on identifying racial differences in factors that may hinder or facilitate continuous employment of these nationally representative sample members. For sample members who were no longer employed, the self-reported reasons for their non-work are also analyzed. In addition, factors associated with reentry into the labor force among those who were previously disengaged from it are analyzed. The findings will help us understand differential patterns of and reasons for continued work versus non-work among low-income elders of color, helping us to further evaluate the potential consequences of the reform proposals for them.

A Brief History and Significance of Social Security for People of Color

The institution of the national Old-Age Benefit Program by the 1935 Social Security Act was hastened by the worsened situation of the aged during the Great Depression. (The Old-Age Benefit Program was renamed the Old-Age Insurance Program in 1937, and the latter became the Old-Age and Survivors' Insurance [OASI] in 1939.) Although OASI began as (and still is) the largest, most important social insurance system in the United States, its coverage was not extended to a large proportion of low-income people of color who most needed the economic protection provided by a guaranteed source of retirement income. The exclusion, most notably of agricultural workers and domestic employees from the pool of covered workers until September 1954, was largely a result of racially charged politics during the formative years of Social Security. Because President Franklin D. Roosevelt needed support from southern congressmen to move his Social Security programs past the key House and Senate committees, he gave in to their pressure to exclude agricultural workers and domestic servants—mostly Black men and women—from both Old-Age and Unemployment Insurance Programs (Quadagno, 1994).

Later amendments to the 1935 Social Security Act not only extended OASI coverage to initially excluded groups but also offered Disability Insurance (DI) benefits to disabled workers and their dependents. However, these social insurance programs were never intended to disrupt existing economic gaps between races and classes. As an employment-, earnings-, and contribution-based system, OASDI has, in fact, ensured the existing inequality structure in retirement and in disability (see Cates, 1983). Economic hardship among low-income elders has rarely been included as a topic in the discussion of Social Security. The prevailing assumption and attitude among scholars and policymakers has been that the needs of low-income elders should be met by public assistance programs (i.e., Old-Age Assistance [OAA] and later, Supplemental Security Income [SSI]) rather than by social insurance/Social Security programs. The lack of sufficient attention to potential impacts on low-income minority workers of various Social Security reform measures that have been recently debated reflects the very same assumptions and attitudes. In reality, Social Security is the most significant source of income for low-income elders of color, and more attention needs to be paid to potential effects of proposed Social Security reform measures on low-income minority workers.

Social Security retirement benefits provide only a partial replacement of lost earnings and thus, economic security in old age is supposed to rest on a three-legged stool: savings, a public or private pension, and Social Security (Villa, Wallace, & Markides, 1997). Often, however, low-income elders have accumulated few assets beyond equity in housing nor have they earned any public or private pension rights to carry into old age. In 2000, only 11% of aged units aged 65 or older in the lowest income quintile, as opposed to 68% of those in the highest quintile, received income from public or private pensions, or both (including veterans' benefits). In the same year, 24% of those in the lowest quintile versus 87% of those in the highest quintile received income from assets (Grad, 2002).

Needless to say, lack of income from assets and pensions among low-income elders reflects their low preretirement income—mostly earnings—status. Many previous research findings show that pension coverage is significantly lower among minority and female workers than among White male workers (Chen, 1994; Chen & Leavitt, 1997; Morrison, 1990; National Economic Council, 1998). A more disturbing finding is that the percentage of Blacks covered by private pensions dropped from 45.1% in 1979 to 33.8% in 1993 and coverage among Hispanics dropped from 37.7% to 24.6% for the same period (Chen & Leavitt, 1997). Thus, it does not appear that income from pensions will increase for elders of color in the near future.

For lack of income from assets and pensions, low-income elders tend to rely on Social Security as their most significant source of income. Unlike income from assets and pensions, which are highly positively correlated with individuals' preretirement earnings levels, Social Security's progressive benefits-computation formula allows higher replacement rates for lower earnings. In this regard, Social Security functions as an important income-redistribution mechanism not only among workers and retirees, their dependents, and their survivors, but also among different classes of dependents and survivors (see Hogan, Kim, & Perrucci, 1997; Moore, 2000). The cost-of-living adjustment (COLA) provision of Social Security also guarantees stability of its purchasing power.

For many Social Security reform proposals that have been discussed, raising the retirement age is only a part of a more comprehensive package of revisions to both the revenue collection and the benefits payment systems. However, given the significant racial disparities in health and employment status, the effect of raising the Social Security eligibility age is likely to be especially detrimental to the economic well-being of minority older persons. A 1999 report prepared by the General Accounting Office (GAO) for the U.S. Senate Special Committee on Aging showed that raising the retirement age would increase the number of older workers in the labor force, and thus increase payroll tax revenues and reduce the Social Security benefit outlay. But the report, based on an analysis of data from the Health and Retirement Study, also concluded that raising the Social Security retirement age could create the potential for increased unemployment among blue-collar workers with health problems, inhibiting continued employment at older ages. This would quite possibly increase caseloads for DI and SSI, although the increased costs from a higher DI caseload would not offset the significant cost savings that would accrue to the OASI portion of the Social Security Trust Fund. Because people of color make up a disproportionate share of blue-collar workers, they are more likely to be adversely affected by retirement age increases. In Washington's conservative political environment, however, the potentially adverse consequences for low-income, minority persons are often pushed to the back-burner of policy debates.

The increasing racial/ethnic diversity of the U.S. population has already been shown in the racial/ethnic composition of the work force. Despite improvements in their educational level, people of color still lag behind Whites in terms of educational preparation and, consequently, level of earnings and private retirement income prospects. When these minority workers retire, they, like their parents, need Social Security as the major source of income. This makes it more important for the country to pass sound reform measures to ensure the long-term financial health of the Social Security system. Any reform measures may inevitably require some degree of financial sacrifice from workers/payroll tax payers and Social Security beneficiaries. Nevertheless, the burden of reform should not be too harsh and the consequences not too detrimental to those who are the most dependent on the system.

Retirement Trends, Factors Associated With Withdrawal From the Labor Force, and Conceptual Framework

Although people are living longer and enjoying a healthier old age than the previous generations, labor force participation rates among men age 55 or older declined steadily between the mid-1960s and the mid-1980s. At age 62, for example, the labor force participation rate for men was nearly 80% in both 1950 and 1960, but the rate declined to nearly 50% by the mid-1980s. In 1950, nearly three quarters of all 65-year-old men were in the labor force; by 1985, fewer than one third were (Quinn, 1997). By the mid-1980s, the declining trend appeared to have stopped and older men's participation rate appears to have stabilized since then (Burtless & Quinn, 2001). Older women's labor force participation rates was stable between 1970 and 1985, but the rate has since increased somewhat for all age groups, owing possibly to a strong economy in the 1990s (Burtless & Quinn, 2001).

Declining labor force participation rates have been attributed largely to the early retirement incentives embedded in Social Security retirement and disability benefits and employer pension plans (Herz & Rones, 1989; Quinn, Burkhauser, & Myers, 1990; Stock & Wise, 1990). An analysis of Social Security benefits records shows that an increasing proportion of older persons (e.g., a little over two thirds in 1993 as compared to a little over one half in 1980 for White males) opted to receive Social Security benefits at ages 62 through 64 (Gendell & Siegel, 1996). Social Security has been a reliable alternative income source that allowed older persons to opt for retirement and leisure instead of continued work. Moreover, when older workers face challenges in keeping their jobs in times of high unemployment rates or rapid technological changes and industrial restructuring, Social Security, sometimes in combination with private pensions, can be an especially attractive incentive for early retirement for both workers and their employers. It was also found that nearly two thirds of those who begin receipt of disability benefits are between ages 50 and 65 (Hennessey & Dykacz, 1989).

In addition to the institutional incentives for early retirement embedded in Social Security and employer pensions and labor market conditions, an individual's decision to withdraw from the labor force, reduce work efforts, or reenter the labor force is influenced also by a complex array of individual, family, occupational, and economic factors (Henretta & Lee, 1996). A large body of empirical research on retirement processes and behaviors shows that older persons continue to work, retire, or reenter the work force following retirement for a variety of reasons, including those of individual strengths and constraints, social–structural opportunities and constraints, and economic need and desire for status maintenance. The indicators of *individual strengths and constraints,* as antecedents of retirement or continued work, include health, level of education, and marital and other family status, as well as psychological commitment to work. For example, good health, a high level of education, a strong psychological commitment to work and a corresponding "distaste" for retirement, and being married to a working wife were found to increase the probability of men's working in old age (Beck, 1985; Henretta, Chan, & O'Rand, 1992; Parnes & Sommers, 1994). On the other hand, poor health has been found to be an especially important determinant of retirement among older workers and lack of post-retirement employment among retired men (Beck, 1985).

Social–structural opportunities and constraints refer to preretirement work histories and occupational structures that provide differential opportunities, resources, and rewards in labor force withdrawal and post-retirement employment patterns. Behavior at given stages of life is likely to result from patterns or trajectories of related behavior at earlier time points (Elder, 1985). Early work experiences, like the patterns of transition in and out of the labor force, shape the patterns of work behavior in later life, including retirement and beyond (O'Rand, 1996; Rindfuss, 1991). Studies also found that workers in unpleasant, difficult jobs tend to retire at a different rate than do those in pleasant, easy jobs, and that people with more marginal work histories are less likely to sustain work efforts after retirement (Hardy, 1991; Hayward et al., 1989; Holden, 1988; Morrow-Howell & Leon, 1988). In addition, retirement patterns often depend on a worker's ability to vary the volume of work on the same job and on the availability of alternative jobs with different hour-and-wage combinations (Hurd & McGarry, 1993). Those in professional or executive positions are more likely than those in nonprofessional and nonexecutive positions to have options for time reductions in their career job or for transferring work skills to another job (Elder & Pavalko, 1993).

Economic need and/or *status maintenance* reasons are supported by the findings that older persons who have inadequate retirement income are more likely to work out of economic necessity than are their well-off counterparts. Pension coverage and the level of pension benefits and income in general, including Social Security benefits, have been found consistently to be the most significant determinants of retirement versus continued work or post-retirement employment in old age (Myers, 1991; Ruhm, 1990). In their study of working-class retirees, Calasanti and Bonanno (1992) found that many worked because they lacked adequate economic resources to survive and wanted to maintain their previous status and that they were responding to their families' and communities' needs.

Overlapping and intersecting with each of the above antecedent variables is the effect of race and gender. Research on work and retirement patterns among Hispanics is scant, but studies have generally shown that Black retirement processes reflect their poorer health, poorer work histories, and lesser economic resources. Older Black men are less likely to participate in the labor force than their White counterparts, and this racial gap in older men's labor force attachment, especially after age 45, is accounted for by Blacks' higher rate of disability both when they are older and when they are younger (Hayward, Friedman, & Chen, 1996). The higher rate of disability among Blacks may result from self-ascribed disability status—out of psychological need and social desirability—especially among those who have had discontinuous patterns of lifetime work and have dim prospects for future employment (Gibson, 1987, 1991). However, according to Hayward et al. (1996), "the adoption of disability status among Blacks is not simply a socially desirable response to constrained economic opportunities, because Blacks, once disabled, are no more or less likely to die than Whites" (p. S9). Based on an analysis of data from the 1984 and 1985 Survey of Income and Program Participation, Burr, Massagli, Mutchler, and Pienta (1996) also found that Black men have objectively poor health and that associations between labor force status, on the one hand, and health and socioeconomic status, on the other, differ by race. Their discontinuous work experiences earlier in life and the necessity to work in old age would make it difficult for some Black individuals to draw a clear line between work and retirement, especially when older Black persons are predominantly self-supporting (Jackson & Gibson, 1985).

Men and women also display quite different patterns of retirement and post-retirement employment, reflecting socially structured gender differences in work histories and economic status (Moen, 1985, 1996; O'Rand, 1996). For example, Pienta, Burr, and Mutchler (1994) report that women's work patterns in later life are particularly responsive to employment histories earlier in the life course, which are in turn closely tied to family histories. Atchley (1982) found that unmarried women of average health and in lower-status occupations were more likely than men to say that they did not plan to retire, indicating that the economic aspect of retirement was of even greater concern for women than for men.

This study employs a conceptual framework in which individual strengths and constraints, social–structural opportunities and constraints, and the economic need or desire for status maintenance are expected to determine the likelihood of older persons' employment activities. Furthermore, the study examines whether or not race/ethnicity compounds the effects of those variables on the likelihood of work. Because of the complex interplay among this variety of factors influencing an individual's work and retirement behavior, amendments to Social Security raising the eligible age for full benefits, extending the benefits-computation period, and providing generous delayed-retirement credits may not result in a significant increase in the labor force participation rates among all elders. Despite their economic need, many low-income elders may not be able to sustain their work efforts due to disability or other health problems, while others may not be able to do so for lack of necessary educational background and skills. Fair and equitable Social Security reform proposals must include measures to protect these low-income, ill-educated, and/or disabled elders from being penalized with benefit reduction for their involuntary early withdrawal from the labor force.

Method

Data Source and Sample Characteristics

The data for this study came from the 1992 and 1994 interview waves of the Health and Retirement Study (HRS). In 1992, the HRS interviewed a total of 12,652 respondents from 7,702 households. The respondents comprised 2,373 single men and women; 5,234 married men and women born between 1931 and 1941; and 5,045 spouses (partners), regardless of their age, of the married respondents. In 1994, these respondents participated in a second interview wave (Institute for Social Research, 1998). With questions regarding demographic information on respondent and spouse, their health and disability status, changes in family circumstances, employment status and work history, type and nature of jobs and job satisfaction, pension coverage, reasons for non-work, and income and assets, the HRS data system provides a large amount of rich longitudinal panel data.

The study focuses on both single and married respondents and spouse-respondents who were age eligible (born between 1931 and 1941) and interviewed in both 1992 and 1994 waves. The racial composition was 6,394 non-Hispanic Whites, 1,468 Blacks, 755 Hispanics, 76 Native Americans, 93 Asian Americans, and 19 other or unknown. (Because of their small numbers, Native Americans, Asian Americans, and "other" or unknown races are excluded from the study.) The HRS oversampled Blacks and Hispanics but for the purpose of ensuring large enough sample sizes for multivariate analysis of within-group differences, weights are not applied in this study. Both univariate and bivariate analyses of selected variables showed no significant difference between weighted and unweighted outcomes.

The race groups of both genders did not differ significantly in age, but Whites reported better health than the people of color—Blacks and Hispanics—regardless of their work status. Whites and Hispanics were significantly more likely than Blacks to be married. As expected, Whites of both genders also reported significantly higher education and higher earnings than did the people of color. White households also reported significantly higher net worth and total household income, including capital income and pension benefits. The only income source from which the people of color drew higher amounts than did the Whites was SSI. That is, non-working Black males and non-working Black and Hispanic females received significantly higher SSI benefits than did their White counterparts. With respect to the Social Security Disability Insurance income, no significant racial difference was found.

Variables and Method of Analyses

Taking advantage of the longitudinal nature of the data set, gender- and race-specific logit models were employed to analyze factors associated with: (1) work status (working=1, not working=0) in 1992, and (2) work status in 1994 among those who worked in 1992 (working in both 1992 and 1994=1, worked in 1992 but no longer working in 1994=0). Because employees and self-employed persons are likely to be affected by different sets of variables, employment-type–specific logit models were analyzed, but the findings section will focus on employed and formerly employed (as opposed to self-employed) persons. Gender-specific logit models were also employed to examine factors associated with work status in 1994 for those who did not work in 1992 (reentered the labor force since 1992 and working in 1994=1, worked neither in 1992 nor in 1994=0). Because of a relatively small sample size, all races and employed and self-employed persons are pooled in this model. Also, a small percentage of respondents—1.7% of males and 13.3% of females—who had never worked or who had last worked prior to 1972—were excluded because their long-term detachment from the labor market set them apart from the rest of the respondents.

The respondent's answer to the question whether or not he or she had done any work for pay in the given year, rather than his or her self-designation of worker versus non-worker (including retiree) status, was chosen to be the dependent variable to capture those who continued to participate in or who reentered the labor force following their "official" retirement.

Many older persons would define themselves as retired although they may be engaging in post-retirement employment. It is a well-established fact that although a majority of men and women retire from their career job unilaterally and completely, a significant minority stretch their retirement process by gradually reducing work efforts over a period of a few or so years. One fifth to one third of retirees have been found to continue working for pay in a bridge job or reenter the labor force after a short hiatus, usually at a lower category on the occupational ladder, at lower pay, or at reduced hours, or some combination of these (Choi, 2000; Han & Moen, 1998; Hayward, Hardy, & Liu, 1994; Mutchler, Burr, Pienta, & Massagli, 1997; Myers, 1991; Parnes & Less, 1985; Quinn et al., 1990; Quinn & Kozy, 1996; Ruhm, 1990). (In this study, 79.6% of White males, 63.9% of Black males, and 69.6% of Hispanic males defined themselves as workers in 1992, while 82.0% of White males, 68.3% of Black males, and 73.0% of Hispanic males in the same year gave a positive answer to the question, "Are you doing any work for pay at the present time?")

Independent variables representing individual strengths and constraints in 1992 are age; marital status in 1992 (married=1, single=0); years of education (0 through 17 with all years beyond 17 counted as 17); self-rated health status in 1992 (on a scale of 1=excellent to 5=poor); and permanent disability limiting the kind or amount of paid work, or both (yes=1, no=0) in 1992. (When the sample sizes for specific logit models are small, marital status and race are collapsed into dichotomous categories—married versus unmarried and White versus non-White.) The respondent's attitude toward work (how likely it was that he or she would continue working regardless of economic need, on a scale of 1 to 4, with 4=most likely) was also entered into the model estimating the predictors of continued work between 1992 and 1994.

Independent variables representing social–structural opportunities and constraints are present occupation for the currently working (either in 1992 or in 1994) or the last occupation for the non-working (sales, clerical, administrative support, or services=1; mechanical, repairing, construction, machine operation, farming, forestry, fishing, or armed services=2; managerial, professional, or technical support=3); the year the respondent started the type of current or last work; the last year when the non-working respondent worked; annual hours of work in the current or the last job; and whether or not the respondent had ever been laid off or unemployed in the preceding 10 years (yes=1, no=0). In the models estimating the predictors of continued work between 1992 and 1994, the characteristics of the 1992 job were also entered: the type of earnings (salaried versus hourly); the degree of physical effort required by the job (on a scale of 1=none of the time to 4=all or almost all of the time); the degree of stress involved in the job (on a scale of 1=none of the time to 4=all or almost all of the time); and how strongly the respondent felt that he/she could do a better job if he/she had received training (1=strongly disagree to 4=strongly agree). In addition, among those who did not work in 1992, the self-reported reasons for non-work (unemployed or laid off; disabled; or retired, or some combination) were entered in the models estimating the predictors of the likelihood of resuming work in 1994.

Independent variables representing economic/status maintenance need are pension coverage from the current, last, or any other previous job (yes, covered=1; no, not covered=0); and net worth (in $10,000). For those who did not work in 1992, total amount of their pension was also entered in the model estimating their likelihood of resuming work in 1994.

Findings

Work Status in 1992 and 1994 and Self-Reported Reasons for Non-work

Data in Table 1 show that in 1992, 79.1% of male respondents reported that they were currently working, 19.2% reported that they were not currently working but had last worked for pay between 1972 and 1991, and 1.7% reported that they had never worked for pay or had last worked prior to 1972. For female respondents, the corresponding percentages were 60.4%, 26.3%, and 13.3%, respectively. A majority of those who did not work in 1992 but had worked since 1972 listed the last year of their work as 1989, 1990, or 1991. In 1994, the proportion of those who worked decreased to 72.0% for males and to 55.2% for females. In both years of observation, a significantly higher proportion of White than Black and Hispanic males were working. Similar proportions of White and Black women worked in both years, while a much lower proportion of Hispanic women did.

Further analysis shows that 87.0% of men and 83.8% of women who worked in 1992 were still working, but 13.0% of men and 16.2% of women who worked in 1992 were no longer working for pay in 1994. Of those who did not work in 1992 but had worked between 1972 and 1991, 15.9% of men and 14.2% of women were working again in 1994. Breakdowns by race showed that 87.6% of White, 82.2% of Black, and 88.6% of Hispanic males who worked in 1992 were still working in 1994 ($p<01$). The corresponding percentages for women were 84.4% for Whites, 82.9% for Blacks, and 84.8% for Hispanics; the difference was not statistically significant. And 16.8% of White males, 11.5% of Black males, and 17.7% of Hispanic males who last worked between 1972 and 1991 were found to be working again in 1994. The corresponding percentages for women were 15.6% for Whites, 9.9% for Blacks, and 12.3% for Hispanics.

According to Table 2, in both 1992 and 1994, White men and women were more likely to report retirement than disability as a reason for non-work, whereas Black and Hispanic men and women were more likely to report disability than retirement as a reason for non-work. In

Table 1. Engagement in Paid Work Activities in 1992 and 1994 by Gender and Race (N=8,617)

		Working		Not Working	
		1992	1994	1992	1994
	n	%	%	% (a, b)	%
Male					
White	3,058	82.0	74.7	18.0 (17.0, 1.0)	25.3
Black	593	68.3	59.9	31.7 (27.8, 3.9)	40.1
Hispanic	337	73.0	69.1	27.0 (23.4, 3.6)	30.9
All	3,988	79.1	72.0	20.9 (19.2, 1.7)	28.0
Female					
White	3,336	62.0	57.3	38.0 (25.7, 12.3)	42.7
Black	875	62.2	54.4	37.8 (26.6, 11.2)	45.6
Hispanic	418	45.2	40.7	54.8 (29.2, 25.6)	59.3
All	4,629	60.4	55.2	39.6 (26.3, 13.3)	44.8

Note. a = last worked between 1991 and 1972; b = never worked or last worked before 1972.

addition, 49.9% of White, 30.9% of Black, and 24.4% of Hispanic males who were not working in 1992 reported that they were retired in that year; in 1994, the corresponding percentages increased to 59.1% for White, 37.7% for Black, and 31.7% for Hispanic males. In the case of female non-worker respondents, 24.9% of Whites, 21.1% of Blacks, and 8.3% of Hispanics in 1992, and 27.4% of Whites, 27.2% of Blacks, and 11.4% of Hispanics in 1994 reported that they were retired.

In both 1992 and 1994, almost one and one half times as many Black and Hispanic non-working men as White non-working men reported disability as a reason for not participating in the labor force. Almost three times as many Black women and twice as many Hispanic women reported disability as a reason for their detachment from the labor force as their White counterparts. Further analysis shows that as many as 50.7% of White, 63.6% of Black, and 62.0% of Hispanic males who did not work in 1992 affirmatively answered the question whether or not they had "any impairments or health problems limiting the kind and/or the amount of paid work they could do." The corresponding percentages for women were 37.5% for Whites, 55.4% for Blacks, and 48.4% for Hispanics.

Bivariate Results of Key Independent Variables

Of those who worked in 1992, 77.9% of men and 86.9% of women were employees, whereas 22.1% of men and 13.1% of women were self-employed. Of those who did not work in 1992 but had worked between 1972 and 1991, 88.9% of men and 91.4% of women were employees in their last job. The average number of work hours of those who worked in 1992 was 2,201 (SD=541) for employed men; 2,310 (SD=968) for self-employed men; 1,869 (SD=604) for employed women; and 1,768 (SD=1,070) for self-employed women. The average number of

Table 2. Self-Reported Reasons for Non-work in 1992 and 1994 by Gender and Race

	White		Black		Hispanic	
	1992	1994	1992	1994	1992	1994
Male (n)	(519)	(771)	(165)	(236)	(78)	(104)
Unemployed, looking for work	16.8	9.1	16.4	11.9	24.4	16.3
Laid off, sick or other leave	2.3	1.3	1.8	1.3	3.8	5.8
Disabled	39.3	36.2	52.7	51.3	55.1	47.1
Retired	49.9	59.1	30.9	37.7	24.4	31.7
Homemaker	0.6	0.4	1.8	0.8	—	—
Other	1.0	2.9	4.2	2.5	1.3	5.8
Female (n)	(850)	(1,426)	(232)	(397)	(120)	(245)
Unemployed, looking for work	8.2	4.0	9.9	6.3	15.0	6.5
Laid off, sick or other leave	1.3	0.5	1.7	0.8	1.9	0.8
Disabled	19.1	16.	46.1	43.6	31.7	28.6
Retired	24.9	27.	21.1	27.2	8.3	11.4
Homemaker	54.6	57.9	28.8	29.7	38.4	54.3
Other	2.6	4.0	1.3	3.5	3.3	3.3

Note. Reason categories are not mutually exclusive.

work hours in their last job of those who did not work in 1992 were 2,191 (*SD*=671) for employed men; 2,531 (*SD*=1,137) for self-employed men; 1,721 (*SD*=722) for employed women; and 1,806 (*SD*=1,036) for self-employed women.

The average number of work hours in 1994 of those who continued to work in 1994 were not significantly different from those in 1992 for both genders. But the average number of work hours in 1994 of those who did not work in 1992 but resumed working in 1994 were about one half the number the continuously working group put in, at an average 1,297 (and a median of 1,000) hours for employed men and an average of 1,084 (and a median of 960) hours for employed women.

White males, regardless of their current work status, were found to have worked significantly more years and more hours than did minority males. White females were not significantly different from minority females in average number of annual work hours. Black women had joined the labor force significantly earlier, but Hispanic women joined the labor force significantly later than White women. Thus, Black women had worked the most years of all three groups of women. A significantly higher proportion of Hispanics of both genders than their White and Black counterparts reported that they had been laid off or unemployed, or both, in the preceding 10 years.

With respect to the types of occupation, 36.6% of White males employed in 1992, as compared to 14.2% and 12.8% of their Black and Hispanic counterparts, respectively, were in managerial, professional, and technical support positions. The corresponding percentages for women were 32.2% for Whites, 22.1% for Blacks, and 13.7% for Hispanics. The racial difference was even wider in the case of the last occupation of those who did not work. With respect to the nature of their job, Black and Hispanic workers of both genders were significantly more likely than White workers to report that their jobs required lots of physical effort, whereas White men and women were significantly more likely than the people of color to report that their jobs involved a lot of stress. Hispanic men were significantly more likely than White and Black men to indicate that they could do a better job if they received more training. Racial difference was not found in men's attitude toward work, but White women were found to have more positive attitudes toward work than Black women, indicating that they would continue to work even if they did not need the money.

The differences in the types of occupation and work histories may also explain the significant racial difference in pension coverage: 74.4% of White males working in 1992, as compared to 69.4% and 51.2% of their Black and Hispanic counterparts, indicated that they had pension coverage from either their current or their previous job. The corresponding percentages for non-working males were 75.1% for Whites, 57.6% for Blacks, and 36.7% for Hispanics. For females working in 1992, 63.2% of Whites, 63.4% of Blacks, and 47.1% of Hispanics had pension coverage; for non-working females, 38.2% of Whites, 40.8% of Blacks, and 21.3% of Hispanics had pension coverage. (More detailed bivariate analysis results for other independent variables can be obtained from the author.)

Multivariate Logistic Regression Results

1. Determinants of work status in 1992. As shown in Table 3, although having a disability was a consistently significant determinant of work status for all races and genders, there were some racial differences in factors determining the likelihood of work within each race. Age was not a significant factor for Hispanics and self-rated health was not a significant factor for Blacks. Marital status was a significant factor for White women only. White men in semi-skilled jobs were more likely to work than White men in managerial, professional, or technical support positions. Among Black men, those in mechanical and machine-operating or blue-collar jobs were less likely to work than their white-collar counterparts. Black men who had started work-ing later were also more likely to still be working. The amount of net worth was significant for Whites only, but pension coverage was significant for all women regardless of race. The odds ratios indicate that women with pension coverage were 58% (Blacks) to 286% (Hispanics) more likely than those without it to be working in 1992. The variables showing no statistical significance in determining work likelihood included years of education, annual hours of work (in 100 hours), and whether the respondent had ever been laid off in the preceding 10 years. The model chi-squares (*df*) for the logistic regression models are: 470 (*12*) for White men; 182 (*12*) for Black men; 105 (*12*) for Hispanic men; 521 (*12*) for White women; 243 (*12*) for Black women; and 110 (*12*) for Hispanic women.

2. *Determinants of continued work in 1994 among those who worked in 1992.* As shown in Table 4, age was a significant factor for all races and genders with the exception of Hispanic males. Marital status and having disabilities were significant factors for White males only. Self-rated health was significant for White males, White females, and Black females. Interestingly, the number of years of education was negatively associated with the likelihood of continued work among Black men. Attitude toward work was significant for White men and women only, and the number of hours of work in 1992 was significant for White and Black women only. Black men who indicated that they could do a better job with more training were more likely to

Table 3. Determinants of Work Status in 1992 for Employees: Odds Ratios for Significant Logistic Regression Coefficients

	Men			Women		
Variable	White (2,321)	Black (470)	Hispanic (269)	White (2,464)	Black (680)	Hispanic (263)
Age	.86	.90*		.86	.87	
Marital status						
• Married				.42		
• (Single)						
Disabled	.13	.07	.06	.21	.06	.06
Self-rated health	.78		.58	.77		
Current/last occupation						
• Sales/clerical/service	1.38					
• Mechanical		.63*				.40
• (Professional)						
Year started work	1.03				1.05	
Have pension coverage				2.74	1.58	3.86
Net worth ($10,000)	.99			.99		

Note. Those variables which were entered into the model but are not shown were excluded from the table because of lack of statistical significance.

*$p<.05$; all others are significant at $p<.01$.

continue to work than Black men who did not so indicate. Hispanic women who had previously been laid off or unemployed were less likely to continue to work than Hispanic women who had not been laid off or unemployed. Net worth was negatively associated with the likelihood of continued work among Hispanic women only. The variables showing no statistical significance in determining likelihood of continued work included current/last occupation (sales/clerical/ service, mechanical, and professional), earnings type in 1992 (salaried versus hourly); degree of physical efforts required by the 1992 job; degree of stress involved in the 1992 job; and year the respondent started the type of current or last work. The model chi-squares (*df*) for the logistic regression models are: 134 (*17*) for White men; 36 (*17*) for Black men; 16 (*17*) for Hispanic men; 100 (*17*) for White women; 54 (*17*) for Black women; and 38 (*17*) for Hispanic women.

3. *Determinants of resuming work in 1994 among those who last worked between 1972 and 1992.* As reported in Table 5, age was significant only for women and marital status and self-rated health was significant only for men. Race was not a significant factor. In terms of occupational characteristics, the more recently a respondent had worked for pay, the more likely it was that he or she would resume work; this was true for both men and women. Those men who started

Table 4. Determinants of Work Status in 1994 Among Those Who Were Employed in 1992: Odds Ratios for Significant Logistic Regression Coefficients

	Men			Women		
Variable	White (1,864)	Black (320)	Hispanic (199)	White (1,707)	Black (478)	Hispanic (154)
Age	.83	.85		.88	.86	.82
Marital status • Married • (Single)	2.05					
Years of education		.82				
Disabled	.60*					
Self-rated health	.80		.58	.81	.43	
Would work even if money not needed	1.29			1.36		
Annual hours of work (unit=100)				1.04	1.05	
Could do better if received job training		1.72				
Have ever been laid off						.24*
Net worth ($10,000)						.95*
Model chi-squre (df)	134 (17)	36 (17)	16 (17)	100 (17)	54 (17)	38 (17)

Note. Those variables which were entered into the model but are not shown were excluded from the table because of lack of statistical significance.

*p<.05; all others are significant at *p<.01.*

working in later years were also more likely to resume work in 1994. As expected, men and women who reported that they were unemployed or laid off in 1992 were three times (men) to twice (women) as likely to resume working in 1994 as those who did not so report. For women, those who reported that they were disabled in 1992 were less likely to resume working in 1994 than those who did not so report. The amount of pension benefits received by female respondents, or their spouses, or both was negatively associated with the likelihood of their resuming work in 1994. The variables showing no statistical significance in determining likelihood of work resumption among those who had previously worked between 1972 and 1992 included race (White versus non-White); years of education; last occupation (categories explained above); type of last work (employed versus self-employed); annual hours of work in the last job (in 100 hours); whether the respondent reported retired in 1992; and net worth (in $10,000). The model chi-squares (*df*) for the logistic regression models are: 180 (*16*) for men and 166 (*16*) for women.

Discussion

The findings of this study confirm those of previous studies with regard to low labor force participation rates among older men and women as well as gender and racial differences in those rates. In 1994, when the respondents were between 53 and 63 years old, 25.3% of White, 40.1% of Black, and 30.9% of Hispanic males did not engage in any employment activities. Between 1992 and 1994, the nonparticipation rates increased 7.3, 8.4, and 3.9 percentage points for White, Black, and Hispanic males, respectively. Understandably, women's labor force participation rates were even lower than men's, and their nonparticipation rates increased 4.7, 7.8, and 4.5 percentage points between 1992 and 1994 for Whites, Blacks, and Hispanics, respectively. By 1994, only a little over half of women in the sample were working for pay.

Table 5. Determinants of Resuming Work in 1994 Among Those Who Last Worked as Employees or Self-Employees Between 1972 and 1992: Odds Ratios for Significant Logistic Regression Coefficients Only

Variable	Men (*n=744*)	Women (*n=1,156*)
Age		.91
Marital status		
Married	2.46	
(Single)		
Self-rated health	.62	
Year started the work (last job)	1.02	
Year last worked for pay	1.25	1.19
Reported unemployed/laid off in 1992	3.58	2.20
Reported disabled in 1992		.23
Total amount of pension received in 1992 (unit=$100)		.99*

Note. Those variables which were entered into the model but are not shown were excluded from the table because of lack of statistical significance.
*p<.05; all others are significant at p<.01.

But the increase in the nonparticipation rates between 1992 and 1994 does not mean that the rates went up unilaterally. About one sixth of men and women who reported in 1992 that they had last worked between 1972 and 1991 were found to be working again in 1994. Apparently, these people had not exited the labor force permanently and they subsequently reentered the labor force. Some nonparticipants were willing to rejoin the labor force. One sixth of White and Black males and one fourth of Hispanic males who did not work in 1992 identified themselves as unemployed; in 1994, one tenth of White, one eighth of Black, and one sixth of Hispanic male nonparticipants reported that they were unemployed and thus, they were involuntary nonparticipants who would rather be working than not working, if given the choice.

Two factors—age and disability—were found to be significant predictors of work versus non-work status for most groups in 1992. The relatively large magnitude of the effect of age (5% to 15% decrease in the likelihood of working per 1-year increment), even with health status and other antecedent variables controlled for, reflects the retirement patterns that have been significantly shaped by chronological age for the past 3 or 4 decades. Eligibility for Social Security retirement benefits as well as other public and private pensions is based on chronological age. Societal norms and expectations as to an appropriate age when people can disengage themselves from the work role may have been shaped in conjunction with the official sanction and incentives for retirement that are embedded in the Social Security and other pension systems. For example, those who were working in 1992 reported that the average retirement age for their job was 63 (*SD*=3) and they planned to reduce work hours or stop working at about 62, which coincides with the age when they would be eligible for Social Security. Less than 8% of the respondent-workers in 1992 indicated that they would never stop working. It appears that, according to the prevailing social norms, reduction in or disengagement from the work role and transition to a more leisurely life path in old age is often construed as a desirable sequence within the life course, a well-deserved reward and privilege that many workers look forward to.

The predictive power of disability was especially salient when those who worked were compared with those who did not work in 1992, but it was somewhat subdued when those who continued to work were compared with those who did not continue to work in 1994. In fact, having a disability was a significant determinant of the 1994 work status among White males only. This finding implies that many disabled persons, especially people of color, had already exited from the labor force by 1992, the first year of observation. Given the magnitude of the significance of disability as a determinant of labor force participation in 1992, racial differences, especially, in men's labor force participation rates, may be due in large part to significant racial differences in disability rates. Apparently because those who had withdrawn from the labor force for reasons of disability were less likely to reenter it (see Table 5), the labor force participation rates among minority men continued to be lower than those among White men in 1994.

Contrary to the findings of previous studies, job characteristics, that is, the degree of physical effort required by the job and job-related stress, were not found to be significant factors determining the likelihood of continued work between 1992 and 1994. Given the age range of the sample members, it is possible that those in physically demanding jobs, for example, had already retired prior to 1992 or had switched to a different job prior to 1992 or between 1992 and 1994. Further research is needed on this topic. Data also show that the attitude toward work explained within-group differences among Whites only. Among blacks and Hispanics, the work attitude was not a predictor of the likelihood of continued work. Given the high prevalence of disabilities among people of color, it is quite probable that their attitude toward work or psychological commitment to work takes a back seat compared to the physical/functional incapacities to work.

As in the case of attitudes toward work, the relationship between the amount of net worth and the likelihood of work turned out to be significant only for Whites in 1992. Net worth was not a determinant of continued or resumed work in 1994 for all race and gender groups with the exception of Hispanic women. While net worth had race-specific effects, pension coverage had gender-specific effects. The finding that women, but not men, who had pension coverage, regardless of their race, were more likely to work in 1992 may be interpreted as indicating that these women were working to ensure their future pension benefits. It is also likely that women with pension coverage are in good-paying, possibly unionized jobs with job security and stability, and thus, they are likely to work longer than women without pension coverage.

In summary, this study shows that racial and gender differences exist in labor force participation rates. Regardless of gender and race, however, disability status was consistently found to be a significant determinant of non-work among those who were between 51 and 61 years old in 1992, often eclipsing the importance of other individual strength/constraints, social–structural opportunities/constraints, and economic need variables.

Implications for Social Security Reform

This study has several very important implications for Social Security reform measures that are currently being debated—raising further the eligibility age for full Social Security benefits and, therefore, extending the benefits computation period. Raising the age and extending the benefits computation period is tantamount to a benefit reduction for those who are not able to extend their work-life span to reach the eligible age. This study shows that most older workers who would have difficulty extending their work career are low-income, disabled, or unemployed persons. Moreover, given the higher rates of disability and unemployment among people of color, the potentially adverse effects of benefit reduction are likely to be disproportionately borne by low-income, minority older persons. Although the adverse consequences may be ameliorated by the protective cushion of DI to a certain extent, policies and programs are needed to help those who would otherwise fall through the cracks. In the following, I discuss the potential consequences of reform measures on low-income elders as well as steps to remedy their possibly adverse effects.

First, considering the overriding significance of disability as a barrier to work among men and women between ages 51 and 61, raising the age for full Social Security benefits is quite likely to result in increased numbers of DI claimants. That is, many would rather opt for DI than Old Age Insurance (OAI), even if they would become eligible for reduced OAI benefits, because the latter would be smaller than DI. Because the nature and severity of disabilities were not analyzed in this study, the proportions of those who would actually qualify for DI and those who may be pushed to continue to work are not known. Nevertheless, an increase in the DI rolls is quite likely given the increasing share of minority workers in the population and the higher rates of disabilities among people of color. Under the circumstances, the DI application and claims procedures may need to be made more user friendly and simplified for those over a certain age.

Second, as discussed, when the eligible age is raised, early retirement would result in a substantial benefit cut for persons who would not qualify for DI because their disabilities are not severe enough to prevent them from engaging in substantial gainful activities (SGA). Reduced benefits are likely to create economic hardship for low-income retirees and their dependents who do not have other sources of income to supplement Social Security. Following the death of their husbands, surviving wives would also be forced to live with even less. Thus, increase in the age for full benefits needs to be accompanied by relaxation of the strict SGA criterion to allow these low-income retirees to qualify for DI until they become old enough to be eligible for retiree benefits. An increase in the unearned income disregard for SSI is another alternative that needs to be considered for low-income Social Security beneficiaries.

Third, when the eligibility age is raised, programs and services must be provided to assist healthy older individuals who are involuntarily out of work, so that they may not be unfairly penalized by the Social Security system for their involuntary nonparticipation in the labor force. Supportive services need to be provided to help unemployed older persons find jobs and receive job training. The study shows that a sizable proportion of non-working people of color were unemployed rather than retired. It is also possible that many who claimed that they were retired may have reluctantly taken the retiree role following frustrating and futile attempts to find a job. Without supportive services, the unemployment period may extend to the point that their long-term detachment from the labor market would make it very difficult for these people to rejoin the labor force (refer to the significant association between the year the respondent last worked for pay and the likelihood of his/her resuming work). In addition, rehabilitation services need to be provided to enable older persons who have a good prognosis for recovery if given appropriate care to continue or return to work. Provision of continuing education and job-skills enhancement training is also needed to help low-income, ill-educated workers to extend their work-life span. Educational and skills deficiencies definitely put these low-income workers at a high risk for premature termination from a job in the face of changing technologies and industrial restructuring.

Fourth, we also need to pay attention to the fact that older workers will eventually reach the physical limits of their ability to do heavy-duty, physically demanding tasks. Despite the increase in human longevity and the decrease in morbidity in old age, the gradual decline in physical strength during the aging process poses a barrier for older workers engaging in physically demanding work activities. In many occupations, even age 65 can be an extremely unrealistic retirement age. In the interest of older workers who are approaching their "natural" retirement age in those occupations, formalized occupational transition services may be needed to help the workers continue to work. Another alternative is development of a graded eligible age system for Social Security under which certain occupational categories may be exempt from stiff benefit reduction for early retirement.

Fifth and finally, policymakers need to be careful not to draw sweeping conclusions from aggregate or average statistics in which different races and genders are pooled. As shown in the findings section, race-specific models reveal that the variables determining work status among Blacks and Hispanics are quite different from those determining work status among Whites. Debate on Social Security reform needs to continue to examine differential potential effects of various reform measures on different genders, races, and classes.

References

Atchley, R. C. (1982). The process of retirement comparing women and men. In M. Szinovacz (Ed.), *Women's retirement* (pp. 153–163). Beverly Hills, CA: Sage.

Beck, S. H. (1985). Determinants of labor force activity among retired men. *Research on Aging, 7,* 251–280.

Burr, J. A., Massagli, M. P., Mutchler, J. E., & Pienta, A. M. (1996). Labor force transitions among older African American and White men. *Social Forces, 74,* 963–982.

Burtless, G., & Quinn, J. F. (2001). Living longer, living better: The policy challenge of an aging work force. *The Public Policy and Aging Report, 11*(3), 5–11.

Calasanti, T. M., & Bonanno, S. A. (1992). Working "over-time": Economic restructuring and retirement as a class. *The Sociological Quarterly, 33*, 135–152.

Cates, J. R. (1983). *Insuring inequality: Administrative leadership in Social Security, 1934–1954.* Ann Arbor: University of Michigan Press.

Chen, Y.-P. (1994). Improving the economic security of minority persons as they enter old age. In *Minority elders: Five goals toward building a public policy base.* Washington, DC: Gerontological Society of America.

Chen, Y.-P., & Leavitt, T. D. (1997). The widening gap between White and minority pension coverage. *The Public Policy and Aging Report, 8*(1), 10–11.

Choi, N. G. (2000). Determinants of engagement in paid work following Social Security benefit receipt among older women. *Journal of Women & Aging, 12*(3/4), 133–154.

Diamond, P. A. (1997). Proposals to restructure Social Security. *Journal of Economic Perspectives, 10*, 67–88.

Elder, G. H. (1985). Perspectives on the life course. In G. H. Elder (Ed.), *Life course dynamics: 1960s to 1980s.* Ithaca, NY: Cornell University Press.

Elder, G. H. & Pavalko, E. K. (1993). Work careers in men's later years: Transitions, trajectories, and historical change. *Journal of Gerontology, 48*, S180–191.

Ferrara, P. J. (1997). Privatization of Social Security: The transition issues. *Social Philosophy and Policy, 14*, 145–164.

Friedland, R. B. (1996). Privatizing social insurance. *The Public Policy and Aging Report, 7*(3), 11–15.

Gendell, M., & Siegel, J. S. (1996). Trends in retirement age in the United States, 1955–1993, by sex and race. *Journal of Gerontology, 51B*, S132–S139.

Gibson, R. C. (1987). Reconceptualizing retirement for Black Americans. *The Gerontologist, 27*, 691–698.

Gibson, R. C. (1991). The subjective retirement of Black Americans. *Journal of Gerontology, 46*, S204–S209.

Grad, S. (2002). *Income of the population 55 or older, 1998.* Washington, DC: U.S. Social Security Administration, Office of Research, Evaluation, and Statistics.

Gramlich, E. M. (1997). Different approaches for dealing with Social Security. *Journal of Economic Perspectives, 10*, 55–66.

Institute for Social Research (1998). *Health and retirement study, Wave 2: Full public release, version 1.0, Data description and usage.* Ann Arbor, MI: University of Michigan. Retrieved December, 1, 1999, from http://hrsonline.isr.umich.edu/meta/1994/core/desc/hrs94dd.pdf

Han, S., & Moen, P. (1998). *Clocking out: Multiple time in retirement* (BLCC Working paper No. 98-03). Ithaca, NY: Cornell Careers Institute.

Hardy, M. (1991). Employment after retirement: Who gets back in? *Research on Aging, 13*, 267–288.

Hayward, M. D., Friedman, S., & Chen. H. (1996). Race inequities in men's retirement. *Journal of Gerontology, 51B*, S1–S10.

Hayward, M. D., Hardy, M. A., & Grady, W. R. (1989). Labor force withdrawal patterns among older men in the United States. *Social Science Quarterly, 70*, 425–448.

Hayward, M. D., Hardy, M. A., & Liu, M. (1994). Work after retirement: The experience of older men in the United States. *Social Science Research, 23*, 82–107.

Hennessey, J. C., & Dykacz, J. M. (1989). Projected outcomes and length of time in the Disability Insurance program. *Social Security Bulletin, 52*(9), 2–41.

Henretta, J. C., Chan, C. G., & O'Rand, A. M. (1992). Retirement reasons versus retirement process: Examining the reasons for retirement typology. *Journal of Gerontology, 47*, S1–S7.

Henretta, J. C., & Lee, H. (1996). Cohort differences in men's late life labor force participation. *Work and Occupations, 23,* 214–235.

Herz, D. E., & Rones, P. L. (1989). Institutional barriers to employment of older workers. *Monthly Labor Review,* 14–21.

Hieger, M., & Shipman, W. (1997). *Common objectives to a market-based Social Security system: A response* (SSP No. 10). Washington, DC: Cato Institute.

Hogan, R., Kim, M., & Perrucci, C. (1997). Racial inequality in men's employment and retirement earnings. *Sociological Quarterly, 38,* 431–438.

Holden, K. (1988). Physically demanding occupations, health, and work after retirement: Findings from the New Beneficiary Survey. *Social Security Bulletin, 51*(11), 3–15.

Hurd, M., & McGarry, K. (1993). *The relationship between job characteristics and retirement* (Working Paper No. 4558). Cambridge, MA: National Bureau of Economic Research.

Jackson, J. S., & Gibson, R. C. (1985). Work and retirement among the Black elderly. *Current Perspectives on Aging and the Life Cycle, 1,* 193–222.

Jones, T. W. (1996). Strengthening the current Social Security system. *The Public Policy and Aging Report, 7*(3), 1–6.

Kijakazi, K. (1998). *African Americans, Hispanic Americans, and Social Security: The shortcomings of the Heritage Foundation reports.* Retrieved April 1, 2002, from http://www.cbpp.org/10-5-98socsec.htm

Mashaw, J. L., & Marmor, T. R. (1996). The great Social Security scare. *The American Prospect, 29,* 30–37.

Moen, P. (1985). Continuities and discontinuities in women's labor force participation. In G. H. Elder, Jr. (Ed.), *Life course dynamics: 1960s to 1980s* (pp. 113–155). Ithaca, NY: Cornell University Press.

Moen, P. (1996). Gender, age, and the life course. In R. H. Binstock & L. K. George (Eds.), *Handbook of aging and the social sciences.* New York: Academic Press.

Moore, K. L. (2000). Redistribution under the current Social Security system. *University of Pittsburgh Law Review, 61,* 955–990.

Morrison, M. (1990). Economic well-being and the aging of minority populations. In E. P. Sanford, F. Torres-Gil & S. A. Schoenrock (Eds.), *Diversity in an aging America: Challenges for the 1990s.* San Diego: National Resource Center on Minority Aging Populations.

Morrow-Howell, N., & Leon, J. (1988). Life-span determinants of work in retirement years. *International Journal of Aging and Human Development, 27,* 125–140.

Munnell, A. H. (1998). *Why Social Security privatization would hurt women.* Boston College, Carroll School of Management. Retrieved April 1, 2002, from http://www.socsec.com/library/mun_women.htm

Mutchler, J. E., Burr, J. A., Pienta, A. M., & Massagli, M. P. (1997). Pathways to labor force exit: Work transitions and work instability. *Journal of Gerontology, 52B,* S4–S12.

Myers, D. A. (1991). Work after cessation of career job. *Journal of Gerontology, 46,* S93–S102.

National Economic Council (1998). *Women and retirement security.* Washington, DC: The National Economic Council Interagency Working Group on Social Security.

Niggle, C. J. (2000). Political economy of Social Security reform proposals. *Journal of Economic Issues, 34,* 789–809.

O'Rand, A. M. (1996). The cumulative stratification of the life course. In R. H. Binstock & L. K. George (Eds.), *Handbook of aging and the social sciences* (pp. 188–207). New York: Academic Press.

Parnes, H. S., & Less, L. J. (1985). Economic well being in retirement. In H. S. Parnes et al. (Eds.), *Retirement among American men* (pp. 91–118). Lexington, MA: Lexington Books.

Parnes, H. S., & Sommers, D. G. (1994). Shunning retirement: Work experience of men in their seventies and early eighties. *Journal of Gerontology, 49,* S117–S124.

Pienta, A., Burr, J., & Mutchler, J. (1994). Women's labor force participation in later life: The effects of early work and family experience. *Journal of Gerontology, 49*, S231–S239.

Porter, K. H., Larin, K., & Primus, W. (1999). *Social Security and poverty among the elderly*. Washington, DC: Center on Budget and Policy priorities. Retrieved April 1, 2002, from http://www.cbpp.org/4-8-99socsec.htm

Quadagno, J. (1994). *The color of welfare: How racism undermined the War on Poverty*. New York: Oxford University Press.

Quinn, J. (1997). Retirement trends and patterns in the 1990s: The end of an era? *The Public Policy and Aging Report, 8*(3), 10–14.

Quinn, J. F., Burkhauser, R. V., & Myers, D. A. (1990). *Passing the torch: The influence of economic incentives on work and retirement*. Kalamazoo, MI: W. E. UpJohn Institute for Employment Research.

Quinn, J. F., & Kozy, M. (1996). The role of bridge jobs in the retirement transition: Gender, race, and ethnicity. *The Gerontologist, 36*, 363–372.

Quinn, J. F., & Mitchell, O. S. (1996, May-June). Social Security on table. *The American Prospect, 26*, 76–81.

Rindfuss, R. (1991). The young adult years: A view of structural changes and fertility. *Demography, 28*, 493–512.

Ruhm, C. J. (1990). Bridge jobs and partial retirement. *Journal of Labor Economics, 8*, 482–501.

Schieber, S. J. (1996). A new vision for Social Security. *The Public Policy and Aging Report, 7*(3), 1–14.

Smeeding, T. M. (1999). *Social Security reform: Improving benefit adequacy and economic security for women* (Center for Policy Research Policy Brief Series #16). Syracuse, NY: The Maxwell School, Syracuse University.

Stock, J. H., & Wise, D.A. (1990). Pensions, the option value of work and retirement. *Econometrica, 58*, 1151–1180.

U.S. Census Bureau. (1996). *Population projections of the United States by age, sex, race, and Hispanic origin: 1995 to 2000* (Current population Reports No. P25-1 130). Washington, DC: U.S. Government Printing Office.

U.S. Census Bureau (2000). *Poverty in the United States: 1999* (Current Population Reports, Consumer Income). Retrieved February 11, 2004, from http://www.census.gov/hhes/www/poverty.html

U.S. Census Bureau (2001). *Overview of race and Hispanic origin 2000* (Census 2000 brief). Retrieved August 15, 2002, from http://www.census.gov/prod/2001pubs/c2kbr01-1.pdf

U.S. Census Bureau. (2002). *Poverty in the United States: 2001*. Current Population Reports, P60-219. Washington, DC: U.S. Government Printing Office.

U.S. General Accounting Office. (1999). *Social Security reform: Implications of raising the retirement age* (Report to the Chairman and Ranking Minority Member, Special Committee on Aging, U.S. Senate, GAO/HEHS-99-112). Washington, DC: Author

Villa, V. M., Wallace, S. P., & Markides, K. M. (1997). Economic diversity and an aging population: The impact of public policy and economic trends. *Generations, 21*(2), 13–18.

Weller, C. E. (2000). Risky business? Evaluating market risk of equity investment proposals to reform Social Security. *Journal of Policy Analysis and Management, 19*, 263–273.

Williamson, J. B. (1997). A critique of the case for privatizing Social Security. *The Gerontologist, 37*, 561–571.

Williamson, J. B., & Rix, S. E. (2000). Social Security reform: Implications for women. *Journal of Aging and Social Policy, 11*(4), 41–68.

Chapter Six

Social Policy Implications of Racial Disparities in the Criminal Justice System

Nkechi Taifa

In 1900 W.E.B. DuBois accurately predicted that the problem of the 20th century would be the problem of the color line. And now, more 100 years later, this prophecy is just as ominous, particularly with respect to the criminal justice system. Social and criminal justice policy decisions about drugs have caused racial disparities that are having devastating effects on people of color and poor people.

To demonstrate such effects, this chapter profiles Miz Pearl and her family, in a highly stylized, exaggerated composite of different persons and events portrayed as occurring in one family affected by the grim realities of today's criminal justice system. This is not, of course, the typical case study; most families fortunately do not experience such compounded trauma. Far too many, however, are subjected to a taste of it. Although the saga's characters are purposely stereotyped to dramatize the context of their lives, the issues they are confronted with are based on actual scenarios that have occurred as the result of current policy and legislation. The information relative to specific cases that supports the saga is found throughout the sections that follow. The chapter then analytically critiques the issues raised in the case study and suggests a number of remedies.

The Saga of Miz Pearl

Miz Pearl is a 70-year-old matriarch from the South currently residing in a massive housing project in a major city. Pearl is the mother of three children (Bobby, Beverly, and Sharon); three grandchildren (Tyrone, Sharmeka, and Bay-Bay), and one great-grandchild. While down South, Pearl's brother Bubba was executed in 1958 for the rape and murder of a White woman. Pearl's family knew Bubba had not committed the gruesome crime, because he was 50 miles away at a family reunion at the time. However, it was their word against the dead woman's husband, who identified Bubba as the murderer. Unfortunately,

---

For their invaluable assistance with this chapter, the author thanks Dr. Tricia Bent-Goodley, associate professor at Howard University School of Social Work, along with Howard University School of Law graduates Nareissa Smith and Robin Konrad.

Bubba's lawyer fell asleep during substantial portions of the trial and failed to conduct any meaningful investigation. Bubba was executed, proclaiming his innocence to the end.

After that incident, Pearl and her husband left the South for what they thought would be more promising opportunities in the North. Shortly after the birth of her youngest daughter, Sharon, Pearl's husband died, the victim of a rare form of cancer associated with the illicit dumping of toxic waste where he played as a child. Bobby, her eldest, had just returned from Vietnam, not clear on why he was fighting the war, yet suffering the effects of frontline combat. He had constant headaches and problems sleeping. When he did sleep, he had intense nightmares. He found it difficult to concentrate. Bobby started shooting heroin to ease his physical and mental pain. Eventually, he was arrested, convicted, and sent to prison on drug and robbery charges.

Miz Pearl's youngest daughter, Sharon, never knew her father because of his premature death, never knew her Uncle Bubba because he was executed, and never got to know her big brother Bobby because he was in prison. Although she was a bright girl and had been captain of the cheerleading squad at her neighborhood school, after the advent of bussing she could not make the new school's team. Her grades deteriorated; she began to suffer problems of self-esteem and, to feel popular and important, began running with a fast crowd. She got pregnant and dropped out of school.

Miz Pearl insisted that her daughter get her life together. Enrolling in a prenatal care program, Sharon became friends with nine other young Black women in the program. Coincidentally, all the women were expecting boys. After a general overview of what to expect during pregnancy and childbirth, the coach told them that she had some news regarding the future of their children: "Ladies, 3 out of 10 of your boys will spend time in prison. I can't predict which of your sons will be among the three, but national statistics suggest that this is how their lives will turn out."

Sharon gave birth to her son and named him Tyrone. Tyrone's sister, Sharmeka, was born 2 years later. With two children, no degree, and limited skills, Sharon found it increasingly hard to make ends meet. She wanted to work, but could not find a job that would allow her to stay within the income range to receive public assistance. She finally accepted a deal from a friend to allow him to use her apartment to sell drugs, in exchange for him taking care of her needs and the needs of her children. Soon, part of Sharon's needs included drugs. By the time she was pregnant for the third time, she was addicted to crack. Sharon needed the extra money her boyfriend was giving her to raise her children and to support her habit, but she desperately wanted to stop using drugs. Unable to receive drug treatment and unable to stop using drugs, she gave birth to a crack-addicted baby. The public hospital reported her to the prosecuting authorities, and Sharon was convicted and sent to prison under a drug trafficking statute for delivering drugs to her baby through the umbilical cord. Despite the fact that it was not the prenatal care that sent Sharon to prison, after learning of this predicament, her friends vowed they will never seek prenatal care.

Sharon's baby, Benjamin, was taken away from her before she even got a chance to hold him. He, Tyrone, and Sharmeka were placed in separate foster homes. It took more than a year for Miz Pearl to plow through the red tape and lengthy neglect proceedings to get custody of her grandchildren. In the meantime, young Tyrone was physically beaten and his sister Sharmeka sexually assaulted at their respective foster homes. They were finally sent to live with their grandmother. So, at age 65, Miz Pearl found herself raising her daughter's newborn, Benjamin, whom everyone called "Bay-Bay," 13-year-old Tyrone, and 11-year-old Sharmeka.

In school, Tyrone started to misbehave, partly because, although he was in the seventh grade, he read at the third-grade level. Tyrone began to emulate the drug dealers and hustlers he saw on the street and the rappers he watched on television. By the time he was 16, he was a statistic—one of the three young Black men warned about in his mother's childbirth class. He had been stopped by the police countless times, had been entered into the police gang index although he had never actually been a member of a gang, and finally was detained as a juvenile for stealing a car, yet housed in a facility with adult offenders. It was during this detention that he became acquainted with a man who boasted of big-time crack cocaine contacts, and after his release, Tyrone became involved in dealing crack. Tyrone's "friend," however, neglected to explain to him that sentences for crack cocaine were extremely long, even for first-time offenders. So, 2 years later, at age 18, Tyrone found himself back in prison, this time serving a mandatory minimum sentence of 10 years, even though it was his first adult conviction.

Miz Pearl's oldest son, Bobby, got out of prison the day her grandson Tyrone began serving his 10-year mandatory sentence. Bobby had contracted AIDS in prison but was unaware of it. He assumed that the escalation of headaches, nausea, and pain emanated from his earlier experiences in Vietnam. It was hard to settle into a permanent relationship with a woman, so he didn't even try, contenting himself with sporadic sexual encounters with lonely women. In prison he had been housed in a Special Housing Unit—a prison within a prison—because no one associated his erratic behavior with Post-Traumatic Stress Disorder from the war or provided appropriate treatment. In the later years of his incarceration, Bobby was transferred to a prison run by a private corporation, where he participated in labor which generated millions of dollars in profits for the corporation, yet he personally made only $1 an hour.

After his release from prison, the conditions of life confronting Bobby appeared calculated to ensure he would not succeed. Every time he admitted he had been convicted of a felony on a job application or during an interview, he was not hired or, if he lied to get a job, when his record was discovered, he was fired. Bobby had received his GED while imprisoned and upon release wanted to enroll in some college courses, but he was unable to receive financial aid because of his drug conviction. He was released from prison with no medical insurance and, again, because of his prior conviction, was ineligible to qualify for public housing. There appeared to be no opportunities available to him. To make matters worse, when Bobby went out to look for a job, he was often stopped on the streets by the police and harassed for no apparent reason.

Ms. Pearl's granddaughter, Sharmeka, although only 16, appeared to have a penchant for falling in love with men who abused her. The last boyfriend who beat her up got her pregnant. Sharmeka was scared of him and did not question how he made his money. She thought she would be safe as long as she did not know what was going on. Indeed, after seeing what had happened to her mother and the disintegration of their family, Sharmeka had vowed that she would never use or sell drugs. But she was unaware that with the advent of the new drug conspiracy laws, one does not have to actually sell drugs to be guilty as a principal. Answering a telephone and taking a message can suffice as conspiracy. Sharmeka was eventually arrested and convicted on such charges. Ironically, she received more time than those actually involved in the drug ring because she had no information to trade to the government for a lighter sentence.

With Sharmeka's imprisonment, Miz Pearl tried to get custody of her great-grandchild. The state, however, determined that Miz Pearl was too poor and too old to be raising a newborn, that Sharmeka's baby was at risk, and that having him raised by his great-grandmother would not be in the best interests of the child. As such, he was placed in a White foster home with influential parents who were intent on adopting him. Sharmeka was devastated with the removal of her son but because she had a mandatory sentence of 3 years and the child was not being cared for by a family member, the state began the process of terminating her parental rights to free him for adoption.

By this time, Miz Pearl knew more about courtrooms and laws than Perry Mason himself. The previous year her grandson Bay-Bay had gotten in trouble at school. Although he was addicted to crack at birth, that condition was overcome with the devotion, love, and attention of Miz Pearl. With the exception of excruciating bouts of asthma, he was growing up normally. He loved his grandmother very much and was embarrassed that the principal had to call her. He knew she was going to scold him and braced himself for what he knew would be a stern lecture. But when he got home, his Aunt Beverly was there. After working with the NAACP, Miz Pearl's second-born had been inspired to further her education so she would have the skills to help make a difference in society. Beverly was a student at Howard University School of Social Work. During the summers and holidays, she came to get Bay-Bay. She took him to museums and concerts. She told him about her work with organizations working for social change. Her colleagues in the NAACP helped and tutored him in reading and mathematics. They taught him great things about his heritage and instilled in him positive values and pride. Benjamin told his grandmother that his friends at school were calling him a nerd, but he didn't care. He knew who he was and what kind of person he wanted to grow up to be: just like his Aunt Beverly. This was the first time in a long time that Miz Pearl smiled.

The importance of the extended family and community is critical for African Americans (Hill, 1997; Martin & Martin, 1995). Due to the caring support of a community and an extended family structure, at least one of this saga's children will have a solid chance at a bright future. Unless there are major shifts in policy, however, the future for the others appears bleak. It is important to emphasize that this grimly exaggerated scenario does not represent the circumstances of every African American family. However, aspects of the story do reflect the experiences of far too many.

Disproportionate Racial Imprisonment

As of mid-year 2002, the total U.S. prison and jail population was 2,019,234 (Harrison & Karberg, 2003). Nearly half of that population (43%) is African American (Harrison & Karberg, 2003). African American men in the United States are incarcerated at a rate five times higher than Blacks were under apartheid in South Africa (Mauer, 1994). Alarmingly, there were more young Black men in prison and jail than in college in 1992—583,000 African American males incarcerated, compared with 537,000 enrolled in higher education (Mauer, 1994). By 1999–2000, that number increased to 791,600 African American men in prison and jail, compared with 603,000 in higher education (Zeidenberg & Schiraldi, 2002). The increase in the prison population is not evidence of rising crime and not an indication of more criminal activity by African Americans (Mauer, 1999; Weich & Angulo 2000), but a reflection of more stringent sentencing policies, possibly fueled in part by the motivation of the private prison industry to maintain high occupancy rates for profit, regardless of need (The Sentencing Project, 2002)

Tyrone's arrest and incarceration as a juvenile for car theft is not an aberration. The research is indisputable that youth of color are overrepresented at every stage of the justice system, from intake to secure confinement, with the disparities increasing at each successive stage (Poe-Yamagata & Jones, 2000; Weich & Angulo, 2000). A 1990 Florida study determined that despite no difference among juveniles with respect to age, gender, seriousness of offense, and prior record, African American teenagers received the harshest disposition at each stage of the juvenile justice process when compared to White youth (Bishop & Frazier, 1990).

Among young people who have never been involved in the juvenile system, African American youth are at least six times more likely than White youth to be sentenced to prison (Poe-Yamagata & Jones, 2000). African American teens charged with violent crimes are nine times more likely than Whites to be sentenced to juvenile prison and those charged with drug offenses are 48 times more likely than White youth to be sentenced to juvenile prison (Poe-Yamagata & Jones, 2000). Latino youth spend 143 days longer incarcerated compared with White youth with similar charges and are incarcerated at a rate 13 times higher than White youth in public facilities (Villarruel & Walker, 2002). If youth like Tyrone in Miz Pearl's story are sent to an adult prison, they are 500% more likely to be sexually assaulted, 200% more likely to be beaten by staff, and 50% more likely to be attacked with a weapon than if they are confined in a juvenile facility (American Civil Liberties Union [ACLU], 1996).

As the result of far-reaching policy changes initiated during the 1990s, more juveniles are being tried as adults. In 1998, Congress expressly encouraged the practice of juvenile transfer by making federal grants contingent on states implementing policies which would allow for the prosecution of juveniles over age 14 as adults (Weich & Angulo, 2000). A total of 77% of juveniles sent to adult prison are youth of color: 60% African American, 15% Latino, 1% American Indian, 1% Asian. Seventy-five percent of juvenile defendants charged with drug offenses in adult court are African American, and 95% of youth sentenced to adult prison for drug offenses are children of color.

Race and Innocence in Death Penalty Applications

Miz Pearl's brother Bubba executed for killing a White woman, is representative of hundreds of Black men who have been convicted of killing Whites and sentenced to die (Death Penalty Information Center [DPIC], 2003b). While the facts may differ in individual cases, the constant factor—death penalty sentence where the race of the victim is White—remains. While Blacks and Whites are victims of homicide in about equal numbers (Amnesty International, 1995), more than 80% of those individuals executed or sentenced to die have been convicted in cases involving White victims (U.S. General Accounting Office [GAO], 1990).

The United Nations (U.N.) Special Rapporteur on Extrajudicial, Summary, or Arbitrary Executions filed a report with the U.N. Commission on Human Rights after his visit to the United States in 1998 stating that race, ethnic origin, and economic status appear to be key determinants of who will and will not receive a sentence of death (Olsen, 1998). Findings have confirmed that racism plays a role in death penalty cases. The U.S. General Accounting Office found a pattern of evidence indicating racial disparities in the charging, sentencing, and imposition of the death penalty and concluded that those who murdered Whites were more likely to be sentenced to death than those who murdered Blacks (GAO, 1990). This finding was consistent regardless of the data sets, method of data collection, techniques for analysis, states studied, and quality of the study (GAO, 1990). This point was poignantly illustrated in the landmark 1987 case of *McCleskey v. Kemp*, in which a Black man in Georgia was convicted of killing a White police officer and sentenced to die. McCleskey's attorneys argued that the Georgia death penalty was racially biased and produced a comprehensive study that strongly indicated that the victim's race was the most significant factor in determining whether someone convicted of capital murder would be sentenced to death in Georgia. Despite these findings, the Supreme

Court upheld the Georgia death penalty and, based on this cue, federal courts have declined to grant relief based on a racial application of the death penalty in any case (Dieter, 1998).

In addition to issues of race, there are also issues of innocence when one examines the application of the death penalty. Miz Pearl's brother Bubba maintained his innocence to the end. The record is replete with cases in which execution of the innocent has been narrowly averted. In the United States since 1900, there have been on average four cases per year in which an entirely innocent person was convicted of murder and dozens of these persons were sentenced to death. Since 1973, 111 people in 25 states have been released from death row with evidence of their innocence (DPIC, 2003a). A 1982 *Stanford Law Review* study (as cited in ACLU, 1999) documents 350 capital convictions in the 20th century in which it was later proven that the person had not committed the crime. Of those, 23 were executed, while others spent decades of their lives in prison. The number of innocent defendants released from death row has been steadily increasing over recent years. Between 1973 and 1993, an average of 2.75 innocent persons per year was released from death row. Since 1993 an average of five innocent persons per year have been released (DPIC, 2003a).

A disturbing study of the death penalty by Liebman, Fagan, & West (2000) reported that courts found serious mistakes in two thirds of all capital cases—the most common errors being incompetent representation by defense attorneys and prosecutorial misconduct (Liebman, Fagan, & West, 2000). Indeed, the scene in Miz Pearl's saga depicting Bubba's lawyer falling asleep at counsel table is factually illustrative of such incompetence (see *Burdine v. Texas*, 2001). In 2002, the second part of Professor Liebman's report was issued, detailing why the death penalty system in the United States makes so many mistakes and how those mistakes can be prevented (Liebman et al., 2002).

There is currently momentum in the courts, Congress, and the states to reform the system of capital punishment. In 2002 the Supreme Court ruled it unconstitutional to execute the mentally retarded (*Atkins v. Virginia*, 2002) and held that it was the province of juries, rather than judges, to determine whether a person would be executed (*Ring v. Arizona*, 2002). Also in 2002, a federal judge in New York, Jed. S. Rakoff, held that the federal death penalty was unconstitutional (Death Sentence, 2002). In addition in 2002, then-Illinois Governor George Ryan and former Maryland Governor Parris Glendening both imposed a moratorium on the imposition of capital punishment in their states until findings from state commissions on the fairness of the death penalty could be reviewed. In Maryland, despite a University of Maryland study that found compelling statistical evidence of racial bias, Governor Robert Ehrlich, Jr., rescinded the moratorium on executions in that state (Montgomery, 2003). In Illinois, just prior to leaving office at the beginning of 2003, Gov. Ryan emptied the state's death row by pardoning four men and commuting the sentences of 167 others, after a commission found persistent problems and called for reform (Turow, 2003). After several years of negotiations, the U.S. House of Representatives overwhelmingly passed the Innocence Protection Act on November 5, 2003, as part of the Advancing Justice Through DNA Technology Act. Included within the bill is a post-conviction DNA testing program, which will assist in establishing systems that ensure death penalty trials are fair and accurate.

Astronomical Rise of Women of Color in the Criminal Justice System

The portions of Miz Pearl's saga portraying her daughter Sharon and granddaughter Sharmeka, fictitious first-time offenders, are representative of thousands of young Black women.

Until recently, however, there has been little research and analysis of the negative social impact that criminal justice policy decisions have on women of color.

The Sentencing Project, a national nonprofit organization that conducts research on criminal justice issues, reports that from 1989 to 1994 the criminal justice control rates for African American women increased 78%—a rate greater than for any other demographic group studied. This was more than double the increase for African American men and for White women and more than nine times the increase for White men (Mauer & Huling, 1995). African American women are 2.5 times more likely than Latinas and 5 times more likely than White women to be incarcerated (Harrison & Karberg, 2003). Statistics from the Department of Justice reveal that the number of women in prison has more than doubled since 1990, with an annual rate of growth averaging 8.1%, higher than the 6.2% average increase of men in prison. Between 1990 and 2000, the number of men in prison grew by 77%, while the number of women in prison escalated by 110% (Beck & Karberg, 2001).

The greatest contributor to this mass influx of women of color in the criminal justice system has been irrational policy decisions mandated in furtherance of the war on drugs. Perhaps the most senseless of these directives has been the implementation of mandatory minimum sentences for first-time, nonviolent drug offenders such as Sharon and Sharmeka. A mandatory minimum sentence is a prison term predetermined by Congress and automatically levied for a crime primarily involving drugs and firearms. Laws requiring mandatory minimum sentences prohibit judges from considering any of the facts of a case when sentencing other than the type of drug and its weight or the presence of a firearm (Taifa, 1993; USSC, 1991).

Having no discretion to consider the minor or peripheral role of the defendant in the offense or any other factor traditionally found relevant to sentencing, judges have been constrained under mandatory sentencing laws to treat both the "drug mule" and the "drug kingpin" as equals in sentencing despite obvious differences in knowledge, motive, access, and control (Taifa, 2001b; USSC 1991). The only way to escape the imposition of a mandatory sentence is to provide "substantial assistance" to the government. However, as portrayed in Miz Pearl's story, less culpable individuals or arguably innocent persons convicted pursuant to drug conspiracy statutes rarely have valuable information to provide and, as such, often receive sentences higher than major players.

The real-life case of Dorothy Gaines is illustrative of this point. Gaines, a grandmother, had no prior record and there was no physical evidence of any drugs found in her possession. The government offered her a deal: a 5-year sentence for all she knew about a drug trafficking ring in and around Mobile, Alabama. She was a suspect because she once dated a crack user who knew the alleged leader of the cocaine ring. She turned the offer down, saying she was innocent of charges that she helped supply the ring with cocaine. She received a 19-year and 7-month sentence. Her felony conviction was based solely on the uncorroborated testimony of admitted drug dealers who received reduced sentences in exchange for naming "co-conspirators." Because she had no information to trade, she received the total mandatory sentence. The real life story of Kemba Smith is yet another example of the harshness of these drug laws. Kemba, a college student with no prior criminal involvement, received 24 years in prison for her very peripheral role in a drug conspiracy case involving her former boyfriend. Both Gaines and Smith were granted clemency by President Clinton at the conclusion of his term.

Eighty percent of women entering state prisons are mothers who are often the sole caretaker of their children and their primary source of financial and emotional support. The children most often end up in foster care or kinship care (Bent-Goodley, 2003). The Bureau of Justice

Statistics reports that in 1997, more than half (54%) of mothers in state prison had never been visited by their children, and nearly half (40%) of mothers in federal prison had never been visited since admission (Mumola, 2000). This situation may be the consequence of geography, as the majority of both men and women in state prison (62%) as well as federal prison (84%) were imprisoned more than 100 miles from their last place of residence. African American children (7.0%) were nearly nine times more likely to have a parent in prison than White children (0.8%), and Latino children (2.6%) were three times as likely as White children to have a parent in prison (Mumola, 2000).

Although nearly all fathers in federal prison cited the child's mother as the current caregiver (92%), a mere 31% of incarcerated mothers reported the child's father as the current caregiver, resulting in a significant percentage of children being raised by grandparents, other relatives, or the state through foster care (Mumola, 2000). For women who give birth in prison like Sharmeka, forced separation from the infant usually comes within 24 to 72 hours after birth. For those who are drug dependant while pregnant, the result in some instances is criminal prosecution (Roberts, 1991).

Since poor women are subjected to increased government supervision through public hospitals, which screen for drug use, their drug use is more likely to be discovered and reported (as Sharmeka's was) than the drug use of affluent women who frequent private physicians (Roberts, 1991). Interestingly, however, based upon the results of toxicology tests of pregnant women in Pinellas County, FL, who received prenatal care in public health clinics and in private obstetrical offices, researchers determined that there was little difference in the prevalence of substance abuse by pregnant women along either racial or economic lines and there was no significant difference in the prevalence of substance abuse between public clinics and private offices. The study revealed that although the rates of abuse among women of varying ethnic and socioeconomic backgrounds were similar, African American women were 10 times more likely than White women to be reported to public health officials for substance abuse during pregnancy (Roberts, 1991). This trend, however, may be changing. In March 2001, the Supreme Court in *Ferguson v. South Carolina* ruled that a South Carolina hospital overstepped its bounds in 1989 when it tested the urine of pregnant women for drugs and forwarded the results to the police.

Perhaps the most far-reaching consequence for primary caretakers facing sentences of more than 1 year is the Adoption and Safe Families Act of 1997. Provisions within this policy directive accelerate the termination of parental rights by requiring such termination when a child has been in foster care 15 of the previous 22 months (Mauer, Potler, & Wolf, 1999). For women serving mandatory sentences like Sharmeka, this often means the automatic end of the parent/ child relationship if no acceptable relative is able to provide care for the child and no compelling reason exists to halt the termination process (Mauer, Potler, & Wolf, 1999). On average, parents incarcerated in state prison are expected to serve 80 months, and those incarcerated in federal prison 103 months (Mumola, 2000). This length of time far exceeds the 15-month requirement in the statute's threshold, greatly increasing the risk of a governmental petition for the termination of parental rights.

Women find themselves placed in even more vulnerable positions as the result of domestic violence (Richie, 1996). It is well established that numerous women arrested for drug use during pregnancy have been victims of abusive relationships (Harlow, 1999; Mauer, Potler, & Wolf, 1999). Studies show that drug-addicted pregnant women are also likely to have been sexually abused as children and to be in battering relationships as adults (Paltrow, 1993). Women of color experience barriers to obtaining domestic violence services and are often afraid to engage the criminal justice system due to previous or perceived discriminatory treatment by law enforcement (Bent-Goodley, 2001). More than half (57%) of the female state prison population has been abused, either physically or sexually or both (Mauer, Potler, & Wolf, 1999). Although many women such as Sharon and Sharmeka desperately want help dealing with the substance abuse, domestic violence, and stress that characterize their lives, appropriate and accessible comprehensive treatment programs are virtually nonexistent for women, with many of the current programs based on gender-specific male-model constructs that fail to address the myriad issues confronting women in the criminal justice system (American Bar Association & National Bar Association 2001; Richie, 1996; Roberts, 1991).

Barriers to Reentry

According to the Bureau of Justice Statistics, more than 600,000 people return home each year from state and federal prisons (Hughes & Wilson 2002). The successful reintegration of these individuals is one of the most formidable challenges facing society today. Many of these individuals who return home have spent long terms behind bars, are unprepared for life on the outside, and receive little assistance in the reintegration process. Recent legislative initiatives have made the transition process from prison life to societal member more difficult, creating challenges that not only negatively affect the formerly incarcerated person but have a rippling effect on the family and community as well. Many of these barriers to reentry into society arise in the areas of housing, employment, public benefits, education, family reunification, and participation in the political process. For example, the Personal Responsibility and Work Opportunity Reconciliation Act, enacted in 1996, bars those with a drug-related felony conviction from receiving federal cash assistance and food stamps during their lifetime (Allard, 2002; Hirsch et al., 2002; Jacobs, 2001; Mauer, Potler, & Wolf, 1999). Although states have the opportunity to opt out of this lifetime ban, the majority of states have not done so (Allard, 2002; Hirsch et al., 2002; Jacobs, 2001; Mauer, Potler, & Wolf, 1999). States are also prohibited from providing Temporary Assistance for Needy Families (TANF), Supplementary Security Income (SSI), housing, and food stamps to people with convictions who are in violation of a condition of their probation and parole (Hirsch et al., 2002; Jacobs, 2001).

The Higher Education Act of 1998 delays or denies students convicted of any drug-related offense from being eligible to receive any grant, loan, or work assistance (Hirsch et al., 2002; Jacobs, 2001; Mauer, Potler, & Wolf, 1999). Interestingly, violent, predatory, and alcohol-related offenses do not result in such automatic denials of federal financial aid eligibility. Despite a positive correlation between education and lack of recidivism, the schoolhouse door is shut on former prisoners like Miz Pearl's son Bobby, who was unable to receive federal funding to further his education after release from imprisonment. Criminal records also create barriers to employment for the rest of one's life, with certain occupations strictly prohibiting the participation of people with criminal records through the denial of licenses (Hirsch et al., 2002; Love & Kuzma, 1996; Rubinstein, 2001).

People with certain types of convictions are also precluded from living in government-subsidized public housing, and some jurisdictions have instituted criminal background checks for persons applying for Section 8 certificates, which allow tenants with limited income the opportunity to live in non-public housing (Center for Law and Social Policy, 2002; Jacobs, 2001). Additionally, as the result of strict "one strike" policies, entire families, including innocent residents, can be evicted from subsidized housing for the alleged criminal conduct of another family member or guest of a family member on or near the premises (Hirsch et al., 2002). Thus, Miz Pearl could lose her public housing as the result of the actions of one of Tyrone's friends. This was, in fact, the case underlying the Supreme Court's 2002 decision in *Department of Housing and Urban Development v. Rucker* (2002), which upheld the strict enforcement of HUD's one-strike housing policy. The *Rucker* case involved four tenants: a 63–year-old woman, Pearline Rucker, who had lived in public housing since 1995 with her daughter, grandchildren, and great-grandchild. Her mentally disabled daughter was found with cocaine three blocks from the apartment. Willie Lee (age 71) and Barbara Hill (age 63) lived in public housing more than 25 years, both living with their grandsons who, without prior knowledge of their drug activity by Lee or Hill, were caught smoking marijuana in the parking lot. The fourth tenant the case was based on was Herman Walker, a disabled 75-year-old who relied on the help of a caregiver. The caregiver was found with cocaine in Walker's apartment. Eviction proceedings commenced against all of these tenants. The Supreme Court upheld the right of the local Public Housing Authorities to evict tenants "for the drug-related criminal activity of household members and guests, whether or not the tenant knew or should have known about the activity."

The long-range implications of the multiple barriers to reintegration into society are staggering. African Americans and Latinos are disproportionately represented in the criminal justice system due to discrimination encountered from arrest to adjudication (The Sentencing Project, 2000). Increased incarceration not only results in more African Americans and Latinos living with stigmatizing felony records which ensure negative consequences for employment, but it also negatively affects access to public benefits, public housing, student loans, and child custody, and, in many instances, leads to disenfranchisement for large segments of African Americans and Latinos while imprisoned and upon release (Fellner & Mauer, 1998). The historical exclusion from the vote included not only enslaved persons, but also White women, the illiterate, people who did not own property, and convicted felons. Only one group, however, remains disenfranchised—convicted felons. According to a joint report issued by the Sentencing Project and Human Rights Watch, approximately 4.2 million people in the United States are currently disenfranchised and of these, 1.4 million are African American men—representing 14%, or one in seven, of the 10.4 million African American men of voting age (Fellner & Mauer, 1998). And, disturbingly, formerly incarcerated persons seeking re-enfranchisement encounter a myriad of seemingly irrational barriers to regaining their right to vote (Taifa, 2002). Such long-term impact on voting rights, coupled with the disruption and disintegration of families and diminished life prospects, results in incalculable damages to people of color. Warehousing entire generations behind bars is not the solution to societal problems, particularly when the results of such incarceration have such a negative and disproportionate impact on particular racial groups.

The War on Drugs and Sentencing Policy

Drug trafficking and drug abuse transcend all social, economic, and racial barriers. Indeed, Whites sell most of the nation's illegal drugs and account for most of the nation's drug abusers (Taifa, 1996; USSC, 1995). Yet the war on drugs has been targeted at inner-city poor communities, causing a disproportionate number of persons from these communities to be arrested, prosecuted, and convicted (Lusane, 1991; Miller, 1992; Taifa, 1996).

One particularly blatant example of the racial disparity in drug sentencing is the federal mandatory minimum sentence for crack cocaine. Had Tyrone been convicted of trafficking in powder cocaine, his sentence would not have been so severe. The penalties for crack, however, are 100 times more severe than the sentences for the same amount of powder cocaine (Taifa, 1996; USSC, 1995). Simple possession of more than 5 grams of crack is a felony and generates an automatic mandatory sentence of 5 years without parole for a first-time offender; possession of the same amount of powder cocaine, a misdemeanor, requires no jail time (Taifa, 1996; USSC, 1995). Crack has not been found to be more addictive or dangerous than the powdered form of cocaine; indeed no medical or scientific distinction has been found between the two (USSC 1995; Hatsukami & Fischman, 1996; Taifa, 1996).

According to a 1993 survey conducted by the National Institute on Drug Abuse (NIDA), the greatest number of documented cocaine users are White. Of those reporting cocaine use in 1991, 75% were White, 15% were African American, and 10% were Latino. Of those reporting crack cocaine use in the same year, 52% were White, 38% were African American, and 10% were Latino (NIDA, 1993). Despite the evidence that more Whites than people of color use crack, a study issued by the U.S. Sentencing Commission in 1995 revealed that 96.5% of those convicted of federal crack offenses were people of color (USSC, 1995). The commission's 2002 report updating its demographic data found that in 2000, 84.7% of those convicted were people of color (USSC, 2002). A 1993 report on federal sentencing commissioned by the Justice Department disclosed that the higher proportion of African Americans charged with crack offenses was the single most important difference accounting for the overall longer sentences imposed on African Americans relative to other racial groups (McDonald & Carlson, 1993).

Policy Implications for Social Workers

The Leadership Conference on Civil Rights is the nation's oldest, largest, and most diverse civil and human rights coalition. In 2000, the organization produced a report concluding that racism in America's criminal justice system is the number one civil rights issue facing the nation in the 21st century and that criminal justice reform is a civil rights challenge that can no longer be ignored (Weich & Angulo, 2000). Public education that addresses negative stereotypes and erroneous propaganda pertaining to race and crime is key to this reform. Shifts in policy, which combat the unequal administration of justice, are paramount. Such reform can be expressed under three constructs critical to the social work profession: policy advocacy, policy research, and program development (Jansson, 1999).

Social workers can play a key role in advocating for policies that are humane and equitable, while also respecting the need to address crime. As the impact of punitive criminal justice policies broadens, there must be a strengthened intersection between the disciplines of law and social work. The fight for fair and equal treatment within the criminal justice system must be a priority for the profession. Social workers should advocate for federal funding shifts that stress prevention and treatment over incarceration and for a repeal of mandatory minimum sentencing, particularly when such sentencing results in severe ramifications for parental rights.

In light of current research that speaks to discrimination and innocence in death penalty cases, social workers should advocate for the abolition or, at a minimum, a moratorium on the death penalty.

Social workers should advocate for the repeal of automatic barriers which impede the formerly incarcerated person's successful re-entry into society, such as the denial of public benefits, financial aid, employment licenses, housing, and voting rights for people with convictions, and any other civil disability unrelated to the offense that unfairly restricts or stigmatizes persons after they have already paid their debt to society. Finally, the effects of drug policy have been devastating to people of color. Social workers must include promotion of a serious dialogue on drug policy as a major emphasis for advocacy.

Programmatic development is also critical for social workers in the criminal justice arena. Culturally competent training programs, such as job training and reentry initiatives, are needed in communities of color. These services should be community based, with additional resources placed toward community alternatives to incarceration programs. In addition to these efforts, a component of programs could be the development of independent civilian review boards to oversee allegations of police brutality and misconduct.

Social workers can have a direct impact on prisoners through program development in prisons. Increased prisoner access to programs that combine education, life survival skills, vocational training, and stress management are needed. In addition, social workers should be in the forefront of advocacy in support of gender-specific approaches addressing the needs of women of color in the criminal justice system.

Conclusion

All of the characters in Miz Pearl's saga, although exaggerated, personify the impact of racial disparities in the criminal justice system and demonstrate the far-reaching consequences of the misguided policy decisions that affect their lives. The actual case studies that support the story provide evidence of the reality of the impact of the criminal justice system on people of color, particularly African Americans. The statistics provided point to the need for increased information sharing, advocacy, and social change in the criminal justice system. The fact that these disparities continue to proliferate is a testament to the continuing problem of race in 21st century America. Society as a whole must seriously consider shifts in policy to begin the process of eliminating racism in the administration of justice and rectify the criminal justice system's disproportionate impact on people of color.

References

Adoption and Safe Families Act of 1997. 42 USCS 675 (E).

Allard, P. (2002). *Life sentences: Denying welfare benefits to women convicted of drug offenses.* Washington, DC: The Sentencing Project.

American Bar Association, & National Bar Association. (2001). *Justice by gender: The lack of appropriate prevention, diversion and treatment alternatives for girls in the juvenile justice system.* Washington, DC: Author.

American Civil Liberties Union. (1996). *Fact sheet on the juvenile justice system.* New York: Author.

American Civil Liberties Union. (1999). *The death penalty* (Number 14: ACLU Briefing Paper). New York: Author.

Amnesty International (1995). *U.S. human rights violations: A summary of Amnesty International's concerns.* New York: Author.

Atkins v. Virginia, 536 U.S. 304 (2002).

Beck, A. J., & Karberg, J. C. (2001). *Prison and jail inmates at midyear 2000.* Washington, DC: U.S. Department of Justice, Bureau of Justice Statistics.

Bent-Goodley, T. B. (2001). Eradicating domestic violence in the African American community: A literature review and action agenda. *Trauma, Violence and Abuse, 2,* 316–330.

Bent-Goodley, T. B. (2003). Criminal justice policy: Issues for African Americans. In T. B. Bent-Goodley (Ed.), *African American social workers and social policy* (pp. 137–161). New York: Haworth Press.

Bishop, D., & Frazier, C. (1990). *A study of race and juvenile processing in Florida*. Report submitted to the Florida Supreme Court racial and ethnic bias study commission.

Burdine v. Johnson, 262 F. 2d 336 (2001) cert. den.

Cockrell v. Burdine, 122 S. Ct. 2347 (2002).

Death Penalty Information Center. (2003a). *Innocence and the death penalty*. Washington, DC: Author.

Death Penalty Information Center. (2003b). *Race of death row inmates executed since 1976*. Washington, DC: Author.

Death sentence faces powerful argument [Editorial]. (2002, July 3). *The Washington Times*, p. A18.

Department of Housing and Urban Development v. Rucker, 122 s. Ct. 1230 (2002).

Dieter, R. C. (1998). *The death penalty in black and white: New studies on racism in capital punishment*. Washington, DC: Death Penalty Information Center.

DuBois, W. E. B. (1903/1999). *The souls of Black folk*. Chicago: McClurg.

Fellner, J., & Mauer, M. (1998). *Losing the vote: The impact of felony disenfranchisement laws in the United States*. Washington, DC: The Sentencing Project & Human Rights Watch.

Harlow, C. W. (1999). *Prior abuse reported by inmates and probationers*. Washington, DC: U.S. Department of Justice.

Harrison, P. M., & Karberg, J. C. (2003). *Prison and jail inmates at midyear 2002* (NCJ 198877). Washington, DC: U.S. Department of Justice, Bureau of Justice Statistics.

Hatsukami, D., & Fischman, M. (1996). *Crack cocaine and cocaine hydrochloride: Are the differences myth or reality? Journal of the American Medical Association, 276*, 1580.

Higher Education Act, 20 U.S.C. § 1091 (1988).

Hill, R. (1997). *The strengths of African American families: Twenty-five years later*. Washington, DC: R & B Publishers.

Hirsch, A., Dietrich, S., Landau, R., Schneider, P., Ackelsberg, I., Bernstein-Baker, J. et al. (2002). *Every door closed: Barriers facing parents with criminal records*. Center for Law and Social Policy & Community Legal Services. Washington, DC.

Jacobs, A. L. (2001). Give 'em a fighting chance: Women offenders reenter society. *American Bar Association, Section of Criminal Justice, 16*, 1.

Jansson, B. S. (1999). *Becoming an effective policy advocate: From policy practice to social justice* (3rd ed.). Pacific Grove, CA: Brooks/Cole.

Liebman, J. S., Fagan, J., & West, V. (2000). *A broken system: Error rates in capital cases, 1973–1995*. Retrieved February 11, 2004, from http://justice.policy.net/cjedfund/jpreport

Liebman, J. S., Gelman, A., Davis, G., Fagan, J., West, V., & Kiss, A. (2002). *A broken system: Part II: Why there is so much error in capital cases and what can be done about it*. Retrieved February 11, 2004, from http://justice.policy.net/cjedfund/jpreport

Love, M. C., & Kuzma, S. M. (1996). *Civil disabilities of convicted felons: A state-by-state survey*. Washington, DC: Office of the Pardon Attorney.

Lusane, C. (1991). *Pipe dream blues: Racism and the war on drugs*. Boston: Southern Press.

Martin, E., & Martin, J. (1995). *Social work and the Black experience*. Washington, DC: NASW Press.

Mauer, M. (1994). *Americans behind bars: The international use of incarceration 1992–93*. Washington, DC: The Sentencing Project.

Mauer, M. (1999). *Race to incarcerate*. New York: The New Press.

Mauer, M., & Huling, T. (1995). *Young Black Americans and the criminal justice system: Five years later*. Washington, DC: The Sentencing Project.

Mauer, M., Potler, C., & Wolf, R. (1999). *Gender and justice: Women, drugs and sentencing policy.* Washington, DC: The Sentencing Project.

McCleskey v. Kemp, 481 U.S. 279 (1987).

McDonald, D., & Carlson, K. (1993). *Sentencing in the federal courts: Does race matter? The transition to sentencing guidelines, 1986–90.* Washington, DC: U.S. Department of Justice.

Miller, J. (1992). *Hobbling a generation: Young African American males in the criminal justice system of America's cities.* Alexandria, VA: National Center on Institutions and Alternatives.

Montgomery, L. (2003, January 31). Md. attorney general asks for end to death penalty. *The Washington Post,* A1.

Mumola, C. (2000). *Special report: Incarcerated parents and their children.* Washington, DC: U.S. Department of Justice, Bureau of Justice Statistics.

National Institute on Drug Abuse (1993), *Overview of the 1991 National Household Survey on Drug Abuse.* Washington, DC: Author.

Olsen, E. (1998, April 7). U.N. report criticizes U.S. for racist use of death penalty. *New York Times,* p. p. A17.

Paltrow, L. (1993). *Criminal prosecutions against pregnant women.* New York: American Civil Liberties Union Foundation.

Poe-Yamagata, E., & Jones, M. (2000). *And justice for some.* Washington, DC: Building Blocks for Youth.

Richie, B. (1996). *Compelled to crime: The gender entrapment of battered Black women.* New York: Routledge.

Ring v. Arizona, 536 U.S. 584 (2002).

Roberts, D. E. (1991) Punishing drug addicts who have babies: Women of color, equality and the right to privacy. *Harvard Law Review, 104,* 1419–1482.

Rubinstein, G. (2001). *Getting to work: How TANF can support ex-offender parents in the transition to self-sufficiency.* New York: Legal Action Center.

Taifa, N. (1993). Mandatory minimum sentences open up a Pandora's box. *The National Prison Project Journal, 8*(3), 3–6.

Taifa, N. (1996). Cracked justice: A critical examination of cocaine sentencing. *University of West Los Angeles Law Review, 27,* 107–164.

Taifa, N. (2001a). Journal introduction: The impact of the criminal justice system on women and their families. *Center for Research on African American Women Journal, 2,* 11–12.

Taifa, N. (2001b). Criminalization of drug dependent pregnant Black women. *The New Barrister, 37*(5), 6.

Taifa, N. (2002). *Re-enfranchisement! A guide for individual restoration of voting rights in states that permanently disenfranchise former felons.* Washington, DC: The Advancement Project.

The Sentencing Project. (2000). *Reducing racial disparities in the criminal justice system: A manual for practitioners and policymakers.* Washington, DC: Author.

The Sentencing Project. (2002). *Prison privatization and the use of incarceration.* Washington, DC: Author.

Turow, S. (2003, January 17). Clemency without clarity. *The New York Times,* p. A27.

U.S. General Accounting Office. (1990). *Death penalty sentencing: Research indicates pattern of racial disparities.* Washington, DC: Author.

U.S. Sentencing Commission. (1991). *Special report to the Congress: Mandatory minimum penalties in the federal criminal justice system.* Washington, DC: Author.

U.S. Sentencing Commission. (1995). Special report to the Congress: Cocaine and federal sentencing policy. Washington, DC: Author.

U.S. Sentencing Commission. (2002, May). *Report to the Congress: Cocaine and federal sentencing policy.* Washington, DC: Author.

Villarruel, F., & Walker, N. (2002). *Donde esta la justicia? A call to action on behalf of Latino and Latina youth in the U.S. justice system.* Washington, DC: Building Blocks for Youth.

Weich, R. H., & Angulo, C. T. (2000). *Justice on trial: Racial disparities in the American criminal justice system.* Washington, DC: Leadership Conference on Civil Rights/Leadership Conference on Civil Rights Education Fund.

Zeidenberg, J., & Schiraldi, V. (2002). *Cellblocks or classrooms? The funding of higher education and corrections and its impact on African American men.* Washington, DC: Justice Policy Institute.

Chapter Seven

Mental Health Policy and People of Color: The Surgeon General's Supplement on Culture, Race, and Ethnicity and Beyond

Lonnie Snowden

In *Mental Health: A Report of the Surgeon General* (U.S. Department of Health and Human Services [DHHS], 1999), Surgeon General David Satcher affirmed that mental health is a legitimate and high-priority national concern. He defined mental health as "the successful performance of mental functioning, resulting in productive activities, fulfilling relationships with other people, and the ability to adapt to change and to cope with adversity" (DHHS, 1999, p. 19). In this definition and elsewhere, Surgeon General Satcher made it clear that mental health is an integral aspect of human biological, psychological, and social functioning and an important component of general health.

The surgeon general addressed issues of particular concern to people of color in a supplemental report. *Race, Culture, and Ethnicity and Mental Health: A Supplement to* Mental Health: A Report of the Surgeon General (DHHS, 2001) reiterated the importance of mental health to human well-being and noted obstacles to mental health and mental health treatment facing people of color. From a review of the best available scientific evidence, the supplement called attention to many disparities in access between Whites and people of color, quality, and other areas. Whether African American, Latino, Asian American or Native American, few persons of color were determined to have received treatment when suffering from mental health problems. Fewer still were found to receive treatment adhering to the highest standards of contemporary practice.

These disparities are troubling. They can be closed through a multifaceted approach that includes, as perhaps its key element, analysis and action at policy levels. The supplement is a rich source of ideas for profitable policy analysis and for making recommendations for corrective action.

Four areas are especially important to consider. The first is a shift, foreshadowed in the supplement, from emphasizing rates of mental illness in communities of color to understanding differences in the *burden* of mental illness. A focus on burden enlarges our scope of concern beyond mental illness per se and invites consideration of the social and economic consequences of mental illness. The consequences—often reflected in impaired functional status—are of special interest to scholars and advocates concerned with the fate of communities of color.

The most widely cited strategy for improving access in communities of color is to increase insurance coverage for mental health care (Thomas & Snowden, 2001) and insurance coverage is a second area for consideration. Developments like parity legislation (Feldman, Bachman, & Bayer, 2002) help us to recognize that expanding mental health coverage does not in itself guarantee better access, no matter how justified on moral and economic grounds. In attempting to increase access of people of color, what is the role of greater insurance coverage?

A third area for attention is managed care. Managed care is widespread and of such consequence that it has provoked a backlash, leading national policymakers to put forward proposals for controlling the strategies available to managed care organizations.

While attention paid to managed care has increased, little attention is paid to the experience of people of color. It is important to consider whether managed care's impact has been beneficial or detrimental to the most vulnerable groups in society as a guide to possible reform of mental health managed care.

Quality of care, evidence-based practice, and outcomes orientation all mark an increasing orientation toward implementing treatments of proven effectiveness (Steinwachs, Flynn, Norquist, & Skinner, 1996). Policymakers have encouraged this trend as a rational approach to allocating scarce resources. They are joined by employers and by consumer and family advocates seeking to make the mental health system more accountable. How are these developments to be implemented in communities of color? Although considered infrequently, this question must be addressed if we are to avoid mistaken impressions about levels of improvement and intervention quality among communities of color.

Weighing the burden of mental illness, adjusting the scope and mix of mental health insurance benefits, addressing the impact of managed care, and assessing the effectiveness and quality of treatment are important to any understanding of contemporary mental health policy. They have been relatively neglected in the literature on racial and ethnic disparities but as presented by the surgeon general, they are equally if not more important to an understanding of disparities between White populations and people of color. Each of these issues is considered below.

Mental Illness, Burden, Functional Status, and Quality of Life

Poverty, unemployment and employment in marginal jobs, lack of education, poor health, racism and discrimination, and other stressors occur more among people of color than in other populations (DHHS, 2001). Because of well-established links between these stressors and mental illness, it is reasonable to expect that people of color would suffer from mental illness at high rates—higher than those found among Whites who are, on average, exposed less.

Yet the surgeon general could not document consistent associations between ethnic minority status and higher rates of mental illness (DHHS, 2001). After reviewing epidemiological studies, he noted that researchers have reported few differences between African Americans and Whites in rates of mental illness. Indeed, in selected instances researchers have reported *lower* rates of disorder for African Americans. Mexican American rates have been found to vary sharply with level of acculturation: persons who are least acculturated—and therefore poorest and most vulnerable—have lower rates of mental illness than other Mexican Americans, and lower rates than those of Anglos. Rates between Asian Pacific and Native Americans are more difficult still to establish because of limited evidence but appear to vary with the nationality considered. Theoretical and methodological explanations for these paradoxes have been debated without definitive resolution.

When left untreated illnesses of all kinds impose a burden (Murray & Lopez, 1996). Illness impairs the ability to function in day-to-day living, exacting a toll on affected persons as individuals and as contributing members of their communities.

Technically speaking, burden is defined by two components (Murray & Lopez, 1996). One of them is life expectancy and the other is quality of life. An index of burden combining these elements is "quality-adjusted life years," reflecting life expectancy, reduced by level of disability and impairment.

Because of burden, the World Health Organization has become increasingly concerned about mental illness worldwide: "According to a landmark study by the World Health Organization, the World Bank, and Harvard University, mental disorders are so disabling that, in established market economies like the United States, they rank second only to cardiovascular disease in their impact on disability" (DHHS, 2001, p.3).

The concept "quality of life" emphasizes functioning in domains of living associated with personal fulfillment and community well-being: work, relationships with family and friends, and legal entanglement, and others. By studying quality of life, one group of investigators (Wells et al., 1989) demonstrated that depression was as at least as detrimental, if not more detrimental, than other conditions commonly treated in outpatient medical practice.

The surgeon general did document disparities in access to outpatient mental health treatment. Unambiguous evidence indicated that whether African American, Latino, Asian American, or Native American, few people of color suffering from a mental health problem received treatment and fewer still received care from a mental health specialist. Even fewer were treated with care adhering to the highest standards of contemporary practice.

The surgeon general (DHHS, 2001) concluded that the burden of mental illness was greater for minorities: "*A major finding of this supplement is that racial and ethnic minorities bear a greater burden from unmet mental health needs and thus suffer a greater loss to their overall health and productivity*" (p.3, italics in original). His justification was that even if mental illness were not especially prevalent among people of color, length and quality of life must be lower due to treatment disparities, and therefore burden must be especially great.

Quality of life provides an important link between mental health, people of color, and recognized policy goals. Improvements in education, employment, crime, and family well-being are widely accepted as legitimate objectives for policy initiatives. In each of these areas, disputes are heated about what is an appropriate scope for government action and about acceptable and effective means to achieve societal improvement. However, there is little controversy that promoting education, employment, crime-reduction, and family well-being are legitimate goals.

Although rarely acknowledged, improvements in a population's mental health can further societal well-being by improving the functional status of persons suffering from mental illness. The scale of potential improvement is suggested in estimates of the national cost of mental illness, which economists have placed in the hundreds of billion of dollars (DHHS, 2000).

To observe that the burden of mental illness is greatest in communities of color is to say that mental illness has a disproportionate impact on the social and economic condition of communities of color. By reducing levels of untreated mental illness in communites of color, we can cause a disproportionate increase in social and economic conditions and in overall quality of life.

Financing

Insurance coverage is a target of choice for policymakers, advocates, and others concerned with the problem of access to health and mental health treatment. When discussing financing of mental health care, Surgeon General Satcher commented poignantly on the current state of affairs: "Today, the nation's patchwork of health insurance programs leave more than one person in seven with no means to pay for health care other than out-of-pocket and charity payments. The consequences of the patchwork are many holes in the health care system through which a disproportionately greater number of poor, sick, rural, and distressed ethnic minority families fall" (DHHS, 2001, p. 164).

Concerned parties have proposed various measures, including universal coverage, to increase the number of people who are insured and to increase the generosity of mental health benefits: "Efforts are currently underway to create more systematic approaches for states and local communities to extend health and mental health care to their uninsured residents" (DHHS, 2001, p. 164).

In thinking about the role of insurance, it is important to distinguish between public and private sources, especially when focusing on financing of mental health treatment delivered to people of color (Thomas & Snowden, 2001). Private insurance pays for most of the mental health care delivered in the United States. Most private health insurance policies also cover mental health services and out-of-pocket payments represent only 10–20% of charges (DHHS, 1999).

Public sources are even more important as a source of financing for mental health treatment, especially for people of color. For groups for whom evidence exists, African Americans and Latinos, data indicate that 54% of persons receiving publicly financed care belong to one of these groups (Thomas & Snowden, 2001).

Among public programs, the federal–state Medicaid program pays for a large share of publicly financed mental health treatment. Like its coverage for general medical disorders, Medicaid fully covers acute inpatient services for mental health diagnoses. States may limit mental health services but at minimum must cover outpatient services, including hospital-based outpatient care. On an optional basis, all but a handful of states cover medication and outpatient clinic-based treatment. A few states also cover case management and rehabilitative services.

Persons of color lack private coverage and are especially reliant on public sources of financing (DHHS, 1999). However, public coverage does not eliminate the insurance gap between Whites and people of color (DHHS, 2001). Because peope of color are more likely than Whites to be uninsured, some commentators believe that lack of coverage is the most important explanation for disparities in access (DHHS, 2001). People of color tend to be poor, they argue, and payments for health or mental health treatment therefore are especially burdensome. Insurance comes to play a critical role for people of color because it reduces the price of care—it reduces competition for scarce dollars from other sorely needed goods and services.

Economists have assessed the impact of insurance coverage on the use of health care services (McGuire, 1989). Evidence indicates that people respond to insurance-conferred reductions in the price of mental health care as they respond to reductions in the price of general medical care. Thus, people with mental health problems do not seek treatment in overwhelming numbers or at excessive levels when treatment is covered at the same level as treatment for health problems. This equivalence helps to justify parity legislation, mandating that mental health insurance benefits be set at the same level as benefits for other problems in health (Feldman, Bachman, & Bayer, 2002).

What does research tell us about the role of insurance in explaining the minority–White disparity in treatment seeking for mental health problems? Several studies have examined the role of Medicaid. Taube, Kessler, and Burns (1986) reported that even among persons with Medicaid coverage, people of color continued to be less likely than Whites to use services. Taube and Rupp (1986) found similar results in another national study. Focusing on African Americans, Temkin-Greener and Clark (1988) discovered that among Medicaid-eligible persons in Monroe County, New York, race continued to be a strong determinant of ambulatory utilization, with African Americans seeking less treatment than Whites. In a later study using a national sample, Snowden and Thomas (2000) reported that African Americans and Whites sought outpatient treatment equally when covered by Medicaid, but African Americans were considerably less likely than Whites to seek treatment when covered by private insurance.

Other investigators have studied private health insurance plans. They have found that African American and Latino plan members continue to be less likely than Whites to seek outpatient treatment (Padgett, Patrick, Burns, & Schlesinger, 1994), and that African Americans are less responsive than other groups when provided with a more generous level of mental health coverage (Scheffler & Miller, 1989).

Thomas and Snowden (2001) addressed the issue of insurance and minority–White access in a comprehensive study using a representative national sample. The data confirmed that persons of color with private coverage were far less likely than Whites with private coverage to seek outpatient mental health treatment. The data also indicate that persons of color with private coverage were less likely than persons of color with public coverage to seek treatment.

Evidence indicates that insurance coverage, whether from public or private sources, does not eliminate disparities. The relative lack of responsiveness by people of color to insurance suggests that insurance may be a less effective mechanism than previously believed to encourage self-initiated treatment seeking among persons of color.

Along with earlier findings comparing African Americans and Whites (Snowden & Thomas, 2000), the results point to the private sector as the arena where disparities are especially pronounced. When covered under private insurance plans, people of color remain considerably less likely than Whites to seek mental health care and they are less encouraged than Whites to do so by provision of a more generous benefit.

Managed behavioral health care firms largely control privately financed care. In response, policymakers should consider regulations and incentives to promote help seeking by persons of color.

In general policymakers must learn more about the relative importance of non-financial barriers to help seeking and the extent to which they can be modified. The Surgeon General discussed personal and family beliefs, including attitudes toward mental illness and beliefs about the appropriateness and effectiveness of treatment, and indicated that belief systems might help to explain differences in help seeking from professional caregivers. He indicated that the structure of the mental health system also needs to be examined, especially access to understanding treatment personnel who are aware of the beliefs and practices of people of color and are welcoming of them as clients. These are hypotheses to be further explored and translated into outreach strategies as we seek to understand why people of color do not respond as much as Whites do to private insurance coverage when seeking treatment for mental health problems.

In the end, it appears that increasing insurance coverage to people of color will not eliminate racial and ethnic disparities in outpatient mental health care. Providing more people with coverage would almost certainly increase the total number of people receiving treatment. More persons of color would seek help as well as more Whites, but data suggest that newly covered Whites would seek care in greater numbers. Rather than shrinking, the size of the minority–White differential could grow. We cannot rely solely on financing to equalize access.

Managed Care

Management of behavioral health benefits, or managed care, expanded greatly over the past 2 decades such that by the late 1990s, most insured people in the United States had behavioral health services that were managed (Findlay, 1999). Previous arrangements, under which providers and clients enjoyed greater discretion, have receded.

Managed care is not monolithic. It is a family of structures and practices oriented, in general, toward achieving two related goals. One is to increase planning, oversight, and coordination in the provision of mental health care, transforming what had previously been a haphazard and erratic process of mental health service delivery into a more orderly one. A second goal is to control and ultimately to reduce treatment-related costs.

Both objectives are facilitated by capitation—that is by risk-based, capitated financing (Masland, Piccagli, Snowden, & Cuffel, 1996). Capitation schemes vary, but under most, a payer pays a fixed fee to a provider for all treatment necessary for each eligible person for a specified time period. Because treatment needs might exceed what can be paid for under the capitation rate, the provider is exposed to financial risk. Under capitation, the provider must continue to care for clients even when necessary treatments cost more than the capitated payment.

On the other hand, funds are paid prospectively under many forms of capitation and can be used flexibly for any necessary treatment-related purpose (Masland et al., 1996). Flexible use of funds comes about when to implement capitation, funders consolidate monies provided under categorical programs. They thereby spare providers the burden of what are often rigid and complex rules.

Providers gain flexibility on the one hand, but on the other hand they are exposed to risk. This trade-off is expressed in incentives.

According to proponents of capitation, increased flexibility and the prospect of losing money focus attention on long-term planning, efficiency, coordination, and cost-effective, innovative programming (Masland et al., 1996). Incentives introduced by capitation promote early identification of needs, the use of low-intensity services, and the adoption of alternatives to usual care, such as respite care, home-based crisis intervention, and family support services, in an effort to reduce high-cost services, such as out-of-home placements.

According to critics, capitation encourages undesirable tactics for lowering costs. Capitation creates incentives for "creaming," or avoiding difficult and costly clients; "dumping," or eliminating such clients; and "shifting" of treatment responsibility onto an outside agency which would pay for care (Libby, Evans-Cuellar, & Snowden, 2002; Scott, Snowden, & Libby, 2002).

What is the impact on peope of color of managed care and capitation? Some critics have argued that consequences will be negative but others have argued they will be positive (Snowden, 1998).

Those with reservations propose that managed care and capitation will increase well-documented and troubling disparities. With some empirical support, advocates sometimes say that people of color are disproportionately affected by what may seem excessively bureaucratic and impersonal experiences and by incentives for cost-cutting inherent in capitation. For these reasons they believe that managed care could impede service delivery to people of color.

Others claim that under managed care and capitation, disparities will shrink. They propose that oversight and coordination may benefit people of color, especially those who are vulnerable to "falling through the cracks" and that capitation might facilitate the development of innovative, culturally oriented programming.

The Surgeon General commented on the opportunities and risks inherent in managed care. He observed that: "Evidence cited in this supplement suggests that managed mental health care is perceived by some racial and ethnic minorities as creating even greater barriers to treatment than fee-for-service plans. However, more systematic assessment of the treatment experiences, quality, and outcomes of racial and ethnic minorities in managed care may help to identify opportunities for using this mechanism to improve access and quality of services" (DHHS, 2001, p. 165).

Indeed the issue is best understood through research. The literature includes only a handful of studies that have evaluated minority–White differences in mental health treatment delivered under managed care. Snowden and Thomas (2000) used data from the National Medical Expenditure Survey to examine African American–White disparities. Whether treatment was fee-for-service or managed care there was an African American–White disparity and the magnitude was about equal. Under either arrangement, African Americans received little outpatient mental health care.

Other research has focused specifically on state Medicaid programs. In Massachusetts (Crawford, Fisher, & McDermott, 1998) investigators found a shift toward private inpatient care marked by a growing minority–White differential: people of color were more likely to be admitted to public facilities and Whites to private facilities. Focusing on children, Scholle and Kelleher (1998) discovered that people of color enrolled in managed care—African American for the most part—were less likely than Whites to make a specialty mental health visit and that the differential was greater than that existing under fee-for-service. From Philadelphia on the other hand, Rothbard and Azarian (1997) reported a *decrease* in adult racial disparities in specialty care: participation in managed care was associated with smaller differentials than fee-for-service participation.

Two studies addressed the question of differential impact in a transition to capitated managed care in the Colorado Medicaid program. Both compared the experience of African American and Latinos with that of Whites. Snowden, Wallace, Kang, and Bloom (2000) demonstrated that for adults, there was a drop in use of outpatient care among African American users of services; African Americans proved less likely to seek care after the transition to capitated managed care. However, the disparity was transitory: it occurred during the initial 9-month study period but not during the second.

Further analysis revealed that the disparity reduction was associated with the introduction of culturally oriented programming. The finding is open to several interpretations. It remains unclear whether culturally oriented programming *caused* the improvement in African American access or whether the increase in access by people of color was coincidental. Nevertheless, it is plausible to believe that the shift toward culturally oriented programming caused the increase in access and consistent with results from previous research.

A second Colorado study considered the transition to capitated managed care among children and youth. For persons in foster care (Snowden, Evans-Cuellar, & Libby, 2003), a high-risk group accounting for most Medicaid-financed treatment for people of color, few minority–White differences were found. There was, however, a greater reliance on residential treatment centers for children of color after the shift to capitated managed care. Previously existing disparities, which found African American and Latino children and youth to be underrepresented in treatment, were largely unaffected.

Research currently available is inconsistent but indicates overall that managed care and capitation rarely widen excising disparities. Despite some shifting in sources of care, disparities remain unaffected for the most part, and in one instance, were found to have been reduced. For persons of color, there appears to be little impact more or less than that felt by other groups.

Nevertheless, lessons can be learned from our experience with managed care and capitation. Disparities are robust; they are unlikely to shrink as a byproduct of general reorganization of mental health treatment systems. They must be targeted separately for elimination. Efforts to overcome them should move forward through the design of strategies for that particular purpose and through the evaluation of these strategies.

As managed care predominates and the prevalence of capitated financing increases, monitoring and evaluating the impact on vulnerable populations remains a critical task. People of color in particular rely heavily on public-sector care. With the advent of capitated managed care in state Medicaid programs, we must be especially vigilant in monitoring consequences for members of these groups.

Outcomes, Effectiveness, Quality

The supplement noted a lack of evidence on outcomes of care for African Americans receiving mental health treatment. It called for more research evaluating the African American response to novel, standardized treatments, as well as mental health care delivered under usual conditions of community practice.

The surgeon general also stressed a related concern for a greater emphasis on investigating quality of care. Quality is crucial because when suffering from mental health problems, people of color ought to receive treatment that truly is beneficial—that affords the greatest likelihood that recipients enjoy the highest level of relief possible.

Rigorous evidence that treatments work comes from controlled studies of treatment outcomes. The Surgeon General expressed concern that there be greater participation by people of color in randomized clinical trials.

Increasingly, findings from outcomes research have been translated into quality of care indicators and studies of quality have followed. Indicators reflect biomedical agents more than psychosocial interventions following a skew in the knowledge base. In several of these studies the focus is on people of color and whether they are as likely as Whites to receive treatments conforming to quality-of-care guidelines.

The research is reviewed in the supplement and elsewhere (Snowden & Pingitore, 2002). Studies indicate that when treated for anxiety-related problems and depression, African Americans and Latinos are less likely than Whites to receive guideline-based care. Other studies point to a contrasting pattern, wherein practitioners prescribe certain psychotropic medications to African Americans at what appear to be excessive levels.

In his call for more outcomes research, the surgeon general stressed the need for studies of two kinds. One kind of needed study was mentioned previously: for randomized clinical trials, testing standard interventions but with greater inclusion of people of color. The surgeon general recommended that, "In the future, evidence from randomized clinical trials that include sizeable racial and ethnic minority samples may lead to treatment improvements, which will help clinicians to maximize real-world effectiveness of already-proven psychiatric medications and psychotherapies" (DHHS, 2001, p.160).

Greater participation by people of color in randomized clinical trials would permit researchers to evaluate whether treatments are equally efficacious or effective with Whites and people of color. Sufficiently large samples of Whites and people of color would permit researchers to investigate whether there were interactions between, on one hand, ethnicity or culture, and on the other, treatment, in explaining outcomes.

Before analyzing data to address this question, researchers face the task of clarifying why they expect interaction to occur. They should be asked to specify which aspects of the treatment ought to lead to a distinctive ethnocultural response. In the end, formulating and answering questions about possible ethnocultural differences to standard interventions will draw from and contribute to ethnocultural theory.

A second kind of research was also advocated. The surgeon general called for intervention evaluations of treatments and programs designed specifically for racial and ethnic minorities: "At the same time, research is essential to examine the efficacy of ethnic- or culture-specific interventions for minority populations and their effectiveness in clinical practice settings" (DHHS, 2001, p. 160).

Although it is rarely acknowledged, policymakers ask questions going beyond efficacy and effectiveness. Denied the luxury of assuming unlimited resources, they must concern themselves with allocation under conditions of scarcity. They are led to take account of the financial commitment required to bring about improvement. To discharge this responsibility they require information on cost-effectiveness of interventions (Hargreaves, Shumway, Hu, & Cuffel, 1999).

Cost-effectiveness, too, can vary with the racial, cultural, and ethnic background of the person being treated. Even when effectiveness is equal, cost effectiveness may vary. A treatment might prove equally effective for minority persons and Whites, but might be less acceptable when given to people of color. Coping with this lack of minority acceptance might make the intervention more costly for minorities and therefore *less cost-effective*. Ultimately, another more acceptable treatment might prove more cost-effective.

Yet another treatment might again prove equally effective for people of color and Whites but might promote social well-being more among socially vulnerable minorities—it might better prevent clients of color from needing public social services or prevent family members from entering the child welfare system. This treatment might prove *more cost-effective* for minorities.

These questions are crucial to improving the mental health of people of color. Each can be answered only by studies comparing persons of color and Whites on the cost efficacy and cost effectiveness of intervention. Theorists must clarify when and why outcomes might vary based on racial, cultural, and ethnic factors; investigators can then design studies that test these expectations.

Answers are necessary to guide policymakers seeking to bring effective care to people of color. As federal, state, and local policymakers encourage adoption of practices supported by evidence—whether in the name of best practices, practice guidelines, or evidence-based practices—they must be mindful that unless questions about possible differential impacts are answered, their evidence-based stance might promote interventions of differential and possibly lesser efficacy and effectiveness for people of color than for Whites. However inadvertently, the new and desirable orientation might create new disparities of its own.

Conclusion

The Surgeon General's *Supplement on Culture, Race, and Ethnicity* is a landmark in the effort to improve access and effectiveness of mental health care to persons of color. It consolidated what is known and pinpointed disparities in access and quality. It provided a foundation to develop strategies focused on closing disparities, many best addressed as matters of mental health policy.

The supplement began to draw attention to *burden* when thinking about the impact of mental illness on communities of color. In common use by the World Health Organization and other bodies concerned with international health, burden focuses on the social and economic impact of mental illness, addressing the functional status of persons suffering from mental illness.

Burden takes us beyond clinical and cultural considerations and provides a key link between mental health among people of color and the socioeconomic well-being of communities of color. Burden views mental health from a societal perspective and associates it with broader concerns of policy makers.

The supplement briefly called attention to financing and to the role of insurance in overcoming disparities. The scope and conditions of coverage are central concerns of policymakers at federal and state levels, as indicated by a national agenda that featured universal coverage as a defining issue of the 1990s and includes prescription drug benefits and health–mental health parity as high priority issues at present.

When considering minority–White disparities in access, insurance is justifiably regarded as a key lever for producing a greater and more even distribution of mental health treatment. Persons of color are more likely than Whites to be uninsured. If insured they are more likely to rely on public coverage, especially the Medicaid program. Expanding, insurance to cover more people of color and providing a more generous benefit will increase minority access to mental health care.

On the other hand, there are limits on how much progress can be made through expanded insurance coverage. People of color respond less than Whites to insurance-based changes in price. Although more likely to be poor, they are kept from seeking mental health care by sociocultural and other non-economic factors more than Whites and are induced less to seek treatment through reductions in cost. Wider and more generous coverage will increase minority access, but will not decrease minority–White disparities.

Managed care has changed the landscape of health and mental health care delivery, greatly reducing the scope of independent, fee-for-service practice. When contemplating this widespread transformation, few have considered the experiences of persons of color. We know little at present about whether persons of color benefited or lost differentially, or about when and how.

There is increasing concern with regulating the activities of managed care organizations. The present environment might be favorable for considering the policies of managed behavioral health care organizations with respect to the existence of disparities: to consider market-based (differential capitation rates) and regulatory (rules about minority participation) responses that promote greater participation by people of color.

Reflecting concerns of consumers, employers, and family members, as well as policy makers, the current mental health policy environment also features increasing emphasis on outcomes, effectiveness, and quality of care. All seek reassurance that mental health care is truly beneficial—that persons suffering from mental health problems are better off after treatment than before and to a greater extent than if they had undertaken another form of treatment or no treatment at all. They wish either a direct demonstration of positive results or an indication that treated persons received effective treatments as demonstrated previously.

Little attention has been paid to the possibility that effective treatments may not be equally effective for Whites and people of color. Rarely has outcomes research asked the question of differential effectiveness.

If motivated to examine differential effectiveness, researchers must confront issues that are more complex than they might seem at first glance. Studies require careful consideration of when and how differences in race, culture, and ethnicity might lead to differences in treatment outcomes. Introducing the necessary element of cost can overturn conclusions seemingly settled after initial analysis of data. No matter how thorny, researchers and policymakers must engage problems of differential cost-effectiveness if they are to avoid new disparities and close existing ones.

References

Crawford, K., Fisher, W. H., & McDermeit, M. (1998). Racial/ethnic disparities in admissions to public and private psychiatric inpatient settings: The effect of managed care. *Administration and Policy in Mental Health, 26,* 101–109.

Feldman, S., Bachman, J., & Bayer, J. (2002). Mental health parity: a review of research and a bibliography. *Administration and Policy in Mental Health, 29,* 215–228.

Findlay, S. (1999). Managed behavioral health care in 1999: An industry at a crossroads. *Health Affairs, 18,* 116–124.

Hargreaves, W. A., Shumway, M., Hu, T. W., &Cuffel, B. (1998). *Cost-outcome methods for mental health.* San Diego: Academic Press.

Libby, A., Evans-Cuellar, A., & Snowden, L. R. (2002). Cost substitution in a Medicaid mental health carve-out. *Journal of Health Care Finance, 28,* 11–23.

Masland, M., Piccagli, G., Snowden, L. R., & Cuffel, B. (1996). Planning and implementation of capitated mental health services in the public sector. *Evaluation and Program Planning, 19,* 253–262.

McGuire, T. (1989). Financing and reimbursement for mental health services. In C. A. Taube, D. Mechanic, & A. A. Hohmann (Eds.), *The future of mental health services research* (pp. 87–111, DHHS Pub. No. [ADM] 89-1600). Washington, DC: U.S. Government Printing Office.

Murray, C. J. L., & Lopez, A. D. (Eds.). (1996). *The global burden of disease: A comprehensive assessment of morbidity and disability from diseases, injuries, and risk factors in 1990 and projected to 2020.* Cambridge, MA: Harvard School of Public Health.

Padgett D. K., Patrick C., Burns B. J., & Schlesinger, H. J.(1994). Ethnicity and use of outpatient mental health services in a national, insured population. *American Journal of Public Health, 84,* 222–226.

Rothbard, A. B., & Azarin, K. (1997, October). *Race influences access and intensity of behavioral health care in a Medicaid managed care program.* Paper presented at Association for Health Services Research annual meeting, Washington, DC.

Scheffler, R. M., & Miller, A. G. (1989). Demand analysis of mental health service use among ethnic subpopulations. *Inquiry, 26,* 202–215.

Scholle, S., & Kelleher, K. (1998, November). *Managed care for seriously emotionally disturbed children.* Paper presented at Substance Abuse and Mental Health Administration Managed Care Seminar, Washington, DC.

Scott, M. R., Snowden, L.R., & Libby, A. (2002). Alcohol and juvenile justice contacts: A comparison of fee-for-service and capitated Medicaid mental health services. *Journal of Studies on Alcohol, 63,* 44–48.

Snowden, L. R., Evans-Cuellar, A., & Libby, A. (2003). Minority youth in foster care: Managed care and access to mental health treatment. *Medical Care, 41*, 264–274.

Snowden, L, Wallace, N., Kang, S., & Bloom, J. (2000, October). *Ethnic minorities under public sector managed care in Colorado.* Paper presented at the Association for Health Services Research annual meeting, Los Angeles, CA.

Snowden, L. R. (1998). Managed care and ethnic minority populations. *Administration and Policy in Mental Health, 25*, 581–592.

Snowden, L. R., & Pingitore, D. (2002). Frequency and scope of mental health service delivery to African Americans in primary care. *Mental Health Services Research, 4*, 123–130.

Snowden, L. R., & Thomas, K. (2000). Medicaid and African American outpatient mental health treatment. *Mental Health Services Research, 2*, 115–120.

Steinwachs, D., Flynn, L., Norquist, G. S., & Skinner, E. A. (Eds.) (1996). *Using outcomes to improve mental health and substance abuse services.* San Francisco: Jossey-Bass.

Taube, C. A., Kessler, L.,& Burns, B. (1986). Estimating the probability and level of ambulatory mental health use. *Health Services Research, 21*, 321–340.

Taube, C. A., & Rupp, A. (1986). The effect of Medicaid on access to ambulatory mental health care for the poor and near-poor under 65. *Medical Care, 24*, 677–686.

Temkin-Greener, H., & Clark, K. T. (1988) Ethnicity, gender, and utilization of mental health services in a Medicaid population. *Social Science and Medicine, 26*, 989–996.

Thomas, K., & Snowden, L. R. (2001). Minority response to health insurance coverage for mental health problems. *The Journal of Mental Health Policy and Economics, 4*, 35–41.

U.S. Department of Health and Human Services. (1999). *Mental Health: A report of the Surgeon General.* Rockville, MD: Author.

U.S. Department of Health and Human Services. (2000). *National estimates of expenditures for mental health and substance abuse treatment 1997.* Rockville, MD: Author.

U.S. Department of Health and Human Services. (2001). *Mental health: Culture, race, and ethnicity—A supplement to* Mental health: A report of the surgeon general. Rockville, MD: Author.

Wells, K. B., Stewart, A., Hays, R. D., Burnam, M. A., Rogers, W., Daniels, M. et al. (1989). The functioning and well-being of depressed patients: Results from the Medical Outcomes Study. *Journal of the American Medical Association, 262*, 914–919.

PART TWO. Case Analyses

— Public "Liberation" Policy and American Indians

— Mexican American Access to Health Care

— Pacific Islanders and Juvenile Justice

— African Americans and Welfare Reform

Chapter Eight

The Effect of Public "Liberation" Policy on American Indians: Health Care, Sovereignty, and Self-Determination

Ann Pollock, Rebecca Weaver, and Catherine Levandosky

Toward the end of the 19th century, many spectators felt confident in predicting that Native Americans were destined for extinction. After all, as a result of disease, warfare, famine, and outright genocide, the Native American population had been reduced from millions in 1500 to less than 250,000 in 1890 (Snipp, 1998). Epidemic diseases carried from Europe by the Anglo-Americans (Berkhofer, 1979) wiped out an estimated 90% of the entire Native American population. Part of the decimation of the Native American population came also from deliberate efforts to spread infectious diseases by the American military (Thornton, 1987). In regard to these alarming estimates and policies that prompted them, Deneven (cited in McLemore & Romo, 1998) concluded, "The discovery of America was followed by possibly the greatest demographic disaster in the history of the world" (p. 320).

Those Native American tribes that miraculously survived their interactions with Euro-Americans were left frequently without intact families, homes, land, and culture and instead were forced to subordinate themselves to and accept an alien, dominant way of life (Berkhofer, 1979). The process by which Indians were incorporated into Euro-American society via policies that forced resettlement to reservations resulted in centuries of poverty, hunger, and economic dependency for a historically self-sufficient people (McLemore & Romo, 1998). Improvements in the socioeconomic status of Indians have taken place only within the last decade (U. S. Census Bureau, 2001). The magnitude by which the Native Americans, from all tribes and different cultures, suffered at the hands of the Anglo policy is alarming and unconscionable and yet remains a painful reality at the start of the 21st century.

It is hardly debatable for most Americans that diseases, bullets, alcoholic beverages, and industrial civilization have taken their toll on the lives and culture of Native Americans and other populations of color (Diamond, 1997). However, the way in which *public policy* has unjustly and fatally dictated the lives of Native Americans remains cryptic for many Americans. Moreover, it is questionable whether 20th-century policies and programs that have attempted to correct past institutional and social injustices have been successful in protecting Native American sovereignty, self-determination, or economic self-sufficiency brought about improvements in their health status. Unfortunately, what has undoubtedly been reinforced through the American educational system, as well as the media, are the stereotypes concerning Native Americans that manage to clump hundreds of different tribes together, despite their distinct cultures and languages (McLemore & Romo, 1998).

The purpose of this chapter is to discuss and analyze how public policy—from the colonial era up until the present—has affected Native Americans sovereignty, self-determination, and health status, while keeping in mind the existing diversity among the various tribes. After reviewing the generic policy direction that massacred, desecrated, and stripped the dignity of the Native Americans, two important policies initiatives that have attempted to correct these injustices will be evaluated. These policies are Public Law 83-538, titled the Transfer Act of 1954, and Public Law 93-638, titled the Indian Self-Determination and Education Assistance Act of 1975. The latter public law was encouraged by President Richard Nixon and supported the right of self-determination among the Indians without the threat of losing their culture.

The two policies selected here for analysis were chosen because they sought to chart different directions from the genre of policies developed by the United States throughout most of the 20th century. These two policies appear to break precedent with the broader processes and outcomes from hundreds of related public policies that marked the relationships between the federal government and Native American tribes (see Davis, chapter 1 of this volume). Despite their innovations, these two policies also reflect the uneven distribution of decision-making power between the tribes and the government of the United States. This power differential and the outcomes from federal policy decisions remained a seminal part of the legal disputes between the federal government and tribes at the beginning of the 21st century (*Cobell v. Babbit*, 1999). Other related acts, including the Child Welfare Act of 1975, are examined by Ruth McRoy in chapter three in this volume. Max Weber's (Neuwirth, 1969) theory of community formation and closure will be used as a frame of reference for the monopolization of the policy process. Recommended ways in which the social work profession can address these problems are addressed in the final section of this chapter.

Historical Events, Assumptions, and Policies: The Colonial Period

Ironically, when the English founded the Jamestown settlement in Virginia during the early 17th century, the Powhatans were engaged in warfare with other tribes. In hoping to align themselves with the English for further support, they helped the colony survive through their first winter. While the Jamestown settlers did not have a fixed policy toward the Native Americans during these early years of simply trying to survive in a foreign land, the English beliefs and values around which future policy would be formed regarded Native Americans as inferior to the English. However, if they willingly became Christian and a labor force for the English, Native Americans were more than welcome to the "superiority" and benefits of the English culture (Berkhofer, 1979).

Native Americans, of course, would not succumb to this belief system and were unwilling to be the labor force for the Jamestown settlers. When the settlers attempted to force the Native Americans to work, conflict between the two groups emerged. With tobacco production having commenced and the English demanding more land, the Powhatans realized they had made a fatal mistake regarding the intentions of the English. During a full-scale effort to drive them out, the Powhatans killed one third of the English settlers (McLemore & Romo, 1998).

Similarly, the initial relationship between the Puritans, and Native Americans of the Massachusetts Bay region was amiable, having developed trade relations and military alliances. However, as the main migration occurred in the 1630s, the policy of the English toward Native Americans became ambivalent to an even greater extent in comparison to Virginia. While having a strong desire for the Native American's land, the English also wished to force Native Americans to discontinue their "savage beliefs and rituals" and adopt the "civilized, superior culture and religion" of the English. The latter desire required that the Native Americans stay close to the English settlers (this history is discussed in McLemore & Romo, 1998).

In 1675, the Anglo-American colonists of Virginia and England concocted a "two-pronged" policy toward all Native Americans: the Native Americans were expected either: (1) to give up whatever lands the colonists wanted and move peacefully beyond the frontier; or (2) to remain within the confines of Anglo-American settlements under "watchful eyes" (McLemore & Romo, 1998, p. 52). In refusing, Native Americans would be annihilated or forcibly removed from the area to reservations.

Conclusion of these conflicts always occurred with the negotiation of treaties, which, in effect, initiated the reservation system—a form of conquest in disguise at the time. McLemore and Romo (1998) describe the process:

> In this way, the Whites set into motion a method of conquest that was used repeatedly for more than two centuries. As a rule, major conflicts were ended through the signing of treaties that assured the Indians certain "reserved lands," which after a while would be infiltrated, seized, and occupied. Each time, new reservations would be created over which the Indians would be guaranteed permanent control. Soon, however, a new round of encroachments would begin. (p. 51)

It is evident that from the very beginning of Indian–White relations, the tribes were regarded inferior as well as "inassimilable and ineligible for full membership in the new host society being created" (p. 51). Although this separatist mentality shaped much of the Indian policies during the colonial period, there were a minority of Anglos who continued to believe and hope that the Native Americans would become "civilized" and assimilated into mainstream society. This ethnocentric ideology, while counter to the dominant separatist ideology of the day, would regain popularity with policymakers at the end of the 19th century. McLemore and Romo (1998) propose as an explanation for the difficulty Native Americans had with assimilation that "[m]inority groups that have a strong sense of group identity and are socially self-sufficient at the time they become subordinate are likely to resist assimilation strongly for long periods of time" (p. 53).

Despite threats to Native American sovereignty by the English settlers, support for their rights was under consideration. When news of Native American resistance was brought to the attention of the English King, he called for a uniform policy somewhat in favor of Native American rights. Known as the Proclamation of 1763, the colonies were forbidden to move onto Indian land (i.e., land west of the crest of the Appalachian Mountains) without the approval of the representatives of the king and the consent of Native Americans. A similar policy—the Northwest Territory Ordinance of 1763—promised that Native American lands would not be taken without their consent, except in the case of a just and lawful war as authorized by Congress. Moreover, on the homefront, the Native American leader Tecumseh was urging all tribes to unite and turn away from the White man's evil ways (McLemore & Romo, 1998).

Nevertheless, colonists continued to roam on Indian lands in defiance of the king's policy. Native Americans, in turn, felt conflicted about reporting the treaty violations. While wishing the Anglos had never set foot on their precious land, many of them were reluctant to complain because of the alcohol they received in return for their land and other possessions (McLemoe & Romo, 1998). As Josephy (1961; cited in McLemore & Romo, 1998) states, "almost overnight large segments of once proud and dignified tribes became demoralized in drunkenness and disease" (p. 324).

When the English lost the War of 1812 and the Native American leader Tecumseh died, the Native Americans would never again have the support of a European power against the United States. The character of Indian–American relations would be forever changed as the federal government increased its political and military capabilities (Snipp, 1998). Instead, their lives would be dictated by the policies implemented by the United States of America, home of the "free" and founded on the principles of democracy and freedom.

From Separatism to Assimilation

Aware that the Indian population was becoming extinct in the 19th century, reformers urged the federal government to create more "humane" policy measures to help "civilize" American Indians living in poverty on the reservations. While creation of a reservation system had required a separatist policy, the federal government acquiesced to establish a new, contradictory policy—one calling for the assimilation of Indians into American society. Through boarding schools and allotment procedures of the land, the new goal of the federal government became to Christianize, educate, introduce to private property, and make Indians into farmers but not necessarily citizens (Snipp, 1998).

In 1824, the Bureau of Indian Affairs (BIA) was established, a federal organization that would prove to have enormous power on the way in which the Indians lived (Jackson & Galli, 1997). As expected, Native Americans became increasingly dependent on the BIA agents living on the reservations, thereby making the relationship between the federal government and the Indian tribes even more confusing (McLemore & Romo, 1998; Snipp, 1998).

While reformers with good intentions called for federal help and guidance to stimulate assimilation for Native Americans, such a policy backfired for Native Americans. It was assumed by the government that Native Americans, having become increasingly dependent on the BIA for material needs on the reservations, were incompetent to make decisions on their own and therefore, incapable of negotiating treaties. Now considered to be "wards" of the government, the notion that treaties should no longer be negotiated with Native Americans became increasingly popular and would shape future policy (McLemore & Romo, 1998; Snipp, 1998).

According to the Indian Appropriation Act of 1871 (supported by many who were against a separatist movement), Congress decided that, while previous treaties would continue to be enforced, the government through legislation rather than negotiation would decide all new arrangements concerning Native American land. Once it passed, Native Americans found themselves even more powerless at the hands of a government that arrogantly regarded them as inferior. In the following passage, McLemore and Romo (1998) explain the progression of logic regarding the status of Native Americans:

> If Indian tribes were not sovereign nations and could not negotiate treaties, then why should they continue to live on reservations apart from other people? Land speculators and potential settlers wondered why the Indians should continue to occupy more land than they were "using"; political conservatives, forgetting the agreements to pay the Indians for their earlier land cessions, wondered why the government should continue to pay out "doles" to support the Indians; and reformers wondered if the "civilizing" process would not be hastened if the reservations were divided up so each family would have its own plot of land. (p. 332)

Amazingly, both greed and sincere humanitarian concern were the core motives for breaking up the reservations, ending the policy of separatism and instituting a new policy of Anglo conformity and assimilation.

The central effort to bring the "incapable," "uncivilized," and "incompetent" Native Americans into mainstream society climaxed with the passage of the Dawes Act of 1887. The law legalized the division of land into tracts which were then allotted to the members of the tribes in parcels of various sizes. Any land left over was declared "surplus" and handed over to the federal government. After 25 years, if Native Americans could prove their capability in managing their own affairs, they were to be awarded citizenship (McLemore & Romo, 1998; Snipp, 1998).

With the help of the Dawes Act, policy makers intended for the disruption of tribal life once and for all and the transformation of individual members of tribes into American citizens; however, the main effect of this law was the transference of the majority of plots of Native American land to White people, accomplished primarily through widespread deceit and fraud in real estate transactions. According to Jackson and Galli (1977), Native Americans lost an estimated 87 million acres of land during the period of 1887–1934—approximately two thirds of their collective holdings before the enactment of the Dawes Act.

Another important effect of the allotment policy was the increase in power and control of the BIA over the Native people, a significant shift for the tribes, considering that decision making in the past had always been the responsibility of chiefs and tribal councils. McLemore and Romo (1998) state, "Even the rations to which the Indians were entitled could be withheld if BIA agents felt the Indians were not moving satisfactorily toward Anglo conformity" (p. 333). Thus, the Dawes Act strengthened other policies already in place (e.g., BIA) that were designed to force Native Americans to accept the dominant culture. While few Native Americans willfully accepted assimilation, most became increasingly dependent on the federal government to meet their material needs.

The Indian New Deal and Reorganization

As the 20th century approached, the policy of Anglo conformity was in full sway. The Native American population had declined to less than 250,000, with the majority of their lands having been allotted and sold (McLemore & Romo, 1998). Astonishingly, despite the government's goal of assimilating the Indians, they remained reluctant to accept citizenship. After thousands of Native Americans fought in World War I, Congress passed the Indian Citizenship Act in 1924. However, Native American leaders viewed this policy as just another attempt of the federal government to destroy their culture and capture more of their land (McLemore & Romo, 1998).

The Meriam Report of 1928 (an analysis published by the Institute for Government Research in 1928 concerning the effects of the federal policy on the plight of the Native Americans), authored by Indian voters, showed in detail how the land allotment policy had failed in its purpose in neither helping the tribes overcome the problems of ignorance, poverty, and disease or helping them move into the mainstream culture. The report was responded to with the passage of the Indian Reorganization Act (IRA) of 1934, a policy embracing a pluralist philosophy and abandoning the effort to help Indians adopt the dominant group's lifestyle.

The IRA restored the right of Native tribes to self-govern, provided they modeled a democratic self-government and stimulated active participation in the American business economy. Of even greater significance were the beliefs underlying the passage of the IRA; that is, for the first time in the history of relations between Native Americans and the federal government, Native American culture and tribal life were not regarded as something incompatible with contemporary American life. In contrast to the intentions of the educational system and boarding schools under the BIA, McLemore and Romo (1998) state, "[t]he Indians were encouraged to develop their language, renew their skills in arts and crafts, revive and have the opportunity to transmit their ancient rituals and ceremonies, and participate in community life on an equal footing with other Americans" (p. 337).

The reorganization of the Native American tribes did not have an automatic effect on their educational level and standard of living, as policymakers had hoped; however, the policy did initiate programs that enabled Native Americans to recover some of their lost lands and acquire loan funds to help finance college education or help with the development of individual corporations. Most importantly, these programs, unlike the ones initiated by the BIA, were planned and executed by Native Americans (McLemore & Romo, 1998).

However, it should be stated that the BIA was still very much in control of reservation life, still receiving annual appropriation funds from Congress, assisting the tribes to organize representative governments, and playing a strong role in the administration of justice and determination of tribal governments. Thus, it is the contention of some historians that IRA did the opposite of supporting Native American culture and instead, attempted to reproduce U.S. forms of government on the reservations. As Champagne (1986) illustrates, "When the U.S. government introduced elections, rules of parliamentary procedure, constitutions, and other features of the Western political tradition, the government was, in effect, asking reservation Indians to undertake a major reorganization of their social, cultural, and political relations" (p. 25). Disapproval of the BIA and support for the IRA among the American Indians steadily grew. Congress recognized that a change in policy direction was required. Two key policies aimed at "transfer" and "termination" were initiated over the next 20 years.

The Transfer Act of 1954

The Transfer Act of 1954 transferred responsibility for Indian health policy and services from the Bureau of Indian Affairs (BIA) to the Department of Health, Education and Welfare (HEW), now known as the Department of Health and Human Services (DHHS). Analysis of this act identifies and explores the causes of the policy that transferred health services from an agency that focused exclusively on Indian affairs to an agency with broad responsibilities. The analysis also examines what the federal government and Indian nations hoped to gain from the transfer, and the actual outcomes that came as a result of it. To more fully understand the impact of this public law, the discussion includes an overview of Native American health care services, the federal government's relationship with Indian nations, and the implications of working with this displaced population. This policy is vital to our understanding of the development and direction of social welfare policy in the United States because it provides information on how a vulnerable population handles differing levels of power over the provision of their health care funds and services. Throughout the history of health care for Native Americans, their level of power over the appropriation of health services and funding has shifted tremendously. The Transfer Act of 1954 played an important role in redistributing decision-making power over Native American health care, despite the fact that it was transferred from an agency designated as specifically focused on Indian affairs. The intention of this analysis is to examine the positive and negative effects of the act on Native American health care, whether or not it has resulted in sufficient health care improvement for Native American populations, and whether it continues to do so.

Background of Native American Health Care

Before the arrival of Europeans to the Western Hemisphere, Native Americans are described as remarkably disease free (Berkhofer, 1979). When they did have physical ailments, local herbs were used as the major curative agent. When Native Americans developed a disease, it came about primarily through harsh weather or from such hardships as famine or disease (Wyatt, 1994). It was only after the arrival of European populations that the Native Americans' system of medicine broke down and they became vulnerable to new diseases for which they lacked immunity.

The inability to combat new diseases brought to them from Europe was not the only reason that the Native American health care system became non-functional. Colonialists disliked traditional Native American approaches to medicine and worked hard to destroy their indigenous system of health care. When American doctors began working on reservations and Indian schools in the 1800s, they considered traditional tribal medicine to be uncivilized and inferior to their own. These views reflected the general set of beliefs in American society that Native American progress lagged behind that of Euro-Americans (Berkhofer, 1979). Political leaders of the nascent federal government shared the attitude of American doctors and created policies to outlaw the practice of traditional tribal medicine. In its place, the United States sought to educate Native Americans in "White man's" more superior health care (Association of American Indian Physicians, 2000). Despite U.S. policies, traditional healers (medicine men) continued to use traditional medicine and healing to care for ill Native Americans, often with reports of success. At Fort Hall Boarding School in Idaho, Dr. Henry Wheeler reported to the Office of Indian Affairs that "some of the means still in use by the 'Old Medicine Men' have a telling effect upon a share of these patients and often hasten a fatal termination of these diseases of the critically ill" (National Library of Medicine, 2000). However, government health care services remained the primary source of services for Native Americans.

The United States Army, toward the end of the 18th century, first provided government health care for Native Americans. Through the War Department, Native Americans living near military posts received vaccinations and other basic health services (Davis, 1999; National Library of Medicine, 2000; IHS, 2000). However, the provision of health care for Native Americans was not of primary importance at that time. The United States seemed more interested in the linear task of counting the number of people who died from diseases and estimating how many Native Americans were left (National Library of Medicine, 2000). It would not be the last time the United States assisted Native Americans while harboring a covert agenda that endangered their existence.

In 1824, Congress authorized $12,000 to be used for Native Americans to receive smallpox vaccinations. However, reducing or ceasing Native American deaths from smallpox was not the primary reason the United States provided them with immunizations. The primary reason was to protect soldiers at the nearby fort from becoming infected. Smallpox and other European diseases were rampant, forcing the United States to take notice as soldiers were also becoming infected. This devastation was due largely to the fact that Native Americans had no natural immunity to European diseases. The Mandan tribe, for example, was nearly decimated by the smallpox epidemic, which reduced their population of 1,600 to only 125 (National Library of Medicine, 2000). On a larger scale, the population of Native Americans dropped from between 20–70 million at the time of first contact with Europeans to under 250,000 by 1900, primarily due to smallpox and other diseases (Henderson, 1991). The United States provided minimal health assistance. It was not enough to save the majority of the Native population from death.

In 1849, the Office of Indian Affairs (now the BIA), was transferred from the War Department to the Department of the Interior (BIA, 2000). Originally created to deal with the administration of Indian programs, the BIA became the primary source of health care for Native Americans (Davis, 1999). Through the BIA, the first hospitals and clinics were built for Native Americans. In addition, physician services were extended to Native Americans by the establishment of a corporation of civilian field employees. By 1875, about half of the Indian agencies had a physician (Indian Health Service [IHS], 2000). Field matrons also began to be employed at this time, giving instruction in sanitation and hygiene, providing emergency nursing services, and prescribing medicine to treat minor illnesses (IHS, 2000). However, not all reservations fared so well. In many areas, government doctors struggled with heavy caseloads and disease prevalence to the extent that issuing pills was all they could provide. For example, at Pine Ridge Agency, South Dakota, one doctor took care of 10,000 Sioux and Cheyenne by dispensing medicine after cursory examinations made through a hole in his office wall (Henderson, 1991). Some reservations had no medical services at all. By 1911, Congress made the first federal appropriation specifically for health care services to Native Americans and Alaskan Natives. However, they failed to provide recurring appropriations (IHS, 2000). As a result, health services for Native Americans remained inconsistent, under-financed, and a low priority.

While BIA health services struggled to become more established, Native Americans were being placed forcibly on reservations in response to the Indian Removal Act of 1830 (Removal of the Indians Act, 1830). Reservation life for Native Americans meant increased risk of disease due to poor living conditions, thus creating a major challenge for the BIA. In addition, reservation health services were often poorly equipped to combat serious cases of tuberculosis, trachoma, smallpox, and other contagious and infectious diseases. Towards the end of the 19th century, a federal government program of assimilation of Native Americans into White–culture dominated reservation health care (Aberdeen Area IHS, 2000; Galen, 2000; National Library of Medicine, 2000). Against BIA demands, Native Americans remained traditional with regard to home, child rearing, and treatment of illness instead of conforming to "White ways." The BIA decided then that health care would be most effective if administered off the reservation. As a result, in some Native American communities, patients were forcibly removed to receive more "civilized" care.

With the establishment of Indian boarding schools, health care was provided to Native Americans who attended. In some instances, Native American children were removed from their homes and sent considerable distances away to boarding homes, without parental agreement. Once there, they were forced to adopt the ways of White "civilization" and abandon their own indigenous traditions (Henderson, 1991; National Library of Medicine, 2000). The Carlisle School in Pennsylvania was an example of this type of boarding school. Carlisle School, in addition to providing medical treatment to its students, functioned as a preliminary nurse training facility, preparing Native American women to move on to regular nursing schools (National Library of Medicine, 2000). The boarding schools also educated its students on sanitation, lecturing them on bathing, diet for the sick, ventilation, cleanliness, care of infants, and how to aid victims of various accidents.

The basis of federal action to provide Native Americans with health care was a series of provisions within treaties signed between the two nations. Tribes traded and exchanged real property through treaties to obtain pre-paid or guaranteed health care services. More than 350 treaties were signed by the United States and Indian tribes between 1784 and the late 1800s (IHS, 2000). Treaties signed in the latter half of the 1800s revealed an evolution of increasing federal government involvement in and control over Indian health issues. For example, while some of the first treaties allotted Native Americans such items as rifles, blankets, and kettles, later treaties provided for the building of hospitals and the provision of medical personnel on reservations (Galen, 2000). The most common language used in later treaties between the United States and the Indian nations stated that health care and education would be provided "as long as the grass grows and the river flows" (Davis, 1999). However, the treaties masked the interest of the United States in the land held by Indians and were frequently ignored or modified to suit "White man's" needs.

Another problem encountered with treaties has been the time limits under which health care was provided to Native Americans. Many of the early Indian treaties imposed time limits of 5–20 years during which the United States agreed to provide health care (Henderson, 1991; IHS, 2000). An example of this can be seen in a treaty with the Sioux which states, "at any time after 20 years, the U.S. shall have the privilege of withdrawing the physician" (Galen, 2000). But as serious health problems ensued after these benefits periods expired, the federal government adopted a policy of continuing services. However, in 1871, the federal government abolished independent treaties due to mounting concern over the amount of foreign aid the president had been agreeing to in treaties (Galen, 2000). Once again, Native American rights were abandoned in favor of the economic and political interests of the United States government and its White citizens.

In 1921, the Snyder Act was passed into law. This policy called for the Bureau of Indian Affairs to "direct, supervise, and expend such monies as Congress may from time to time appropriate, for the benefit, care, and assistance of the Indians" (Snyder Act, 1921). This included the expenditure of money for the "relief of distress and conservation of health" for Native Americans, in addition to the employment of physicians on Indian reservations (Snyder Act, 1921). While the appropriation of funds remained limited, the Snyder Act created the BIA Health Division in 1924, along with the appointment of district medical directors (Galen, 2000; IHS, 2000). The division was established to address the special needs of the Native American population. A couple of years later, the Institute for Government Research received funding to examine the needs of Native Americans. The results of the research were shocking enough for the United States to pursue implementation of new policies to ensure their involvement in Native American health care.

Native American Health Care

The seriousness of the problem of Native American health clearly became evident with results from surveys conducted under the Institute for Government Research. Specifically, the Meriam Commission of 1927, a survey team comprised of specialists from various fields including medicine, inspected reservations, schools, and hospital settings throughout the United States (National Library of Medicine, 2000). The report documented substandard living conditions and health care for Native Americans. Commissioners observed an example of these poor conditions at the Canton Asylum for Insane Indians in Canton, OH. At this facility, the commissioners found the personnel to be untrained and limited in number, patients receiving a minimum of care, no precautions being taken to protect patients from individuals infected with tuberculosis, manual labor being done by patients, and patients being observed eating food off the floor (National Library of Medicine, 2000). The results of the Meriam Report documented that substandard health conditions were due to government inefficiency and lack of adequate funding. The commission recommended that a policy be designed for Native Americans to receive a minimum standard of health and decency.

The Meriam Commission's report transformed Indian health care policy in important ways. It reversed the trend established in 1871 when the U.S. government chose to ignore Indian sovereignty and re-emphasized federal obligation through treaties. In addition, the Meriam Commission got the attention of prominent politicians. In 1933, Harold Ickes, Secretary of the Interior, stated that the diseases Native Americans suffered from were due in large measure to contacts with Whites and that Congress had assisted in creating the current status of Indian health (Galen, 2000). The United States appeared to be finally taking notice of the poor health status of Native Americans and recognizing their part in its development and maintenance.

The high mortality rate from tuberculosis among Native Americans brought greater attention to the problem of Indian health. Statistics on the Navajo reservation showed a rate of 200 cases per 100,000 compared to 34.6 per 100,000 for the White population (Bergman, Grossman, & Erdich, 2000). During the 1940s, facilities were created to combat the devastation tuberculosis had on Native Americans. While the number of cases was significantly decreased, the irregular appropriation of funds from the BIA kept rates much higher than for the general population.

The BIA continued to be an obstacle in the establishment of appropriate health care for Native Americans. For example, in 1929 the BIA interfered with the building of a hospital in Forest County, WI, after a bill was introduced authorizing the expenditure of $125,000 to fully equip a hospital (National Library of Health, 2000). The bill was never passed, largely because of recommendations of the BIA to the Indian Affairs Committee that the hospital not be built. The BIA also did not always appropriate funds to where they were intended to go. An example of this occurred in Arizona in 1933, when Senator Hayden authorized $30 million to treat Native Americans with tuberculosis (Bergman et al., 2000). The money was never used for this purpose since the BIA claimed it was needed in other areas. The BIA also did very little about sanitation problems on reservations, despite the lack of sanitation facilities and Native Americans frequently drinking contaminated water. Although the BIA had drilled wells for livestock, they did not do so for consumption by Native Americans (Bergman et al., 2000). Another problem with the BIA was their difficulty in recruiting and retaining qualified physicians. This was due mainly to the low pay, workload, and poor medical facilities the BIA provided.

Because Native Americans did not have much faith in the BIA, they established and directed a campaign to abolish it (National Library of Medicine, 2000). Concern over what to do about Indian health problems mounted over several decades within the tribes and in the White community.

The Transfer Act of 1954

During the 1950s, "termination" became the dominant Native American issue. Many believed that if health care administration were transferred out of the BIA, an Indian-focused agency, into a federal agency with a broader base, health care appropriations from the federal government would eventually be eliminated. While this was something that many politicians at the time hoped would occur, Native Americans did not. The Transfer Act actually received very little outside support. The only organized support came from the Association of State and Territorial

Health Officers, the National Tuberculosis Association, and the Association on American Indian Affairs, all of which had very little political power (Bergman et al., 2000). These agencies believed that a transfer would result in the improved status of Native American health. But the majority of these organizations were very opposed to the act. HEW did not wish to take on responsibility for Indian health. In addition, most tribal leaders were opposed to the transfer out of fear of termination. While they disliked the BIA, at least it was "their" agency.

Two Republican senators introduced the act. They also received strong support from Senator Hayden of Arizona, chairman of the Appropriations Committee. Their public intent was to increase the health status of Native Americans (Snyder, 1998). On July 1, 1954, Congress passed the Transfer Act with strong bipartisan support, transferring Native American health from the BIA to HEW's Public Health Service (Jackson & Galli, 1977). The Public Health Service (PHS) adopted the challenge of improving the health status of the 315,000 Native Americans and 35,000 Alaskan Natives who survived (Snyder, 1998).

The initial priorities after transfer were to: (1) assemble a competent health staff; (2) establish adequate facilities where services could be provided; (3) institute extensive curative treatment for the many people who were seriously ill; and (4) develop and initiate a full-scale preventive program aimed at reducing the excessive rates of illness from early deaths by preventable diseases and conditions (IHS, 2000). More long-term goals involved the increased political role of tribal leaders in the administration of health services.

One year after the Transfer Act was passed, a new agency was established for Native Americans under the PHS called the Indian Health Service (IHS, 2000). The goal of IHS was and remains to raise the health status of American Indian and Alaskan Natives to the highest level possible. To carry out these goals, the IHS assists Indian tribes in developing their own health programs, facilitate and assist Indian tribes in the coordination of health planning and obtaining the resources available to them, and provides for comprehensive health care services. And IHS also serves as the principal federal advocate for Indians in the health field (IHS, 2000). More short-term goals involved the improvement in the quality of clinical care, expanding prevention programs, and bridging the gap between tribal members and health facilities.

The IHS proved to be a success, as statistics show major improvements in health care and health status. By the 1980s, infant mortality rates had decreased 83%, the mortality rate from tuberculosis had decreased by 96%, and life expectancy had increased from 60 years to 73.2 years (IHS, 2000). This success has primarily been attributed to the employment of the "iron triangle" in establishing the IHS program. The iron triangle is a political term used to describe the linkages that exist between mid-level bureaucrats in a cabinet department, powerful legislators and their staff members, and outside beneficiaries of government programs (Bergman et al., 2000). Ray Shaw, the first director of the service, skillfully used this tactic to increase the support for Native American health. Although tribal leaders did not necessarily play a major political role after the inception of the IHS, primarily due to their mistrust, within 10 years they proudly claimed ownership of the service (Kunitz, 1996). As the quality of medical care on reservations improved, Native American tribal leaders slowly began to have a reasonable expectation that the Indian Health Service was on their side and they became more actively involved (Kuntiz, 1996).

Other improvements that came as a result of the IHS included improved sanitation and increased appropriations of funds. To improve sanitation, the IHS pushed for and obtained the Indian Sanitation Facilities Construction Act of 1959 (Kunitz, 1996). The appropriation of funds to Native American health also increased, with a new budget of $60 million for the IHS in 1962.

This was a huge improvement from the Snyder Act, which only distributed funds on an intermittent basis. As a result, the increase of sufficient clinics, hospitals, and environmental health services was possible (Kunitz, 1996).

Another addition that came as a result of the IHS was Community Health Representatives (CHRs). CHRs are trained members of each community that served as a part of the health team. Created in 1968, these representatives were developed to help deal with the problem related to transportation and communication in American Indian and Alaskan Native communities (IHS, 2000). They help in providing early intervention, direct primary care, and follow-up services. CHRs are often the primary means through which Native Americans gain access to the direct health care system provided by the IHS. In addition, they represent the first time in American history that tribes have managed their own programs.

Despite the significant improvements as a result of the Transfer Act of 1954 and the development of the IHS, the health status of Native Americans continues to rank lower than that of other Americans (Plepys & Klein, 1995).

Analysis of Policy

Throughout American history, Native Americans have been exploited, marginalized, disempowered, and subjected to cultural imperialism. Europeans first exploited Native Americans by taking advantage of their generosity and kindness in sharing the land. In fact, they took it away. Europeans have also exploited the Native American's lack of modern weaponry and other devices to more effectively fight Indians in battle and force them off their lands (Diamond, 1997). Finally, Native Americans were and continue to be exploited by the federal government, withholding appropriate health care that is rightfully theirs through treaty agreements.

The passage of the Snyder Act was not very controversial. This was due to the fact that two very different outcomes were predicted once implementation took place. While the intention was to provide improved health care to Native Americans, many were skeptical that the new law would do this. Because the policy would transfer responsibility from an agency identified as an Indian agency to a broad-based governmental agency, many Native Americans feared termination. This fear was not unfounded, as many politicians openly spoke for the termination of federal obligations to Native Americans, claiming that assimilation into the general society would be in their best interest. However, Native Americans believed that termination would result in their complete abandonment, not assimilation (Berkhofer, 1979; Deloria, 1969). Fortunately, this was not the case and improvements were actually made in the health of Native Americans and Alaskan Natives through this act.

The most positive outcome of the Snyder Act was the creation of the IHS in 1955 (Jackson & Galli, 1977). This prevented termination while improving the provision of health care to Native populations. With the inception of the IHS came major improvements in sanitation, a decrease in infectious diseases, and the creation of a more positive relationship between Indian health and the federal government with the employment of CHRs. In addition, it helped foster a greater sense of self-determination in tribal governments by providing the means for nations to control appropriation of funds from the IHS to develop their own health care services (Kunitz, 1996).

The historical politics of the relationship between Native Americans and the federal government have been extremely turbulent and inconsistent, as shown through various public policies over the decades. Their relationship is unique when compared to other people of color in the United States. This is due to the fact that American Indians and Alaskan Natives have a direct government-to-government relationship with the United States. This is based on Article 1, Section 8 of the United States Constitution and has been given greater substance through numerous Supreme Court decisions, treaties, legislation, and executive orders (IHS, 2000). As a result, they have a specific recognition status that other oppressed populations do not.

Native Americans suffer a great deal economically and their health status remains below that of the general American population in many areas. They are the poorest group in the United States and have higher than average rates of unemployment. In 1980, the total per capita income for Native Americans was $16,500, compared to $23,000 for the rest of the U.S. population (Greeley, 1991). In addition, despite the vast improvements that the IHS has made in their lives, their health status is still not comparable to the rest of the population of the United States. At 71, their life expectancy is 5 years less than the national average (Association of American Indian Physicians [AAIP], 2000). The AAIP (2000) reports that death rates for Native Americans from tuberculosis are 475% higher, while deaths from accidents are 212% higher, and suicide and homicide rates are 70% and 41% higher, respectively, than for the U.S. population as a whole.

Despite the devastation that Native Americans still encounter concerning the status of their health care, funding is substantially less than the national figure. In 1994, the amount spent per capita on health services for Native Americans was substantially less than that spent on health care for the entire U.S. population. For the nation as a whole per capita health care expenditures exceeded $2,629, while per capita expenditures for the IHS were $976 (Kunitz, 1996). In addition, a reduction in funding was made from 1994 to 1995, with the IHS budget reduced by 6% (Noren & Kindig, 1998). Although the IHS was created to provide medical coverage to all Native Americans not covered elsewhere, Native Americans have less access to health care than the overall population. Another obstacle encountered is due to the uneven distribution of IHS resources across all service areas. This is because the method of distribution is based on historical funding patterns, rather than current needs (Noren & Kindig, 1998). But even in those areas with the highest allocations, health care for this population remains considerably less than for the average citizen of the United States.

The provision of Native American health care has been greatly influenced by social, cultural, and spiritual factors. Socially, Native Americans lead a substantially different way of life due to their residency on reservations. Reservations keep them separated from the rest of American society. In addition, it makes access to health care services very difficult as currently designed.

The culture and spirituality of Native Americans has also influenced how they perceive health, disease, and health care. Traditionally, spirituality and medicine were one and the same. Healing occurred through blessings from the old Medicine Man and Great Spirit. In addition, one was thought to be sick spiritually if one were found to be physically ill. Also inherent in Indian culture is the concept of gift giving and sharing of one's self. Traditional healing of sickness by Medicine Men involved putting much personal time and effort into developing a relationship with the patient to facilitate healing. In exchange, gifts were given to the Medicine Man and the Great Spirit, making the interchange mutual (Aberdeen Area IHS, 2000). Also, traditional medicine rests on the assumption that sickness and disease represent being out of balance with the natural order of living. As a result, healing is holistic and employs certain ceremonies and rites utilizing herbs and roots to assist the sick into returning to wellness and wholeness (Aberdeen Area IHS, 2000). In addition, healing was very much of a group effort, as family and community were frequently involved. IHS health workers were advised that they take the time to listen to Navaho patients to facilitate medical treatment.

To successfully incorporate western medicine into Native American culture, traditional healing practices needed to be understood and respected. The first director of the IHS did this by creating tribal health committees, which bridged the gap between traditional and modern healing practices (Jackson & Galli, 1977). Today, both types of health care can be found on the reservation and both are often utilized for healing (Aberdeen Area IHS, 2000).

The Termination Act of 1975

During the two presidential terms of Dwight Eisenhower, a policy of Anglo conformity through termination gained popularity. To set Native Americans free from federal supervision and control, Congress suggested that all laws and treaties currently binding the United States government to Native Americans be nullified. Known as "termination," the policy was made official with the passage of House Concurrent Resolution 108. The United States Congress implemented its termination policy with passage of the Indian Self-Determination and Education Act in 1955. This act was subsequently amended and expanded in 1975 and is commonly know as the "termination" act.

The 1975 act is another example of a unilateral decision by the government to avoid its part in past treaty agreements. Under this law, Native Americans were no longer entitled to the payments and services for the land they had handed or ceded to the federal government (Svensson, cited in McLemore and Romo, 1998). However, the termination of services under this policy would only occur if a tribe was adequately assimilated, willing to cut ties to the federal government, and able to survive economically with only local and state help. Not surprisingly, there were few tribes that actually met these standards and few that went out of their way to make it known if they had (McLemore and Romo, 1998).

As with the allotment policy (Dawes Act of 1887), the termination policy was a disaster in attempting to help Native Americans participate fully in the mainstream of American life. As McLemore and Romo (1998) state, the ironic tragedy of these two policies, which sought to end abruptly the special relationship of Native Americans to the U.S. government, was that they "served in fact, only to take away from the Indians the resources they needed to create the very independence the policies tried to enforce" (p. 338).

The problem was not the federal government's attempt to liberate Native Americans from their aid and supervision, most notably the interference and regulation of the BIA. In fact, many Native Americans endorsed a termination policy, having wished they would be forever free from constraints of the BIA to regain their sovereignty. The problem was the very means created by these policies used to obtain the end goal of termination. Not only were Native Americans fearful that the government would deny their treaty entitlements, resulting in even greater destitution, they were afraid that termination from government aid would mean an end to tribal life and therefore their existence as Native Americans (Deloria, 1969). In other words, while Native Americans did not want to be wards of the government, they also did not want to conform to an American mainstream way of life to avoid a life of continued destitution. Moreover, Native Americans did not accept that Euro-American culture was superior and, in fact, pointed to problems relating to air and water pollution, soil erosion, energy exhaustion, ecological imbalance, and widespread feelings of loneliness and powerlessness as signs of the impermanence and inferiority of the alien culture (McLemore & Romo, 1998). As McLemore and Romo (1998) state, "The policy of termination did not take into account the strong wish among the American Indians to fashion a mode of participating in American society that would not sacrifice their distinctiveness as Indians" (p. 339).

Self-Determination

Luckily, during the 1960s War on Poverty, governmental actions to effect reorganization were brought to a standstill with the passage of the Indian Civil Rights Act of 1968 and President Johnson affirming the right of Indians "to remain Indian while exercising their right as Americans" (McNickle, cited in McLemore & Romo, 1998, p. 339). Then, in 1970, President Nixon attacked the past policies that had allowed for the unilateral termination of Indian tribes' relationship to the government and instead expanded the notion that government policy should encourage self-determination among the Indians without threatening their sense of community (Jackson & Galli, 1977). Calling for a renunciation of the House Concurrent Resolution 108, Nixon's beliefs regarding the importance of Indian self-determination and culture are exemplified in the following statement made in1970 (Indian Record, cited in Forbes, 1980):

> Down through the years, through written agreements and through formal and informal agreements, our government has made specific commitments to the Indian people . . . to strengthen the Indian's sense of autonomy without threatening his sense of community. We must assure the Indian that he can assume control of his own life without being separated involuntarily from the tribal group.

In 1975, Congress enacted the Indian Self-Determination and Education Assistance Act in support of President Nixon's pluralist policy, implicit in self-determination. Known as the greatest victory for Native American activists in American history, this act established a new relationship between the Native Americans and the government (Olson & Wilson, cited in McLemore & Romo, 1998) that now respected their desires for self-determination.

The creation and implementation of policy does not occur in a vacuum; rather, it is precipitated and influenced by environmental events, timing and/or other factors. We have seen that much of the policy concerning the relationship between Native Americans and the federal government was influenced by assumptions concerning the inferiority of Native Americans coupled with economic greed.

The following questions remain: (1) What contributed to the shift in policy towards self-determination and respect for Native American culture during the Nixon Administration; (2) How is it possible that between 1900 and 2000, the Native American population grew eightfold, with much of the growth occurring after 1960 and is now the fastest growing population in the United States (U.S. Census Bureau, 2001); and, (3) What has contributed to the revival of traditional Native American culture, as evidenced by the development of 48 tribal newspapers and newsletters published by Native Americans or organizations and efforts of tribal leaders to restore lost languages which disappeared hundreds of years ago (Nagel, cited in McLemore & Romo, 1998)? Factors influencing Nixon's policy of self-determination and its consequential effects on Native American culture will be explored in the following paragraphs.

The New Tribalism

Nixon's proclamation for Native American self-determination came during a time of intense advocacy and protest. Known by historians as the Indian Movement, the protesting occurred from 1969–1972 during the Vietnam War and the war at home for civil rights (Forbes, 1980). Alongside the Indian Movement were sincere efforts by Euro-Americans and other well-meaning groups, many whom never consulted Native Americans to see what they thought or wanted (McLemore & Romo, 1998).

A discussion concerning the development of policy and Native Americans would be incomplete without an exploration of a policy created by Native Americans themselves: that is, *tribalism*. While the basic social unit in Native American life has been the tribe, with one's loyalty to the tribe as primary, nevertheless Native Americans did realize the advantages of acting together in broader groups to fight for their rights and culture (Hertzberg, 1971). More specifically, many Native Americans, highly educated under White influence and living bi-culturally in both worlds, believed the following:

> [T]he White dominated–industrial American society would change all things Indian unless the Indians joined together, accepted the reality of the changed conditions, and attempted to fashion a new "Indian identity beyond the tribe and within the American social order." (Hertzberg, cited in McLemore & Romo, p. 340)

In 1961, tribalism, otherwise known as "tribal nationalism" or "Red Power," commenced its first official gathering at the American Indian Chicago Conference (Laurie, 1961). This historical meeting would precipitate the success of many future court cases concerning the issue of Indian sovereignty pertaining to fishing and hunting rights, religious and burial rights, and tribal land claims, water rights, and contract disputes (Laurie, 1961).

While the majority of Native Americans agreed on the right to sovereignty and maintenance of their identity as well as the binding nature of treaties, the members differed on tactics to win these rights (Hertzberg, 1971). The older members of the conference did not want to consider themselves as just another group of persons of color fighting for civil rights and demanding to be treated like all other Americans. In contrast, the younger members considered their fight to be, in many ways, a part of the larger battle for social justice between the dominant society and all other oppressed groups, and that Native Americans, like all other oppressed groups, must exercise their rights (James, 1986).

Despite the differences among Native Americans, the next several years were characterized by a sharp increase in organized Indian actions to protest various conditions or violations of civil rights. A great majority of these actions were conventional; that is, they were nondisruptive efforts to improve the lives of American Indians; however, some of these actions were direct and confrontational, such as when a group of 89 young Indians seized Alcatraz Island in 1969, identifying themselves as "Indians of all Tribes" (Indians of All Tribes; James, cited in McLemore & Romo, 1998). In arguing that their actions were lawful, they drew upon a previous law that verbalized their right to reclaim any unused land.

While this action did not achieve the purpose of establishing a title and a pan-Indian cultural center on on Alcatraz Island as the young Indians had hoped, it did communicate to the nation their serious demands for self-determination, tribal lands and tribal identities (Olson & Wilson, 1984). Undoubtedly, their efforts contributed to a turning point for the federal government to support a policy in favor of their ethnic pride and dignity (McLemore & Romo, 1998).

In 1970, triggered by the events at Alcatraz, the American Indian Movement (AIM) was established in Minneapolis, MN. A militant new body that grew quickly into a national organization, AIM argued for Indian sovereignty, insisted on the protection of the treaty rights of Indians, and challenged the validity of the tribal governments formed under the Indian Reorganization Act of 1934 (Bonney, 1977). Like other civil rights groups in the past, AIM held their first protest march in Washington, DC, which came to be known as "The Trail of Broken Treaties." The march turned into a 6-day seizure during which Native Americans occupied the offices under the BIA. On the interior walls of the BIA building, it was written: "In building anew, one must first destroy the old. This is the beginning of a new era for the North American native people" (Forbes, 1981).

With the purpose of protesting violations of the Sioux Treaty of 1868, AIM in 1973 seized the Wounded Knee village on the Pine Ridge Reservation. The occupation of the reservation lasted for 70 days and climaxed with an armed face-off, attracting widespread media attention. Finally, federal officials sent a team of investigators to discuss the problem of broken treaties, ending the occupation.

As McLemore and Romo (1998) point out, there were several long- and short-term occupations, many of which occurred on reservations and involved tribal factions associated with AIM or urban tribal members. Throughout the 1980s and into the 1990s, AIM was a constant strength for American Indian activism and remained at the forefront for organizing and participating in protests over land and grazing rights, the rights of tribes to sell cigarettes without state or federal taxes, and protests over athletic team Indian mascots, gestures, logos, and slogans. However powerful their protests were, federal and local law enforcement agencies continued to repress their efforts, and consequently the AIM leaders began to use less direct-action protest and more legal action, a tactic that has continued to this day (Bonney, 1977).

The Nixon Administration

There was hope that the Indian Self-Determination and Education Assistance Act of 1975 might stabilize previous policy actions that had wavered among ideologies of equality, extermination, domination, assimilation, and termination (Joe, 1986). Through Nixon's policy, tribes now had the right to subcontract or administer certain programs and services operated by the federal government, giving some reaffirmation to the concept of self-government for the tribes. The policy also brought to the forefront support for tribal sovereignty and government-to-government relations. However, it is the contention of Forbes (1981) that Nixon's words were hollow and that in fact his strategy was designed to simply stabilize and pacify Native American protests and destroy militancy to eventually pave the way for the exploitation of Native American resources. Moreover, it is possible that rather than being one of self-determination, Nixon's policy was actually a reflection of the values of neocolonialism, moving toward the goal of political and economic control (Forbes, 1981).

The following questions remain: Why the rhetoric of self-determination? Why the switch from termination policy to one whose rhetoric claimed to be for Native American rights and the continuation of their culture? Were Native Americans that much of a threat to United States corporations or the government? Forbes eloquently responds to these questions:

> Perhaps the Nixon strategists surmised that successful American Indian struggles would shatter the ideological basis for economic control. More starkly than any other group in the United States, Indian issues expose the fundamental contradictions in United States "democracy," as well as the nature of its historical development via theft of Indian land and resources. Indian peoples successfully organizing and winning public support for their demands would crack the myth of United State's history and power, and even give added strength to the toiling millions of Indians and mestizos in Latin America whose cheap labor serves to produce enormous profits for the United States-based corporations. (p. 10)

He reminds readers that the United States military and the Central Intelligence Agency had made a point of hunting down and killing Ernesto Che Guevara and his small guerrilla unit in

Bolivia in 1967 and that obviously these two dozen freedom fighters posed a real threat to United States power in Latin America.

In agreement with Forbes (1981), Gross (1986) proposes that not only did American Indian militancy, helped by the media, draw attention to the Indian affairs agenda of the Nixon legislation, but the civil rights era in and of itself created a national mood that was receptive to do something about the dilemma faced by all people of color. However, in contrast to Forbes (1981), she argues that Nixon was sincerely invested in improving chances and independence for Native Americans.

The restoration of Blue Lake to the Taos Pueblo serves to illustrate just how sympathetic the Nixon Administration was to the plight of Native Americans. In 1906, the federal government forcibly appropriated 48,000 acres of Indian land at and around Blue Lake, NM, for a national forest. Until Nixon granted them restoration in the early 1970s, the Pueblo Indians had been trying for 64 years to reclaim their land. Moreover, the Menominee tribe had been fighting for the restoration of their tribal status until 1973, until Congress, following the president's example, finally consented to it being reinstated.

According to Gross (1986), Nixon's support for Indian self-determination was precipitated by his strong dislike for the previous termination policy. He believed it was wrong for several reasons: (1) the trusteeship responsibility of the federal government should not and could not be unilaterally nullified without the consent of Indians; and (2) the tactics of termination were clearly harmful and unsuccessful at establishing the very goal of self-sufficiency (i.e., the fear of termination negatively influenced tribal progress as well as the Indians' willingness to pursue political, economic, and social autonomy).

Despite this obvious commitment to self-determination of Native Americans, the question that Forbes proposed remains: Why Nixon of all people and all politicians? Some argue, according to Gross (cited in Joe, 1986), that his conservative political orientation was highly compatible with Native American values of local control, self-determination, autonomy, and independence. Others, in fact, point to Nixon's personal advocacy for Native Americans as having its roots in his youth when he had played football at Whittier College with Wallace "Chief" Newman. As quoted by Gross (cited in Joe, 1986), in Nixon's own words, "I think that I admired him [Wallace 'Chief' Newman] more and learned more from him than from any man I have ever known aside from my father" (p. 59).

Current Attempts for Sovereignty

Despite the shift in policy during the Nixon Administration in favor of Native American sovereignty and self-determination, tribes have continued to fight for their rights. One illustration of their continued fight for sovereignty concerns their operation of gambling casinos, a main source of income during the past 2 decades. According to Bordewich (cited in McLemore & Romo, 1998), there are 160 tribes throughout the country with gambling businesses generating profits of about $6 billion per year, known to many Native Americans as "the new buffalo economy" (p. 344).

According to the Indian Gaming Regulatory Act of 1992, federal law required the states to grant permission to operate certain games. When Native Americans refused to gain state approval, arguing that it was their land to self-govern as they saw fit, FBI agents raided several reservations across Arizona to seize the games that were generating an estimated $1.4 million per year in revenue for the Yavapai-Apache tribe. A similar dispute occurred in New Mexico when 11 tribes refused to discontinue operation of their casinos, despite orders from the state Supreme Court and three federal appeals judges ruling that the gambling pacts the tribes signed with a former governor were illegal. As a sovereign nation, the tribes argued, they would deal directly with the U.S. government and insisted that the gaming act gave too much power to the states. Signing an agreement with U.S. Attorney John J. Kelly, 9 out of the 11 tribes agreed not to block federal projects. In return, the government agreed that the casinos could remain open. However, in 1996, Judge Martha A. Vazquez of the Federal District Court ruled that such an agreement was invalid but agreed the casinos could remain open while the case was appealed. These jurisdictional conflicts are just some of the many examples of the efforts of the tribes "to define and enlarge the area within which they may determine the direction of their own lives" (McLemore & Romo, 1998, p. 345).

Another illustration concerns sovereignty for Alaskan tribes. For 3 decades now, the Alaskan Natives have attempted to regain their tribal status, as have many other Indians. While the Alaskan Natives were certain they could prove that the 226 tribes in Alaska were modern-day successors to historically sovereign bands of Native Americans, to hire lawyers, historians, and anthropologists on a tribe-by-tribe basis would have been too expensive. However, since the U.S. Supreme Court has repeatedly ruled that the courts must defer to the judgment of the executive or legislative branch for recognition of a tribe, Ada Deer, the Assistant Secretary for Indian Affairs of the Department of the Interior and a Menominee Indian woman, did precisely that. In 1993, Deer published a list of the federally recognized tribes in Alaska, an action that would move one step closer toward promoting tribal sovereignty in Alaska (McLemore & Romo, 1998).

Theory of Community Formation

Data included in the 2000 Census (U. S. Census, 2001) illustrate the extent to which there have been a number of positive changes in the socioeconomic circumstances of Native Americans within the past decade. The Census shows increases in mean income, lowering of unemployment rates among some tribes, an increase in utilization of primary health care, and a major increase in overall population. In fact, the Native American population has increased at twice (26%) the rate of growth (13%) for the population as a whole. However, the rate of poverty has remained steady at close to 25% over the last decade. These data, particularly the rate of population increase, suggest clearly that change has occurred on an unprecedented scale within the lives of this population within the last decade. Theory developed by Max Weber is helpful in placing these and related changes in context.

Weber (Neuwirth, 1969) developed a theory to help explain how communities formed out of conflict between groups with differing levels of power and control. Key to Weber's theory is the idea that groups that differ along some identifiable characteristics often engage in conflict and competition for resources: land, minerals, control, space, and wealth. Some groups are able to dominate competition for resources to the extent that they control and consume disproportionately large amounts of societal resources. Although Weber's theory was born out of his observations of Jewish and German ethnic groups, his major concepts and hypotheses provide a valuable context for understanding the history and outcomes of conflict between Native Americans and Euro-Americans, as well as the changes in the nature of Native American communities in the last decade.

Community formation is conceptualized by Weber as both a goal and a process sought by most populations that share characteristics in common. The achievement of community appears to reinforce the processes that led to its formation and gives groups a sense of honor—interpreted as a subjective sense of accomplishment, esteem, and belief in their ability to thrive. Weber proposes that the effort to achieve community is characterized by varying levels of competition between groups, which includes overt and covert efforts to limit the ability of outgroups to control access to resources. Obviously, the more successful one group is in achieving community formation, there is a risk that the groups that do not achieve community will reflect the negative effects of having their access to resources denied or limited. These effects can be increased rates of poverty, ill health, malnutrition, depression, high death rates, and possibly extinction. Community formation is often marked by what Weber terms community closure, a condition or status in which opportunities and access to resources is denied to outgroups. The ability to close communities to outsiders is also seen as increasing the sense of honor, as well as the sense of safety and control by, in-group members. Community closure can take the form of segregating competing groups, establishing separate geographic communities, placing groups on reservations, or the use of internment or concentration camps. Community formation and closure are seen as the key processes that eventually increase the status of a community and increase the ability of its members to meet individual needs. Another related concept used by Weber is monopolization. Monopolization is said to exist when a community that has achieved closure is able to control access, power, policies, processes, and resources.

Historically, the relationship between Native Americans and Euro-Americans reflected Weber's concepts of intense competition for community, closure, and monopolization. The most significant factor in this historical relationship was the desire and effort on the part of Euro-Americans to establish monopoly control of land, minerals, and opportunities to the exclusion of Native Americans. Part of the justification for this control and the eventual segregation on reservations was the attribution of negative status to the tribes based on the extent to which their cultures differed from European expectations (Berkhofer, 1979). Within just a few decades, the effort to establish monopoly and closure of White communities was achieved, as reflected in the Indian Removal Act of 1830. A key mechanism for establishing Euro-American monopolization was their ability to create and enforce a plethora of public policies favorable to their interests. Many of these policies were reinforced by decisions in state courts, federal courts of appeal, and the Supreme Court. Christian religious beliefs were used to help justify the extreme closure of Euro-American communities. The result of this intense monopolization and closure was seen in the extent to which Native Americans were pushed to the brink of extinction, although they had considerable wealth held in trust by the federal government that grew out of land leases and mineral rights (*Cobell v. Babbit*, 1999).

The Transfer Act of 1954 and the Indian Self Determination and Education Act of 1975 suggest that a discernable change has occurred in the condition of Native Americans within the past decade. These changes imply that Native Americans are closer to developing a sense of community formation as defined by Weber. Evidence of their ability to formulate a community shows in changes in wealth accumulation, mean income, lower rates of unemployment, increased utilization of primary health care, and a modest change in the number of standard housing units. The most illustrative change has been in the increase in population within the past decade. Consistent with Weber's hypotheses, these changes can be explained by the interaction of several factors:

- An increase in the sense of honor within Native American tribes. Weber proposes that there is a direct correlation between the sense of honor and the ability to formulate and sustain a sense of community.

- The ability of Native Americans to establish a semblance of community closure. Increasingly over the past several decades, Native Americans have been able to build economic wealth and protect opportunities and resources within their communities from external encroachment and seizure.
- Native American community formation has been aided by lawsuits and advocacy that has resulted in significant legal victories in the courts and the passage of legislation aimed at liberation.
- Community formation has also progressed from the ability of Native American tribes to form networks that transcend narrow tribal identities that formerly resulted in inter-tribal competition.
- Euro-American demand for closure and monopolization has declined in response to legal, social, economic, and human rights demands of people of color.

The Role of Social Work

It is clear that the creation of a just policy is limited in reversing past injustices—the very reason why social workers are needed as advocates is to ascertain that such policies are actually implemented for oppressed peoples. Finding creative and fair ways to compensate for past injustice has become part of the active legal efforts to recover damages based on the imposition of illegal policies by the federal government. The role of the social worker is complex, however, because many of the major problems Native Americans face stem from their transformation from self-sufficiency to dependency on the government. In this circumstance, how do social workers help Native Americans recover their economic and psychological losses without threatening their need for self-sufficiency and dignity? Advocacy may be the wisest way for social workers to help alleviate the suffering of the Indians.

As Department of the Interior Assistant Secretary for Indian Affairs, Ada Deer was in an authoritative position that enabled her to advocate and take action on behalf of Native American rights. Social workers as well can make use of their own positions in government to advocate for Native American rights for self-determination. Moreover, social workers serving as lobbyists can make a concerted and continuous effort to lobby Congress and the executive branch. Rhetoric is not only powerful among policymakers to influence policy; it can be just as powerful among lobbyists who, by influencing the policymakers, indirectly shape policy. Social workers can be instrumental in promoting the value of self-determination for Indians, as self-determination is a goal and value of the social work profession. As social workers, we have an obligation to preserve this value and see that oppressed groups, like Native Americans, are allowed to exercise their rights.

While observers believed that the Native Americans were likely to become extinct, their growth in the past decade has refuted all predictions. Moreover, they have regained a greater sense of self-sufficiency, autonomy, and honor as shown in the form of tribal governments and networking. Perhaps one of their greatest strengths has been their perseverance throughout centuries of persecution and oppression by American citizens and their government. Despite the deleterious effects of unjust public policies—which have waffled between trying to assimilate the Native Americans or trying to separate them from mainstream society—they have gathered together, despite the differences between tribes, and fought the policies that have governed their lives for hundreds of years.

Vast improvement in Native Americans' health status is socially, economically, and politically feasible. The IHS seems to have demonstrated an ability to work effectively with Native American tribal communities to improve the health of the population. However, future success will require an increased level of involvement in health care services by the tribes and greater integration of traditional approaches with Native American customs and medicine. These combined approaches will be a vast improvement over previous approaches provided by the BIA (Kunitz, 1996).

Economically, the IHS continues to struggle. Obviously, part of this economic struggle is based on the politics of getting adequate funds to take care of Native American health care needs in a continuously reluctant political environment. It is apparent that the United States does have the financial resources to meet its commitment to improve the health status of the Native American population. The political reality, however, may be that this will never truly be feasible. The history of American policy toward this population is a reflection of a deep cultural ambivalence toward social justice, even though there are hundreds of legal documents, treaties, agreements, and a moral imperative that should dictate the course to follow.

However, as long as Native Americans are forced to fight for their culture and sovereignty, social workers have a special obligation to advocate on their behalf. Thus, insofar as human beings and the oppressed groups from which they come are complex, there exists neither a single policy nor social work intervention that will sufficiently serve all Native Americans, whose cultures, tribes, and languages differ significantly from each other.

References

Aberdeen Area Indian Health Service. (2000). *History and tribal movement.* Retrieved January 21, 2004, from http://www.ihs.gov/FacilitiesServices/AreaOffices/Aberdeen/Aberdeen-history-tribal-movement.asp

Association of American Indian Physicians. (2000). *Legislative health policy.* Retrieved January 21, 2004, from www.aaip.com

Bergman, A. B., Grossman, D., Erdrich, A., Todd, J. G., & Forquera, R. (2000). *A political history of the Indian Health Service.* Retrieved January 21, 2004, from http:///http://www.sihb.org/ihs27.html

Berkhofer, R. F. (1979). *The White man's Indian.* New York: Vintage Books.

Bonney, R. A. (1977, Autumn).The role of AIM Leaders in Indian nationalism. *American Indian Quarterly*, 209–244.

Bureau of Indian Affairs. (2000). *Short history of the BIA.* Retrieved January 21, 2004, from http://www.doiu.nbc.gov/orientation/bia2.cfm

Champagne, D. (1986). American Indian values and the institutionalization of IRA governments. In J. R. Joe (Ed.), *American Indian policy and cultural values: Conflict and accommodation* (pp. 25–34). Los Angeles, CA: UCLA Publications Services Department.

Cobell v. Babbit. No. 96-1285 (D.C. Oct. 14, 1999).

Davis, D. J. (1999). Health care for Alaska Natives and Native Americans: Historical perspective. In J. M. Galloway, B. W. Goldberg, J. S. Alpert, & M. H. Trujillo (Eds.), *Primary care of Native American patients: Diagnosis, therapy, and epidemiology* (pp. 3–5). Boston: Butterworth-Heinemann..

Dawes General Allotment Act, ch. 818, 25 U.S.C. Stat. 392 (1887).

Deloria, V. (1969). Custer died for your sins: An Indian Manifesto. New York: Avon Books.

Deneven, W. M. (1992). *The native population of the Americas in 1492* (2nd ed.). Madison, WI: University of Wisconsin Press.

Diamond, J. (1997). *Guns, germs and steel.* New York: Norton.

Forbes, J. D. (1981). *Native Americans and Nixon.* Los Angeles: UCLA Publications Services Department.

Galen, L. (2000). *The reorganization of the Indian Health Service.* Retrieved January 21, 2004, from http://members.tripod.com/~nezperce/indian.htm

Greeley, C. (1991). Health status of Native Americans. *Journal of the American Medical Association, 265,* 2272.

Gross, E. (1986). Setting the agenda for American Indian policy development, 1968–1980. In J. R. Joe (Ed.), *American Indian policy and cultural values: Conflict and accommodation* (pp. 47–51). Los Angeles: UCLA Publications Services Department.

Henderson, J. (1991). Native American health policy: From U.S. territorial expansion to legal obligation. *Journal of the American Medical Association, 265,* 2272–2273.

Hertzberg, H. W. (1971). *The search for an American Indian identity.* Syracuse: New York University Press.

House Concurrent Resolution 108, 67 U.S.C. Stat. B132 (1953).

Indian Appropriations Act, ch. 120, 16 U.S.C. Stat. 544 (1871).

Indian Citizenship Act, ch.233, 43 U.S.C. Stat. 253 (1924).

Indian Civil Rights Act, ch. 15, 25 U.S.C. 1301 (1968).

Indian Gaming Regulatory Act, 25 U.S.C. 1701 (1992).

Indian Health Service. (2000). *Comprehensive health care program for American Indians and Alaska Natives.* Retrieved January 21, 2004, from www.ihs.gov

Indian Re-Organization Act, ch. 576, 48 Stat. 984 (1934).

Indian Sanitation Facilities Construction Act, Public Law86-121, ch. 56, 73, Stat. 267 (1959).

Indian Self-Determination and Education Assistance Act, Public Law 67-85, 42 U.S.C. 1450 (1955).

Indian Self-Determination and Education Assistance Act of 1975. Public Law 93-638, 88 Stat. 2203 (1975).

Institute for Government Research. (1928). *The Meriam Report: The problem of Indian administration.* Baltimore, MD: Johns Hopkins University Press.

Jackson,C. E., & Galli, M. J. (1977). *A history of the Bureau of Indian Affairs and its activities among Indians.* San Francisco: R & E Research Associates.

James, L. (1986). Activism and Red power. In K. R. Phillip (Ed.), *Indian Self-Rule* (pp. 229–231). Salt Lake City, UT: Howe Brothers,.

Joe, J. R. (Ed.). (1986). *American Indian policy and cultural values: Conflict and accommodation.* Los Angeles: UCLA Publications Services Department.

Josephy, A. M.(1961). The patriot chiefs. New York: Viking Press.

Kunitz, S. J. (1996). The history and politics of U.S. health care policy for American Indians and Alaskan Natives. *American Journal of Public Health, 86,* 1464

Laurie, N. (1961). American Indian Chicago Conference. *Current Anthropology, 2*(5), 478–500.

McLemore, S. D., & Romo, H. D. (1998). *Racial and ethnic relations in America.* Boston: Allyn & Bacon.

McNickle, D. (1973). Native American tribalism. London: Oxford University Press.

National Library of Medicine. (2000). *If you knew the conditions: Health care to Native Americans.* Retrieved January 21, 2004, from http://www.nlm.nih.gov/exhibition/if_you_knew/if_you_knew_01.html

Neuwirth, G. (1968). A Weberian outline of a theory of community: Its application to the Dark Ghetto. *British Journal of Sociology, 20,* 148–163.

Noren, J. (1998). Challenges to Native American health care. *Public Health Reports, 113,* 22–33.

Northwest Territory Ordinance of 1787 (n.d.). *Supplement to First Volume of Columbian Magazine.* Retrieved Jan. 24, 2004, from http://earlyamerica.com/earlyamerica/milestones/ordinance

Olson, J., & Wilson, R. (1984). *Native Americans in the 20th Century.* Urbana: University of Illinois Press.

Plepys, C., & Klein, R. (1995). *Health status indicators: Differentials by race and Hispanic Origin.* Atlanta, GA: Centers for Disease Control.

Proclamation of 1763 (1763, October 7). *The Royal Proclamation on North America.* Retrieved January 25, 2004, from http://www.yale.edu/lawweb/avalon/proc1763.htm

Removal of the Indians West of the Mississippi Act, ch. 148, 4 Stat. 411 (1830).

Snipp, C. M. (1998). The first Americans: American Indians. In M. L. Andersen & P. H. Collins (Eds.), *Race, class, and gender: An anthology* (3rd ed., pp. 357–364). Belmont, CA: Wadsworth.

Snyder Act, Public Law 67-85, ch. 115, 42 Stat. 208 (1921).

Snyder, L. (1998). Integrating American Indian and Alaska Natives into the body politic? *Public Health Reports, 113,* 365–368.

Thornton, R. (1987). *American Indian holocaust and survival: A population history since 1492.* Norman: University of Oklahoma Press.

U.S. Census Bureau. (2001). *Overview of race and Hispanic origin 2000.* Retrieved January 21, 2004, from http://www.census.gov/population/www/cen2000/briefs.html

U.S. Constitution. Article 1, Section 8.

Wyatt, J. (1994). *The roots of North American medicine.* Retrieved January 21, 2004, from http://www.yvwiiusdinvnohii.net/articies/medroots.html

Chapter Nine

What Will Ensure Mexican Americans Equal Access to Health Care?

Llewellyn J. Cornelius and Larry P. A. Ortiz

The data from the 2000 Census have confirmed highly publicized expectations of growth in the Latino population in the United States. While the U.S. population as a whole increased 13.2% between 1990 and 2000, the Latino or Hispanic population increased 57.9% (from 22.4 to 35.3 million). As of 2000, Latinos represent 12.5% of the U.S. population. Although growth had been predicted, growth of this magnitude had not been expected for at least another decade. According to the Census data, Latinos, as an ethnically heterogeneous group, will surpass African Americans as the largest group of color in the United States (U.S. Census Bureau, 2001).

But the group commonly labeled "Latino" is neither monolithic nor easily defined. Although its members are often called "Hispanic," this is a government-generated term that refers to several different ethnic groups. Latinos vary significantly by and within countries in such areas as socioeconomic class, geopolitical orientation, ethnic histories, diet, and religious holidays. Generally, Latinos are presumed to include Cuban Americans, Mexican Americans, Puerto Ricans, and others from the Caribbean and Central and South America.

According to the recent U.S. Census data, 58.5% of the Latino population is Mexican American. Puerto Ricans constitute 9.6%; Central Americans 4.8%; South Americans 3.8%; Cubans 3.5%; and persons from the Dominican Republic 2.2%. The remaining 17.6% are from other Spanish-speaking countries in the Western Hemisphere (U.S. Census Bureau, 2001).

Much of the discussion about Latinos has centered on the possible increase in demand their population growth implies for U.S. social and economic institutions. Though xenophobes in politics and elsewhere have expressed concern about the heavy impact the United States' growing Latino population will have on, for example, public and social services for health care, this increase has simply not happened. In fact, Latinos in the United States tend to underutilize health care services, often to their own detriment.

To improve Latinos' access to health care in the United States, providers must understand the differences in Latino groups. Without a systematic analysis of specific groups, there is an increased chance that data will be misinterpreted, resulting in inadequate and perhaps even contra-indicated health care. Although measurement of health needs by ethnic groups has become moderately more sophisticated in recent years, there is still a clear need to improve data collection methods.

Because the future vitality of many large U.S. cities depends upon the contributions of this growing population of color, policymakers and professionals must rethink the structure and delivery of health care, social services, and public education. This chapter summarizes trends in Latino access to health care, particularly among Mexican Americans, with an eye toward formulating policies that can improve this access.

Background

Historical Problems in Latino Access to Care

Historically, the major limitation to assessing health care for Latinos has been the lack of data differentiated by race and ethnicity. Before 1965, no distinction was made among the non-White ethnic groups in the United States. From the mid 1960s through the 1980s, gross comparisons were made between Caucasian Americans and African Americans; finally, beginning in the mid-1980s, the need to focus on differences between subpopulations was recognized.

Reports on access to care published before the 1980s did not look specifically at Mexican Americans, Cuban Americans, Puerto Ricans, or other Latinos in the United States, so very little is known about how they fared and their status has to be interpreted based on how the data were reported. One of the earliest studies indicated that non-Whites received worse access to medical care than Whites because they were disproportionately poor (Committee on the Costs of Medical Care, 1933). Studies published between the Depression and the late 1970s reported that non-Whites were less likely than Whites to have health insurance, to see a physician, or to have a regular health care provider (Andersen, Lion, & Anderson, 1975; National Center for Health Statistics, 1994, 1998). By the 1970s the data being collected made it possible to compare Latinos in general with other groups, and studies found them less likely than Whites to have health insurance, to see a physician, or to have a regular health care provider and more likely to face language barriers in obtaining care, to perceive they were discriminated against, to wait longer to see a provider, and to delay seeking care (Cornelius, 1993a, 1993b, 2000; Cornelius, Beauregard, & Cohen, 1991; Kasper & Barrish, 1982; National Coalition of Hispanic Health and Human Service Organizations, 1990; Short, Cornelius, & Goldstone, 1990). By the 1980s, it was clear that Latinos fared worse than African Americans and Whites on measures of access to medical care and that Latinos, like African Americans, were more likely to rely on hospital emergency rooms and outpatient departments (Cornelius, 1993a, 1993b).

In the last 20 years, there has also been disproportionate growth in the number of uninsured Latinos in the United States. Between 1977 and 1996, the number of uninsured Latinos increased from 2 to 9 million, while the number of uninsured African Americans increased from 4 to 7 million and the number of uninsured Whites increased from 18 to 24 million (Short, Cornelius, & Goldstone, 1990; Vistnes & Monheit, 2001). However, while it was known that Latinos were encountering barriers to medical care, it was unclear how these barriers were affecting each Latino subpopulation.

In a landmark study, Schur, Bernstein, and Berk (1987) reported that the health needs, problems, and barriers for Cuban Americans are different from those of Puerto Ricans and Mexican Americans. They concluded that there should be different policy options for the Latino subpopulations, because each group has distinct needs.

A Framework for Access to Care

A widely used framework for analyzing access to care was created by Ronald Andersen and Lu Ann Aday (Aday, Begley, Lairson, & Slater, 1998; Andersen, Aday, Lyttle, Cornelius, & Chen, 1987). Access to care for Latinos is influenced by their predisposing characteristics (age, gender, educational status, race, or ethnicity), their ability to pay for medical care (insurance and income), the existence of a regular place to go for medical care, and their need for medical care (as reflected by health status and number of days of work missed due to disability). The ability to obtain care is further influenced by such barriers as discrimination, lack of convenient care, or lack of available providers. Although these factors all affect an individual's ability to obtain health services, the ultimate proof of access to care is whether a person has contacted a provider or been admitted to a hospital. These definitive factors are examined in this chapter to reveal how Latinos are faring on issues of access to care.

Health Care Needs of Latino Subpopulations

Historical trends suggest that there has been growth in the number of uninsured Latinos and that this growth might affect some Latino subpopulations more than others. Mexican Americans fare worse than other Latinos on measures of access to care (health insurance, language barriers, and the use of preventive health care services; see Table 1) (Collins & Hall, 2000). In 1996, more than one third (36.7%) of Mexican American adults aged 18–64, were uninsured, compared to 14.4% of Puerto Ricans and 17.6% of Cuban Americans ($p<.05$) (National Center for Health Statistics, 1998).

Table 1. Percent of Adults Over 18 Who Had Encountered Barriers to Obtaining Health Care by Race/Ethnicity and Gender, 1994

	White	African American	Mexican American	Cuban American	Puerto Rican	Asian American
Males						
Saw a physician	81.1	83.9	71.6	83.3	86.4	73.9
Barriers to care						
• Limited in where they could go for health care	37.0	51.6	55.4	50.0	60.9	39.1
• No access to specialty care	8.1	12.8	20.5	16.7	21.7	11.9
• Language barriers	3.4	5.6	8.5	—	8.7	23.9
• Paperwork	8.2	10.3	11.0	—	13.0	13.3
Females						
Saw a physician	91.8	90.8	83.7	66.7	77.3	78.0
Barriers to care						
• Limited in where they could go for health care	41.5	54.5	52.9	50.0	77.3	43.1
• No access to specialty care	10.0	16.7	18.4	40.0	28.6	28.0
• Language barriers	4.1	4.5	11.5	16.7	4.8	29.4
• Paperwork	7.6	12.2	12.8	16.7	13.6	16.0

Note. —= data not available. Source: Lou Harris and Associates (1994).

Health Care Needs of Latinas

Mexican American (11.5%) and Cuban American women (16.7%) were more than twice as likely as Puerto Rican women (4.5%) to have difficulty obtaining medical care because of language barriers ($p<.05$) (Monheit & Vistnes, 2002). Language barriers were problematic among all people of color in the United States, regardless of gender.

While Cuban American women were more likely than Mexican American women to indicate that they did not have access to specialty care, Table 2 illustrates that they were also more likely to have completed a physical examination within the previous year (Monheit & Vistnes, 2002). Like general data on access to care, data on preventive care for women also support the notion that there are differences among Latinos. As Table 2 shows, in 1996 Puerto Rican women (28.1%) were more likely than Mexican American women (17.2%) to have had a flu shot within the previous year ($p<.05$) (Monheit & Vistnes, 2002).

Current Barriers to Health Care Access for Mexican Americans

It is clear that in spite of Mexican Americans being the largest Latino group in the United States, they are less likely to have health insurance and more likely to face language barriers to care than other Latinos. In addition, Mexican American women are less likely than other Latinos to obtain a mammogram, a breast exam, a physical exam, or a flu shot. These trends are influenced by socioeconomic trends, social policies, and cultural differences between Latino populations based on notions of disease etiology, problem recognition, and primary care.

A major reason why a smaller proportion of Mexican Americans have health insurance than Cuban Americans or Puerto Ricans is that they are more likely to be employed in jobs that do not provide it; Mexican Americans are more likely than other Latinos or Whites to be employed in farming, fishing, or forestry (Knouse, Rosenfield, & Culbertson, 1992), industries in which the average 1999 wage was $7.10 an hour (Bureau of Labor Statistics, 2001a). A smaller proportion of Mexican Americans than Cuban Americans or Whites are employed as managers or professionals (Knouse, Rosenfield, & Culbertson, 1992), whose average 1999 wage was $33.17 per hour (Bureau of Labor Statistics, 2001b). The industries in which Mexican Americans are employed tend to be seasonal, rely on day labor, and pay cash to avoid giving benefits, paying taxes, or checking immigrant documentation. Almost three out of five uninsured adults in the United States (58.0%) are persons who earn less than $10 an hour (Monheit & Vistnes, 2002). By contrast, only 2% of uninsured adults are persons who earn $20 or more per hour (Monheit & Vistnes, 2002).

It should be noted, however, that the type of employment is only one of the factors that influence access to care for Mexican Americans. "Official language" and immigration policies also present barriers to Mexican Americans and other immigrants. One example of an immigration policy that has negative health consequences for Mexican Americans is the inclusion in the Personal Responsibility and Work Opportunity Reconciliation Act of 1996 of a provision that allows states to deny immigrants public health coverage (Kilty & Vidal De Haymes, 2000). This type of policy disproportionately affects Mexican Americans because Mexico is the "leading country of origin for recent immigrants to the U.S., with almost one fourth of all current immigrants coming from that country" (Kilty & Vidal de Haymes, 2000, pp. 3–4).

Of the three major Hispanic groups in the United States (Cubans, Puerto Ricans, and Mexicans), Mexican Americans have been disproportionately affected by formal and informal policies that limit their access to health and social services. To be admitted legally into this country,

Table 2. Percent of Women Over 18 Who Had Selected Preventive Exams in 1996, by Race/ Ethnicity and Poverty Status

	White	African American	Mexican American	Puerto Rican	Cuban American	All Asian/ Pacific Islanders
Overall population						
Population (in thousands)	72,235	11,784	5,326	1,109	393	3,055
Mammogram	65.5	64.8	59.5	72.2	79.9	49.9
Breast exam	75.4	77.4	65.3	78.1	79.5	60.1
Pap smear	90.6	89.9	83.4	89.3	86.8	69.3
Blood pressure	84.9	79.2	95.4	93.3	99.0	72.7
Physical exam	49.5	59.7	41.8	63.5	70.1	44.8
Cholesterol screening	95.7	93.5	95.4	93.3	99.0	90.9
Flu shot	30.8	17.8	17.2	28.1	23.7	29.9
Below poverty						
Population (in thousands)	8,259	3,494	1,598	463	67	506
Mammogram	54.5	57.5	56.0	68.9	72.8	31.9
Breast exam	65.9	70.8	61.4	77.0	74.6	47.0
Pap smear	92.0	88.7	80.5	92.4	75.5	50.7
Blood pressure	83.4	77.8	68.6	83.0	81.0	60.8
Physical exam	45.9	61.5	39.0	66.9	81.1	24.4
Cholesterol screening	96.6	96.3	98.0	98.2	100.0	87.5
Flu shot	26.9	20.8	13.2	23.2	14.2	25.5
100–200% poverty						
Population (in thousands)	12,919	2,988	1,304	195	87	403
Mammogram	51.8	63.3	51.6	61.6	84.5	59.7
Breast exam	66.8	74.4	56.2	77.9	71.1	63.0
Pap smear	88.5	89.0	78.5	75.2	92.4	76.0
Blood pressure	83.3	79.0	67.1	74.9	74.5	82.2
Physical exam	49.8	54.9	33.8	58.3	59.7	65.7
Cholesterol screening	95.0	91.8	93.8	84.1	95.5	97.4
Flu shot	33.5	21.9	15.7	30.3	28.7	22.5
>200% Poverty						
Population (in thousands)	51,057	5,300	2,425	451	239	2,146
Mammogram	70.5	69.5	64.8	81.6	81.2	54.9
Breast exam	79.1	83.4	72.8	82.4	81.5	62.7
Pap smear	91.0	91.3	88.0	92.3	87.9	72.5
Blood pressure	88.5	80.2	80.5	81.7	86.5	73.8
Physical exam	50.0	61.1	48.0	62.4	70.8	45.7
Cholesterol screening	95.8	92.5	94.7	92.3	100.0	90.4
Flu shot	30.7	13.4	20.8	32.2	124.6	32.3

Source: Monheit & Vistnes, 2002.

they need immigration papers and getting them is a lengthy, costly, bureaucratic process. Consequently, many Mexicans and people from Central American countries migrate into the United States by illegally crossing the United States–Mexico border.

Many of these immigrants come to the United States because jobs in their countries are scarce and, for the few jobs that do exist, the compensation is poor. Moreover, these immigrants' labor is much sought after by U.S. employers, who spend little time trying to determine whether a worker is a legal resident of the United States. Yet there is an overwhelming and biased belief on the part of many U.S. citizens, promoted by conservative politicians, that these immigrants are taking advantage of public social services and creating a huge burden for taxpayers. Consequently, many mean-spirited laws have been passed to restrict the access of Mexican and Central American immigrants to such services. Some services are restricted to U.S. citizens alone, excluding even documented residents who are not U.S. citizens; others are available to any documented resident of the United States. While many Mexican Americans are indeed documented residents, they often have family members or friends in the United States who are not. Thus, these legal residents may be reluctant to seek out the services to which they are entitled for fear that the Immigration and Naturalization Service (INS), known as *la migra*, may investigate their social network and apprehend and deport undocumented friends and relatives.

Language policies, like immigration policies, create barriers to care for Latinos. One such policy is legislation that makes English the official and only language of a state, thereby minimizing or eliminating the commitment to bilingual programs and translation services (Kilty & Vidal de Haymes, 2000). There have also been administrative attempts to create language barriers, but these have been more a result of omission than commission. A 1990 study of the Medicaid program in the seven states that include 84.4% of the Latino population (Arizona, California, Florida, Illinois, New Jersey, New York, and Texas) found that one third of the Medicaid sites in these states provided no special services to help staff work with multilingual Latinos and those who speak only Spanish (National Coalition of Hispanic Health and Human Services Organizations, 1990).

While some of the differences in access to medical care have socioeconomic or social policy causes, others may be due to cultural differences between Latino subpopulations. A good example is preventive health care. Just as there were differences between Mexican Americans and other Latino groups in the percent of women receiving mammograms, breast exams, and flu shots, there are other differences in preventive health care.

This information suggests that health programs, interventions, and policies need to reflect the different needs and interests of the heterogeneous Latino populations. While all people of color face barriers to accessing quality health care, Mexican Americans' experiences tend to have common themes: low-skilled, low-wage, no-benefit jobs; policies designed to prevent immigrant access to publicly funded health care; language barriers; and other cultural impediments.

Removing Barriers to Health Care Access for Mexican Americans

There is no single, simple solution to the problem of Mexican American access to health care. Although a number of policies would improve such access, legislation alone will not resolve the problem. Community action and vigorous, targeted outreach designed to provide culturally competent services that take into account language and cultural norms are also needed. Without them, the outcome of policy activities will be at best insufficient and at worst destructive.

The United States needs a new paradigm for service delivery that considers the cultural nuances of each population group to be served. Legislators, health professionals, and social workers that serve subpopulations must recognize that models of service delivery must be tailored to each specific ethnic group. Programs designed to serve people of color in general will not be effective. The same is true of heterogeneous groups like Latinos; a program designed to serve Cuban Americans may not be effective for Puerto Ricans, Mexican Americans, or Central Americans. The essence of culturally competent programs is finding the natural cultural fit for service delivery. One size does not fit all.

Three factors identified in the previous section perpetuate health access barriers for Mexican Americans: the nature of the industries in which many Mexican Americans are employed, language and cultural barriers, and public policies designed to discourage immigrants from obtaining services. This section focuses on policy approaches and social interventions that may reduce the negative effects of these factors.

Employment Solutions

Close to 70% of health insurance in the United States is employment based (Caroll, 2001). Employed persons who are uninsured typically labor for little pay in positions that require few skills. The companies for which they work tend to be small and unable to afford insurance benefits; some companies, on the other hand, avoid paying benefits by limiting the number of hours employees can work or by paying cash to keep workers off the books, thus avoiding tax reporting and document reviews. Immigrants are also more likely than others to be paid for their work in cash. As part of the cash economy, they not only have no benefits but they are also ineligible to receive publicly funded support (Kilty & Vidal de Haymes, 2000).

This problem spans several domains: commerce, immigration, public assistance, and health care. Any new legislative action needs to have as its premise the right to health care for all members of society. Health care viewed as a right rather than a privilege should be patterned after the World Health Organization's assertion that the purpose of health systems is "to improve health goodness and fairness" (Aguirre-Molina, Falcon, & Molina, 2001, p. 463). In the United States, there are several creative ways that health support might be made available to those who work in low-wage, unskilled positions or for small businesses. For example, legislation could make it mandatory for all employers to offer health insurance to their workers. If the employer is too small or otherwise unable to afford the benefits, the government could subsidize health care directly to the employer through tax credits, grants, or other financial incentives.

Another approach would be to relax the Personal Responsibility and Work Opportunity Reconciliation Act regulations that restrict aid to immigrants. Whether immigrants are documented or not, they clearly play a very important role in the U.S. economy. Without hardworking Mexican Americans laboring in the fields; making beds in hotels; preparing and serving meals in restaurants; cleaning floors and emptying trash cans; building highways, houses, and apartment, office, and manufacturing buildings; and caring for the private and public landscape, the economy of this country would collapse. For this back-breaking work, these immigrants deserve more than laws designed to make their lives even more miserable.

Specific health care programs targeted to meeting the endemic needs of Mexican Americans should also be considered. This population suffers disproportionately, for example, from diabetes and cardiovascular diseases. Primary prevention programs in the form of screening and early detection, without regard for health insurance, could help increase these individuals' health and longevity. The ultimate social policy solution is the passage of a universal health care bill that provides for medical care at low or no cost.

Culturally Competent Service Solutions

Cultural competence goes beyond mere awareness and sensitivity and is a process of personal reflection on one's own culture that leads to understanding and valuing differences in other cultures. This reflection ultimately results in cultural interaction that responds to this analysis and a new awareness. Cultural competence can apply to many types of interactions, including language, the value placed on relationships, arranging appointments, time management, and privacy policies. The U.S. Office of Minority Health initiated standards for culturally and linguistically appropriate services to create a framework for culturally competent services by better preparing health care personnel to work effectively with diverse populations. Its work has resulted in comprehensive standards and guidelines for a culturally and linguistically competent workforce (Office of Minority Health, 2002).

Collins and Hall (2000) have specified cultural competence at three levels for health care organizations: (1) ensuring there is a racial and ethnic mix throughout the health care workforce; (2) establishing a minimum standard for cultural competence in the workforce and supporting it with training programs; and (3) collecting data on morbidity and health outcomes for specific populations.

Language is a common barrier for Mexican Americans in gaining access to health care but it need not be the central issue if there are structures in place (e.g., translators) to compensate for linguistic differences between health care provider and patient (Falcon, Aguirre-Molina, & Molina, 2001). A better solution is access to health care professionals who reflect the racial and ethnic background of the patient. When there is racial and ethnic similarity between Latinos and health care professionals, patient satisfaction and self-rated quality of service are higher (Carrillo et al., 2001). When language is a barrier and provider and patient must communicate without a translator, the number of patient misunderstandings and misinterpretations are higher and patient satisfaction and compliance are lower (Carrillo et al., 2001).

How appointments are arranged and how much time health care providers spend with their patients is also very important. Mexican American patients prefer face-to-face encounters; they need to develop a trusting relationship with their provider, which demands more from the attending physician than a passing diagnosis. Guendelman and Wagner (2000) report that less acculturated Mexican Americans interpret health symptoms differently from those in an acculturated sample. This finding suggests that health care facilities need to understand the sociocultural context of symptoms, how health care is promoted in the community, and the roles of family and other forms of support. Primary prevention programs that fail to offer literature in Spanish or to take into account the educational level of the reader and the cultural nuances of the subject matter are not likely to succeed.

The whole issue of cultural relevance and competence really depends on awareness and thinking outside of one's cultural assumptions. Everyone approaches life with certain assumptions but this perspective is not ubiquitous across cultures and populations. Without conscious awareness, therefore, individuals are unlikely to think beyond their cultural orientation. For a health care organization, employing people from diverse backgrounds to provide insight from the perspective of the "other" is critical. Carrillo and colleagues (2001) report that racial and ethnic diversity in the leadership and the workforce of health care delivery systems is well correlated with quality care for diverse populations. Moreover, Latinos in leadership positions are more likely to recruit and hire other qualified Latino health care professionals and implement policies and procedures that are culturally appropriate.

Obtaining improved data on diversity experiences (Collins & Hall, 2000) would further reduce the cultural distance between patients and health care professionals. It would also go a long way toward increasing Latino patients' confidence and trust in health professionals, which would inevitably have a positive effect on their access to care.

Legislative Solutions

As already noted, several federal and state laws passed within the last decade have been designed to prevent governmental support of health and welfare services to immigrants. For example, immigration law prohibits the use of Medicaid funds to provide services to undocumented workers, although states can use their funds to test for, immunize against, and treat communicable diseases. Proposition 187, passed in 1994 in California, prohibits the state from using any of its funds to provide services to undocumented immigrants.

The federal Balanced Budget Act of 1996 went one step further, reducing the budget allocation for welfare services like food stamps, disability insurance, and other forms of critical assistance even to documented immigrants (Guendelman & Wagner, 2000). Further, the INS monitors the status of all immigrants receiving services and can use its investigations against undocumented immigrants treated in medical facilities. This type of INS intimidation reverberates throughout the Latino community and it is an obstacle to health care access for immigrants in general.

On October 27, 2000, Representative Ciro Rodriguez (D-TX) introduced a bill to help overcome these barriers. The Hispanic Health Act of 2000 (H.R. 5595) primarily targets specific diseases for which Latinos are particularly at risk, with a focus on diabetes, HIV/AIDS, and mental health. The bill "requires the Secretary of Health and Human Services to annually provide a report to Congress on programs carried out through the Public Health Service for improving the health status of Hispanics regarding diabetes, HIV infection, AIDS, substance abuse, and mental health" (Hispanic Health Act, H.R. 5595, 2000, p. 2), but it also requires the federal government to take the following steps:

- Create and implement a program for training bilingual health professionals;
- Make grants available to certain health professional schools to recruit and enroll Latinos;
- Design a curriculum for cultural competence that would include: "(1) educational materials on providing health services in a culturally competent manner; (2) establishing a Center for Linguistic and Cultural Competence in health care; and (3) implementing cultural competence demonstration projects at two hospitals" (Hispanic Health Act, H.R. 5595, 2000, p. 2);
- Amend the Public Health Service Act to collect and maintain health care data by race and ethnicity; and
- Craft outcome measures "to evaluate, by race and ethnicity, the performance of health care programs and projects to individuals under Medicare and Medicaid programs" (Hispanic Health Act, H.R. 5595, 2000, p. 2).

This bill addresses many of the previously mentioned barriers to access. For example, it identifies specific diseases for which Latinos are most vulnerable and seeks to establish programs to address them through education, primary prevention, and follow-up care. It also addresses cultural barriers by emphasizing cultural competency and would increase the number of providers available to deliver services to Latinos by encouraging recruitment and training of Latino health care professionals to work where there are significant Latino populations. Another very important provision is the bill's directive to collect data that document services delivered to Latinos. Without this meaningful data, it is impossible to track epidemiological trends among Latinos. This bill was referred to the Subcommittee on Health on November 2, 2000, with no further action.

A bill introduced in the House of Representatives in 2001 by Representative Gene Green (D-TX) would amend the Personal Responsibility and Work Opportunity Reconciliation Act of 1996 to give states and localities discretion to provide primary and preventive care to all individuals, documented or not (H.R. 2635). The bill does not require states or localities to provide services; it merely gives them the option. If it passes, however, the bill could not only effectively end discriminatory practices but would remove the INS from its role in monitoring medical services. Removing INS intimidation would dismantle one important barrier to health care access for both documented and undocumented immigrants.

The Hill-Burton Act, included as part of the Community Service Assurance under Title VI of the Public Health Service Act, "authorizes assistance to public and other nonprofit medical facilities" (Office for Civil Rights, 2000). It prohibits any type of discrimination by recipients on the basis of race, color, national origin, creed, or any other grounds unrelated to the individual need for service. This has several implications for Mexican Americans and others seeking assistance:

1. All persons residing in a facility service area have the right to medical treatment without regard for their race, color, national origin, or creed.
2. A facility receiving funds under the Hill-Burton Act must post notices in English and Spanish informing the public of its community service obligations.
3. These facilities may not deny emergency services to any person residing in their service areas on the grounds that the person is unable to pay for those services.
4. A Hill-Burton facility may not adopt patient admissions policies that have the effect of excluding persons on grounds of race, color, national origin, creed or for any other reason unrelated to the patient's need for the service or its availability (Office of Civil Rights, 2000).

Presently in committee in the House of Representatives is a bill, H.R. 663, that would establish a National Center for Social Work Research (National Center for Social Work Research Act, H.R. 663, 2001). Former Representative Asa Hutchinson (R-AR) sponsored the House version (National Center for Social Work Research Act, H.R. 663, 2001) and Senator Daniel K. Inouye (D-HI) sponsored the Senate version (National Center for Social Work Research Act, S. 70, 2001). The House bill was referred to the Subcommittee on Health on March 14, 2001, and the Senate version was referred to the Committee on Health, Education, Labor, and Pensions on January 22, 2001. Neither version has had any further action. The proposed legislation would appropriate money to support social work research. Latinos and the poor and underserved could benefit in many different ways from the passage of this legislation because funding would be directed to the empirical examination of best practices for increasing access to services for the underserved (S. Hoechstetter, personal communication, August 27, 2001). Social workers perform many important functions in health arenas. In rural areas, they are often the primary mental health practitioners, and in hospital and outpatient settings they provide important information, especially for the poor; they help patients received preventive care; they counsel patients facing traumatic health problems; they support families of stricken relatives; and they are often the first to respond to medical crises and disaster situations. The social work research bill could thus work to improve access to care for Latinos, because it would help social workers understand how to better promote medical services for them. Discussions of this bill should emphasize how it can support people of color and not just fund research conducted by and with White, non-Hispanic people.

A variety of policy options have been offered to improve the plight of Latinos in general and Mexican Americans in particular. Short of universal health insurance, which would be the best solution, we stress the importance of mandating health insurance, whether subsidized or not, for all who are employed. A second option is to clarify the true value of immigrant labor. There is more dependence on immigrant labor than is well understood and hostile immigrant policies thus only hurt the United States in the long run. A third option is to increase programmatic dollars to decrease the health disparities between Latinos and other ethnic groups in the United States. A fourth option is to increase the number of bilingual, bicultural health professionals, especially in communities with significant Latino populations.

Political and Community Action

Because legislative authorization of funds to build and support community initiatives are essential to removing existing barriers to health care access for Mexican Americans, one of the most important actions the Latino community can take is to organize politically to advocate for its health care agenda, which should include advocacy for more responsive, equitable, and accessible health care and for holding health care organizations and the government accountable for their policies, regulations, and services to the Latino community. Such an agenda should also insist upon the creation of an educational infrastructure to provide cultural competence training for health care providers and a new generation of Latino providers, administrators, and educators.

Communities should also support providers of the traditional health care safety net, such as public hospitals and community health centers (Collins & Hall, 2000). Historically, these facilities have served the indigent when other facilities have catered only to the insured. Medicaid has moved to a managed care model and there is now more competition from other hospitals (Collins & Hall, 2000). As these facilities have lost revenue, they have had to cut back on services and personnel, decreasing their ability to serve non-revenue-producing patients. These individuals, disproportionately people of color, then go unserved.

Another way to reduce barriers to access while promoting primary prevention and health education is to identify key people in the Latino community and the networks they affect. Using respected leaders to act as liaisons between the community and health care facilities can serve an important and culturally competent health educative and outreach function. Further, aggressive outreach should consider ways for the health care system to connect with nontraditional medical practitioners, such as those practicing with herbs, prayers, and incantations (*curanderos* or *curanderas*). Less acculturated Latinos may be more inclined to access such practitioners as a preventive or primary source of care. *Curanderas* and *curanderos* tend to have a trusted reputation in the community, can relate to their clients linguistically and culturally, and do not charge, ask probing questions, or require complicated procedures for obtaining service. Most responsible folk practitioners are also aware of the limits of their craft; they know when to suggest that their clients seek more formal medical service. Whether or not this advice is always taken, incorporating these healers into the primary prevention programs of health care facilities could be valuable in identifying individual and community needs, educating clients, and providing specific referrals.

Such aggressive outreach projects could also be extended to Mexican border towns. Pharmacists and dentists in Mexico play very essential roles in the health care of Mexican Americans. They are popular because of their accessibility, non-bureaucratic service, low costs, and cultural compatibility, and Mexican Americans are known to travel back across the border to obtain their services. A creative, aggressive health care outreach program could establish relationships with these facilities in Mexico as a necessary linkage between primary prevention, education, and advanced care.

Building, understanding, and utilizing natural supports in the Latino community is an important variable in reducing barriers to health care access. Such capacity building requires cultural competence, creativity, and desire for change on the part of both the United States in general and the Latino community.

Conclusion

Does population growth lead to a better future for Latinos? Unfortunately, the answer is not yet. Although the number of Latinos in the United States is increasing disproportionately compared to other racial and ethnic groups, they still encounter significant barriers to health care. The reasons are multifaceted and solutions will differ for each ethnic group within the Latino population. This chapter suggests a series of recommendations that would make the health care system more equitable for Latinos, particularly Mexican Americans. Much depends, however, on the political will not only of federal and state legislators, but also of Latino communities themselves.

References

Aday, L. A., Begley, C. E., Lairson, D. R., & Slater, C. H. (1998). *Evaluating the heath care system: Effectiveness, efficiency and equity.* Chicago: Health Administration Press.

Aguirre-Molina, M., Falcon, A., & Molina, C. W. (2001). Latino health policy: A look to the future. In M. Aguirre-Molina, C. W. Molina, & R. E. Zambrana (Eds.), *Health issues in the Latino community* (pp. 461-467). San Francisco: Jossey-Bass.

Andersen, R. M., Aday, L. A., Lyttle, C. S., Cornelius, L. J., & Chen, M. S. (1987). *Ambulatory care and insurance coverage in an era of constraint.* Chicago: Pluribus Press.

Andersen, R. M., Lion, J., & Anderson, O. W. (1975). *Two decades of health services: Trends in use and expenditures.* Cambridge, MA: Balinger.

Bureau of Labor Statistics. (2001a). *National industry-specific occupational employment and wage estimates SIC 07—agricultural services.* Retrieved January 26, 2004, from http://stats.bls.gov/oes/2001/oesi2_07.htm#b45-0000

Bureau of Labor Statistics. (2001b). *National industry-specific occupational employment and wage estimates SIC 899—services not elsewhere classified (management occupations).* Retrieved January 26, 2004, from http://stats.bls.gov/oes/2001/oesi3_899.htm

Caroll, W. (2001). The health insurance status of U.S. workers. Retrieved January 24, 2004, from http://www.meps.ahrq.gov/papers/st11/stat11.pdf

Carrillo, J. Trevino, F., Betancourt, J., & Coustasse, A. (2001). Latino access to health care: The role of insurance, managed care, and institutional barriers. In M. Aguirre-Molina, C. W. Molina, & R. E. Zambrana (Eds.), *Health issues in the Latino community* (pp. 55-74). San Francisco: Jossey-Bass.

Collins, K., & Hall, A. (2000). A look to the future. In C. Hogue, M. Hargraves, & K. Collins (Eds.), *Minority health in America: Findings and policy implications from the Commonwealth Fund minority health survey* (pp. 274-292). Baltimore, MD: Johns Hopkins University Press.

Committee on the Costs of Medical Care. (1933). *Medical care for the American people: Final report on the Committee on the Costs of Medical Care.* Chicago: University of Chicago Press.

Cornelius, L. J. (1993a). Ethnic minorities and access to medical care: Where do they stand? *Journal of the Association of Academic Minority Physicians, 4*(1),16-25.

Cornelius, L. J. (1993b). Barriers to medical care for White, Black, and Hispanic American children. *Journal of the National Medical Association, 85,* 281-288.

Cornelius, L. J. (2000). Financial barriers to health care for Latinos: Poverty and beyond. *Journal of Poverty, 4*(1/2), 65–83.

Cornelius, L. J., Beauregard, K., & Cohen J. (1991). *Usual sources of medical care and their characteristics* (DHHS Publication No. PHS 91-0042). Washington, DC: U.S. Government Printing Office.

Falcon, A., Aguirre-Molina, M., & Molina, C. (2001). Latino health policy: Beyond demographic determinism. In M. Aguirre-Molina, C. W. Molina, & R. E. Zambrana (Eds.), *Health issues in the Latino community* (pp. 3–22). San Francisco: Jossey-Bass.

Guendelman, S., & Wagner, T. (2000). Hispanics' experience within the health care system: Access, utilization, and satisfaction. In C. Hogue, M. Hargraves, & K. Collins. (Eds.), *Minority health in America: Findings and policy implications from the Commonwealth Fund minority health survey* (pp. 19–46). Baltimore, MD: Johns Hopkins University Press.

Hispanic Health Act of 2000, H.R. 5595, 106th Cong. (2000). Retrieved July 19, 2002, from http://thomas.loc.gov/cgi-bin/t2GPO/http://frwebgate.access.gpo.gov/cgi-bin/getdoc.cgi?dbname=106_cong_bills&docid=f:h5595ih.txt.pdf

H.R. 2635, 107th Cong. (2001). Retrieved July 19, 2002, from http://thomas.loc.gov/cgi-bin/t2GPO/http://frwebgate.access.gpo.gov/cgi-bin/getdoc.cgi?dbname=107_cong_bills&docid=f:h2635ih.txt.pdf

Kasper, J. A., & Barrish, G. (1982). *Usual sources of medical care and their characteristics* (DHHS Publication No. PHS 82-3324). Washington, DC: Government Printing Office.

Kilty, K. M., & Vidal de Haymes, M. (2000). Racism, nativism, and exclusion: Public policy, immigration and the Latino experience in the United States. In M. Vidal de Haymes, K. M. Kilty, & E. A. Seigal (Eds.), *Latino poverty in the new century: Inequalities challenges and barriers* (pp. 1–26). Binghamton, NY: Haworth Press.

Knouse, S. B., Rosenfield P., & Culbertson, A. L. (Eds.). (1992). *Hispanics in the workplace.* Newbury Park, CA: Sage.

Lou Harris and Associates. (1994). Health care services and minority groups: A comparative survey of Whites, African Americans, Hispanics, and Asian Americans. New York: Author.

Monheit, A. C., & Vistnes, J. (2002, January). *Research findings #2: Health insurance status of workers and their families: 1996.* Rockville, MD: Agency for Healthcare Research and Quality. Retrieved January 26, 2004, from http://www.meps.ahrq.gov/papers/rf2_97-0065/rf2.htm

National Center for Health Statistics. (1994). *Health United States, 1994.* Hyattsville, MD: Author.

National Center for Health Statistics. (1998). *Health United States, 1998.* Hyattsville, MD: Author.

National Center for Social Work Research Act of 2001, H.R. 663, 107th Cong. (2001). Retrieved July 19, 2002, from http://thomas.loc.gov/cgi-bin/t2GPO/http://frwebgate.access.gpo.gov/cgi-bin/getdoc.cgi?dbname=107_cong_bills&docid=f:h663ih.txt.pdf

National Center for Social Work Research Act of 2001, S. 70, 107th Cong. (2001). Retrieved July 19, 2002, from http://frwebgate.access.gpo.gov/cgi-bin/useftp.cgi?IPaddress=162.140.64.88&filename=s70is.pdf&directory=/disk2/wais/data/107_cong_bills

National Coalition of Hispanic Health and Human Services Organizations. (1990). *And access for all: Medicaid and Hispanics.* Washington, DC: Author.

Office for Civil Rights. (2000). *Fact sheet: Your rights under the community service assurance provision of the Hill-Burton Act.* Rockville, MD: U.S. Department of Health and Human Services. Retrieved January 26, 2004, from http://www.hhs.gov/ocr/hburton.html

Office of Minority Health. (2002). Final national standards on culturally and linguistically appropriate services in health care published. Retrieved June 26, 2002, from http://www.omhrc.gov/OMH/Programs/2pgprograms/cultural4.htm

Schur, C. L., Bernstein, A. B., & Berk, M. L. (1987). The importance of distinguishing Hispanic populations in the use of medical care. *Medical Care, 25,* 627–641.

Short, P. F., Cornelius, L. J., & Goldstone, D. G. (1990). Health insurance of minorities in the United States. *Journal of Health Care for the Poor and Underserved, 1,* 9–24.

U.S. Census Bureau. (2001). *The Hispanic population: Census 2000 brief.* Suitland, MD: U.S. Census Bureau. Retrieved January 26, 2004, from http://www.census.gov/prod/2001pubs/c2kbr01-3.pdf

Vistnes, J., & Monheit, A. C. (2001, April). *Health insurance coverage in America—1996* (AHCPR Publication No. 98-0031). Rockville, MD: Agency for Healthcare Research and Quality. Retrieved January 26, 2004, from http://www.meps.ahrq.gov/papers/hl4_98-0031/hl4.htm

Chapter Ten

Pacific Islanders and the Juvenile Justice System

Halaevalu Ofahengaue-Vakalahi and Meripa T. Godinet

Pacific Islander Americans are one of the fastest growing ethnic communities in the United States. According to the 2000 Census, Pacific Islanders constitute about 0.3% of the total U.S. population (874,414 individuals), a growth of approximately 140% since 1990 (U.S. Census Bureau, 2000). By 2010, the projected combined population of Asian Americans and Pacific Islanders in the United States will be approximately 16 million (5%); and by 2050 that figure will increase to approximately 38 million (9%). Although this growth offers tremendous opportunities for progress and contributions to society, it also presents challenges. One of the greatest challenges is building a juvenile justice system that is culturally competent in responding to Pacific Islanders in relation to issues such as crime and delinquency (Bilchik, 1998; Devore & Schlesinger, 1999; Green, 1999). At the same time, this challenge presents new opportunities to build collaborative partnerships between professionals in the juvenile justice system and Pacific Islander communities. As a profession that promotes cultural competency, self-determination, and social and economic justice, social workers, with their expertise in policy, administration, practice, and research, are needed in the juvenile justice system to work collaboratively with Pacific Islander communities in advocating for a juvenile justice system that is culturally competent, particularly in terms of policies that affect Pacific Islander youth (Vakalahi, Godinet, & Fong, in press).

Juvenile delinquency is a growing problem in the United States. With the exception of African American and non-white Hispanic youth, information about various ethnic groups with high rates of juvenile crime is surprisingly sparse (Godinet, 1998). This lack of information trivializes the significance of juvenile delinquency among Pacific Islanders and hinders the development of culturally sensitive juvenile justice policies, programs, and research that appropriately and effectively responds to the needs of this population. Indeed, existing policies reflect systemic privileges for certain groups and individuals, which often exclude Pacific Islanders (i.e., Samoan, Tongan, Kanaka Maoli, Chamorro, Papua New Guinean).

Nonetheless, the limited information that does exist regarding delinquency among Pacific Islanders suggests that delinquency is a major problem. A report by the Center for Youth Research indicated that Samoan and Hawaiian youths in Hawaii were greatly overrepresented in secured detention facilities, family court, secured confinement facilities, arrests, and referrals for family court relative to their proportion in the general population. For example, Hawaiians represent 31% of the juvenile population in the state of Hawaii but account for 35% of juvenile arrests and 53% of juveniles in secure facilities. Samoan juveniles represent the greatest disproportionality in secure facilities compared to any other group (Kassebaum et al., 1995). Likewise, studies on people of color with risk factors similar to Pacific Islander groups indicate that they are arrested, charged, and convicted in higher percentages than Caucasian youth; they also serve longer prison sentences than Caucasians despite similarities in crimes, criminal histories, and socioeconomic backgrounds (Medley, 1998; Sickmund, 1997; Snyder, 1997).

The literature clearly demonstrates that youth of color are politically disadvantaged, receive more severe sentences, and have higher rates of incarceration and probation than White youth (Allen-Hagen, 1991; Fagan, Slaughter, & Hartstone, 1987; McCabe et al., 1999). Furthermore, the literature confirms that youth of color are at greater risk for juvenile crime and delinquency because of contributing factors such as low economic status, educational failure, racism, institutional discrimination, and lack of political power (Bridges, Conley, Engen, & Price-Spratlen, 1995; Hawkins & Catalano, 1992; Medley, 1998; Pope & Feyerherm, 1993).

This chapter attempts to discuss what is currently known about Pacific Islander Americans and the juvenile justice system. The discussion analyzes the sociocultural context, challenges of existing paradigms, and relevant policies and programs for Pacific Islander juveniles. Key issues are identified as implications for policy, practice, and research. Information provided in this chapter, although limited, is offered to assist juvenile justice personnel in designing systems and services that will better meet the needs of Pacific Islander American communities.

Sociocultural Context

For decades, Asian and Pacific Islanders were aggregated in government documents, social services, juvenile justice systems, educational systems, and other sectors in American society. The political, ideological, and demographic aggregation of these two distinct ethnic and racial groups seems to have had some positive outcomes, such as Asians being labeled "model minorities"—leading to social, economic, and educational privileges and greater access to more resources than other ethnic groups. Unfortunately, the aggregation presented a misleading portrait of Pacific Islanders, thus contributing to not meeting their needs appropriately (Vakalahi, Godinet, & Fong, in press). For instance, the title of "model minority" given to Asian Americans and Pacific Islanders has actually been in reference to Asians only, whereas Pacific Islanders have often been perceived by many people in the general population as lazy, unmotivated, and violent (McDermott, Tseng, & Maretzki, 1980). Furthermore, according to the U.S. Census Bureau (2000), Asian Americans and Pacific Islanders as an aggregated group are the highest educated ethnic and racial group with the highest median of household income in the United States. However, Asian and Pacific Islanders have higher rates of poverty for all ages, are underemployed (earning less than non-Hispanic Whites), and because of larger family size (multiple generations living in one residence), they have lower income per household member (Mokuau, 1995; U.S. Census Bureau, 2000). Thus, socioeconomic status is one of the most misunderstood factors for Asians and Pacific Islanders because of its mismatch with high educational achievements (Chow, 2001). Moreover, despite the high educational achievement of the Asian group, Pacific Islanders alone generate lower numbers in educational achievement compared to Asians and the larger U.S. population (Mokuau, 1995). For example, Tongans had the lowest number of high school diplomas earned (about 64%) compared to Hawaiians (80%). Tongans also had the lowest number of bachelor's degrees earned at 6% compared to 58% for Asian Indians (U.S.

Census Bureau, 1999). Additionally, statistics of the Hawaii school system indicated that Samoan women have the lowest high school completion rate of all ethnic groups in the study. Similarly, the high school completion rate for Samoan men is the second lowest, surpassed only by the rate for Filipino men (Franco, 1991). Nationally, Pacific Islander Americans alone are overrepresented in crime, poverty, and health problems (Mokuau, 1998; Zane, Takeuchi, & Young, 1994). Certainly, these factors contribute to the involvement (e.g., arrest, detention, court appearance, secure facility commitment) of Pacific Islanders in the juvenile justice system. As noted, this aggregate data has hindered the development of culturally competent policies and programs that respond to the needs of Pacific Islanders who live and practice in diverse cultures of origin combined with their American culture (Vakalahi, Godinet, & Fong, in press).

The 2000 Census was the first time Pacific Islander Americans were recognized on Census documents as a separate group. The political implications of this course of action are yet to be realized. According to the 2000 Census, Pacific Islanders were the smallest ethnic or racial group in the United States. Because of its relative size, any misreporting could have a large effect on the Pacific Islander population. Pacific Islanders belong to three major groups, including Polynesians (e.g., Native Hawaiian, Samoan, Tongan, Tahitian, Maori, Fijian, Tokelauan), Micronesians (e.g., Chamorro or Guamanian, Mariana Islander, Saipanese, Palauan, Carolinian, Kosraean, Pohnpeian, Chuukese, Yapese, Marshallese, I-Kiribati), and Melanesians (e.g., Papua New Guinean, Solomon Islander, Ni-Vanuatu). In terms of age, Pacific Islanders are a fairly young population, with the largest age group between 25 and 44 years. In terms of gender, Pacific Islanders are about proportional in numbers of men and women. The largest Pacific Islander group in the United States is Native Hawaiian, followed by Samoan and Chamorro. Three-fourths of the total number of Pacific Islanders live in the West, mainly in Hawaii and California. Other locations with a fair number of Pacific Islanders include the South, Midwest, Northeast, and Puerto Rico (Bureau of the Census, 2000).

Colonization and Immigration

The story of Pacific Islander Americans is one of dealing with enormous historical, cultural, political, and socioeconomic diversity that has led to challenges in appropriately meeting the needs of children and families involved in the juvenile justice system (Bilchik, 1998; Conley, 1994). The present status of Pacific Islanders and their mistrust of foreign systems is linked to their historical and cultural experiences of colonization, immigration, oppression, marginalization, and racial discrimination. For example, early immigrants to Pacific Island nations brought diseases and foreign practices that destroyed many native Pacific Islander populations. Likewise, Pacific Islanders who migrated to the United States experience the consequences of language barriers, poor health, lack of job skills leading to lower paying jobs, lack of education, and involvement in criminal activities as a form of survival. Discrimination from government entities and White American communities is faced by every new generation of Pacific Islander immigrants (Millett & Orosz, 2001). Today at 140,652 individuals, Kanaka Maoli are overrepresented in prison populations and among public assistance recipients (Furuto, San Nicolas, Kim, & Fiaui, 2001; Office of Hawaiian Affairs, 1998; U.S. Census Bureau, 2000). Similarly, Samoans are overrepresented in prison, juvenile arrests, family violence incidences, family court cases, and public housing. In the state of Hawaii, Samoan high school students have the second highest rate of suspension of all ethnic groups. Also, the unemployment rate among Samoans is nearly as high as 80%. In the workforce, they are underrepresented in professional jobs and in universities. Furthermore, in-migration has contributed to oppression, exploitation, and the disintegration of cultural identity of Chamorro (Furuto et al., 2001). Evidently, diversity in historical, migratory, and sociopolitical experiences contributes to differences in socioeconomic status and educational achievement as sources of risk for involvement in juvenile crime and delinquency (Vakalahi, Godinet, & Fong, in press).

Although the literature is limited, for immigrants and people of color who still maintain their culture practices, acculturation issues become very important in their adjustment to the United States. Studies of delinquency have indicated the importance of including acculturation in research on delinquency among immigrants of color and refugees (Berry, 1997; Fridrich & Flannery, 1995). Sommers, Fagan, and Baskin (1993) report that acculturation is positively correlated with participation in interpersonal violence and theft and lower acculturation is associated with drug use (Vega, Gil, Warheit, Zimmerman, & Apospori, 1993). As defined by Berry (1997), acculturative stress is caused by the accommodations that must be negotiated by the demands of the host culture and those of the culture of origin. Such stress is marked by a reduction of the physical and mental health status of individuals or groups undergoing acculturation (Nwadiora & McAdoo, 1996). Thus, when an adolescent experiences significant levels of acculturative stress as a result of acculturation to the host culture, the adolescent may steer away from the host norms and values. An adolescent can also be in a state of confusion when he or she can't come to terms with or understand the acculturation process. Acculturative stress is therefore an important construct when examining the development and adjustment of adolescents from families of first- or second-generations immigrants. Equally important when studying first- or second-generation immigrant youth are the effects of transcultural adaptation. Because many of these immigrants and their children are still in the process of adjusting to their new environment, emotional and physical stress may hinder healthy development among some adolescents (Vakalahi, Godinet, & Fong, in press).

Cultural Strengths and Protective Factors

Despite the many challenges faced by Pacific Islander Americans, there are strengths in the values and practices of the culture of origin that may serve as a guide for policy decisions and protective factors for involvement in the juvenile justice system. The diversity among Pacific Islanders makes it difficult to identify a set of cultural practices that is adhered to by the entire population. However, common themes emerge from values of all Pacific Islander cultures that emphasize harmony in family relationships, love for children, respect for the elderly, and communal responsibility (Chow, 2001). For instance, in Pacific Islander culture, family is first and the center of all relationships. In the Chamorro family or *y familia*, love and support are not demanded but are simply there. The family is the agent of socialization where individuals learn to trust, respect, and be responsible for each other. Because of such a heavy responsibility, family members do their best to nurture, honor, respect, collaborate with, and sacrifice for the family. Similarly, in the Samoan culture, the unit of organization is the extended family or *aiga*, consisting of several nuclear families related by blood, marriage, or adoption and headed by a chief or *matai*. The *matai* of various *aiga* make up the council or *fono* that governs the family community (Furuto et al., 2001; McDermott, Tseng, & Maretzki, 1980). As a result of a sometime hostile U.S. environment, the extended family and informal networking have become the primary support systems for new Pacific Islander immigrants (Millett & Orosz, 2001). Clearly, interdependency and harmony in relationships in families and communities rather than individual independence is the ultimate achievement in Pacific Islander cultures (Furuto et al., 2001). In addition, Pacific Islander families have great love for children. In fact, Pacific Islanders believe that a house without children is a house without life. All children are embraced, paid attention to, and are where the first human bonds are developed. In Samoan culture, children are taught from childhood to respect the elderly and older siblings are held responsible for their younger siblings (McDermott, Tseng, & Maretzki, 1980).

Certainly the range of challenges faced by Pacific Islander Americans in relation to cultural transitions and demographic changes have affected their experiences with the juvenile justice system (Bridges & Steen, 1998; Devine, Coolbaugh, & Jenkins, 1998; Hsia & Hamparian, 1998). Unfortunately, the juvenile justice system has not recognized and maximized the use of Pacific Islander cultural strengths to meet their needs, particularly in terms of policies that affect Pacific Islanders.

Challenges of Existing Paradigms

Historically in the delinquency literature, theories attempting to explain delinquency have been very limited in their approaches. As a result, policies have often been insufficient in meeting the needs of juveniles involved in crime and delinquency, particularly those from disenfranchised groups such as youth of color and impoverished youth. The major drawback of these theories is their inability to integrate varying sources of influence on delinquency. For example, some theories examine structural challenges that influence the potential for involvement in delinquent activities (Figueira-McDonough, 1992; Merton, 1938), whereas others focus on intermediate-level factors such as family and community (Hirschi, 1969), and still others focus on individual psychological factors such as locus of control. When theoretical explanations focus on one particular set of factors, other factors that may be essential to an adequate analytical perspective are often ignored (Giddens, 1991). Such limitations have hindered the development of culturally relevant policies for people of color, particularly Pacific Islanders. Over the years, the focus on theoretical explanations of delinquency has changed to become more integrative in nature as a way to account for varying influences on delinquency. This trend reflects the notion that delinquency is influenced by multiple factors, therefore requiring a multifaceted approach to policies that direct prevention and intervention.

Theories that have been widely used to guide policy making, such as social control (Hirschi, 1969) and social learning theories (Bandura, 1977), are useful in explaining the influence of systems on individuals, particularly youth. Social control theory and social learning theory are eclectic in the sense that social systems (e.g., family, school, and community) central to the adolescent can be tested to determine their effects in the deterrence of deviancy. The appeal of social control theory in explaining delinquency among Pacific Islander adolescents is its focus on bonding. Traditional culture is a crucial part of the lives of Pacific Islander emigrants, regardless of where they settle. Although modernization and acculturation processes have altered Pacific Islander customs to accommodate their new environments, basic customs, and social structures still constitute important elements of life among Pacific Islander emigrants (Fitzgerald & Howard, 1990; Hanna & Fitzgerald, 1993; Hanson, 1973; Holmes, 1978; Janes, 1990). Evidently, competing demands of substantially different ways of life often lead to cultural conflict, a contributing factor to delinquency. When the host culture is in conflict with the traditional culture, a child is forced to either adhere to the host society's norms and values, which may alienate the child from his or her traditional ethnic culture, or to behave in ways consistent with traditional ethnic culture, thus risking alienation from the host society. In this context, an adolescent who bonds with the host society's norms and values may not have a strong bond with his/her traditional ethnic culture. Families or parents that maintain their traditional ethnic cultural practices may find themselves in conflict with their children, which may impair family-child bonding, a contributing factor to delinquency (Godinet, 1998).

Although these theories are useful to explain the influences of systems on youth, there are limitations. Social control theories do not critically assess school systems and the juvenile justice system and their differential treatment of youth of color. Social learning theory also does not take into account social structural difficulties, such as adjustment issues for immigrants, lack of resources, discrimination, and other factors that are relevant to studies on Pacific Islander youth. Both theories can be criticized for perpetuating cultural imperialism insofar as they assume a universality of conduct defined by the dominant (White, middle class) group's experience and culture and its hegemony as the normative standard for all people (Young, 1990). Definitions of appropriate behavior are assumed not to differ among varying countries and cultures, thus the behaviors of people of color that maintain their cultural practices, as well as new immigrants, may be seen as deviant.

Labeling theory (Hamilton & Rauma, 1995), conflict theory (Bridges & Myers, 1994; Lilly, Cullen, & Ball, 1995), and bias theory (Harris & Hill, 1982) attempt to address the limitations of the aforementioned theories in examining structural and process inequities within a system. For example, bias theory offers an explanation of how embedded perceptions about a group of people inform decision-making (Harris & Hill, 1982). Researchers of this perspective have suggested that decision makers, in cases where discretionary decisions are made, create typescripts about certain groups and classes that are used in decision-making situations when little information is known about such groups. For example, when a Pacific Islander youth is arrested and shows passive resistance toward an intake or probation officer, the officer, given little information regarding the youth's specific situation, makes decisions based on presumptions, personal knowledge about Pacific Islander youth (whether misinformed or informed), and generalizations about the Pacific Islander American population. The youth may then receive a harsher punishment due to the negative picture that is painted by society about Pacific Islander American youth. Thus, bias theory is useful in examining the decision-making structure of the juvenile justice system in explaining the differential assessments that youth receive due to race. Yet, the one limitation of this theory is its inability to predict or explain delinquency before involvement with the juvenile justice system.

As noted, when theoretical explanations focus on one particular source, other sources that may be essential to a comprehensive analytical perspective in informing policies are often ignored (Dear & Moos, 1994; Giddens, 1991). Due to the limitations of existing theories, a paradigm shift is warranted to appropriately address the problem of delinquency in terms of prevention and intervention policies and programs. Because of multiple influencing factors, these authors advocate an integrative approach of diverse theories to better understand delinquency among Pacific Islander adolescents and create culturally competent policies and programs.

The Juvenile Justice System

The history of the penitentiary system in the United States can be traced to the work of the Philadelphia Society for Alleviating the Miseries of the Public Prisons, organized in 1787 under the direction of Dr. Benjamin Rush (Fox, 1972). Initially, this system emphasized solitary confinement and prayer and was later replaced by a system that emphasized solitary confinement at night and labor during the day (Goebel, 1976; Rusche & Kirchheimer, 1968). Alternatives to incarceration are community corrections programs that include services such as mental health treatment, parenting skills training, halfway houses, probation, and parole (Coggins & Fresquez, 2001).

In early U.S. history, juvenile criminals were treated like adult criminals. Children 7 years old and older were tried and, if found guilty, could be sentenced to prison or death. In about 1825, the Society for the Prevention of Juvenile Delinquency advocated for the separation of juveniles from adult criminals. In 1899, the first juvenile court was established in Chicago. The doctrine of *parens partiae* allowed the state to intervene in the lives of children, providing protection for children whose parents were not able to provide care or supervision. Thus, the focus was on child welfare (Snyder & Sickmund, 1999). By 1910, 32 states had juvenile courts and/or probation services focused on providing treatment that would turn delinquents into productive citizens. During the 1950s and 1960s the effectiveness of the juvenile justice system was under public scrutiny. Consequently, in the 1960s, the U.S. Supreme Court ruled to formalize juvenile courts to include formal hearings, providing juveniles protection against self-incrimination, and rights to receive notice of charges, and present witnesses, have an attorney, and require proof beyond a reasonable doubt. However, the Supreme Court acknowledged that a jury was not necessary in juvenile court hearings (Snyder & Sickmund, 1999).

The 1974 Juvenile Justice and Delinquency Prevention Act (P.L. #93-415, as amended) and subsequent legislation called for the separation of juvenile and adult offenders in detention facilities, thus creating the Office of Juvenile Justice and Delinquency Prevention. In addition, the act required that those juveniles committing status offenses (behaviors that are legal for adults but not legal for minors) not be placed in locked detention or correctional facilities but instead be diverted to community-based programs with an emphasis on diversion and de-institutionalization (Garvin & Tropman, 1998). During the 1980s, national concerns related to crime and delinquency resulted in the passage of more punitive laws that handled certain classes of juvenile offenders as adults and other juvenile offenders as criminals but adjudicated in juvenile court. During the 1990s, state legislatures cracked down on juvenile crime even further. State legislation determines the age limit for inclusion in the juvenile justice system and many state legislators have proposed lowering the age limit at which a juvenile can be considered an adult for purposes of adjudication. Currently, states will try juveniles as adults under certain circumstances. However, imposition of the death penalty for crimes committed at age 17 or younger is rare (Sickmund, Snyder, & Poe-Yamagata, 1997). Given state and federal legislation and public scrutiny, the juvenile justice system has experienced significant modifications in the past two decades. For Pacific Islander American youth and families, particularly recent immigrants, the unfamiliarity with and blatant changes in the juvenile justice system have led to uncertainty, disorder, and maladjustment; thus, resulting in increased involvement with and overrepresentation in the justice system.

Juvenile Justice Policy Foundation

Specifically for Pacific Islander Americans, policy and program approaches to juvenile crime and delinquency must include the cooperation of families and communities, new training, new systems designs, and capacity building models that the promote goals of safety, protection, and empowerment (Briar-Lawson, 1998). Numerous policies serve as a foundation for juvenile justice services, including the Juvenile Justice and Delinquency Prevention Act of 1974 (P.L. 93-415, as amended), the Child Abuse Prevention and Treatment Act of 1974, Title XX that provides grants to states, and the Adoption Assistance and Child Welfare Act of 1980.

One of the most influential policies affecting juvenile justice services is the Juvenile Justice and Delinquency Prevention Act of 1974. This act was established to provide needed resources, leadership, and coordination to develop and implement effective methods of preventing and reducing juvenile delinquency. A special purpose of this act was to support efforts related to the overrepresentation of youth of color in the juvenile justice system. Amendments were made in 1988 and 1992 to identify causes of disparate treatment of youth of color in the juvenile justice system and options to combat such disparities. Thus, addressing the problem of the overrepresentation of youth of color became a core requirement of this major juvenile justice policy. Unfortunately, the amendments made to the Juvenile Justice and Delinquency Prevention Act of 1974 did little to decrease the overrepresentation among youth of color, including immigrant Pacific Islander American juveniles (Harms, 2002).

Racial Bias in the Juvenile Justice System

According to Adams, Bell, and Griffin (1997), racial bias refers to a system of oppression that, based on their race, violates rights of individuals to self-determination and development. Such violation of individual rights occurs through overt prejudice and discrimination, as well as unconscious attitudes and behaviors of both individuals and societal institutions. Pratt (1992) suggested that one explanation for the overrepresentation of youth of color in the juvenile justice system in the United States and Britain could be found in the structure of the systems. Both systems have three main components: (a) involvement of a variety of individuals and agencies with different and often conflicting objectives; (b) discretionary decision making; and (c) use of subjective discretionary factors. The disproportionate representation of youth of color in the juvenile justice system in light of these three components leads to suspicion about intentional and unintentional racial discrimination. That is, systemic structures such as discretionary powers may allow racial stereotypes to influence decisions about a youth of color juvenile (VanVleet, Vakalahi, Holley, Brown, & Carter, 1999).

Since the 1960s, studies have indicated that the American juvenile justice system incorporates biases that make certain that youth of color and juveniles of lower socioeconomic status are targets for discriminatory treatment (Cicourel, 1968; Platt, 1969). Many studies have found a direct influence of race on the experiences of youth of color in the juvenile justice system (Austin, 1995; Leiber & Woodrick, 1995; McCarter, 1997), whereas some studies have not (Barton, 1976; Piven, 1979). Sources of conflicting findings may be attributed to methodological and conceptual differences or deficiencies (Pratt, 1992). The majority of studies support the proposition that institutional discrimination in relation to race impacts the overrepresentation of youth of color in the juvenile justice system (Albonetti, 1997; Gastwirth & Nayak, 1997; Liff, 1999; Nobiling, Spohn, & DeLone, 1998). In a study conducted by Bridges and Steen (1998), it was found that racial stereotypes influenced decisions of probation officers regarding Black and White juvenile delinquents. Furthermore, Leiber and Woodrick (1995) found that overt racial bias has been replaced with subtle or covert racial discrimination. As such, social policies that were intended to decrease the problem of the overrepresentation of youth of color in the juvenile justice system have not been effective. The statistics on youth of color, particularly Pacific Islander Americans, will continue to escalate unless a more culturally competent approach is integrated into policies and programs.

Action-Based Research: Relevant Strategies

According to Mokuau (1995), providing services to Pacific Islander Americans require several considerations, including service accessibility, culturally valid content, and culturally valid delivery. For example, for services to be accessible, they must be established within the community rather than in areas where driving or plane rides are required. Also, given the high poverty rate among Pacific Islanders, affordability of services is critical. Furthermore, validity in content and delivery requires the incorporation of Pacific Islander cultures (e.g., spirituality, family, cooperation) into the program curriculum and using agencies with high involvement rates of Pacific Islanders to deliver prevention and intervention services. Based on these considerations and given the limited literature on Pacific Islander Americans in relation to juvenile crime and delinquency, a few strategies are highlighted herein that encompass key elements relevant to Pacific Islander cultures in general.

Ho'oponopono

Ho'oponopono is a Hawaiian family-centered, family empowering, problem-solving model (Mokuau, 1990). Ho'oponopono means to set right. This indigenous model has been used widely in Hawaii in the child welfare system with Native Hawaiians. Many forms of this model are used by other Pacific Islander cultures. Stages of Ho'oponopono include the following (Fong, Boyd, & Browne, 1999):

1. *Pule* (prayer). The process begins by asking God for a blessing in the problem-solving effort. Sincerity and truthfulness are imperative.
2. *Kukulu Kumuhana* (statement of the problem). The *kupuna* (elderly) leads the session and reaches out to everyone, including any resistant individuals, to establish a proper climate for the *hala* (transgression) to be stated. It is critical that the initial transgression is articulated to avoid further misunderstandings. The *kupuna* selects one issue to focus on throughout the discussion, simultaneously uncovering other concerns and resolving relationship troubles.
3. *Mahiki* (discussion). The *kupuna* leads an in-depth discussion, yet prevents direct confrontations that may generate additional emotional eruption and confusion. Each member is allowed to share his or her *mana'o* (feelings) but with extreme caution in avoiding reproach and recrimination.
4. *Ho'ike i ka hana hewa i hana ia* (confession of wrongdoing). After the discussion, a sincere confession of wrongdoing and the seeking of forgiveness takes place.
5. *Panina* (restitution). When necessary, restitution is discussed and agreed upon.
6. *Mihi* (forgiveness). Mutual forgiveness by both parties occurs.
7. *Kala* (release). A mutual release occurs when there is confession and forgiveness. Both parties are expected to engage in mutual release for proper *Ho'oponopono* to occur.
8. *Pani* (summary). In the final phase, the occasion and the family's strengths are summarized. After the problem is resolved, further discussion about the matter is forbidden. In closure, a closing prayer is offered and a meal is shared among participants.

Family Decision-Making and Family Group Conferencing

The Family Decision-Making Model originated in New Zealand among the native Maori people. Many forms of this model are used by other Pacific Islander cultures. This model has a cultural base in that the Maori people developed a culture that included childrearing practices and family decision-making shaped by their relationship to the land. Such a cultural base gives the Maori people the preeminent right to be heard, to participate, and to decide what happens to their own. This model is based on the premise that each family is the "expert" on itself. Each family has the power to make decisions on its own. The family knows itself better than anyone else does, including those in the external environment. The family is a natural and perhaps the best place to determine needs and resources for addressing areas of family dysfunction. This model proposes that the best decisions can only be made by the family. This model has been successful in helping families resolve social problems, including juvenile crime and delinquency, substance abuse, and family violence (Wilcox et al., 1991).

Discussion

The limited nature of the existing literature on the intersection of substance abuse, family violence, and child welfare for Pacific Islander Americans has major implications for policy, practice, and research. The ethnic and racial status of Pacific Islanders amplifies their vulnerability for and the effects of crime and delinquency (Conley, 1994; Pratt, 1992). Discriminatory and stereotypical beliefs held by officials of institutions such as the juvenile justice system may be seen to increase the likelihood of Pacific Islanders being labeled by these systems as criminals or deviants (Albonetti & Hepburn, 1996; Chesney-Lind et al.,1995). Risk factors for social problems such as crime and delinquency commonly associated with being a person of color, including that of Pacific Islanders, include racism, institutional discrimination, low educational commitment, low family income, substance abuse, and language barriers (Millett & Orosz, 2001; Wordes, Bynum, & Corley, 1994). In the United States, Pacific Islanders are an oppressed group and as a means of coping they may become involved in criminal activities and other illegitimate means of making a living. Immigrant Pacific Islanders are at greater risk for crime and delinquency and other social problems because of linguistic difficulties, pressure of balancing dual cultures of origin, poverty, and intergenerational conflicts (U.S. Department of Health and Human Services, 2001). Despite these many challenges, strong family and community supports among Pacific Islanders may serve as protective factors associated with positive behaviors among Pacific Islander juveniles. Thus, solutions must be focused on all levels including policy, practice, research, and organization and economic infrastructures (Chow, 2001).

Implications for Policy

In general, existing policies have done little to advance the interests of vulnerable Pacific Islander American juveniles. Progress has been minimal for Pacific Islander Americans. Thus, there is an urgent plea for effective policies that address the inequality and injustice in the juvenile justice system and in society as a whole.

First, juvenile justice policies must reflect cultural competency in advancing the interests of vulnerable Pacific Islander American juveniles. For example, policymakers must advocate for funding to create programs for Pacific Islander juveniles and their families that integrate original cultural values and practices into program curriculum. Furthermore, culturally competent policies must create initiatives that include staff diversity training, language translations, family and community collaborations, accurate record keeping, and the involvement of staff of color in the justice system (Medley, 1998). In terms of addressing the overrepresentation of youth of color in the juvenile justice system, the State of Pennsylvania found programs such as Positive

Choice, the Hispanic Center After-School Program, Dreams of Tomorrow, and the Great Start Program to be culturally effective and relevant (Hsai & Hamparian, 1998).

Second, policies could reflect the need for multi-systemic efforts with Pacific Islander Americans, including provisions for higher education, employment training, and mental health services. Finally, juvenile justice policy needs to mandate timely decision-making in the system. Pacific Islander youths and families should receive juvenile justice services quickly and accurately. In other words, policies could mandate the system to adjust to the needs of Pacific Islander Americans rather than Pacific Islander Americans accommodating the system.

Implications for Practice

Any discussion of juvenile justice has implications for people of color involved in the justice system. This is especially true for Pacific Islander Americans, who account for less than 1% of the U.S. population, yet are increasingly engaged in or at-risk for crime and delinquency and involvement in the justice system. Given the commonality among Pacific Islander cultures, many interventions (i.e., *Ho'oponopono*, Maori Family Group Conferencing) would be relevant to most or all Pacific Islander cultures. As stated earlier, to meet the needs of Pacific Islander Americans, service providers must consider historical and cultural experiences such as colonization, immigration, oppression, shame and stigma that occur on multiple systemic levels during all stages of services (i.e., assessment to treatment). Traditional juvenile justice modalities have denied adequate service capacities for Pacific Islander American juveniles and professionals alone have not been able to meet the needs of Pacific Islander American families and communities.

Despite these barriers, social workers have long known that indigenous experiences are significant because of their giving and benefiting ethos (Reisman, 1997). Pacific Islander values promote reciprocity, advocacy for the whole, and interdependency. Thus, expansion of professional theories and practices for Pacific Islander Americans would build family capacity to deal with the effect of juvenile crime and delinquency. Both professionals and Pacific Islander communities are sources of expertise for filling gaps in traditional juvenile justice services, and advocacy, and mobilizing Pacific Islander American families and communities. Certainly, to make a difference in the lives of Pacific Islander Americans, we must include more people and more skills at greater levels (Briar-Lawson, 1998). Emphasis should be focused on a holistic, collaborative, systemic, strengths-based, and multi-service practice approach reflecting the original cultures of Pacific Islander Americans.

VanVleet et al. (1999) provide the following recommendations for practice within the juvenile justice system. First, at the conceptual level, the juvenile justice system must implement a strengths-based approach, as the current use of aggravating and mitigating circumstances are perceived to be bias against youth of color and those of lower socioeconomic status, which are realities for Pacific Islander Americans. Second, there is a need to increase the number of staff of color and of the same ethnicity as the youth who are served. On the direct service level, an increase of staff of color would allow youth and staff ethnic matching (culture, language, gender). Increased numbers of people of color at administrative and management levels can lead to developing policies and procedures that are more culturally competent. Administrators could actively recruit, mentor, and retain staff from communities of color and local universities. Of course, simply adding staff of color without modifying policies, procedures, and interventions cannot be effective. Thus, administrators must critically examine hiring and promotional practices for the unconscious effect of racial bias, educate staff about the nature of covert as well as overt racism, and develop an environment conducive to addressing such bias when it arises. Finally, the juvenile justice system could collaborate with ethnic communities of color and organizations to assess their needs, identify resources, and develop programs such as after-school programs and youth employment programs to help prevent involvement in crime and delinquency. Likewise, family advocacy programs could be established to help low-income parents to learn about their rights and responsibilities within the juvenile justice system. This is particularly critical for recent immigrant Pacific Islander Americans who are not familiar with nor adjusted to the justice system.

Implications for Research

The limited nature of the existing literature on Pacific Islanders and the juvenile justice system is a desperate call for further research. First, studies are needed to focus on the complexity of juvenile crime and delinquency intertwined with Pacific Islander cultures and historical experiences. A major part of grappling with complexity is to improve existing databases because the lack of complete data prevents a thorough understanding of Pacific Islander juveniles in the context of the system. Second, additional research is needed to examine specific risk and protective factors for juvenile crime and delinquency among Pacific Islanders. There is a need to evaluate factors such as systemic biases, racism, socioeconomic status, employment, and higher education as sources of risk or protection for crime and delinquency among Pacific Islander Americans. A risk factor for the involvement of youth of color in the system is the use of aggravating and mitigating circumstances. According to VanVleet et al. (1999), aggravating and mitigating practices are not culturally sensitive and lead to more severe sentences for youth of color. Research is needed to examine racial and social class biases as aggravating and mitigating circumstances and the relationship of such circumstances to dispositions of juveniles of color. The use of a strengths-based approach in place of or in addition to the aggravating and mitigating circumstances is recommended. Another risk factor requiring examination is racial profiling. Studies are needed in terms of police calls, people of color compared with Caucasian arrests, types of arrests, and officers' attitudes toward racial profiling. Finally, there is a need to examine the relationship of socioeconomic status to arrest and disposition. The issue of socioeconomic status is critical for Pacific Islander Americans, who are among the most disadvantaged individuals in the United States today.

Conclusion

This chapter has focused on the experiences of Pacific Islander youth in the juvenile justice system. The primary emphasis has been placed on understanding the sociocultural and historic experiences and current circumstances of Pacific Islander Americans in an effort to determine policies that will better support this population. Pacific Islander Americans possess a rich culture, full of possibilities, to change the life courses of many in this population.

References

Adams, M., Bell, L. A., & Griffin, P. (1997). *Teaching for diversity and social justice: A source book.* New York: Routledge.

Albonetti, C. A. (1997). Sentencing under the federal sentencing guidelines: Effects of defendant characteristics, guilty pleas, and departures on sentence outcomes for drug offenses, 1991–1992. *Law and Society Review, 31,* 789–822.

Albonetti, C. A., & Hepburn, J. R. (1996). Prosecutorial discretion to defer criminalization: The effects of defendant ascribed and achieved status characteristics. *Journal of Quantitative Criminology, 12*, 63–81.

Allen-Hagen, B. (1991). Public juvenile facilities: Children in custody. *Office of Juvenile Justice and Delinquency Prevention Update on Statistics, January*, 1–10.

Austin, J. (1995). The overrepresentation of minority youths in the California juvenile justice system: Perceptions and realities. In K. K. Leonard, C. E. Pope, & W. H. Feyerherm (Eds.), *Minorities in juvenile justice* (pp. 153–178). Thousand Oaks, CA: Sage.

Bandura, A. (1977). *Social learning theory.* Englewood Cliffs, NJ: Prentice Hall.

Barton, W. H. (1976). Discretionary decision-making in juvenile justice. *Crime and Delinquency, October*, 470–480.

Berry, J. W. (1997). Immigration, acculturation and adaptation. *Applied Psychology: An International Review, 46*(1), 5–68.

Bilchik, S. (1998, May). A juvenile justice system for the 21st century. *Office of Juvenile Justice and Delinquency Prevention Bulletin*, 1–8.

Briar-Lawson, K. (1998). Capacity building for integrated family-centered practice. *Social Work, 43*, 539–550.

Bridges, G. S., Conley, D. J., Engen, R. L., & Price-Spratlen, T. (1995). Racial disparities in the confinement of juveniles: Effects of crime and community social structure on punishment. In K. K. Leonard, C. E. Pope, & W. H. Feyerherm (Eds), *Minorities in juvenile justice* (pp. 128–152). Thousand Oaks, CA: Sage.

Bridges, G. S., & Myers, M. A. (Eds.). (1994). *Inequality, crime, and social control.* Boulder: Westview.

Bridges, G. S., & Steen, S. S. (1998). Racial disparities in official assessments of juvenile offenders: Attributional stereotypes as mediating mechanisms. *American Sociological Review, 63*, 554–570.

Chesney-Lind, M., Leisen, M. B., Allen, J., Brown, M., Rockhill, A., Marker, N., et al. (1995). *Crime, delinquency, and gangs in Hawaii: Evaluation of Hawaii's youth gang response system: Part I.* Honolulu: Center for Youth Research, Social Science Research Institute, University of Hawaii-Manoa.

Chow, J. C. (2001). Assessment of Asian American/Pacific Islander organizations and communities. In R. Fong & S. B. C. L. Furuto (Eds.), *Culturally competent practice: Skills, interventions, and evaluations* (pp. 211–224). Needham Heights, MA: Allyn & Bacon.

Cicourel, A. V. (1968). *The social organization of juvenile justice.* New York: Wiley.

Coggins, K., & Fresquez, J. E. (2001). *Working with clients in correctional settings: A guide for social workers and corrections professionals.* Dubuque, IA: Bowers.

Conley, D. J. (1994). Adding color to a Black and White picture: Using qualitative data to explain racial disproportionality in the juvenile justice system. *Journal of Research in Crime and Delinquency, 31*, 135–148.

Dear, M. J., & Moos, A. (1994). Structuration theory in urban analysis. In D. Wilson & J. O. Huff (Eds.), *Marginalized places and populations: A structurationist agenda* (pp. 3–25). Westport, CT: Praeger.

Devine, P., Coolbaugh, K., & Jenkins, S. (1998). Disproportionate minority confinement: Lessons learned from five states. *Office of Juvenile Justice and Delinquency Prevention Bulletin, December*, 1–12.

DeVore, W., & Schlesinger, E. G. (1999). *Ethnic sensitive social work practice* (5th ed.). Boston: Allyn & Bacon.

Fagan, J., Slaughter, E., & Hartstone, E. (1987). Blind justice? The impact of race on the juvenile justice process. *Crime and Delinquency, 33*, 224–258.

Figueira-McDonough, J. (1992). Community context and dropout rates. *Children and Youth Services Review, 14*, 273–288.

Fitzgerald, M. H., & Howard, A. (1990). Aspects of social organization in three Samoan communities. *Pacific Studies, 14*, 31–54.

Fong, R., Boyd, C., & Browne, C. (1999). The Gandhi technique: A biculturalization approach for empowering Asian and Pacific Islander families. *Journal of Multicultural Social Work, 7*, 95–109.

Fox, V. (1972). *Introduction to corrections.* Englewood Cliffs, NJ: Prentice Hall.

Franco, R.W. (1991). *Samoan perceptions of work: Moving up and around.* New York: AMS Press.

Fridrich, A.H., & Flannery, D. J. (1995). The effects of ethnicity and acculturation on early adolescent delinquency. *Journal of Child and Family Studies, 4,* 69–87.

Furuto, S. B. C. L., San Nicolas, R. J., Kim, G. E., & Fiaui, L. M. (2001). Interventions with Kanaka Maoli, Chamorro, and Samoan communities. In R. Fong & S. B. C. L. Furuto (Eds.), *Culturally competent practice: Skills, interventions, and evaluations* (pp. 327–342). Needham Heights, MA: Allyn & Bacon.

Garvin, C., & Tropman, J.E. (1998). *Social work in contemporary society* (2nd ed.). Needham Heights, MA: Allyn & Bacon.

Gastwirth, J. L., & Nayak, T. K. (1997). Statistical aspects of cases concerning racial discrimination in drug sentencing: Stephens v. State and U.S. v. Armstrong. *Journal of Criminal Law and Criminology, 87,* 583–603.

Giddens, A. (1991). Structuration theory: Past, present, and future. In C. Bryant & D. Jary (Eds.), *Giddens theory of structuration: A critical appreciation* (pp. 201–221). New York: Routledge.

Godinet, M. T. (1998). *Exploring a theoretical model of delinquency with Samoan adolescents.* Unpublished doctoral dissertation, University of Washington, Seattle.

Goebel, J. (1976). *Felony and misdemeanor.* Philadelphia: University of Pennsylvania Press.

Green, J. W. (1999). *Cultural awareness in the human services: A multi-ethnic approach* (3rd Ed.). Boston: Allyn & Bacon.

Hamilton, V. L., & Rauma, D. (1995). Social psychology of deviance and law. In K. S. Cook, G. A. Fine, & J. S. House (Eds.), *Sociological perspectives on social psychology* (pp. 524–547). Needham Heights, MA: Allyn & Bacon.

Hanna, J. M., & Fitzgerald, M. H. (1993). Acculturation and symptoms: A comparative study of reported health symptoms in three Samoan communities. *Social Science and Medicine, 36,* 1169–1180.

Hanson, A. H. (1973). Political change in Tahiti and Samoa: An exercise in experimental anthropology. *Ethnology, 2,* 1–13.

Harms, P. (2002). Detention in delinquency cases, 1989–1998. *Office of Juvenile Justice and Delinquency Prevention, January,* 1–2.

Harris, A. R., & Hill, G. D. (1982). The social psychology of deviance: Toward a reconciliation with social structure. *Annual Review of Sociology, 8,* 161–186.

Hawkins, J. D., & Catalano, R. F. (1992). *Communities that care: Action for drug abuse prevention.* San Francisco, CA: Jossey-Bass.

Hirschi, T. (1969). *Causes of delinquency.* Berkeley: University of California Press.

Holmes, L. D. (1978). Factors contributing to the cultural stability of Samoa. *Anthropological Quarterly, 29,* 395–406.

Hsia, H. M., & Hamparian, D. (1998). Disproportionate minority confinement: 1997 update. *Office of Juvenile Justice and Delinquency Prevention Bulletin, September,* 1–12.

Janes, C. R. (1990). *Migration, social change and health.* Stanford, CA: Stanford University Press.

Kassebaum, G., Lau, C. W. S., Kwack, D., Leverette, J., Allingham, E., & Marker, N. (1995). *Identifying disproportionate representation of ethnic groups in Hawaii's juvenile justice system: Phase one.* Honolulu: Center for Youth Research Social Science Research Institute, University of Hawaii-Manoa.

Leiber, M. J., & Woodrick, A. C. (1995). Theoretical and empirical developments in the study of race and juvenile court processing. *Social Pathology, 1*(2), 149-164.

Liff, S. (1999). Diversity and equal opportunities: Room for a constructive compromise? *Journal of Human Resource Management, 9,* 65–75.

Lilly, R. J., Cullen, F. T., & Ball, R. A. (1995). *Criminological theory: Context and consequences* (2nd ed.). Thousand Oaks, CA: Sage.

McCabe, K., Yeh, M., Hough, R. L., Landsverk, J., Hurlburt, M. S., Culver, S.W., et al. (1999). Racial/ ethnic representation across five public sectors of care for youth. *Journal of Emotional and Behavioral Disorders, 7,* 72–82.

McCarter, S. A. (1997). *Understanding minority overrepresentation in Virginia's juvenile justice system.* Unpublished doctoral dissertation, Virginia Commonwealth University, Richmond.

McDermott, J. F., Tseng, W., & Maretzki, T. W. (1980). *People and cultures of Hawaii: A psychocultural profile.* Honolulu: University Press of Hawaii.

Medley, T. E. (1998). Utah task force on racial and ethnic fairness in the legal system. *Utah Bar Journal,* 38–43.

Merton, R. K. (1938). *Social theory and social structure.* New York: Free Press.

Millett, R., & Orosz, J. J. (2001). Understanding giving patterns in communities of color. *Fund Raising Management, 32,* 25–27.

Mokuau, N. (1990). A family-centered approach in Native Hawaiian culture. *Families in Society: The Journal of Contemporary Human Services, 71,* 607–613.

Mokuau, N. (1995). *Pacific Islanders.* In Center for Substance Abuse Prevention cultural competence series [special collaborative NASW/CSAP monograph] (DHHS Publication No. SMA 95-3075) (pp. 159–188). Rockville, MD: Substance Abuse and Mental Health Services Administration.

Mokuau, N. (1998). *Responding to Pacific Islanders: Culturally competent perspectives for substance abuse prevention.* Washington, DC: Substance Abuse and Mental Health Services Administration, Center for Substance Abuse Prevention.

Nobiling, T., Spohn, C., & DeLone, M. (1998). A tale of two counties: Unemployment and sentence severity. *Justice Quarterly, 15,* 459–485.

Nwadiora, E., & McAdoo, H. (1996). Acculturative stress among Amerasian refugees: Gender and racial differences. *Adolescence, 31,* 477–487.

Office of Hawaiian Affairs (1998). Native Hawaiian data book 1998. Honolulu: Office of Hawaiian Affairs.

Piven, H. (1979). The status offender controversy: Charges and study evidence. *Child Welfare, LVIII*(8), 485–499.

Platt, A. M. (1969). *The child savers.* Chicago: University of Chicago Press.

Pope, C., & Feyerherm, W. (1993). *Minorities in the juvenile justice system.* Washington, DC: U. S. Department of Justice, Office of Justice Programs, Office of Juvenile Justice and Delinquency Prevention.

Pratt, M. A. E. (1992). *Racial bias in the juvenile justice system in the United States and Great Britain.* Unpublished association paper. Nashville, TN: Vanderbilt.

Reisman, F. (1997). Ten self-help principles. *Social Policy, Spring,* 6–11.

Rusche, G., & Kirchheimer, O. (1968). *Punishment and social structure.* New York: Russell and Russell.

Sickmund, M. (1997). Offenders in juvenile court, 1995. *Office of Juvenile Justice and Delinquency Prevention Bulletin, December,* 1–12.

Sickmund, M., Snyder, H. N., & Poe-Yamagata, E. (1997). *Juvenile offenders and victims: 1997 update on violence.* Washington, DC: U.S. Department of Justice, Office of Justice Programs, Office of Juvenile Justice and Delinquency Prevention.

Snyder, H. N. (1997). Juvenile arrests 1996. *Office of Juvenile Justice and Delinquency Prevention Bulletin, November,* 1–12.

Snyder, H. N., & Sickmund, M. (1999). *Juvenile offenders and victims: 1999 National Report.* Washington, DC: Office of Juvenile Justice and Delinquency Prevention, U.S. Department of Justice.

Sommers, I., Fagan, J., & Baskin, D. (1993). Sociocultural influences on the explanation of delinquency for Puerto Rican youths. *Hispanic Journal of Behavioral Sciences, 15,* 36–62.

U.S. Census Bureau. (1999). Select social characteristics of the population by region and race. *Racial statistics branch, population division.* Retrieved May 1, 2002, from http://www.census.gov

U.S. Census Bureau. (2000). Select social characteristics of the population by region and race. *Racial statistics branch, population division.* Retrieved May 1, 2002, from http:// www.census.gov

U.S. Department of Health and Human Services. (2001). *Child maltreatment 1999: Reports from the states to the National Child Abuse and Neglect Data System.* Washington, DC: U.S. Government Printing Office.

Vakalahi, H. O., Godinet, M., & Fong, R. (in press). Pacific Islander Americans: Impact of colonization and immigration. In R. Fong, R. G. McRoy, & C.O. Hendricks (Eds.), *Intersecting child welfare, substance abuse, and family violence.* Alexandria, VA: Council on Social Work Education.

VanVleet, R. K., Vakalahi, H. F., Holley, L., Brown, S., & Carter, C. (1999). *Minority overrepresentation in the Utah juvenile justice system.* Unpublished report for the Utah State Task Force on Racial and Ethnic Fairness in the Legal System. Salt Lake City: University of Utah.

Vega, W. A., Gil, A. G., Warheit, G. J., Zimmerman, R. S., & Apospori, E. (1993). Acculturation and delinquent behavior among Cuban American adolescents: Toward an empirical model. *American Journal of Community Psychology, 21,* 113–125.

Wilcox, R., Smith, D., Moore, J., Hewitt, A., Allan, G., Walker, H., et al. (1991). *Family decision making & family group conference.* Lower Hutt, New Zealand: Practitioners'.

Wordes, M., Bynum, T. S., & Corley, C. J. (1994). Locking up youth: The impact of race on detention decisions. *Journal of Research in Crime and Delinquency, 31,* 149–165.

Young, I. M. (1990). *Justice and the politics of difference.* Princeton, NJ: Princeton University Press.

Zane, N. W. S., Takeuchi, D. T., & Young, K. N. J. (1994). *Confronting critical health issues of Asian and Pacific Islander Americans.* Thousand Oaks, CA: Sage.

Chapter Eleven

African Americans and Welfare Reform: Success or Failure?

Sandra Edmonds Crewe

Welfare reform is yet another example of social welfare policy that has not escaped the damage of historical and systemic racial discrimination toward African Americans. An examination of 5 years of welfare reform provides further evidence of the continued detrimental effects of racial discrimination inherent in social welfare policy (Gilens, 1999; Handler & Hasenfeld, 1997; Quadagno, 1994, 1996). Steeped in the rhetoric and passion of the Protestant work ethic and the myth of the "worthy poor," welfare reform was introduced in 1996 and 5 years later labeled a success by many. The benefits of welfare reform have been celebrated, in particular the decline of child poverty—especially among African American children (Administration for Children and Families [ACF], 2002). While many African Americans have transitioned from the nation's welfare rolls, there is evidence of disparities and hardships that are rooted in cumulative disadvantage and differential access to resources. The successes of African Americans have been muted by disparate treatment, misinformation, and inadequate resources to maintain their transition to work (Walters & DeWeever, 1999). According to Schram & Soss (2001), "the secret of success for welfare reform has been a frame of reference that suggests positive interpretations of roll decline and leaver outcomes while simultaneously obscuring alternative criteria that might produce more critical assessments" (p. 62). Race is a criterion that must be considered before a verdict of success can be universally imposed on the American public.

This chapter provides a historical overview of welfare policy and its inextricable link to race. It specifically examines the effects of welfare reform on African Americans and calls for a new approach to welfare reform that addresses race-based inequities. Furthermore, the narrow claim that welfare reform is a success because of a decline in caseloads is rejected. Instead, this chapter asserts the need to more closely examine welfare reform policies in terms of their disparate impact and the role such policies have played in the lives of African Americans. Evidence is presented in this chapter to document the continued legacy of unequal treatment of African Americans in social welfare policy.

This chapter's focus on African Americans is motivated by the need to examine welfare reform within the context of a society that has historically enacted laws that have resulted in harm to certain subpopulations. Although most analyses of data show that African Americans are disproportionally represented on welfare rolls, these studies often fail to provide the historical context that explains existing imbalances. In fact, once the history of U.S. social policy is accurately examined, as opposed to the over-scrutiny of the 20% of African Americans who have not escaped poverty, readers may become more inquisitive into the fact that 80% of a population that was enslaved fewer than 150 years ago and guaranteed basic civil rights only 40 years ago has managed to rise out of poverty.

The unforgiving nature of the enslavement of African people requires an analysis of the 1996 welfare reform legislation and its outcomes in terms of the implications for African Americans. The discussion that follows is guided by the awareness that "history is replete with examples of well-intentioned policies that proved to be catastrophic [especially for African Americans]" (Karger & Stoesz, 1998, p. 40). For example, Quadagno (1994) clearly documents how Franklin D. Roosevelt's New Deal and Lyndon B. Johnson's War on Poverty were shaped by the issue of race and reinforced the racial divide in U.S. society. Like these earlier social policies, there is post–1996 welfare reform evidence that all things are not equal (Gooden, 1998) and race appears to matter in terms of key outcomes (DeParle, 1998; Bonds, 2002; Rockeymoore, 2001b; Schram, n.d.; Schram & Soss, 2001).

1996 PRWORA and Reauthorization Proposals

Welfare reform—within the context of the 1996 Personal Responsibility and Work Opportunity Reconciliation Act (PRWORA)—represented one of the most important shifts in welfare policy since the passage of the 1935 Social Security Act. The idea of changing welfare from an entitlement program to one that emphasized work, local control, flexibility, and time limits received bipartisan support and was largely perceived as a much-needed change in U.S. social policy that historically fostered "dependency." However, many opponents viewed this new wave of political thought and action as punitive and driven by capitalism, mean-spiritedness, and racism. To many African Americans, the emphasis on personal responsibility and behavioral controls was not a maturation of public policy, but rather a retrenchment to a time when one's race determined one's worth.

The 1996 PRWORA was set to expire September 30, 2002. Its cornerstone, the block-granted Temporary Assistance to Needy Families (TANF) program is currently operating under a continuing resolution scheduled to expire March 2004. The Bush Administration's 2002 and 2003 reauthorization proposals focus on continuing work requirements with no additional funding for child care transportation or child care (White House, 2002). Both the Senate and House bills (S 108-162 and HR 4, respectively) also mandate stringent work requirements that are opposed by most Democrats and anti-poverty activists (Coalition on Human Needs, 2004). The minority views toward the majority proposals primarily address their inadequacy in moving families out of poverty and into permanent economic independence. They also have concern about the growing dependency on other support programs such as food stamps; Women, Infants, and Children; and other publicly supported programs. The Center for Law and Social Policy (2003) reports that between June 2002 and June 2003, the number of families receiving food stamps increased by 13%, while TANF caseloads increased by only 0.3%. This, coupled with findings that 31 states had increased TANF caseloads (June 2002–June 2003), reflects the increased dependency on foods stamps and other public programs during the economic downturn (Center for Law and Social Policy [CLASP], 2003).

Overall, the opponents of the Republican-authored reauthorization plans call attention to the need for changes that enhance quality of life by focusing on employment, quality child care, job retention, and increasing incomes from services (Committee on Education and the Workforce, 2002). Citing the unheeded wisdom of the highly controversial and debated 1965 U.S. Department of Labor report on the African American family authored by Patrick Moynihan (White House, 2002; Moynihan, 1999), the 2002 Bush administration's welfare reauthorization plan, *Working Toward Independence*, sets forth its new campaign to promote personal responsibility with little or no attention to its disparate and differential effects on African Americans (White House, 2002). *Working Toward Independence*, the Bush Administration's (2002) Reauthorization plan, stated:

> The news on family composition is encouraging. The negative effects of single parent families were brought forcefully to the Nation's attention in 1965 by Daniel Patrick Moynihan, then an Assistant Secretary in the Department of Labor. Moynihan noted the dramatic increase in non-marital births and reviewed evidence to argue that these births were the underlying cause of several of the Nation's leading domestic problems, including violence and welfare dependency. But the public reaction to Moynihan's report was so negative that the problem he diagnosed with such clarity was ignored for three decades. It was not until the welfare reform law of 1996, some three decades later that the Federal Government launched its first major attack on the problem of non-marital births. (p.9)

Despite the strong historical sentiment of the African American community that the Moynihan "Tangle of Pathology" report (Moynihan, 1999) ignored strengths of their communities, it was raised as testimony to the success of welfare reform and its focus on individual pathology. Ironically, the reference to the Moynihan report because of its focus on the pathology of African American families (Hill, 1997) has further documented the lack of sensitivity of policymakers to the African American community and their earned distrust of the system.

Setting the Record Straight

Myths and stereotypes born out of racism can give the U.S. public a biased view regarding the African American experience with welfare. Because of these untruths, many African Americans resist any attempts to examine welfare in the context of the African American experience. These individuals are justifiably concerned that the discourse will be used to pejoratively label the whole race rather than focusing on an important segment of the African American population that has not gained equal access. Racial pride that has been an anathema to social service institutions (Carlton-LaNey, 1999) causes some African Americans to de-emphasize the plight of individuals deemed "embarrassing" or "dysfunctional." Yet other African Americans insist on the importance of racial uplift and focus their energy on highlighting the needs of individuals who are not able to progress. Thus, welfare reform calls forward the debate regarding whether the inequities of the past should be, in the words of James Baldwin, "excavated" ("The 100 Best Writers," 1999).

Other conservative groups are less benign in their "silence" on PRWORA and race. A philosophy of "the less said the better" serves to keep segments of the public from knowing about the disparate negative effects of the new policy. Most African Americans do not receive welfare in the form of cash or non-cash benefits. In fact, "eight out of ten black families today are working class, middle class or upper class; two out of three women who head black families are in the labor force; and four out of five black families are not dependent on welfare" (Hill, 1997, p. xv). Staples (1999) underscores this point by emphasizing the variations within African American subgroups in the United States. His claim that African American families are not monolithic is supported by 2000 Census data that show only 19% of African Americans living below the poverty line. Additionally, only 9% of African Americans report being on welfare within the past 5 years and only 16% report an immediate family member being on welfare during this same period (National Urban League, 2001).

Gilens (1999) affirms that the public has been presented a biased view of the African American experience with poverty. Research on media coverage documents that 65% of poor Americans shown on televised news shows are African American and 54% of newspaper pictures associated with welfare and antipoverty programs depicted African Americans. The October 10, 1999, *New York Times* front page displayed an African American woman facing Wisconsin's welfare deadline (DeParle, 1999). Similarly, a *Washington Post* article on October 30, 1999, showed only an African American woman in its report on child-care payment cuts (Rein, 1999). This and other similar reports distort national statistics that indicate that African Americans and Whites have historically been almost equally represented by percent on welfare rolls (ACF, 2001; Gilens, 1999; Karger & Stoesz, 1998; U.S. Census, 2001) and validate the assertion that public welfare workers have helped to propagate the notion that African Americans have developed a "relief habit" that causes them to seek a handout rather than a job (Martin & Martin, 1995). The 1990 General Social Survey confirmed that 78% of White Americans believed that African Americans preferred living on welfare, thus reinforcing the notion of the "Black Welfare Queen" (Franklin, 1997).

A Historical View of Welfare Policies

Although the passage of the 1935 Social Security Act is considered the beginning of modern public welfare, many authors cite the English Poor Laws as early models for U.S. social welfare (Karger & Stoesz, 1998; Yoo, 1999). Doctrines asserting the value of work, such as the "less eligibility" concept that prescribed that any assistance given must always be less than the lowest working wage, were incorporated in these Elizabethan Poor Laws (Gilens, 1999). Similarly, the Poor Laws were instrumental in bifurcating the worthy versus the unworthy poor through its policies that required able-bodied adults to work, attached eligibility to residency, required menial work for pay, minimized the necessities of life, and made local governments responsible for the poor (Jansson, 1997; Karger & Stoesz, 1998; Katz, 1986; Yoo, 1999). Many of these ideas became part of the early welfare efforts in the colonial United States.

The Social Security Act of 1935 established the Aid to Dependent Children program with a stated mission of providing support for children (Jansson, 1997; Karger & Stoesz, 1998; Katz, 1986). In 1950, this program evolved to include financial assistance for mothers or caretakers and in 1961 the Aid to Families with Dependent Children (AFDC) program was created to allow families to receive assistance in the event of the father's unemployment or incapacitation. In addition to adding "deserving" fathers to welfare rolls, the program's focus shifted to rehabilitation and a mandated treatment philosophy (Karger & Stoesz, 1998). Indicative of this change was the 1972 Separation of Services Amendment that divided services from eligibility with the purpose of facilitating intensive services aimed at rehabilitating the poor. The separation would allow workers more time in assessing and treating individuals needs rather than splitting their attention with income eligibility. Additionally, the separation of services was designed to create units with specialized skills in counseling. In 1988, the Family Support Act (FSA) was passed, and it is this program that is credited for instituting mandatory work and training programs and ending the "entitlement mentality."

By granting waivers to states to experiment with new rules, the FSA fostered the 1996 PRWORA, which was hailed as the "most important piece of welfare legislation to emerge since the 1935 Social Security Act" because "in effect, enactment of the PRWORA rescinded the 60-year-old federal entitlement program to support poor children and families" (Karger & Stoesz, 1998, pp. 273–274). Critics showed their disapproval of the new welfare law by referring to it as a repeal rather than a reform of welfare policy. A key provision of the new act was the replacement of the AFDC program with the Temporary Assistance to Needy Families (TANF) block grant program that limits assistance and mandates work. The 1996 reform also put into place time limits and emphasized the reduction of out of wedlock births. The 1996 PRWORA was the center of many debates. Table 1 summarizes the major changes in the cash assistance programs.

TANF's effectiveness is still being evaluated and debated, especially with its upcoming reauthorization. Although most acknowledge the dramatic decline in the number of people on welfare rolls as an indicator of success, there is no clear consensus as to what factors that contributed to this reduction are most significant. Political persuasion, strict work requirements, the economy, supports made available (e.g., child care/housing vouchers), and discrimination were all cited as primary reasons for the drastically reduced rolls.

The Bush Administration's 2002 plan for the reauthorization of TANF notes "the historic decline in welfare rolls, substantial increases in employment by low-income mothers, unprecedented increases in earnings by low-income female headed families, and a substantial decline in poverty, particularly among African American children" (ACF, 2002, p. 1). The opening statement of a plan titled *Working Toward Independence* states that the welfare reform law of 1996 marked a turning point in welfare policy, encouraging personal responsibility by promoting work, reducing nonmarital births, and strengthening and supporting marriage. This plan sets forth the continuation of the reform with four key components: (1) helping welfare recipients achieve independence through work; (2) protecting children and strengthening families; (3) encouraging innovation by states to help welfare recipients gain independence; and, (4) providing assistance for legal immigrants in need.

Table 1. Historical View of U.S. Cash Assistance Programs

	1935	**1962**	**1988**	**1996**
	Aid to Dependent Chidren	**Aid to Families With Dependent Children and Unemployed Parents**	**Family Suport Act**	**Temporary Assistance to Needy Families**
Focus	Income support	Rehabilitation	Mandatory work and training	Block grants Mandatory work Time limits/repeal of entitlement
Target	Children	Children Mothers Caretakers Incapacitated and unemployed fathers (optionsl—25 states adopted policy)	Children Mothers Caretakers Incapacitated and unemployed fathers	Children Mothers Caretakers Incapacitated and and unemployed fathers Teen parents

The most controversial aspect of the plan is its proposed provision to require welfare recipients to work 40 hours every week. Arguably, this requirement will severely limit the time that can be spent on job training, rehabilitation services, or substance abuse treatment. Democratic proposals generally disagree with these increased work requirements and restrictions on training and services. Instead, these proposals call for increased block grant funding to address new needs and cost increases. Also, counterproposals include substantially more funds for childcare, other dedicated funding, and a call for the elimination of nonmarital birth control incentives.

Ironically, although one of the most debated aspects of the 1996 PRWORA was time limits, none of the major reauthorization proposals call for the elimination of the 60-month lifetime restriction. The debate has instead centered primarily on work participation requirements and removing barriers between and among other federal programs. This change may reflect a sense that the time limit was a key factor in motivating family members to work. The Bush reauthorization plan is flawed by its focus on "get tough on work," rather than emphasizing mixed strategies to link people with employment (Greenberg, 2002, p. 4). Mixed strategies are more desirable because they recognize that individuals have different pathways in and out of poverty and that interventions are more likely to be effective when tied to individuals' unique circumstances (Crewe, 1997). Recognizing the diversity of the group is important. While some TANF parents are continuing a generational cycle of dependency, others are starting the cycle in their family (first-time TANF recipients); these are very distinct subgroups requiring strategies that reflect their family history.

The African American Experience With Welfare Reform

The African American experience with welfare policy has historically been different from that of Whites; African Americans' experience has been defined by racist policies and deals cut to appease others who were deemed politically important (Quadagno, 1994; Yoo, 1999). It is essential that "policy frameworks reflect an understanding that social policy is not created in a vacuum but is. . . context-sensitive and that policy options usually contain a set of competing priorities" (Karger & Stoesz, 1998, p. 40). Thus, while policy shifts affect all poor families, the experiences of African Americans must be examined through the lens of racism during each of the respective periods of transition. This approach lends itself to a person-in-environment theoretical framework of policy analysis (Marcenko & Fagan, 1996). In essence, one must consider the systems and environmental pressures that impact a population when considering policy options. This perspective is particularly critical for analyzing welfare policy and African Americans because of the added stressor of racism.

During the United States' colonial period, most African Americans were enslaved and thus outside of the welfare system available to Whites. By the late 1700s, more than 40,000 Africans were forcibly imported into the United States each year. By the time of the American Revolution, enslaved Africans comprised 40%–60% of the population in southern jurisdictions (Jansson, 1997). Enslaved Africans were considered property and provisions for their welfare were tied to their status as chattel. Within the shackles of slavery, work was expected or punishment was exacted without a debate on whether the offender was "worthy" or "unworthy." In fact, all enslaved Africans were deemed unworthy or undeserving. There are some accounts that show some indigent and older slaves being given less responsibility but other accounts indicate more harsh realities, such as bundling disabled slaves in dozens and selling them at cut-rate prices. Added to numerous other cruelties, the institution of slavery reinforced the belief of many Whites that

African Americans were unworthy of assistance. According to Martin & Martin (1985), enslaved Africans formed a helping tradition among themselves. Enslaved Africans found it necessary to cooperate for survival and thus created their own mutual aid alliance (Carlton-LaNey, 1999; Martin & Martin, 1985). This healing tradition continued among free African Americans and was institutionalized through African American churchs, benevolent societies, and fraternal orders.

The Bureau of Refugees, Freedmen, and Abandoned Land (known as the Freedmen's Bureau) was established in 1865 to assist formerly enslaved Africans with their transition to freedom. The Freedmen's Bureau is recognized as the first systematic effort to involve federal agencies in the development of programs to serve African Americans (Franklin, 1997). Refugees were emphasized because of the concern of President Andrew Johnson and other legislators that the Freedmen's Bureau would do more for African Americans than Whites. The Freedmen's Bureau was then charged with the responsibility of distributing food and clothing and allocating abandoned land (Friedman, 1996). During the 7-year history of the Freedmen's Bureau, it resettled 40,000 enslaved Africans out of a population of 3 million (Friedman, 1996; Jansson, 1997). After the Civil War, however, President Andrew Johnson declared that the abandoned land redistributed through the Freedmen's Bureau was illegally occupied and required that it be returned to its former owners (Friedman, 1996; Jansson,1997). In 1866, there was another thwarted attempt at wealth redistribution through the Southern Homestead Act. This act stipulated that public lands in the states of Alabama, Mississippi, Louisiana, Arkansas, and Flordia be disposed of under the auspices of the 1862 Homestead Act. Because it was post–Emancipation Proclamation, formerly enslaved people were able to take advantage of it. It resulted in some African Americans signing long-term restrictive labor contracts, while others were unable to succeed because they lacked the necessary tools and resources (Friedman, 1996). It was repealed in 1876, and African Americans had to relinquish their land to pardoned Confederates. This postwar period marked the beginning of a chain of broken promises regarding governmental support for African American self-sufficiency, as well as the beginning of a set of orchestrated strategies initiated by the federal government to restrict the ability of African Americans to become independent. The phrase "40 acres and a mule" is widely used among African Americans to sarcastically denote unfulfilled governmental commitments and distrust of governmental programs. Granting 40 acres and a mule was an early attempt by the federal government at land redistribution to formerly enslaved persons under the Freedman's Bureau (Salzman, Smith, & West, 1996). The promise of help through this homesteading program did not materialize and emancipated enslaved persons were left to transition to freedom with little or no support from the government that enslaved them.

The New Deal was also a missed opportunity to right injustices toward African Americans. During the presidency of Franklin D. Roosevelt, a host of programs were instituted to address the economic and social hardships of the Depression era. The relief policies of the New Deal era led to the establishment of programs to put American citizens to work. Programs like the Civilian Conservation Corps, the Federal Emergency Relief Administration, the Civil Works Administration, and the Works Progress Administration were headed by Harry Hopkins, a social worker (New Deal, 2000). These programs benefited African Americans as well as Whites. However, President Franklin D. Roosevelt's belief that discrimination was rooted in poverty and not race (Jansson, 1997; Quadagno, 1994) resulted in New Deal advocates reluctant to support federal civil rights legislation and to develop programs linked to jobs and resources. Also, New Deal policies excluded many African Americans from federal relief programs because the Roosevelt Administration chose to remain silent on race to maintain the political support of southern Democrats. For example, by excluding occupations such as farming and domestic service, which were largely held by African Americans, the 1935 Social Security Act continued the legacy of racism and oppression in social welfare policy (Cates, 1983; Jeff, 1998; Karger & Stoesz, 1998: Skocpol, 1989). Although farmers and domestic workers were finally granted benefits in 1950, the 15 years of exclusion resulted in irreparable damage (Yoo, 1999). Jansson (1997) notes that "an African American social worker ominously predicted in the 1930s that the provision of welfare rights to African Americans without civil rights and jobs legislation risked perpetuating their inferior economic and social status" (p. 187). This prediction has proved to be painfully accurate.

Relaxed program rules and eligibility criteria are credited with the dramatic increase in welfare participation through AFDC. Between 1960 and 1971, welfare rolls increased (Gilens, 1999). Much of this growth, however, can be attributed to the deterioration of economic conditions and not merely the often-cited more liberal changes to program rules such as residency requirements and assistance to unemployed parents (Katz, 1986). This is particularly important because currently decreasing welfare rolls (which have dropped 59% nationwide) can be tied to a strong economy. With the downturn in the economy, states are experiencing increasing TANF rolls. Thus, there seems to be evidence that welfare rolls are reactive to economic trends. As the welfare rolls began to expand in the 1960s (Gilens, 1999), the public's attention was drawn to the disproportionate number of African Americans reliant on such programs. The 1996 welfare reform has exacerbated this by making African Americans clearly the majority group receiving TANF.

The racialization of poverty is reflected in the welfare reforms of the late 1980s and 1990s. Most notably, the PRWORA brought the disproportionate number of African Americans on welfare to the nation's attention. While conservatives relied upon failed morality and a lack of work ethic to describe those on the welfare rolls, liberals focused on the absence of structural supports. Some believed that the conservative agenda was a" "hooded" version of the same mentality expressed by President Franklin D. Roosevelt's New Deal administration—that is, a denial or marginalization of the possibility that for some welfare dependency is a byproduct of racism. Ending welfare as it existed became a common agenda for groups with differing constituencies, the only points of disagreement being the specific strategies and outcomes of such reform. While some groups focused on reducing welfare rolls and ending reliance on the government as the ultimate outcomes, others emphasized a social capital model that championed replacing the old system with one that promoted a livable wage and family well being.

Although U.S. society as a whole is supportive of welfare eligibility based on personal responsibility factors, African Americans continue to strongly support policies that take into consideration structural barriers such as discrimination and job availability (Groskind, 1994). African Americans continue to be less supportive of ending entitlements because they fear that the employment sector, despite a strong economy, is not free of discriminatory practices. Policies such as "last hired, first fired" can have disparate impact on African Americans and other oppressed population that have shorter longevity because of previous policies that denied opportunity based upon race or ethnicity. Employment barriers such as inadequate education, residency requirements, credit checks, and criminal background checks can be proxies for racial discrimination (Hill, 1997).

Racial and ethnic disparities among those on welfare rolls are rooted in a history of racial discrimination (Cates, 1983; Ehrenreich, 1991; Jeff, 1998; Skocpol, 1989). Therefore, the disproportionate number of persons of color must be understood within the context of earlier public policy discrimination. Because of a concern that welfare dependency might be unfairly attributed to people of color, comparisons that examine race often focus on only African Americans and Whites, and these studies often emphasize the fact that more Whites than African Americans have historically been on welfare rolls. Thus, although race and ethnicity are important in examining welfare, historical discrimination and stereotyping have restricted unbiased reporting on race. Some are concerned that raising the claim of racial bias is tantamount to excusing dependency and supporting individuals who abuse the system.

The welfare reform introduced by the 1996 PRWORA had many provisions that particularly caused African Americans to be concerned. Yet, an important political change had taken place among African American leaders and their racially and economically mixed constituencies. While the prior generation of the African American electorate came out of a strong civil rights movement and urgently supported African American issues, the "new [African American] mayors" placed the practical demands of governing over the symbolic rhetoric of racial justice (Thernstrom & Thernstrom, 1997). Although many African Americans agreed that the old welfare system was a failed policy, they were not generally supportive of the new reforms. Their sense of foreboding was grounded in a distrust of state governments to provide needed support, an inadequate supply of jobs offering a livable wage, and neighborhood destabilization. Yet these new leaders were also faced with the political reality of the growing anger and public resentment toward those welfare recipients who were perceived to be "getting over on the system." Welfare reform posed an ethical dilemma for many African Americans because despite their desire to improve the plight of poor people, they feared opening welfare to the public for attack and being labeled as "too welfare compassionate."

African American organizations weighed in on the debate by speaking out against the policy. The National Urban League (1996) stated its opposition to welfare reform, along with the National Association of Black Social Workers, which asserted that "we have here a law of reform void of reformulation. The continued underdevelopment of the African American welfare recipient is the independent variable in the reform equation. . . African Americans on welfare are being treated like aliens in their own land" (Jeff, 1998, p. 49). Similarly, other groups expressed their disapproval of the law before it was signed, such as the National Association of Social Workers, which enlisted 1,000 social workers to take out a full page ad in the *New York Times* to demand either congressional action to kill the Senate bill or a presidential veto (Jansson, 1997).

African American scholars similarly criticized the PRWORA: "Though the act will have devastating consequences for all poor and working-class families, its effects on the African American community will be especially ominous" (Schiele, 1998, p. 1). Hill (1997) pointed out that "unless radical changes are made, this act is not likely to increase self-sufficiency of most welfare recipients, nor will it lift them out of poverty" (p. 184). African American scholars generally did not embrace the welfare reform proposed in the PRWORA. Their reluctance was rooted in a history of policies that failed to address the interests of African Americans and this welfare reform presented itself as yet another example of a policy pregnant with both intended and unintended negative consequences for African Americans. While there are many reasons that African Americans rejected the universal appeal of "ending welfare as we know it," all such reasons seem to be grounded in the general distrust of the government to provide the needed support to move the most vulnerable families to self-sufficiency. This legacy of broken promises demands extreme caution in advocating for policies that deny or terminate assistance based upon the judgement of individuals who have previously promulgated failed policies and are in many cases openly hostile to African Americans. Given the wretched history of public policy, the African American public was justifiably skeptical of President Clinton's claim that PRWORA would end welfare as we know it (ACF, 1996, p. 1).

Studies have begun to show that the concerns of many African Americans about the potential for disparate impact were indeed justified. Bond (2002) cites research showing adverse effects in the areas of leaver disparities, use of sanctions, loss of health insurance, caseworker disparities, work hours, support services, and earnings disparities. Schram (n.d.) also noted a welfare-race connection to "get-tough policies" such as sanctioning, family caps, stricter work requirements, and time limits. These findings compel African Americans and other advocates to advocate for a reauthorization plan that respects the systemic hardships of multiple barriers and an "unequal playing field."

The National Urban League credited the robust economic expansion with the success of shrinking welfare rolls and noted the ongoing barriers that African Americans and Latinos face in accessing services and job markets (Rockeymoore, 2001a). Thus, calls are being made for reforms that would revamp the program to include measures such as education and training to address the reduction or elimination of poverty. The National Association of Black Social Workers (2002) is calling for the reauthorization proposals to have a renewed focus on poverty elimination:

> Most mistaken is the failure of welfare reform policy makers to understand or to use the principles that underpin the strength of Black family. A strong work ethic, strong achievement orientation, buttressed by flexible family roles and kinship bonds, prominently permeate Black community and family life. These anchors have served to assure even in the face of race discrimination and other unfair marketplace practices, the indomitable spirit of Blacks to win and to succeed. (p. 1)

This perspective, a strengths perspective, is missing in the leading reauthorization proposals just as it was missing in the 1965 Moynihan report.

Welfare Reform 5 Years Later: The Report Card on Race

For all of the aforementioned reasons, it is important to examine the first 5 years of the 1996 welfare reform from the perspective of race. This discussion specifically addresses race by looking at changing demographics of the active welfare rolls as well as the characteristics of those leaving the rolls. This discussion will also examine policy implications, especially as they relate to current reauthorization proposals.

Continued Racialization of the TANF Rolls

The claims for welfare reform being a success are largely grounded in the statistics that show 4.7 million Americans getting off welfare between 1996 and 1999 (ACF, 2000). These figures are coupled with the decline in the overall poverty rate from approximately 14% to 11% in this same period to celebrate the unprecedented accomplishments of this reform. At the end of the 2001 fiscal year, there was a 56% decline in the number of people on welfare since 1996 (ACF, 2003) While there has been an upward trend in the size of welfare rolls since 2000 (CLASP, 2003), the new laws and a strong economy and state initiatives drastically reduced the number of families receiving cash assistance since the passage of PRWORA. The question for this section is how African Americans were affected.

African Americans represent the racial group with the largest number of families and children on the TANF rolls (ACF, 2003). This situation, which existed prior to TANF, continued through the first 5 years of the program's implementation. A total of 39% of adult heads of households and 41% of children on TANF rolls are African American, compared to 31% of adult heads of households and 26% of children being White. Table 2 shows the 1996 and 2001 TANF family rolls by race (ACF, 2000). There has been a greater decline in welfare dependency among Whites than among any other racial or ethnic group. While President George W. Bush's reauthorization plan touts the decline in poverty among African American children, it fails to address this inequity. The five annual reports to Congress (1997–2001) have all noted the shift in the racial composition of the welfare rolls. The primary emphasis has been on the increase of Hispanic households. The changes in the African American composition of the rolls have been minimized by language that infers a continuation of existing trends or slight increases. For example, the following statements are included in the 2001 TANF Annual Report to Congress

> The racial distribution of TANF recipient children was slightly changed in recent years. African American children continued to be the largest group of welfare children, comprising about 40% of recipient children. (p. 5)

> There was little change in the racial composition of TANF families. African American families comprised 39% of the TANF families. White families comprised 31% of the families, and 25% were Hispanic. (p. 3)

Caseload trends and analysis of those leaving welfare rolls confirm the existence of differential patterns (Lower-Basch, 2000). While the number of people on welfare for all racial groups have declined, Whites have fared better than any other racial or ethnic group. Lower-Basch reported that African Americans and Whites were relatively equally represented in 1996, but there was a 50.6% decline for White families as compared to a 39.9% decline for African American families. This almost 11% difference is minimized in the ACF's annual reports to Congress and since 1996 their reports have indicated that there has been little change in the racial composition

Table 2. Race and Ethnicity of AFDC/TANF Families and Children, by Percent of Total Population Receiving Benefits

	U.S. Total	White	African American	Hispanic	Native American	Asian	Other
Adult Recipients							
FY 1996	4,553,308	36	37	21	1	3	2
FY 1999	2,648,462	31	38	25	2	4	2
FY 2001	1,408,752	32	39	24	1	2	2
Difference							
1996–2001	3,144,556	(4)	2	3	0	1	0
Child Recipients							
FY 1996	8,685,985	32	38	22	1	4	2
FY 1999	5,318,722	26	40	26	2	5	2
FY 2001	4,054,964	26	41	28	1	3	1
Difference							
1996–2001	4,631,021	(6)	3	6	0	1	1

*Program data for Aid to Families With Dependent Children (AFDC)
**Program data for Temporary Assistance to Needy Families (TANF)

of the welfare rolls. The ACF's *First Annual Report to Congress* (ACF, 1998) cautioned the public not to draw premature conclusions about the increase in the percentage of African American children, which could be attributed to missing state-level data. The ACF's *Third Annual Report to Congress* (ACF, 2000) acknowledged the shift in the proportion of people of color on the TANF rolls; however, this change was explained to be largely related to the growing population of Hispanics. No specific mention was made in any of the ACF's annual reports of the differences in the number of African Americans and Whites leaving welfare—the focus was always on the shift in the composition of the rolls and the data usually reports changes from 1992, thus obscuring the impact of PRWORA. The following excerpt from the 2002 TANF Annual Report to Congress demonstrates the awareness of the shifting demographics of the TANF rolls.

The racial composition of welfare families has changed substantially over the past ten years. In FY 1992, it was 39% white, 37% African American, and 18% Hispanic. In FY 2001, however, it was 30% white, 39% African American, and 26% Hispanic. Viewed over the decade, there has been a shift from White to Hispanic families, which is consistent with broader population trends… In addition, the proportion of African American families has trended up slightly since FY 1996, following a decline that preceded FY 1996. The result of these changes is that over the past decade the proportion of welfare families that are of color has increased from three-fifths to just over two-thirds, primarily driven by the relative growth in Hispanic families. (p. 191)

These aggregate federal totals do not tell the whole story of the 1996 welfare reform's impact on African Americans; state level data are more revealing. Data from the fiscal year 2001 TANF Annual Report (ACF, 2003) when compared with fiscal year 1996 report show that 39 out of 52 reporting jurisdictions met an increase in the percentage of African American families on the rolls. Also, these same data show that four states (Indiana, Missouri, New York, and Ohio) have TANF rolls that have become majority African American following the 1996 PRWORA. These data also show that large urban centers have the largest percentage of TANF recipients and most of the individuals remaining on their welfare rolls are African Americans. Meyers (2001) points out that 72% of Washington, DC-area welfare recipients reside in the actual city of Washington, DC, and 83% of Baltimore-area recipients live in the city of Baltimore. What the article does not mention is that each jurisdiction's caseload is more than 85% African American. The decline in welfare caseloads may be greater in areas with more economic opportunity, thus implying that those remaining on welfare rolls are more likely to be concentrated in distressed neighborhoods. This has been researched by the Joint Center for Political and Economic Studies (2001): "Urban counties containing the 30 largest cities had about 20% of the U.S. population throughout the 1990s. But they accounted for 39% of welfare recipients in 1998, up from 33% in 1994" (pp. 7). The increasing concentration of welfare recipients in major cities is largely connected with the disproportionate number of African Americans residing in those locations. The Joint Center also reported that between 1994 and 1998, the proportion of African Americans on Milwaukee, Wisconsin's welfare rolls increased from 57% to 86%; Chicago's Cook County's from 66% to 74%; New York City's from 68% to 70%; and Baltimore's from 48% to 56%.

Outcomes of Leavers

Research on TANF outcomes has also examined the experiences of individuals leaving the rolls. These projects, called "leaver studies," have examined various aspects of the reform experience and have generally found that African Americans are underrepresented among leavers (Lower-Basch, 2000). The exit rate of African Americans between 1995 and 1996 in Wisconsin, which implemented a highly praised reform plan, trailed Whites by as much as 24%. Ironically, this state was used as the model for the national welfare-to-work agenda and little attention was given to these disparities. Although other studies report smaller differences, they do find that African Americans have exited at slower rates. This difference may in part be attributed to a higher number of African Americans being long-term recipients with multiple barriers to self-sufficiency. Other explanations relate to patterns of discrimination inside and outside of the welfare office. The National Urban League (Rockeymoore, 2001a) attributes these findings to two flawed assumptions: (1) that there would be "level playing grounds" in the administration of the program; and, (2) that recipients would find work in the labor market.

Two pieces of evidence confirm this assertion. First, studies have already uncovered differential sanctioning patterns. For example, the Department of Health and Human Services report on racial differences noted that "one disturbing finding is that those studies that examined reason for exit found that minorities were more likely than Whites to have their cases closed due to sanctions rather than earnings" (Lower-Basch, 2000, p. 17). Second, African Americans are more likely to recidivate than Whites. In Wisconsin, for example, being an African American welfare recipient was associated with an almost 80% likelihood of returning to TANF within 6 months. These data were consistent with pre-TANF findings that showed African Americans returning to welfare rolls at a rate of 65% as compared to the 44% return rate for Whites (Lower-Basch, 2000; Bonds, 2002).

Welfare reform has also resulted in a proliferation of child-only cases. These are cases where the parent is no longer receiving TANF assistance for reasons that include low earnings, their failure to comply with work, or other requirements. Thirty-seven percent of the fiscal year 2001 TANF cases (a 15% increase since PRWORA implementation) were child-only (ACF, 2001). According to the *Year Five Annual TANF Report to Congress*, both the number and proportion of child-only cases increased, with 22% being cared for by grandparents. Nationwide there has been an increase in these cases, with African Americans experiencing a greater impact than other racial or ethnic groups. A specific concern is that this trend is placing extra burden on already fragile family systems such as grandparents in the African American community (Crewe, 2003b). In a study of African American grandparents in the District of Columbia, AARP noted that some grandparents avoid the stressors associated with job search by opting for child-only grants that result in additional financial burdens (Crewe & Stowell-Ritter, 2003).

Understanding welfare leavers also requires looking at poverty rates. Poverty data for 2000 show that the poverty rate for African Americans fell from 24% to 22% (U.S. Census, 2001). The Urban Institute (1999) reported that poverty rates are indicators of income and hardship associated with the PRWORA. In 2000, non-Hispanic Whites had a poverty rate of 5% as compared to the African American poverty rate of 19%. Among female householders with no male present, the poverty rates were 20% for Whites and 35% for African Americans. Interestingly, although African Americans are disproportionately overrepresented among the poor, these data show that out of those below the poverty level, Whites are more likely to receive TANF aid. In summary, these data show that race does matter in welfare reform outcomes. Differential impacts have been discussed that require dismissal of the notion that welfare reform is color blind.

Conclusion

Despite the evidence of growing racialized welfare rolls, little or no attention is given to strategies, research, or programs to better understand the trends. Findings from current national research studies do not provide direct explanations for racial disparities. Some local research has begun to elicit information related to race and the receipt of welfare services. There are reports on the differential experiences of African Americans and Whites concerning the receipt of support services from welfare workers (Bonds,2002; Crewe, 2002; Gooden, 2000, 1999, 1998; Schram, Sorr & Fording, 2001; Walters & DeWeever, 1999). These studies indicate that there are perceived and documented disparities and increases in the proportion of African Americans on welfare that may reflect structural barriers such as employment discrimination, lack of transportation, or health problems. On the other hand, decreases in the number of African Americans on welfare rolls may result from overaggressive sanctioning of people of color, misunderstanding benefits, or other systemic patterns of discrimination within social services agencies. These studies do not negate the strengths and resilience of the African American community and its successes despite the individual and systemic challenges. On the contrary, the studies bring a needed consciousness to racial disparities with the goal of reversing the historical pattern of discrimination that has resulted in substantial numbers of African Americans developing dependency on welfare. This can be achieved by more research efforts undertaken with sensitivity to this cohort of clients and an understanding that exposing and honestly discussing differential impacts is the first step toward resolving inequities.

Despite abundant evidence of differential treatment, the major reauthorization proposals and bills fail to acknowledge these disparities. In fact, race is only mentioned in the Bush Administration's report to note the decrease in African American child poverty (White House, 2002). There are no stated strategies to address these research-confirmed inequalities. Rather, the reauthorization plans present a more determined "get tough on work" approach without acknowledging that declining welfare rolls do not address the quality of life issues that are faced by many African Americans. In fact research has shown that get-tough policies, such as stricter sanctions and family caps, are more heavily utilized in states with relatively high percentages of African Americans and Latinos (Schram, n.d.; Schram, Soss, & Fording, 2001).

The 5-year report card for TANF must use a pass–fail system that awards a passing grade only when all are equally served by the safety net. As long as disparities are tied to race, there cannot be a claim of success. Walters & DeWeever (1999) in their W. K. Kellogg Devolution Project note a "troubling contradiction" about the success of welfare reform. They state that:

> Welfare reform has been a success if one only considers the decline in the number of recipients, however, welfare reform was never touted to be a mechanism to only reduce the rolls. It was also crafted to be a system that would ostensibly provide welfare clients with a sense of accomplishment by building self esteem and social viability through work. However, the reality has been quite different. (p. 35)

In the midst of inspirational individual accounts, policies and practices continue to knowingly produce unequal outcomes for African Americans while being camouflaged by declining welfare rolls. Further, almost no attention has been given to the thousands of individuals who left welfare rolls without finding work and the thousands who have found work with little or no hope of self-sufficiency. These families must also be accounted for before a passing grade can be given. Even a robust economy could not eliminate the discriminatory effect of prior enslavement, deliberate bifurcation in social welfare policy, and absence of cultural sensitivity. The continued marginalization and insensitivity to the effect of cumulative disadvantage and racially disparate policies is evidenced by the Bush administration's heralding of the 1965 Moynihan report as being accurate and ignored. Blaming welfare dependency solely on single parenthood and individual behavior is as misguided now as it was then. For those who feel that enough time has elapsed to correct past discrimination, the following quote from Dr. Martin Luther King, Jr. (1983) is appropriate:

> When millions of people have been cheated for centuries, restitution is a costly process. Inferior education, poor housing, unemployment, inadequate health care—each is a bitter component of the oppression that has been our heritage. Each will require billions of dollars to correct. Justice so long deferred has accumulated interest and its cost for this society will be substantial in financial as well as human terms. This fact has not been fully grasped, because most of the gains of the past decade were obtained at bargain rates. The desegregation of public facilities cost nothing; neither did the election and appointment of a few black public officials. (p. 57)

Although strides have been made and many families have benefited from this reform of welfare coupled with support services and a strong economy, social welfare policy has failed to level the playing field. Gais and Weaver (2002) tell us that:

> contrary to the hopes of some welfare reform proponents, the new welfare law does not seem to have dissipated the image of the program as disproportionately aiding minorities, or the negative impact that this image has on support for the program in many states. (p. 7)

It could not accomplish this because welfare rolls are more racialized than ever. Thus, we cannot support a race-blind policy that fails to acknowledge cumulative disadvantage and systemic problems. Ridding the system of differential treatment and refocusing on poverty eradication are non-negotiable requirements for improved outcomes. This is the new bottom line to be achieved before African Americans can declare the program a success. The danger in the reauthorization proposals is that we are building indiscriminately on our failures and successes. It is not too late to reverse the trend. Lieberman (1995) gives us hope in his analysis of the exclusionary origins of Old Age Assistance under the New Deal and how it traveled a different evolutionary path from public assistance by paying attention to the nature of the institutional apparatus. The ultimate test of the success or failure of welfare reform is its contribution to quality of life for the thousands of African American families, women, and children who are behind the numbers (Crewe, 2003a). Data strongly compel that we review its performance with improved quality of life as the benchmark for success. We need a policy for all people characterized by an understanding that history has charted different pathways to dependency and self-sufficiency and the minority of African Americans who find themselves "on the system" need a policy that is not ahistoric. The final words of advice come best from a TANF mom who asks for a compassionate and understanding policy that will *"help us where it's really needed so we can survive and not throw us into the water and watch us drown."*

References

Administration for Children and Families. (1996). Welfare bill signing (HR3734\PL 104-193) August 22, 1996. Retrieved January 9, 1997, from http:www.acf.dhhs.gov/welfarereform

Administration for Children and Families. (1998). *Temporary assistance to needy families program: First annual report to congress.* Retrieved September 18, 2002, from http://www.acf.dhhs.gov/programs

Administration for Children and Families. (2000). *Characteristics and financial circumstances of TANF recipients¾Fiscal year 1999.* Retrieved October 4, 2000, from http://www.acf.dhhs.gov/programs/opre/characteristics/fy99/analysis.htm

Administration for Children and Families. (2001). *Characteristics and financial circumstances of TANF recipients¾Fiscal year 2000.* Retrieved September 18, 2002, from http://www.acf.dhhs.gov/programs/opre/characteristics/fy00/analysis.htm

Administration for Children and Families. (2002). *Temporary assistance to needy families program: Fourth annual report to congress.* Retrieved September 18, 2002, from http://www.acf.dhhs.gov/programs/ope/ar2001/indexar.htm

Administration for Children and Families. (2003). *Temporary assistance to needy families program: Fifth annual report to Congress.* Retrieved January 23, 2004, from http://www.acf.dhhs.gov/programs/ope/ar2002/indexar.htm

Bonds, M. (2002). Racial disparities in welfare reform: Wisconsin Works (W2) experience in America's heartland. Retrieved January 24, 2004, from http://www.wkkf.org/Pubs/Devolution/Pub3703.pdf

Carlton-LaNey, I. B. (1999). African American social work pioneers' response to need. *Social Work, 44,* 311–321.

Cates, J. (1983). *Insuring inequality: Administrative leadership in Social Security, 1935–1954.* Ann Arbor, MI: University of Michigan Press.

Center for Law and Social Policy. (2003, October 16). Welfare caseloads remains relatively flat in second quarter of 2003. Retrieved January 24, 2003, from http//:www.clasp.org

Coalition on Human Needs. (2002). *Many programs benefiting poor face reauthorization in 2003.* Retrieved on January 22, 2004, from http://chn.org/humanneeds.asp

Committee on Education and the Workforce. (2002). *Minority views to H.R. 4092-Working toward Independence Act 2002.* Retrieved on January 22, 2004, from http:///www.house.gov/eeo_democrats/hr4092views.html

Crewe, S. E. (1997). Unmotivated or unchallenged: An ethnographic study of sanctioned welfare recipients residing in federally assisted housing. *Dissertation Abstracts International, 58*(8), 3307. (UMI No. 9804115)

Crewe, S. E. (2002). Motivated but fearful: Welfare reform, disability, and race. *Journal of Health and Social Policy, 16,* 55–68.

Crewe, S. E. (2003a). Behind the numbers: Welfare reform from an ecological perspective. *International Journal of Public Administration, 26,* 753–771.

Crewe, S. E. (2003b). African American grandparent caregivers: Eliminating double jeopardy in social policy. In T. Bent-Goodley (Ed.), *African American social workers and social policy* (pp. 35–54). Binghamton, NY: Haworth Press.

Crewe, S. E., Schervish, P., & Gourdine, R. M. (2000). *Welfare reform: Risk and resilience indicators of TCA customers in Prince George's County, Maryland.* Washington, DC: Howard University, E. Franklin Frazier Research Center.

Crewe, S. E., & Stowell-Ritter, A. (2003). Grandparents raising grandchildren in the District of Columbia: Focus group report. Retrieved January 24, 2004, from http://research.aarp.org/general/dc_gp.html

DeParle, J. (1998, July 27). Shrinking welfare rolls leave record high share of minorities. *The New York Times,* p. A1.

DeParle, J. (1999, October 10). As benefits expire, the experts worry. *The New York Times,* p. A1, A28.

Ehrenreich, B. (1991, December 16). Welfare: A White secret. *Time,* 84.

Franklin, D. (1997). *Ensuring inequality: The transformation of the African-American family.* New York: Oxford University Press.

Friedman, W. (1996). Forty acres and a mule. In *Encyclopedia of African American culture and history* (Vol. 2, pp. 1032–1033). New York: Simon and Schuster.

Gais, T. & Weaver, R.K. (April, 2002). *State policy choices under welfare reform* (Policy Brief No. 21.) Washington, DC: Brookings Institute Press.

Gilens, M. (1999). *Why Americans hate welfare.* Chicago: University of Chicago Press.

Gooden, S. T. (1998). All things not being equal: Differences in caseworker support toward Black and White welfare clients. *Harvard Journal of African Americans Public Policy, 4,* 23–43.

Gooden, S. T. (1999). The hidden third party: Welfare recipients' experiences with employers. *Journal of Public Management and Social Policy, 5*(1), 69–83.

Gooden, S. T. (2000). Examining employment outcomes of White and Black welfare recipients. *Journal of Poverty, 4*(3), 21–41.

Greenberg, M. (2002). Bush's blunder. *The American Prospect, 13*(13), 1–7.

Groskind, F. (1994). Ideological influences on public support for assistance to poor families. *Social Work, 39,* 81–89.

Handler, J. F., & Hasenfeld, Y. (1997). *We the poor people: Work, poverty and welfare.* New Haven, CT: Yale University Press.

Hill, R. (1997). *The strengths of African American families: Twenty-five years later.* Washington, DC: R & B Publishers.

Jansson, B. (1997). *The reluctant welfare state: American social welfare policies: Past, present, and future* (3rd ed.). Pacific Grove, CA: Brooks/Cole.

Jeff, M. X. J. (1998). The National Association of Black Social Workers' reflection on the new welfare reform law. *Harvard Journal of African American Public Policy, 4,* 49–58.

Joint Center for Political and Economic Studies. (2001). *Devolution.* Retrieved July 26, 2001, from www.jointcenter.org/devolution/devpages/know.htm

Karger, H., & Stoesz, D. (1998). *American social welfare policy* (3rd ed.). New York: Longman.

Katz, M. B. (1986). *In the shadow of the poor house: A social history of welfare in America.* New York: Basic Books.

King, M. L. (1983). *The words of Martin Luther King, Jr.* New York: New Market Press.

Lieberman, R.C. (1995). Race, institutions, and the administration of social policy. *Social Science History, 19,* 511–543.

Lower-Basch, E. (2000). *Leavers and diversion studies: Preliminary analysis of racial difference in caseload trends and leaver outcomes.* Retrieved January 24, 2004, from http://www.aspe.hhs.gov/hsp/leavers99/race.htm

Marcenko, M., & Fagan, J. (1996). Welfare to work: What are the obstacles? *Journal of Sociology and Social Welfare, 23,* 113–131.

Martin J. M., & Martin, E. P. (1985). *The helping tradition in the Black family.* Washington, DC: National Association of Social Workers.

Martin J. M., & Martin, E. P. (1995). *Social work and the Black experience.* Washington, DC: National Association of Social Workers.

Meyers, C. S. (2001). *The District and Baltimore face double whammy in welfare reform: Greater challenges and less funding for needed services.* Retrieved January 24, 2004, from http://www.brook.edu/es/urban/gwrp/welfare_double_whammy_fullreport.htm

Moynihan, D. P. (1999). The study of Black families: The tangle of pathology. In R. Staples (Ed.), *The Black Family* (pp. 7–17). Belmont, CA: Wadsworth.

National Association of Black Social Workers. (2002). *Draft TANF reauthorization policy statement.* Washington, DC: Author.

National Urban League. (1996). *Welfare reform vs. reality.* Retrieved October 26, 1999, from http://www.nul.org/tbe/pqwt/tbe9631.txt

The 100 best writers of the century. (1999, November). *Writer's Digest, 79*(11), 12–25.

New Deal. (2000). *Encyclopedia Americana.* Retrieved January 22, 2004, from http://gi.grolier.com/presidents/ea/side/newdeal.html

Personal Responsibility and Work Opportunity Act, 42 U.S.C. § 110 Stat. 2105 (1996).

Quadagno, J. S. (1994). *The color of welfare: How racism undermined the war on poverty.* New York: Oxford University Press.

Quadagno, J. S. (1996). Race and American social policy. *National Forum, 76*(3), 35–39.

Rein, L. (1999, October 30). Some Virginia families' day-care aid to end. *The Washington Post,* p. B7.

Rockeymoore, M. (2001a). Rethinking welfare reform. *National Urban League: To Be Equal.* Retrieved July 1, 2002, from http://www.nul.org/tbe/tbe2001151.txt

Rockeymoore, M. (2001b). *TANF, race and reauthorization: What do we know about race and welfare reform.* Washington, DC: National Urban League.

Salzman, J., Smith, D. L., & West, C. (Eds.) (1996). *Encyclopedia of African American history and culture* (Vol. 1, 1st ed.). New York: MacMillan.

Schiele, J. H. (1998). The Personal Responsibility Act of 1996: The bitter, the sweet for African American families. *Families in Society, 79,* 424–429.

Schram, S. F. (n.d.). Race and state welfare reform choices: a cause for concern. Unpublished paper. Bryn Mawr Graduate School of Social Work and Social Research. Retrieved January 24, 2004, from http://www.brynmawr.edu/Acads/GSSW/scram/racereform.pdf

Schram, S. F. & Soss, J. (2001, September). Success stories: Welfare reform, policy discourse, and politics of research [Electronic version]. *Annals of the American Academy of Political and Social Sciences,* 49–65.

Schram, S. F., Soss, J., & Fording, C. (Eds). (2001). *Race, welfare and the politics of reform.* Ann Arbor: University of Michigan Press,

Skocpol, T. (1989). The limits of the New Deal's system and the root of contemporary welfare dilemmas. In M. Weir, A. Orloff, & T. Skocpol (Eds.), *The politics of social policy in the United States* (pp. 293–311). Princeton, NJ: Princeton University Press.

Staples, R. (1999). *The Black family: Essays and studies.* Belmont, CA: Wadsworth.

Thernstrom, S., & Thernstrom, A. (1997). *America in Black and White: One nation, indivisible.* New York: Simon and Schuster.

Urban Institute. (1999). *Snapshots of America's families.* Washington, DC: Author.

U.S. Census Bureau. (2000). *Poverty: 1999.* Retrieved on January 24, 2004, from http://www.census.gov/population/www/cen2000/briefs.html

U.S. Census Bureau. (2001). *Overview of race and Hispanic origin.* Retrieved on January 24, 2004, from http:www./census.gov/population//www/cen2000briefs.html

U.S. Department of Labor. (1965, March). *The Negro family: The case for national action.* Washington, DC: Author.

Walters, R. W., & DeWeever, G. E. (1999). *In their own words: Community activists discuss welfare and health care reform.* College Park, MD: Scholar Practitioner Program, University of Maryland.

White House. (2002). *Working toward independence.* Retrieved September 22, 2002, from http://whitehouse.gov/infocus/welfarereform/

Yoo, G. J. (1999). Welfare reform and Black families: The 1996 Personal Responsibility and Work Opportunity Reconciliation Act. In R. Staples (Ed.), *The Black family* (pp. 357–366). Belmont, CA: Wadsworth.

PART THREE. Taking Action

Chapter Twelve

Beyond Cultural Insensitivity and Institutional Racism: An Equipoise Approach to the Delivery of Health and Human Services

Barbara Solomon

The chapters in this book could serve as a virtual encyclopedia of federal and state governmental policies that have effectively institutionalized and thus perpetuated disadvantage and inequity for people of color in the United States. Although it may be argued that other groups have also been subjected to oppressive public policies (based on gender, social class, or sexual orientation), the institutionalization and perpetuation of disadvantage for people of color has been uniquely developed and uniquely resisted (see Davis, chapter one, in this volume). The category, "people of color" is preferred to "race" or even "cultural group" because it avoids any assumption that differences in beliefs, values, and practices correspond systematically to ethnic and racial categories. However, there is strong evidence that dark skin color has been associated historically in the United States and most of the Western world with dispossession and limited social status, whereas light skin has been associated with political and economic power and privilege, particularly for men (Appiah, 1996; Gutman, 1996; Davis, chapter one of this volume).

Social work, like all the helping professions, has been accused of allowing cultural biases to suffuse its theoretical frameworks, models of practice, and service delivery systems (Schiele, 1997). In the literature, these biases are most often referred to as cultural insensitivity and institutional racism and are believed to be responsible for inadequate or ineffective design, delivery, and evaluation of health and human services to people of color. It may be argued that the two phenomena are interrelated and, in fact, institutional racism can be considered a direct consequence of cultural insensitivity. Most important, however, is that the two phenomena may be distinguished by the system level at which they are most likely to be identified: cultural insensitivity is usually identified at the individual or group level, whereas institutional racism is usually identified at the organizational or even societal level.

This article explores the development and implementation of social policy aimed at reducing or eliminating cultural insensitivity and institutional racism in the design, delivery, and evaluation of health and human services. It begins with a brief consideration of sociopolitical theories that are reflected in the various often-conflicting perspectives on social programs that serve people of color. Next, the definition, manifestations, and social policy responses to cultural insensitivity and institutional racism will be detailed. Finally, a reconciliatory approach to policy-making aimed at the delivery of health and human services is proposed that promises not only to be unbiased in regard to people of color but proactively anti-biased.

The Sociopolitical Perspective on Color Bias

The paradox of a nation with a long history of discrimination on the basis of color in almost every aspect of public life, despite a Constitution and Bill of Rights that forthrightly prohibits discrimination on the basis of "race, color or creed," has not gone unnoticed by political theorists. Adams (1997) has presented a compelling explanation of the paradox. He asserts that it is the peculiar combination of liberalism and democracy that has made it so difficult to address the multiple manifestations of racism in American society. Democracy and its related values of equality and justice provided the deeply felt inspiration for those patriots who launched the American Revolution. However, the framers of the Constitution and the state that was built after the Revolutionary War were far more influenced by the principles of classic liberalism—individualism, the notion of rights (particularly to property), the sanctity of contracts, and the rule of law. According to Adams (1997):

> The core value of the more democratic revolutionary period, equality, was given a severe reduction in rank by the founding fathers. And the value of liberty, and its repository in the individual, was elevated and buttressed by law, by contract and by rights." (p. 181)

Scholars who have studied differences between mainstream Eurocentric culture in the United States and traditional cultures of people of color have also identified the tension between the value placed on the collective in these traditional cultures and the primacy of the individual in our mainstream Eurocentric culture (Schiele, 1997). The preoccupation with individualism that has its roots in classic liberalism has been perceived as a major stumbling block to dealing effectively with prejudice and discrimination against stigmatized collectives such as people of color. Communitarians, a political and intellectual movement developed in this country in the past 30 years, suggests that the historic and current emphasis on individualism is pathological, socially and politically, and does not take into account that neither human existence nor individual liberty can be sustained for long outside the interdependent and overlapping communities to which all of us belong (Heller, Sosna, & Wellbery, 1986). However, communitarians have not been the only critics of individualism untempered with an appreciation for the cohesive community.

The countervailing value emphasis to individualism is community. The link between democracy and community has not been challenged. Barber (1993), a political theorist and strong proponent of participatory democracy, has written that the task of democracy is "to transform [interest–motivated individuals] into citizens capable of reassessing themselves and their interests in terms of newly invented communal norms and newly imagined public goods" (p.129). In contrast, the frequent connection made between democratic political philosophy and equality seems strained by contradiction. For example, the founding fathers were nearly all major slave owners who clearly understood that citizens of the new nation would reflect wide ranging differences in regard to gender, age, religion, physical and mental abilities, and wealth. Why would they then state in the preamble to the Constitution that "all men are created 'equal'?"

Patterson (1997) has an intriguing explanation: He asserts that because there is no known criterion for selecting which qualities of the human condition are important, the founding fathers decided "with extraordinary perspicacity to make the assumption of equality which would be proposed as both an end and a means for determining how the new nation was to deal with the problems of difference and inequality" (p. 135).

Their thinking may have gone something like the following: We know that there are numerous differences and inequalities among people. However, we are declaring as an end for the nation the idea that, whatever observable differences there may be between people, it will be accepted that in some profound respects they are to be treated as equal, especially in the legal and political areas of life (Patterson, 1997, p. 135).

Fast forward to contemporary times and the position taken on equality by the founding fathers still seems to have the support of the majority of the American people; however, just as support for the position did not result in setting slaves free, it has not eliminated racism, sexism, anti-Semitism, or related behaviors incongruent with democratic ideals. It is true that no one is prepared to single out for "unequal" treatment or even for any special attention those low-income Whites in Appalachia who score significantly lower on IQ tests than higher-income Whites in the Northeast or the elderly who remain in the workforce despite research that indicates the elderly demonstrate a significant decline in productivity when compared to younger workers (Sowell, 1987). Yet, Hernstein and Murray (1994) were prepared to recommend reduction in public support for programs aimed at reducing the gap between Black–White academic achievement because their analyses of IQ data suggested that Blacks are significantly less intelligent than Whites as a group.

Values are not "either–or" propositions, but rather are hierachical in character. Although one value may take priority over another, each is always dependent on the situation or context. There is ample evidence that discrimination against individuals based soley on their membership in a stigmatized collective occurs despite the strong tradition of individualism in this country. Thus, racism and related behaviors too frequently override commitment to individualism. Similarly, our commitment to democratic principles has not meant that persons of color have always been included either among institutional decision-makers (e.g., grand juries, corporate boards, governors, and legislative bodies) or in the participatory processes that provide input to those decision-makers. Racism and related behaviors too frequently override individual, societal, and governmental commitment to democratic process. For persons of color, it is painfully clear that their best interests may be ignored in the name of either societal value (i.e., individualism) or democracy (Bell, 1992; Guinier & Torres, 2002). In the name of individual rights, it can be argued that the past is history and individuals today cannot be held accountable for the sins or debts of their ancestors. In the name of democracy, the principle of "majority rules" diminishes any justification for the concept of "minority rights," as well as their efforts to restore losses that stem from historical abrogation of these rights (see Fagan, 2002; Gingold, 1999; McAuliffe, 2001; Robinson, 2000).

When there are critical value choices to be made, such choices will inevitably be made on the basis of how the key concept of justice is understood in political theory. Unfettered participation in American political life depends on certain shared opinions about justice. The false assumption by liberal political theorists is that there is a reasonable agreement in the society regarding these first principles of justice. However, Rawls (1993) contends that a modern democratic society is characterized not simply by a pluralism of comprehensive religious, philosophical, and moral doctrines, but by a pluralism of incompatible yet reasonably comprehensive doctrines. Justice as fairness must somehow be established on grounds capable of admitting this pluralism. "Citizens can be brought to accept principles of justice in common without being required to renounce the various doctrines that will naturally arise in a democratic society" (Rawls, 1993, p. 173). A contrary view, however, challenges how citizens can be brought to affirm principles of justice held in common when in reality they hold certain intractable, naturally intolerant, and partisan opinions. How can such emotions as greed, prejudice, and revenge be "tamed by an idea of justice that is constructed by hypothetical rational" and "reasonable" persons subject to "reasonable" constraints (Sowell, 1987, p. 55)?

The answer may lie in a fourth concept, which has been much more apparent in Eastern philosophy than in the Western philosophies of Aristotle, Plato, Hobbes, and Locke. This is the concept of balance, perhaps reflected most comprehensively in the Taoist concept of yin-yang—two polar energies that by their fluctuation and interaction are proposed as the cause of the universe. Moreover, this fluctuation and interaction means that all phenomena is seen as a cyclical process, an endless coming into being and passing away, as everything upon reaching its extreme stage transforms into its opposite. If translated into a perspective on contemporary political theory, yin-yang suggests that Rawls' theory of justice that public affirmation of principles will, in cases of value conflict, provide a means of making the most "just" value choice based on those principles is valid but does not go far enough. It still assumes that the choice will be based on one value or the other; it does not assume that the choice will reflect an effort to balance the commitment to both values.

The set of values that have framed social, political, and economic processes and policy decisions in American society are rooted in a Western tradition while incorporating implants contributed by the non–Western cultural groups (American Indian, African, Asian, and Mexican) that have been absorbed, sometimes without attribution, into the American ethnosystem. The challenge is to experiment with creative ways of organizing the transcultural hierarchy of values as guides to making social policy so that outcomes for all, citizens—regardless of race, color, gender, religion, sexual orientation, or other stigmatized characteristics—are maximized. Lappe (1989) suggests that this means "building upon all that is worthwhile in the Liberal worldview, while incorporating the richer, more relational understanding of human nature and society emerging today" (p.11). From this broadly conceived sociopolitical perspective, policymakers may be better equipped to address the threats and losses in an otherwise cohesive society posed by cultural insensitivity and institutional racism.

Cultural Insensitivity

People of color have frequently been disadvantaged by the lack of cultural sensitivity encountered as clients seeking or receiving human services (U.S. Department of Healthand Human Services [U.S. DHHS], 2001). Pinderhughes (1989) states that the development of cultural sensitivity in service providers requires first an awareness and understanding of one's own cultural background and its meaning and significance to interact with others. It also involves the acquisition of knowledge about specific cultural groups and of skills for working with them. These include skill in assessing the extent to which personal and institutional racism may be involved in problem-solving efforts. DeHoyos, DeHoyos, and Anderson (1986) suggest that it may be sufficient with White clients to focus on issues of individual adjustment such as ego strength, self-image, and perceptions or on issues of clients' face-to-face relationships with people in their support systems, influencing others as they are influenced by them. However, intervention with clients of color may need to focus on the behavior of individual clients within the impersonal social institutions (e.g., government, economy, education, and religion) to help open the opportunity structure to access rewarding roles and opportunities.

Developing a "Working Relationship"

Skill in developing a working relationship with a client or client system is the *sine qua non* of the helping professional. Pinderhughes (1989) has pointed out that "the task of engaging clients will be more successful if procedures are used which are consistent with clients' values" (p. 172). This will frequently require social agencies to allow its practitioners to provide extensive outreach; be prepared to respond immediately to crisis situations; identify and be prepared to help clients use natural supports such as extended family, church, family, and social groups; and adapt professional tasks and work styles to a range of cultural groups, social classes, levels of education, and levels of acculturation.

There is substantial documentation of the over representation of people of color as clients of social agencies, particularly in the public services geared toward low-income populations (see Crewe, in this volume). There is also evidence that there is a higher "drop-out" rate among clients of color than among White clients. The inclusion of people of color among mental health providers is demonstrated to have significant effects on the nature of service delivery (Snowden, 2000; Whaley, 2001). The most straightforward effect of the increased representation of people of color among service providers is the increased participation and retention of people of color in the client population. It would be easy to assume that this is entirely attributable to the belief that only someone of the same racial or ethnic background will be able to understand the nature of their problem and have the expertise to help solve it. However, there is evidence that this is only another manifestation of an apparently universal human response to "trust" those who are similar to ourselves to a greater extent than we trust those who are not.

Some sociopolitical theorists maintain that familiarity is actually a precondition of trust (Fukuyama, 1995). However, familiarity on the basis of racial or ethnic identity may only ease the initial contact. Familiarity of the cultural issues relevant to a particular presenting problem will be even more important. For example, a middle-class Cuban American practitioner who has not absorbed knowledge of the culture of her Mexican American client who has grown up in the barrios of East Los Angeles may begin well with the client until her lack of familiarity with the relevant cultural issues is discovered. The client ultimately may discontinue service usage as a consequence. In contrast, a middle-class, White practitioner who is familiar with Mexican-American cultural issues may take longer to develop the relationship because of initial lack of trust but after it becomes clear to the client that the cultural issues are understood, the client may continue until the problem-solving work is completed.

Familiarity can be developed over time and skill in developing it cross-culturally can be learned. This assumption is a major underlying factor in increased efforts to develop more culturally sensitive service providers. It is assumed that persons of the same cultural background will have a "head start" on the cultural sensitivity problem and there has been a concerted effort to recruit persons of color into the helping professions for at least 3 decades (Manderscheid & Henderson, 1998).

Assessment

Some critics of the mental health services provided to people of color have focused on what is perceived to be differential assessment. Reports indicate that people of color are more likely to be diagnosed as suffering from psychosis, be admitted involuntarily to hospitals, remain for longer periods in hospitals, and be treated with medication rather than by counseling or social rehabilitation (Neighbors, 1992; Ramm, 1989; Ramon, 1996; Snowden, 2000; U.S. DHHS, 2001;

Whaley, 2001). The supportive evidence from empirical research is often ambiguous and controversial, not only because of methodological problems, but because of difficulties in interpreting the data. For example, does underrepresentation among those receiving individual psychotherapy reflect selection bias or because many people of color consider individual psychotherapy to be inappropriate and culturally alien? Even when studies have shown that people of color are more likely than Whites to be characterized individually or as a group as "mentally ill" or "emotionally disturbed," it is not always possible to rule out reasons other than ethnic or cultural bias (Turner & Kramer, 1995, pp. 10–13).

Lopez (1989) has suggested that past conceptual definitions of bias in clinical judgments in therapeutic interventions have been too restrictive, making it difficult to identify bias. It is assumed that the biased clinician is a prejudiced individual who makes judgments based primarily on the racial or ethnic background of the patient. He offers a different conceptualization from a social or cognitive perspective:

The biased clinician is like any other information processor who has to synthesize much complex information to make decisions regarding diagnosis and treatment. Like many decision-makers, clinicians use shortcuts. A contributing factor to the selective information processing of the biased clinician is that clinicians may attempt to consider important group differences suggested by the patients' race, ethnicity, age and even gender. On the one hand, therapists are instructed not to differentially evaluate or treat patients on the basis of their background because this may be reflective of prejudicial attitudes. On the other hand, therapists are instructed to differentially evaluate and treat patients because of the different norms that pertain to patients of different backgrounds. The relevance of this issue for the study of clinical judgement bias is that a clinician who makes errors in adjusting norms or failing to adjust norms is likely to be conceptually distinct from the clinician who makes errors because of prejudicial attitudes (Lopez, 1989, p. 192).

Lopez's concept of "selective information processing" is closely related to the sociological concepts of "stereotyping" and "racial prejudice," but allows for distinctions between information processing that is systematically biased and information processing that is merely inadequate or incomplete in a particular context.

The complexity of issues regarding cultural sensitivity in assessing the problems presented to human services agencies by persons of color is evident when policies around kinship care in the child welfare system are considered (see McRoy in this volume). There are at least two perspectives from which to understand the effect of kinship care policy on families of color, who are much more likely than others to use extended family members as caregivers. From one perspective, a decision to give relatives who care for children enhanced support recognizes that these caretakers, who tend to be poor and receiving public assistance, have been disadvantaged by commitment to a family structure that is atypical in the larger community. A policy of state-supported kinship care could be interpreted as promoting this existing form of diversity in American society. From another perspective, greater state support comes with greater supervision and intrusive intervention and the possibility that a child could be removed on grounds less than those required for birth parents. Rather than supporting diversity, this intrusion could be interpreted as a statement that minority families are less capable of caring for their children than majority families (Edmund S. Muskie Institute of Public Affairs, 1995).

In the assessment of a relative caretaker family of color, it would be cultural insensitivity to ignore an exploration of that particular family's interpretation of the meaning of state support (i.e., cultural insensitivity by omission). In the event that the interpretation is negative, specific interventions could be planned to demonstrate a more positive intent for the support. It would also be cultural insensitivity if it were assumed that a family is making one or the other of these interpretations without any exploration at all and interventions based on that assumption were planned (i.e., cultural insensitivity by commission).

Intervention Strategies

Cultural insensitivity has been studied most often in relation to specific attitudes or behaviors on the part of service providers who reflect a lack of knowledge of relevant cultural issues or "selective information processing." Thus, a service provider may expect a mother in a traditional Mexican American family to have more authority in disciplining her 12-year-old son than is supported by the family's cultural orientation. A therapist may expect an Asian adolescent and his immigrant parents to participate in family group therapy with the same degree of openness and emotional expression that has been observed in White, middle-class families. The preference of an African American client for a White social worker may be interpreted as incorporation of White belief in Blacks' inferiority, rather than concern about confidentiality in an ethnic community where "everybody knows everybody else." Other examples of cultural insensitivity include a range of types of miscommunication that occur between the service provider and client because of cultural differences (e.g., because of differences in perceptions of the time and process required before self-disclosure is acceptable or differences in expectations of the respective roles of the service provider and the client).

The high value placed by the social work profession on the individual and on nonhierarchical egalitarian relationships, including family relationships, is perceived by some to mean that normative practice models are often inappropriately used with ethnic group members whose cultures place the highest value on the collective—the family, the ethnic group, or the nation (Green, 1999; Ho, 1987; Rodriguez & Zayas, 1990). However, it can be argued that the profession's fundamental commitment to individual rights, including the right to self-determination, allows its practitioners to overcome their own ethnocentrism. For example, individuals may exercise the right to self-determination and freely choose to subordinate their desires and aspirations "for the good of" the collective. In such cases, it is the function of the profession to ensure that the decision is an informed one and the person making it is truly aware of all options as well as the costs and benefits attached to each.

Institutional Racism

The concept of institutional racism was introduced to the social science literature by Carmichael and Hamilton (1967) in their book, *Black Power: The Politics of Liberation in America*, in which they state:

> Racism is both overt and covert. The first consists of overt acts by individuals, which cause death, injury or the violent destruction of property. The second type is less overt, far more subtle, less identifiable in terms of specific individuals committing the acts. But it is no less destructive of human life. The second type originates in the operation of established and respected forces in the society, and thus receives far less public condemnation than the first type. (p. 4)

Shortly thereafter, Knowles and Prewitt (1969) presented "an analysis of specific practices appropriately defined as 'institutionally racist'" (p. 6). Institutions were described as stable social arrangements that establish policies that distribute the society's educational, economic, employment, social welfare, political, legal, recreational, technological, religious, and health benefits.

Institutions have great power to reward and penalize They reward by providing career opportunities for some people and foreclosing them for others. They reward as well by the way social goods and services are distributed—by deciding who receives training and skills, medical care, formal education political influence, moral support and self-respect, productive employment, fair treatment by the law, decent housing, self-confidence, and the promise of a secure future for self and children (Knowles & Prewitt, 1969, p. 5.).

These conceptual definitions of institutional racism have been used to explain the manner in which policies and procedures consistently penalize people of color in those formal organizations that are established to carry out our responsibility to care for one another (e.g., family and child welfare services, health and mental health services, and criminal justice services). Soon after Knowles and Prewitt gave shape and depth to the concept, articles began to appear in social work journals that identified manifestations of institutional racism in almost every major social institution.

The criminal justice system has been indicted most recently for racism so deeply embedded in its structure and operations that people of color were seriously disadvantaged even when no individual can be charged with bias or discrimination. Government health statistics show that Black and White Americans use cocaine at a similar rate, but Blacks are more likely to use crack cocaine and Whites are more likely to use powder cocaine (Sklar, 1995; Tonry, 1995). Yet, in 1993 more than 95% of those convicted of federal cocaine offenses were Black (Tonry, 1995). Federal laws call for a 10-year sentence for someone caught selling 500 grams of crack, but the dealer would have to sell 5000 grams of powder cocaine to get the same sentence.

According to the Leadership Conference on Civil Rights, a 50-year-old group that represents 185 human rights organizations, Blacks make up about 13% of the population, but 74% of those sentenced to prison for drug offenses. Among first-time offenders charged with the same crime, young people of color are six times more likely to be incarcerated as young Whites. Between 1985 and 1995, the rate of Latino incarceration nationwide more than tripled. The overrepresentation of people of color among the poor is undoubtedly a factor. A poor youth from a single-parent home who is often unable to bring a family member with him when he goes before a judge for sentencing is likely to be placed in a juvenile facility; however, if the youth comes with both parents who are middle-class and have insurance that will cover drug rehabilitation, the judge has more options (Leadership Conference on Civil Rights, May 2000).

Social policy aimed at increasing cultural sensitivity in human services has placed a priority on increasing the number of people of color among service providers. However, it has been demonstrated that neither cultural insensitivity or institutional racism will be automatically decreased by increasing the number of people of color among service-providers. A recent study (Bridges & Steen, 1999) analyzing racial bias among probation officers found a consistent bias in their written reports on Black and White offenders, regardless of the probation officer's race. The officers routinely described the Black youth in terms of character flaws and the White youth as victims of negative environmental factors such as exposure to family conflict or delinquent friends. The bias, according to the researchers, was rooted in the structure of the probation system itself (Bridges & Steen, 1999).

Extensive research studies have amply linked health status and social inequality (Smith 1990; Plepys, 1995; Wilkinson, 1992). Class membership leads to major differences in political and economic power, which determines the degree to which social groups have to important decisions on public and private issues and ultimately who benefits and who is harmed by their decisions (Packham, 1991; Williams & Collins, 1995). Social inequality may be strongly associated with socioeconomic class; however, the two constructs have different empirical referents. There is evidence that health status may be a function of social inequality rather than a function completely of an absolute standard of economic well-being. For example, although the average annual income in Barbados is less than one-ninth of the average income in the United States, life expectancy in Barbados was 77 years in 1988, whereas it was 63 years for Black men in the United States (Williams & Collins, 1995). The interrelationship between social inequality, institutional racism, and health status was described by Knowles and Prewitt (1969) as determined by the health care system's ration of health according to purchasing power and the lack of representation of people of color among the systems' policymakers shows bigotry in a few cases and ignorance in most cases to prevail at decision-making levels and results in actions that have racist results.

Those academics who initially conceptualized institutional racism as a social phenomenon perceived it to be self-evident when people of color were not treated equally in major social institutions (e.g., they were underrepresented in those insitutions dispensing social benefits and social rewards or overrepresented in those institutions set up to respond to unmet needs or to mete out punishment for violation of social norms). However, inequality was found to be an exceedingly complex construct. The complexity is reflected in the controversies that have swirled around so-called affirmative action policies aimed at reducing institutional racism. Opponents of affirmative action policies consider them to be a serious restriction of individual liberty. However, laws prohibiting employers, university admission committees, landlords, and real estate salesmen from refusing to employ, admit, rent, or sell to people of color also restrict individual liberty. Yet, laws against racial discrimination have been much less controversial than laws or policies commanding affirmative action. Cross (1984) suggests that in the case of affirmative action policy, it is not just that liberty is somewhat abridged, it is the principle of every individual being considered only on merit that is being violated as well. But Cross (1984) contends:

> The fact is that the merit or competence principle does not have an exclusive claim on our sense of justice. An important element of equity is the principle of restitution, of making people whole when they have been wronged. This principle of redress often overrides simple considerations of merit in determining the just outcome of any competitive process. (p. 57)

An Alternative Approach

It is clear that as a society we have embraced fundamental values that at times come into conflict. Given the multiethnic, multicultural nature of the United States, cultural differences may determine whether we are more committed to one value than another (e.g., the rights of the individual or the "good" of the community). Moreover, our interpretation of the best way to express commitment to the same value may also differ even when we have the same cultural orientation. Sowell (1987) has called this latter, "a conflict of visions" (p. 35). In the "unconstrained" vision, the potentialities of human nature are seen as extending far beyond what is currently manifested and the fundamental problem of society is not nature or people, but institutions; in the "constrained" vision, human beings are seen as tragically limited creatures whose selfish and dangerous impulses can be contained only by social contrivances that produce unhappy side-effects (Sowell, 1987). These visions are not commensurate with the usual liberal versus conservative polarity or even the individual versus collective or community polarity, although they tend to be associated with one pole or the other. The differentiating characteristic is the picture of human nature. Thus, the concepts of equality, justice, and power not only differ, but may even have opposite implications in the two visions.

In developing and implementing social policy, the tendency has been to promote one or another of these visions. Cycles or pendulum swings occur almost rhythmically as government or even business adopts policies reflecting an unconstrained vision at one time (e.g., War on Poverty legislation) and a constrained vision at another (Welfare Reform in 1995). It may well be that each of these alternative visions has some intrinsic value and rather than seek to develop policy initiatives based on a "pure" reflection of one or the other, it would be preferable to seek equipoise or balance. An equipoise approach to policymaking may be demonstrated by articulating conflicting positions regarding some social issues and then indicating an equipoise principle, which seeks to find a balance between them.

There are conflicting positions in the delivery of human services as to why people of color share unequally in the benefits of society. From the constrained vision perspective, fewer people of color share in the benefits of society because of their own deficiencies, viewed singularly or collectively as a lack of motivation, intelligence, morality. From an unconstrained vision perspective, fewer people of color share in the benefits of society because of a lack of opportunity. An equipoise principle may be derived from a dilectic in which each of the conflicting positions is considered: The fact that fewer people of color share in the benefits of society is due in some measure to lack of opportunity but in even larger measure to individual deficiencies (e.g., lack of motivation, lack of scholastic aptitude, lack of morality) that are a consequence of past and present societal oppression.

This principle suggests that less emphasis should be placed on simply expanding the opportunity structures. More emphasis should be placed on policies that simultaneously address removing deficiences ("socialization to the workplace") and expanding the opportunity structure.

There are conflicting positions in the delivery of human services as to why governmental efforts to lift people of color out of poverty have failed. From the constrained vision perspective, governmental efforts to lift people out of poverty have failed in spite of massive governmental support that has served primarily to depress individual initiative and fostered dependency. From the unconstrained vision perspective, governmental efforts to life people of color out of poverty have failed because of inadequate governmental support of the kind needed to make a difference. An equipoise principle may be derived from a dialectic in which each of the conflicting positions is considered: Governmental efforts to lift people of color out of poverty must take into account the fact that the capacity of poor persons of color to become socially and economically independent is related to multiple factors—raw intelligence, access to education, nature and availability of a support network.

There are conflicting positions in the delivery of human services as to whether the rights of the individual should take precedence over the rights of the collective or the community. From the unconstrained vision, social justice means that individuals are entitled to some share of the wealth produced by a society simply by being members of the society as a matter of justice, not charity. Therefore, it follows that if the achievement of that end, namely, some share of the wealth for individuals and groups who have been unable to obtain it on their own, requires some other individuals to be forced to share their wealth, the rights of those individuals to keep their wealth should not take precedence over the social good or social justice. Ryan (1985) has supported this point of view that it is not in the best interests of society to have an impoveristhed or destitute class when he states that the redistribution of wealth is not a matter of taking from the "haves" and giving to the "have-nots." Rather, it is taking from the haves and giving to benefit the total society. The constrained vision would argue that deliberately determining social results is beyond the capabilities of human groups and to try to do so will inevitably lead to unintended impacts that may include the "destruction of the rule of law in the quest for an illusory social justice." An equipoise principle may be derived from a dilectic in which each of the conflicting positions is considered: When rights are in conflict, and one is given precedence over another, steps should be taken to mitigate against whatever negative effects can be anticipated as a consequence.

When racist remarks are made or racist literature distributed by persons who are known, the targets of the remarks or printed obscenitites are likely to be supported in their outrage and helped to deal with it. The right of the individual to freedom of speech is in this instance abridged by the right of the community to protect its members from harm—whether the harm is physical or emotional. The perpetrators, however, are more likely to be threatened with punishment than perceived to be in need of help; more likely to be further isolated or left in the company of those with similar prejudices. Yet, the problem if unattended only escalates. More efforts should be made by service providers to provide mechanisms for outreach to those also in need of help and to develop strategies for effecting positive change.

There are conflicting positions in the design, delivery, and evaluation of human services whether ethnic-specific delivery systems are more beneficial or harmful to the ethnic population targeted for service. These positions are essentially "for" or "against" ethnic-specific services. It could be assumed that proponents of ethnic-specific services have for the most part "given up" on mainstream agencies to provide culturally sensitive services. Therefore, the ethnic-specific agency will ensure that those members of an identified ethnic group who are also for the most part culturally different will be assured of receiving adequate and appropriate services. Ethnic-specific service delivery systems provide culturally sensitive services and access to community-based social supports. On the other hand, opponents of the ethnic-specific agency are likely to believe that ethnic-specific service delivery systems perpetuate racial and ethnic segregation and increase the potential for inter-ethnic conflict. An equipoise principle may be derived from a dialectic in which each of the conflicting positions is considered: People of color will benefit most when provided with multiple options for accessing culturally sensitive health and human services.

Priority should be given as a matter of social policy to developing community-based social supports for all and to ensuring that there are culturally senstive practitioners in all human service agencies. Where there are large concentrations of a particular group, the agency may become an ethnic-specific agency by virtue of the ethnic distribution of the population in the community. This is no different than the likelihood that there will be Mexican restaurants in neighborhoods where there are a large number of Mexican Americans or Chinese restaurants in neighborhoods where there are a large number of Chinese Americans. It does not mean that Mexican and Chinese specialities might not also show up on the menus of restaurants that are not particularly designated as Mexican or Chinese and in neighborhoods where there are only a few members of those ethnic groups.

Conclusion

In the conceptual phase of policy planning, there are critical questions that policymakers must answer: How important are specific presenting problems (e.g., the gap between people of color and others in regard to health status)? How will the problem be described or defined (e.g., as a public health problem or a civil rights problem)? What causal or precipitating factors are useful in devising interventions to address the problem (e.g., poverty, lifestyles, or institutional racism)? How can policies and programs be shaped so that social interventions address the needs of specific populations (e.g., How can health care research include people of color in important research that addresses problems that disproportionately affect them given the history of maltreatment of people of color in medical research?)? The answers to these questions will inevitably be influenced by beliefs and values that, if unexplored, may mean that policies will be developed that have negative outcomes for people of color.

The values underlying social, economic, and political decisions in American society include equality, liberty, individualism, and justice. Equality and liberty were driving forces that motivated the proponents of the American Revolution and the framers of the new nation's Constitution. But values are not "either/or" propositions but are more likely to be arranged hierachically in the belief systems of individuals, groups, or nations. They may even be restricted to an in-group and not expected to hold in relationships with out-groups or enemies. In the hierachy of values that have influenced political and economic behavior in the United States, individualism derived from conceptualizations of liberty and freedom has been almost always at or near the top of the rank-order. When values come into conflict, when a commitment to individualism makes it difficult to achieve redistribution of resources in the commitment to equality, it has been proposed that justice becomes the overriding value. Conceptualizations of justice have been shaped by constrained and unconstrained visions of the nature of human groups. In the view of the latter, social justice can be effected by manipulation by elites of legal and institutional structures; in the view of the former, justice lies in adhering to those legal and institutional structures for fear of destroying them.

Human groups are more than likely neither as constrained as one perspective would have us believe or as unconstrained as the other would have us believe. As a consequence, social policies based solely on one or the other view can be doomed to generate a certain inevitable degree of failure, whereas a cyclical pendulum swings between them. Conflicting visions ensure that policies will undergo substantive changes before they might have been corrected to increase the probability of more positive outcomes. And the cycle repeats itself *ad infinitem*. A more balanced approach may be in order. The concept of balance as suggested in the Taoist concept of yin–yang suggests that opposing views may need to be considered simultaneously as two sides of the same coin rather than in sequence as two separate coins.

In the human services, the disadvantages that have been experienced by people of color have been effectively distilled into two primary conceptualizations: cultural insensitivity and institutional racism. Social policies that have been implemented to counteract their pernicious effects have been implemented and eliminated primarily as determined by the cyclical pendulum swings between constrained and unconstrained visions of the nature of human groups that prevail at any given time. There is a need for a commitment to a dialectic in which opposing positions are explored and opportunities created to develop third positions that effectively address the underlying concerns of the original positions in conflict.

In the final analysis, all social policies should ensure that people of color will not be prohibited from enjoying societal benefits and rewards to the same extent as others in the society. Social policies should serve to remove those obstacles that prevent people of color from being able to make the same choices as other people from among reasonable alternatives. Social policies should help the poor and disadvantaged to access and influence the power centers so that they are more responsive to their needs. Social policies should increase opportunities for people of color to participate in, share control of, and influence those who affect their lives and the lives of those they care about. An equipoise approach to the development and implementation of more just social policy is, therefore, warranted.

References

Adams, G. B. (1997). Racism, community, and democracy: The ethics of affirmative action. *Public Productivity and Management, 20*, 243–257.

Appiah, K. A. (1996). Race, culture, identity: Misunderstood concepts. In K. Appiah & A. Guttman (Eds.), *Color conscious*. Princeton, NJ: Princeton University Press.

Barber, B. R. (1993). *An aristocracy of everyone: The politics of education and the future of America*. New York: Oxford University Press.

Bell, D. (1992). *Faces at the bottom of the well: The permanence of racism*. New York: Basic Books.

Bridges, G. S., & Steen, S. (1999). Racial disparities in offical assessments of juvenile offenders: Attributional stereotypes as mediating mechanisms of juvenile offenders. *American Sociological Review, 63*, 554–571.

Carmichael, S., & Hamilton, C. V. (1967). *Black power: The politics of liberation in America*. New York: Vintage Books.

Cross, T. (1984). *The Black power imperative: Racial inequality and the politics of nonviolence*. New York: Faulkner.

DeHoyos, G., DeHoyos, A., & Anderson, C. B. (1986). Sociocultural dislocation: Beyond the dual perspective. *Social Work, 31*, 61–67.

Edmund S. Muskie Institute of Public Affairs. (1995). *Kinship care in America: A national policy study*. Portland, ME: University of Southern Maine.

Fukuyama, F. (1995). *Trust: Social virtues and the creation of prosperity*. New York: Free Press.

Green, J. (1999). *Cultural awareness in the human services: A multi-ethnic approach*. Boston: Allyn & Bacon.

Guinier, L., & Torres, G. (2002). *The miner's canary*. Cambridge, MA: Harvard University Press.

Guttman, A. (1996). *Responding to racial injustice*. In K. Appiah & A. Guttman (Eds.), *Color conscious*. Princeton, NJ: Princeton University Press.

Heller, T. C., Sosna, M., & Wellbery, D. E. (1986). *Reconstructuring individualism: Autonomy, individuality, and the self in Western thought*. Stanford, CA: Stanford University Press.

Herrnstein, R. J., & Murray, C. (1994). *The bell curve: Intelligence and class structure in American life*. New York: Free Press.

Ho, M. K. (1987). *Family therapy with ethnic minorities*. Newbury Park, CA: Sage.

Knowles, L. L., & Prewitt, K. (1969). *Institutional racism in America*. Englewood Cliffs, NJ: Prentice Hall.

Lappe, F. M. (1989). *Rediscovering America's values*. New York: Ballantine Books.

Leadership Conference on Civil Rights (n.d.). *Justice on Trial: Racial Disparities in the American Criminal Justice System*. Unpublished Report.

Lopez, S. R. (1989). Patient variable biases in clinical judgement: Conceptual overview and methodological considerations. *Psychological Bulletin, 106*, 184–203.

Manderscheid, R. W., & Henderson, M. J. (1998). *Mental health United States 1999*. Rockville, MD: U.S. Department of Health and Human Services.

McAuliffe, B. E. (2002). Forcing action: Seeking to "clean up" the Indian trust fund: Cobell v. Babbit, 30 F. Supp. 2d 24 (D.D.C. 1998). *Southern Illinois University Law Journal, 25*, 647–661.

Neighbors, H. W., Bashshur, R., Price, R., Donavedian, A., Selig, S., & Shannon, G. (1992). Ethnic minority mental health services delivery: A review of the literature. *Research in Community and Mental Health, 7*, 55–71.

Packham, J. Power as a neglected variable in the assessment of the class/health relation. Unpublished manuscript.

Patterson, O. (1997). *The ordeal of integration: Progress and resentment in America's racial crisis.* Washington, DC: Civitas Counterpoint.

Pinderhughes, E. (1989). *Understanding race, ethnicity, and power: The key to efficacy in clinical practice.* New York: Free Press.

Plepys, C., & Klein, R. (1995). *Health status indicators: Differentials by race and Hispanic origin* (Rep. No. 10). Hyattsville, MD: Centers for Disease Control and Prevention/National Center for Health Statistics.

Ramm, D. (1989). Overcommitted. *Southern Exposure, Fall,* 14–17.

Ramon, S. (1996). *Mental health in Europe: Beginnings, ends and rediscoveries.* New York: St. Martin's Press.

Rawls, J. (1971). *A theory of justice.* Cambridge, MA: Harvard University.

Rawls, J. (1985). Justice as fairness: Political not metaphysical. *Philosophy and Public Affairs, 14,* 223–251.

Rawls, J. (1993). *Political liberalism.* New York: Columbia University Press.

Robinson, R. (2000). *The debt: What America owes to Blacks.* New York: Dutton Press.

Rodriguez, O., & Zayas, L. H. (1990). Hispanic adolescents and anti-social behavior: Sociocultural factors and treatment implications. In A. R. Stiffman & L. Davis (Eds.), *Ethnic issues in mental health.* Newbury Park, CA: Sage.

Ryan, W. (1985). *Equality.* New York: Random House

Schiele, J. H. (1997). An Afrocentric perspective on social welfare philosophy and policy. *Journal of Sociology and Social Welfare, 34,* 21–39.

Schuhmacher, S., & Woerner, G. (1994). *The encyclopedia of Eastern philosophy and religion.* Boston: Shambhala.

Sklar, H. (1995). The dying American dream and the snake oil of scapegoating. In C. Berloti (Ed.), *Eyes right: Challenging the right wing backlash* (pp. 113–134). Boston: South End Press.

Smith, D. G., Bartley, M., & Blane, D. (1990). The Black report on socioeconomic Inequalities in health: 10 years on. *British Medical Journal, 301,* 373–377.

Snowden, L. R. (2000). Inpatient mental health use by members of ethnic minority groups. In J. M. Herrera, W. B. Lawson, & J. J. Smerck (Eds.), *Cross-cultural psychiatry.* Chichester, England: Wiley.

Sowell, T. (1987). *A conflict of visions: Ideologicalol origins of political struggles.* New York: William Morrow.

Tonry, M. (1995). *Malign neglect: Race, crime and punishment in America.* New York: Oxford University Press.

Turner, C. B., & Kramer, B. M. (995). Connections between racism and mental health. In C. V. Willie, P. P. Rieker, B. M. Kramer, & B. S. Brown (Eds.), *Mental health, racism and sexism* (pp. 3–25). Pittsburgh, PA: University of Pittsburgh Press.

U.S. Department of Health and Human Services. (2001). *Mental health: Culture, race, and ethnicity: A supplement to mental health: A report of the Surgeon General.* Rockville, MD: U.S. Department of Health and Human Services, Substance Abuse and Mental Health Services Administration, Center for Mental Health Services.

Whaley, A. L. (2001). Cultural mistrust and the clinical diagnosis of paranoid schizophrenia in African American patients. *Journal of Psychopathology and Behavioral Assessment, 23,* 93–99.

Wilkinson, R. G. (1992). National mortality rates: The impact of inequality. *American Journal of Public Health, 82,* 1082–1094.

Williams, D. R., & Collins, C. (1995). U.S. socioeconomic and racial differences in health: Patterns and explanations. *Annual Review of Science, 21,* 349–386.

Chapter Thirteen

Building a Common Agenda: Charting a Social Policy Agenda for People of Color

Tricia B. Bent-Goodley, Yolanda Q. Mayo, and Manuel Gonzalez

Previous chapters have illuminated significant issues that bind communities of color and foster the need for a coalition centered on their empowerment. The disproportionate number of children of color in the child welfare and juvenile justice systems is profound (Breggin & Breggin, 1998; Chand, 2000; Cross, Earle, & Simmons, 2000; Dorfman & Schiraldi, 2001; Foster & Furstenberg, 1999; Glasser, 2000; Golden, 1997; Kapp, McDonald, & Diamond, 2001; Weaver & White, 1999). Increasing health disparities and HIV/AIDS among people of color has been persistent and is staggering (Delgado & Santiago, 1998; Gant, Green, Stewart, Wheeler, & Wright, 1998). Drugs have simply devastated communities of color (Amaro, Nieves, Johannes & Cabeza, 1999; Caetano & Rasberry, 2000; Carten, 1996; Kail, Zayas, & Malgady, 2000; Nielsen, 2000; Richie, 1996; Taylor, 2000; Venner & Miller, 2001). Oppressive policies and conservative philosophies have resulted in a criminal justice system composed largely of poor people and people of color (Adams, Onek, & Riker, 1998; Cureton, 2000; Gibbs & Bankhead, 2001; Mauer, 1999). Ultimately, these and other issues should serve as an organizing force for communities of color to work together to create policies that support healthy communities and strong families. The three congressional caucuses—the Congressional Asian Pacific American Caucus, the Congressional Black Caucus, and the Congressional Hispanic Caucus—met for the first time in April 2002 to formulate a collective policy agenda (Congressional Black Caucus Foundation, 2002). Understanding the significance of population trends, these caucus members recognized the need to work together to effect change on behalf of communities of color. The purpose of this chapter is to suggest a collective policy advocacy framework that can form the basis for advancing social change and social justice for people of color.

Conceptual Framework

The proposed policy advocacy framework is supported by the empowerment approach to practice. Empowerment is defined as a "process whereby persons who belong to a stigmatized social category throughout their lives can be assisted to develop and increase skills in the exercise of interpersonal influence and the performance of valued social roles" (Solomon, 1976, p. 6). Empowerment practice implies that individuals and communities have the potential to change and progress. This conceptual framework is important as one begins to engage communities of color. Recognizing the potential for social change, policy becomes one mechanism to engage in social and economic justice. Social workers do not empower individuals and communities; the latter empower themselves. Instead, social workers provide support and resources to assist communities with responding to issues of discrimination and oppression. The skill of the practitioner is evident in the ability to create options, address barriers, and encourage new methodologies for change. Empowerment does not denote that an issue will never re-surface. Instead, true empowerment gives communities an opportunity to develop the skills, competencies, and resources necessary to address issues on a long-term basis.

Empowerment is rooted in principles of option building, capturing self and collective power, and tackling harmful environmental influences. Shared decision-making, understanding historical and contemporary oppression and discrimination across groups, and shared power are critical components of an empowerment perspective (Gutierrez, Alvarez, Nemon, & Lewis, 1996; Gutierrez & Lewis, 1999). The principle of empowerment has not typically been linked to policy practice, as the emphasis of policy practice is typically on larger macro change (Gutierrez & Lewis, 1999). However, "political empowerment consists of social action and social change through a process of social support, coalition building, and praxis. It is based on both the personal and interpersonal levels of empowerment, with the additional goal of transferring power between groups in society" (Gutierrez & Lewis, 1999, p. 11–12). Therefore, the concept of empowerment through the policy process and political navigation is feasible but it requires an emphasis on both individual and collective needs. In order for collective advancement to occur, there must be an emphasis on the empowerment and strengthening of individuals as well. Without a focus on individual empowerment, collective empowerment will be unlikely.

Engaging in empowerment practice on a policy level within communities of color requires an understanding of the shared and different discriminatory and oppressive experiences of people of color. There cannot be a hierarchy of oppression (Lorde, 1984), whereby one group's experiences are highlighted as more oppressive or more significant than another group's experiences. "A rigid line cannot be drawn between racial and national oppression when all victims are people of color. Both are racism, and in combination they generate new varieties of racism. All this suggests why we need to understand more than the Black/White model today" (Martinez, 1998, p. 475). A divisive approach will lead to further disempowerment. The world can no longer be framed in Black and White (Gibbs & Bankhead, 2001; Wilson, 2000); instead, collective experiences and their common consequences should be highlighted. It is through an appreciation of collective struggles that progress can be achieved.

"Social action focuses on power, pursues conflict strategies, and challenges the structures that oppress and disempower constituents" (Fisher, 2001, p. 350). An empowerment approach denotes primacy to social change and social action. True liberation requires individual and collective empowerment, support of mutual aid within communities, and tactical citizen uprisings (Fisher, 2001). The ability to mobilize communities requires strong leadership and organizations to support these movements. An emphasis on the character and capability of leaders to motivate others to work toward social action is necessary. In addition, developing and sustaining organizations that can provide vehicles for change is also critical.

Literature Review

Betancur and Gills (1997) emphasize the need to build "on a broader social basis than on narrow electoral politics" (p. 99). Specifically, communities of color cannot organize around a single issue or campaign, there must be a broader basis for advocacy or such an initiative will fail in the long run. They give the example of Harold Washington's campaign to become the Mayor of Chicago during the 1980s. The authors offer that without shared governance, an effort to address group fragmentation, a clear and common agenda, and discussion of inter-group misunderstandings, this type of coalition building will not be successful. These authors also emphasize the need to establish networks among communities of color prior to undertaking the larger initiative and to create mechanisms for addressing problems early. Without responding to these issues, the authors contend that coalition members may become "less concerned about a social change agenda and more concerned about self preservation and individualized opportunities for power and privilege" (p. 96).

Sales and Bush (1997) submit that "increasing ethnic differentiation...varying perceptions of nationality, communal allegiances, citizenship, and perceived capacity to participate in electoral politics" (p. 137) are barriers to organizing across communities of color. Yet, while some of these communities are segregated, there are also many ethnically diverse communities that can organize around mutual concerns. The authors examine the relationship among Puerto Ricans and African Americans in New York City, as an example. They illustrate how an interethnic collaboration between these groups has led to change in electoral politics, higher education, environmental racism, police brutality, political prisoner advocacy, and local educational struggles. Such examples provide the basis for understanding how different groups can work together for mutually beneficial change.

Wilson (2000) emphasizes the need for multiracial coalition politics as a means to respond to oppressive and discriminatory practices. He stresses the significance of increasing economic inequality as an important consideration. "The development and articulation of an ideological vision that captures and highlights commonalities in basic core values and attitudes are paramount in establishing the case for a progressive multiracial political coalition and defining the opposition of pessimists who promote the more limited advantages of group-specific political mobilization" (p. 87). He suggests that developing coalitions in diverse communities with an established network is critical to the success of this type of endeavor. Furthermore, the author provides a case study of the Industrial Areas Foundation (IAF), a network of influential multiracial coalitions envisioned by Saul Alinsky more than 50 years ago. Using IAF as a model of coalition politics, it is clear that with planning, direction, and vision, such initiatives can be successful.

Gibbs and Bankhead (2001) caution the use of identity politics as an organizing theme. "Identity politics generally has been described as the tendency for each minority group to define issues solely or primarily in terms of their own group interests, values, and priorities" (p. 174). This way of organizing often leads to competition between groups and a minimization of commonalities. Instead, the authors emphasize the need for coming together to work toward policy development that is mutually beneficial. They also suggest that the role of class as a divisive force be addressed to ensure the success of multiracial coalition building.

Advancing a Policy Advocacy Framework

The core elements of a policy advocacy framework are: (1) discerning an ethical code of conduct; (2) agenda building activities; (3) leadership transitioning; (4) policy education and training; (5) funding policy initiatives; and (5) a value-based policy framework. The framework is not stagnant or on a continuum; instead, the core elements require a commitment to an ongoing discussion and compromise.

An Ethical Code of Conduct

An ethical code of conduct is relevant to the advocacy framework in that it determines the collective values of the group and the mutual ethics that will guide behavior. The importance of establishing an ethical code of conduct is paramount to operationalizing common values. An ethical code of conduct can be used to provide guidance on what is acceptable and unacceptable and include consequences of engaging in inappropriate activity.

There is great diversity among and between people of color. A major component of this diversity is differences in language and dialect. It can be a challenge to understand each other, both within and outside of diverse ethnic groups, due to language and cultural nuances. Acknowledging that language is more than speaking different languages but also includes cultural expression is a critical shift in understanding. With demographic shifts and changes, one must consider learning various ways of communicating across groups of color. As opposed to allowing language and cultural expression to serve as barriers, groups of color can begin to educate each other and develop a consensus as to how this issue can be addressed fairly. A true commitment to addressing this barrier requires willingness from all groups to learn different forms of communication styles, languages, and dialects.

Increasingly the need to share diminishing resources has resulted in people of color feeling the need to compete with each other. People of color fear not receiving certain funding or losing political clout due to the increasing numbers of different ethnic groups, depending on the local community composition (Gibbs & Bankhead, 2001). "It is painful to see how prejudice, resentment, petty competitiveness, and sheer ignorance fester. It is positively pitiful to see how often we echo Anglo stereotypes about one another" (Martinez, 1998, p. 466). Thus, fear leads to competing for what is really a small piece of the pie. Instead of wasting time trying to attain a slice of the pie, people of color need to address strategies for owning the pie and dividing the slices through jointly agreed upon formulas. Squabbling over small issues negates the big picture and can lead to manipulation of individuals and groups. As the increasing majority in this country, people of color should be positioning themselves to obtain a larger piece of what the United States has to offer.

People often allow themselves to be limited by history and events. While the historical context is critical to present day decision-making, it should not fully determine the agenda of the community. As part of an ethical code of conduct, people of color need to engage in an honest and full dialogue as to how to move together in the future to meet their collective needs. A true examination of historical events may provide a different perspective when assessed over time. With so much to lose and even more to gain, communities of color must find ways to move beyond history to taking advantage of present and future collective opportunities.

The ethical code of conduct should be centered on shared power and an emphasis on using commonalities to advance a policy agenda, as opposed to focusing on differences (Gutierrez & Lewis, 1999; Wilson, 2000). While fostering an understanding of commonalities, differences should be recognized with a commitment to bridge gaps and encourage understanding. Recognizing the significance of spirituality with communities of color, all efforts should be rooted in a spiritual perspective; that is, there must be an understanding as to how this movement transcends politics and instead is connected and accountable to a higher power.

Included within this ethical code of conduct must be an emphasis on equity across gender, class, sexual orientation, and religion. Women must be treated equally and serve in positions across leadership. Equitable treatment around sexual orientation is also an absolute necessity.

Oppressive actions towards women and discriminatory treatment according to sexual orientation cannot be permitted if the policy agenda will be successful. Religious freedom must also be respected, with people from diverse faith-based communities represented with equal power, and class differences must be perceived as a strength as opposed to a deficit.

Agenda-Building Activities

There appears to be a lack of a defined policy agenda among people of color. Part of this limited collective agenda is a reflection of fragmentation across and within groups of color. The great diversity within each group of color can be an obstacle to developing an agenda that the group can support unconditionally and collectively. Yet, it is this diversity that allows for a holistic and comprehensive policy agenda that can meet needs for different groups.

A limited number of policy position statements that can be used to inform public and political opinion disenfranchises communities from working together. Developing position papers is not simply an exercise but can be used as an opportunity for opening dialogue, sharing diverse opinions, fully exploring issues, and creating realistic compromises. If individuals within a group cannot agree among themselves, it is inconceivable that the group as a whole will find policy options in collaboration with other groups of color. In addition, without understanding one's needs, it is impossible to share in defining collective needs. Thus, the lack of a within-group agenda is a barrier toward fortifying collective strengths to meet shared goals.

In order to develop a collective policy agenda there must be a serious effort to create policy position statements that are agreed upon and can be implemented across groups. These policy position statements should be developed among organizations and community groups. Speaking in one voice, each group of color can establish priorities, make recommendations, determine collective strengths, and acknowledge shared limitations.

Collective agenda building would build upon within-group activities. Bringing these collective strengths to the table, each group can then create policy position statements and establish a policy network. The development of policy position statements encourages people of color to develop priorities and policy positions that will frame dialogue, shape discourse, and inform action. Establishing a policy network promotes fluidity of information and encourages timely responses. Finally, using technology to ensure the flow of information in the network is critical to fostering strong communication.

Leadership Transitioning

Community-based and national leadership should serve as the backbone for policy advocacy. Designated government and non-government leaders cannot resolve issues alone. There needs to be a conscientious effort to pass the leadership baton in these organizations to gain fresh strategies. Understanding that each person is valued, everyone has an important role to play in the advocacy process. More experienced leaders can provide critical mentorship and guidance while simultaneously relinquishing formal and informal control. With the support of more experienced leaders, new leadership can flourish, suggest different approaches, and generate coalition building. While developing new leadership is an important charge, it is even more vital to create genuine opportunities for them to flourish. While there may be initial setbacks as a result of this process, there will be greater success when new leadership actually has the opportunity to lead. With the support of more experienced leaders, new leaders can excel, providing a new voice and diverse perspectives on recurring and emerging issues.

New leadership is not solely reflected in younger leadership but also in less recognized leaders in local communities (Wilson, 2000). These leaders are the heart of change. They create opportunities for growth, demonstrate dedication daily, and have an established network within communities. Redefining leadership will be critical for the advancement of this initiative.

Policy Education and Training

Arguably policy continues to be informally discussed in families and communities of color. For example, policy issues can be heard throughout contemporary rap music, demonstrating the understanding of policy by today's youth (Dixon & Brooks, 2002). Deceased rapper Tupac Shakur often talked about the impact of poverty on communities, changes in welfare policy, and implications of drug and gun policy (Bent-Goodley, 2003). As opposed to focusing solely on his sometimes vile language and offensive stereotypes, which are worthy of dialogue, one can build on these interpretations to connect this knowledge to policy and provide training for young people on how to use the information to create social change.

Building on these collective strengths, policy education can begin early and be connected to specific experiences for young people throughout the age continuum. The establishment of charter schools and after-school programs that promote civic responsibility and increase knowledge of policy advocacy is necessary for young people. Policy education and training is also needed for professionals and community-based advocates through institutes, certificate programs, workshops, and conferences. Such training opportunities, rooted in impartial locales, provide opportunities to train the next generation of community-minded policy advocates.

Funding Policy Initiatives

While there is less wealth in communities of color compared to White communities (Conley, 1999; Wilson, 2000), collective wealth can be used to fund policy advocacy efforts and support political campaigns and ballot initiatives across the country. Pulling together financial resources and creating new funding streams must be a primary effort of this endeavor to achieve success. One opportunity to foster financial independence for this effort is through productive meetings and conferences. With the abundance of annual conferences convened separately by communities of color, the creation of a conference center that houses each of these conferences could produce significant revenue. If groups agreed to use the conference center for meetings and conferences, significant wealth could be developed to fund collective initiatives.

An additional suggestion to engage in collective wealth development would be to collapse national conferences for a specific period of time among organizations with similar constituency groups. Many civil rights organizations enjoy members from the same organizations. Having one conference instead of three or more allows individuals to save money (creating individual opportunities to contribute to the initiative) and allows organizations to spend money and resources more wisely for the coalition's purposes. Funds generated could be used to support policy advocacy and training. Without significant wealth development to fund policy initiatives, this advocacy effort will result in limited success.

Value-Based Policy Framework

Race-based or selective policy initiatives have been regarded as increasingly unsuccessful (Thompson, 1998). Yet, each of the authors in this book suggests the development of policies with respect to race or ethnicity. Race/ethnicity-based policy has merit in creating opportunities for successful and targeted outcomes. For example, health disparities are significant for all groups of color. The Healthy People 2010 initiative (http://odphp.osophs.dhhs.gov/pubs/hp2000/2010.htm), articulated by the U.S. Department of Health and Human Services, was created to address health disparities among people of color and poor people. This initiative has resulted in the establishment of numerous research, prevention, and intervention efforts focused on changing the course of disparities in health care. This type of race- or ethnicity-based policy can produce positive outcomes that improve the health status of people of color. However, the development of race-based policy is often found to receive less support among policymakers and society in general.

Chipungu (1997) identifies a value-based policy framework that includes three criteria: equity, equality, and adequacy of social policy. That is, fairness and "the degree to which benefits provided meet some predetermined level" (Chipungu, 1997, p. 300) are critical to ensuring shared values. People of color share similar additional values: (1) a strong work ethic; (2) a belief in family; and (3) a strong spiritual reliance. These values can be built upon to encourage strong working relationships and mutual understanding. A value-based policy framework supports the development and implementation of policies that promote equity and equal treatment. While policies should be fair, it is naive to think that the playing ground is equitable. Therefore, policy development should emphasize leveling the playing field and proposing policies that are focused on equitable growth and dissemination across groups. Adequacy of policies should be judged by the ability to create equitable opportunities and promote optimal functioning of diverse individuals and communities.

Implications for Social Work Education

Social work educators can support these policy initiatives with policy-based research. Policy endeavors cannot be fully understood without significant, high-quality research that explores policies across communities of color. Social work scholars, uniquely trained as practitioners with an environmental and strengths-based perspective, can offer compelling analysis to inform more educated decision-making and agenda building. Letting the priorities drive the research in collaboration with scholars can produce successful outcomes.

Social work education programs can serve as venues for convening these kinds of endeavors. Programs can facilitate coalition meetings through financial support and a venue to meet, and those that lend administrative support can strengthen this endeavor. Encouraging faculty to participate through increased financial support to attend meetings and a reduced teaching load can increase scholar availability for technical assistance and other types of support. Producing policy scholarship that includes diverse populations is critical to developing fair and equitable analysis. Engaging scholars of color as partners in conceptualizing, conducting, analyzing, and publishing policy-based research enhances opportunities for more thorough and comprehensive analyses.

Training students of color to learn more about social policy and advocacy is critical, regardless of their desire to engage in micro-, mezzo-, or macro-level interventions. Those students of color that demonstrate an interest and commitment to policy and social change should be awarded funding to perfect the craft. Increased and innovative field opportunities are additional means for students to engage in policy advocacy.

Conclusion

The success of communities of color rests in the ability to work together for the good of the collective. Collaboration does not take away from the unique characteristics, experiences, and challenges of these communities; in fact, it allows for better understanding between groups, greater empowerment within society, and the realization of social and economic justice.

The tasks ahead are many. It is not unreasonable to think that people of color will meet the challenges presented in this book with success. It will only be through collective empowerment that people of color will truly evoke policy changes that benefit their communities.

References

Adams, R., Onek, D., & Riker, A. (1998). *Double jeopardy: An assessment of the felony drug provision of the welfare reform act.* Washington, DC: Justice Policy Institute.

Amaro, H., Nieves, R., Johannes, S. W., & Cabeza, N. M. (1999). Substance abuse treatment: Critical issues and challenges in the treatment of Latina women. *Hispanic Journal of Behavioral Sciences, 21,* 266–282.

Bent-Goodley, T. B. (2003). Preface. In T. B. Bent-Goodley (Ed.), *African American social workers and social policy* (pp. XIII-XIV). Binghamton, NY: Haworth.

Betancur, J.J. & Gills, D. C. (1997). Black and Latino political conflict in Chicago. In J. Jennings (Ed.), *Race and politics* (pp. 83–100). New York: Verso.

Breggin, P. R., & Breggin, G. R. (1998). *The war against children of color: Psychiatry targets inner city youth.* Monroe, ME: Common Courage Press.

Caetano, R., & Rasberry, K. (2000). Drinking and *DSM–IV* alcohol and drug dependence among White and Mexican American DUI offenders. *Journal of Studies on Alcohol, 61,* 420–426.

Carten, A. J. (1996). Mothers in recovery: Rebuilding families in the aftermath of addiction. *Social Work, 41,* 214–223.

Congressional Black Caucus Foundation. (2002). Three congressional caucuses hold historic first meeting. *CBCF News, 4,* 1, 3.

Chand, A. (2000). The overrepresentation of Black children in the child protection system: Possible causes, consequences, and solutions. *Child and Family Social Work, 5,* 67–77.

Chipungu, S. S. (1997). A value-based policy framework. In J. E. Everett, S. S. Chipungu, & B. R. Leashore (Eds.), *Child welfare: An Africentric perspective* (pp. 290–305). New Brunswick, NJ: Rutgers University Press.

Conley, D. (1999). *Being Black, living in the red: Race, wealth, and social policy in America.* Berkeley, CA: University of California Press.

Cross, T., Earle, K., & Simmons, D. (2000). Child abuse and neglect in Indian country: Policy issues. *Families in Society, 81,* 49–58.

Cureton, S. (2000). Justifiable arrests or discretionary justice: Predictors of racial arrest differentials. *Journal of Black Studies, 30,* 703–719.

Delgado, M., & Santiago, J. (1998). HIV/ AIDS in a Puerto Rican/Dominican community: A collaborative project with a botanical shop. *Social Work, 43,* 183–186.

Dixon, T. L., & Brooks, T. (2002). Rap music and rap audiences: Controversial themes, psychological effects and political resistance. *African American Research Perspectives, 8,* 106–116.

Dorfman, L., & Schiraldi, V. (2001). *Off balance: Youth, race, and crime in the news.* Washington, DC: Youth Law Center.

Fisher, R. (2001). Social action community organization: Proliferation, persistence, roots, and prospects. In J. Rothman, J. L. Erllich, & J. E. Tropman (Eds.), *Strategies of community intervention* (6th ed., pp. 350–363). Itasca, IL: Peacock.

Foster, E. M., & Furstenberg, F. F. (1999). The most disadvantaged children: Trends over time. *Social Service Review, 73*, 560–578.

Gant, L. M., Green, W., Stewart, P. A., Wheeler, D. P., & Wright, E. M. (1998). *Social workers speak out on the HIV/AIDS crisis: Voices from and to African-American communities.* Westport, CT: Praeger.

Gibbs, J., & Bankhead, T. (2001). *Preserving privilege: California politics, propositions and people of color.* Westport, CT: Praeger.

Glasser, J. (2000, May 8). And justice for some: Minority kids are treated more harshly by the law. *U.S. News and World Report,* 28.

Golden, R. (1997). *Disposable children: America's child welfare system.* Belmont, CA: Wadsworth.

Gutierrez, L., & Lewis, E. (1999). *Empowering women of color.* New York: Columbia University Press.

Gutierrez, L., Alvarez, A. R., Nemon, H., & Lewis, E. A. (1996). Multicultural community organizing: A strategy for change. *Social Work, 41*, 501–508.

Kail, B., Zayas, L., & Malgady, R. (2000). Depression, acculturation, and motivations for alcohol use among young Colombian, Dominican, and Puerto Rican men. *Hispanic Journal of Behavioral Sciences, 22*, 6477.

Kapp, S., McDonald, T., & Diamond, K. (2001). The path to adoption for children of color. *Child Abuse and Neglect, 25*, 215–230.

Lorde, A. (1984). *Sister outsider: Essays and speeches by Audre Lorde.* New York: The Crossing Press.

Martinez, E. (1998). Beyond Black/White: The racisms of our time. In R. Delgado & J. Stefancic (Eds.), *The Latino/a condition: A critical reader* (pp. 466–477). New York: New York University Press.

Mauer, M. (1999). *Race to incarcerate: The sentencing project.* New York: The New Press.

Nielsen, A. (2000). Examining drinking patterns among Hispanic groups: Results from a national survey. *Journal of Studies on Alcohol, 61*, 301–310.

Richie, B. E. (1996). *Compelled to crime: The gender entrapment of battered black women.* New York: Routledge.

Sales, Jr., W. W., & Bush, R. (1997). Black and Latino coalitions: Prospects for new social movements in New York City. In J. Jennings (Ed.), *Race and politics* (pp. 135–148). New York: Verso.

Solomon, B. (1976). *Black empowerment.* New York: Columbia University Press.

Taylor, M. (2000). The influence of self-efficacy on alcohol use among American Indians. *Cultural Diversity and Ethnic Minority Psychology, 6*, 152–167.

Thompson, J. P. (1998). Universalism and deconcentration: Why race still matters in poverty and economic development. *Politics and Society, 26*, 181–219.

Venner, K., & Miller, W. (2001). Progression of alcohol problems in a Navajo sample. *Journal of Studies on Alcohol, 62*, 158–165.

Weaver, H. N., & White, B. J. (1999). Protecting the future of indigenous children and nations: An examination of the Indian Child Welfare Act. *Journal of Health and Social Policy, 10*, 35–50.

Wilson, W. J. (2000). Rising inequality and the case for coalition politics. *Annals of the American Academy of Political and Social Science, 568*, 78–90.

Chapter Fourteen

Social Work's Commitment to Social Justice and Social Policy

King E. Davis

In the first chapter in this book, it was proposed that the Naturalization Act of 1790, at least initially, narrowly outlined the parameters or desired features of American citizenship. For the most part, the Naturalization Act decreed that the privileges of citizenship and the right to vote would be enjoyed only by wealthy White men (Naturalization Act, 1790). The "founding fathers" assumed that only White men of wealth would have sufficient vested interest in building and protecting the emerging nation's infrastructure and institutions and disengaging them from British influence. Thus, citizenship and the right to vote for most other populations of Americans were withheld well into the 20th century. Of equal significance in the Naturalization Act of 1790, however, was the explicit agreement that the most important mechanisms of democratic government (voting, holding office, and creating public policy) should be left permanently in the hands of a relatively small portion of the populace. In subsequent policy instruments, including the United States Constitution and decisions of the Supreme Court, the association between public policy, governing, and wealth was clearly articulated. Legislative action by America's founders guaranteed that their own ethnic and social class characteristics would be reflected in the policies and governance structures they created.

Five important issues did not receive sufficient consideration in the Naturalization Act of 1790 and subsequent debate over the direction of public policies through the end of the 20th century. Largely these five issues, and the disparities that stem from them, form the content and discussion in the chapters included in this book. These issues include: (a) the long-term biopsychosocial effect that circumscribing public policy and governing around wealth, maleness, and whiteness would have on American people who were poor, female, disabled, or members of one of several populations of color covered in this book; (b) the nature of future relationships between powerful White men and others in the population (women, for example) once legislation reinforced and legitimized White male dominance and gave it an air of permanency; (c) the risk to economic equality inherent in developing an intense sense of ownership and privilege by a single class of men who were allowed to monopolize American social institutions; (d) the resistance by this class of men to the ongoing efforts of oppressed groups to reduce the monopolization of government and to increase their inclusiveness and participation in society; and (e) the effect of monopolization on the cherished principles and values on which American democracy was founded. Collectively, these five policy issues are hypothesized as creating and sustaining the disparities in life conditions that affect the majority of social work's clients.

These five issues hold important challenges for the foundation of social work at the start of the 21st century as it seeks to further implement its social justice mandate in an environment in which groups of color feel harmed by the vagaries of current and past public policy. This final chapter underscores the importance of public policy in social work education by examining: (a) the parallels between social workers and consumers; (b) the illusiveness of the concept of social justice; (c) how social justice can be taught in schools of social work; and (d) the important linkages between social justice and clinical social work.

Parallels in Social Work: Gender, Color, and Power

One of the most consistent features in the century-old journey of the social work profession is the realization that the majority of social workers are women who share a major defining characteristic with the people they serve: a relative powerlessness reflected in severe political and economic constraints. In 1910, when the first school of social work opened at Columbia University, its women faculty and students were not allowed to vote in New York State or in federal elections; nor were they able to run for or hold any elective office in the United States (Klein, 1971). In some states, too, women could not own real property or engage in business and commerce. Up to 1919, Congress and the courts had rejected repeated efforts by women to gain access to the ballot. Women, who dominated the emerging social work discipline, could not directly influence the selection of issues in need of legislation nor could they affect the content, direction, or value base of public policy that affected them and their clients. Although early social work theory identified the environment as a causative factor in social problems, social workers could not directly affect the political processes that gave sustenance to such an ethnically adverse environment.

Many social work clients also could not participate in most phases of governance at the local, state, or national level at the turn of the 20th century. Although African American men (rather than women) had been granted the titular right to vote in 1885, that right was of limited merit because the states' rights doctrine effectively denied them the vote. Efforts to register or vote by African American men could bring threats, assaults, or loss of jobs or life. Social workers' efforts to create major changes in public policy were branded as socialistic (Poen, 1979).

The harshness of the responses to social justice advocacy could have led to the conclusion to redirect the movement. In general, people of color and women learned quickly that efforts to secure their right to participate in the formulation of social policy were perceived by the majority population as a threat to the status quo and the monopolization of power and concentration of resources. For social workers, the barriers to policy participation may have made it more acceptable to focus on internal psychological changes in the individual, solidifying the professional status of the discipline, while taking substantially less risk to change those policies that were instrumental in developing and maintaining oppressive conditions and disparities. However, public policy is viewed by many social scientists as one of the most salient causes and cures of the ubiquitous social ills that mark the life conditions of most social work clients, particularly those of color (Day, 1989; Gil, 1970; Schiele, 1997). Austin (1997) proposes that the difficulty of confronting rigid public policies in the early part of the century brought about "tension" in the vision, mission, and educational direction of the field of social work that has carried over into the 21st century. Although seen as a policy profession, social work seems to attract few students with this focus as their main area of interest for practice.

It is clear that women (professional and lay) and people of color were actively and deliberately excluded from participation in almost all phases of public policy formulation during some of the most important formative and fertile stages in American history. The hybrid British-American values that guided public policy were codified in key policy documents from the first Constitutional Congress to the beginning of World War I but without the stamp of critical thought and perspective from American women or people of color (Sapiro, 1986). These barriers are critical examples of the denial of social justice that has historically linked the lower status of social workers with the lower status of most recipients of its services. More than any other profession, social work and its client base have increasingly become comprised of categories of Americans who have the shortest and most contested history of obtaining and exercising their right to vote. In addition, these groups have historically received the least amount of societal support for seeking or holding public office.

One reason proposed for the relative powerless status of social work in public policy is the negative societal response to women as prospective citizens, voters, employees, political office holders, and property owners. As the major recipients of specific social welfare services (e.g., Aid to Families With Dependent Children) that have been marked and distorted by the stigma and myth surrounding personal responsibility for poverty and dependency, women face further rejection. This was seen in the rationale for and language in the welfare reform amendments in 1996.

It is proposed here that the relative powerless status of social workers, their clients, and the legacy of their imposed absence from public policy formulation have hampered the ability of the profession to solve the problems of social justice or ground the social justice vision needed by its clients of color from the beginning of the century. Of equal importance, it seems likely that the negative societal reaction in the past century to the profession, its predominately female workforce, and its stigmatized clients may have caused the profession to underdevelop its theory, research, methods, and investment in public policy education and practice in social work education programs. In-depth study and concentration on public policy is more apt to be a part of the curriculum in schools of public affairs and programs in public policy than in social work programs. In 1991, it was reported (Gibelman & Schervish, 1993) that less than 1% of the membership of National Association of Social Workers were involved in social policy as the primary source of their employment and income.

Examples of the extent and constancy of the exclusion of women social workers and their clients from participation in public policy formulation are found in national data from 1795 to 2000 on the composition of the U.S. Senate and the Supreme Court (U.S. Senate, 2001b). These data are helpful in understanding the nature of the relative powerlessness that has characterized the involvement of women social workers and women generally in the formulation and modification of public policy in this century.

Between 1901 and 2000, approximately 1,400 persons were elected or appointed to serve in the U.S. Senate. However, only 31 women (2.21% of the total) were either elected or appointed to the U.S. Senate during this 100-year period (U.S. Senate, 2001). Part of the explanation for this gap in senatorial representation by women stems from deliberate public policies that disallowed women from holding elective office or voting until after the Nineteenth Amendment to the Constitution was passed in 1919.

The first woman to hold a senate seat was Rebecca L. Felton from Georgia. Felton was appointed to fill a vacancy in 1922 at age 87. However, the term she was appointed to fill lasted only 2 days. Hattie Caraway of Arkansas became the first woman actually elected to the senate. She was initially appointed to complete the term of her deceased husband but subsequently won election in 1932 and 1938. Margaret Chase Smith of Maine was also appointed to complete the unexpired term of her deceased husband but was elected to the Senate in 1949 and served until 1973, the longest term for a woman in American history. Until Nancy Kassenbaum of Kansas was elected by popular vote in 1978, all of the women who served in the Senate had initially filled (and preserved) seats formerly occupied by a husband or were appointed by their husbands (while serving as governor). More than half of all women who have served in the Senate did so for symbolic terms of 1 year of less. Only three women have served more than one term, and 14 of the 17 women who have served in the past 30 years were elected between 1992 and 2001. Clearly, the influence and participation of women in the U.S. Senate is of relatively recent origin. Barbara Mikulski of Maryland and Debbie Stabenow of Michigan are the only social workers to serve in the U.S. Senate. By 2000, women held 13% of the seats in the Senate, a significant increase over their number in 1901 but significantly less than their majority proportion (51%) of the population of the United States (U.S. Senate, 2001b).

Including the abbreviated reconstruction period after the Civil War, only four African Americans have been elected to the U.S. Senate. Of these, only one African American woman (Carol Mosely Braun of Illinois) in U.S. history has been elected to the U.S. Senate. She served only one full term. Ed Brooke of Massachusetts was elected to the Senate in 1967 and served until 1979. When these numbers are compared to the overall number of Senate members elected between 1901 and 2000, it is clear that African Americans have not been elected consistent with their proportion (13%) of the population of the United States. In 2003, there were no African American members of the Senate (U.S. Senate, 2001a).

Five Asian Americans (0.003% of the total) were elected to the U.S. Senate between 1901 and 2000. Of these, four were elected from the state of Hawaii. Three Native Americans have been elected to the U.S. Senate in the past 100 years, whereas three Hispanics have been elected to the Senate since its inception. Of the three Hispanics elected, all three have represented the state of New Mexico (U.S. Senate, 2001a).

The composition of the U.S. Supreme Court, a second major body that influences public policy is also worth examining. From 1795 to 2001, 16 White men were appointed as the chief justice by various presidents. During these years, 107 persons have been appointed to serve on the Supreme Court (including the chief justices). Of this number, only two women and two African American men have been appointed to the Court (Infoplease, 2001).

Obviously, no women or people of color have been elected as either president or vice president in the nation's history. When Elizabeth Dole announced her candidacy for president in 1999, her husband, Senator Bob Dole, expressed reservations about her candidacy and indicated his support for a White male candidate.

The history of the development of social work in the United States shows distinct parallels in a number of areas between social workers and the clients they serve. An overriding issue throughout this history has been how women would define and advance the issue of social justice for themselves as social workers, women, and for the people of color who disproportionately use social work services. Social work increasingly chose clinical services as opposed to reform as the major route for promoting change.

Conceptualizing Social Justice

Historically, the concept of social justice in social work has been easier to define by its absence and its potential rather than by its conceptual clarity or understanding. We seem to know social justice more intimately and passionately when it is absent, denied, reduced, circumvented, threatened, or violently terminated.

The meaning of and need for social justice in social work was associated closely with the desegregation goals of the civil rights movement during the 1960s and earlier in the century with the plight of European immigrants, the urban poor, the mentally ill, and the hungry in America. Although noted in the early part of the century, it was the presence of virulent racism and urban poverty in the 1960s that gave social work part of its passion and platform for social change, action, advocacy, and reform, albeit time-limited and controversial (Ross, 1978; Schiele, 1997). The presence of segregated schools, housing, and public accommodations and the obturation of voting rights for Blacks, Indians, Japanese, Chinese, and Mexicans were so explicitly in contradiction to constitutional guarantees that the meaning of social justice could be discerned as the eradication of such conditions. Social injustice could be defined easily as the absence of civil rights, as demonstrated by the main empirical referent of segregation in varied forms (including internment camps and reservations). In this regard, social justice could be conceptualized as synonymous with racial justice. However, as legally sanctioned segregation ended, the definition of and overt need for actions to guarantee racial justice became more abstract. As violations of rights became more subtle and institutionalized, social justice seemed to become a more elusive and controversial concept in social work and the sustained involvement required to affect policy formulation declined generally in the society (Abramovitz, 1991; McMahon & Allen-Meares, 1992; Pinderhughes, 1989; Swenson, 1998).

The close association between racial justice and social justice may have also made it more difficult to generalize beyond African Americans to other groups, whose current socioeconomic status was not overtly tied to a protracted history of legal segregation. For some groups (women, gays, the disabled, immigrants, Mexicans, Native Americans, and Asians) whose histories have been equally as oppressive as that of Africans but may not reflect a period of legal segregation, there may be less acceptance in American society (and even among Blacks) that their circumstances are indicative of an absence of social justice and warrant "affirmative action" as a remedy (Hamblin, 1996; Swenson, 1998). These differences in life histories may have limited the ability of these groups of color to develop and sustain effective coalitions and networks that could effectively challenge social policies en masse.

Defining social justice and participating in sustained advocacy to achieve it in the more conservative post-segregation era in America represents a major opportunity for the social work profession. Support for such action comes from the accrediting bodies that require social work schools and graduates not only to study social justice but also to participate actively in its achievement and maintenance. This renewed opportunity challenges the social work profession to reexamine the meaning and place of social justice and social policy in its ethos, theory, education, and practice. A number of authors have tried to clarify the concept of social justice and the central role it plays in social work education and practice.

Saleebey (1990) proposed that there are four interrelated factors that constitute the existential *raison d'être* of the social work profession. These include indignation, inquiry, focused compassion, and social justice. Saleebey considers social justice the most important of these four factors in delineating the historic and future direction of the field. However, despite the centrality of social justice in the profession, he suggests that clarifying the meaning of social justice has been a necessary, albeit an elusive, task. To add to the understanding and debate about the meaning of social justice, Saleebey describes social justice in relationship to how resources and opportunities within a society are distributed. Where resource distribution and opportunity are based on need and are "open to all," Saleebey concludes that social justice is evident. This perspective reflects the view of distributive justice as defined by Rawls (1971). Additionally, in Saleebey's perspective, social justice precludes the arbitrary use of power, restrictive policies, and oppressive practices to maintain the current misdistribution of resources and opportunities within a society. Of importance here is the realization that although Saleebey concludes that social justice is at the existential epicenter of the social work field, he notes that the concept has heretofore lacked clear definition.

Reeser and Leighninger (1990) found numerous references in the history of social work to confirm that social justice has been an inveterate goal of the profession. Their work not only traces this history but also the long-term effort to incorporate social justice into the corpus of social work education. These authors note that social work's commitment to the ideal of social justice has origins in the profession's collaborative efforts to remove unfair conditions, practices, and policies toward the poor. (These, too, were conditions faced by many social workers.) To these authors, social work seems to be synonymous with social justice. In some ways, their treatment of social justice parallels the perspective of Gil (1970), when he sees social work as devoid of meaning without social justice and social change at its core. Gil (1990) and Reeser and Leighninger (1990) suggest that social work's commitment to social justice must be operationalized in the social change methods taught in its schools and found throughout social work practice in advocacy, empowerment, community organization, community development, policy development and analysis, political action, and related macro-level strategies to produce change in social institutions. The emphasis placed on macro-level strategies is supported by Figueira-McDonough (1993), who proposes that it is through policy practice and social action that social work can help achieve the goal of social justice.

Although Reeser and Leighninger (1990) provide a logical base for connecting social justice and social work, they do not provide a working definition on which to build curriculum or through which the profession can measure its progress toward social justice. Gil (1990) also makes a strong case for linking social justice and social change strategies in social work, but the conceptual definition of social justice eludes his analysis. Figueira-McDonough (1993) makes an effort to fill this definitional void by assessing social justice as a value or goal that involves "a commitment to ensure equal access to all basic social goals" (pp. 180).

The importance that the social work profession attaches to the elusive concept of social justice is also seen in its prominence in the bylaws of the Council on Social Work Education (CSWE). These bylaws stress that "social justice is to permeate all program activities of the Council" (CSWE, 1989). CSWE's emphasis on social justice is further indicated in the standards that it establishes to determine the accreditation of its member programs. CSWE has two accreditation standards that relate to social justice issues. One of these standards focuses on issues of cultural diversity, whereas the other focuses on women. In the diversity standard, the CSWE indicates that it is important for programs to recognize and teach students about the pluralistic society in which they live, as well as the implications for practice. CSWE also stresses the importance of understanding the common features of racial and ethnic diversity and the contradictory responses of American society to this diversity. CSWE encourages social work education programs to develop their curricula in such ways that they reflect the diversity that is evident in their regions. In its standard on women, CSWE is less explicit. Here, it encourages programs to include content in the curriculum that identifies the changes in the roles and responsibilities of women in American society. Programs are expected to teach students the implications of such changes for social work practice. CSWE also encourages programs to include information through-out the curriculum about the contributions of women to society and the need for the elimina-tion of gender bias.

Further evidence of the importance that social justice issues have within the profession is found in CSWE's (2001) *Educational Policy and Accreditation Standards*. The most explicit state-ment that the Council makes here is the requirement that social work education programs include content about people of color and women in the curriculum. Although CSWE does not dictate how member schools must accomplish this goal, it is firm that to be accredited, a program must have this content in its curriculum. Furthermore, CSWE shows the relationship between this content and the intellectual traditions of the social work profession. For CSWE, social justice is a reflection of the basic values of the social work profession and is replete in is history.

Although social justice is a major value in social work practice and education, the diffusion of its meaning and its relative dormancy since the end of *de jure* segregation has made it difficult for social work education programs to clearly define and implement the concept in curricula or for the practice community to pursue its achievement in clinical or policy practice (Figueira-McDonough, 1993; Wakefield, 1988; Williams, 1993). The absence of a working definition of social justice, a cardinal concept in social work, seems to reinforce the concerns expressed by Piotrowski (1971) that an absence of definitions of critical concepts that form the intellectual and philosophical base of a scientific field can deter and slow its maturity as a science. The absence of a working definition that undergirds the curriculum stimulates the need for an effort here to propose such a definition and show how it illuminates issues of social policy and people of color in the curriculum.

For several decades, efforts have been made in a number of fields to reach a consensus on a definition of social justice, yet no true consensus has been reached nor does a consensus seem to be within reach. Van Soest (1995) provides a comprehensive guide for integrating social justice throughout social work education. However, this effort is likely to have a reduced effect because social justice is not defined within the compendium. Beverly and McSweeney (1987) describe such an effect on the effort to develop a set of coherent social policies in the United States in the absence of a clear definition of social justice. Beverly and McSweeney (1987) view the wide degree of variability in the definitions of social justice as a key factor in explaining the wide variation in social policies. In an earlier article, Van Soest (1994) acknowledges how libertarian, utilitarian, and egalitarian perspectives of social justice offer different conceptualizations of social justice and the policies that emanate from these views.

Efforts to define social justice range from broad philosophical statements by Aristotle (Hospers, 1992), to those more narrowly circumscribed to the role of government (Hospers, 1992). The philosopher John Rawls (1971) has made the most significant efforts to define dis-tributive justice, while indicating that social justice is an unclear term. Rawls tends to view dis-tributive justice as based on such acquired social characteristics and values as merit, wealth, status, and position, whereas more recent policy perspectives (Barker, 1987; Gil, 1990) tend to conceptualize social justice in terms of inherent linkages to such structural characteristics as equality of opportunity and access to societal resources. More conservative social policy views (Glazer, 1988; Hospers, 1992) propose that to define social justice in redistributive and equality terms unfairly penalizes those who are most industrious while obligating the federal govern-ment to implement equality of opportunity policies. Part of the current national debate seems to be a return to this divisive and unproductive philosophical argument about social justice and the proper role of government in affirming opportunity for individuals and groups.

The position taken in this chapter is that justice becomes social when it is applied to the interaction and exchanges between individuals (as well as groups and communities) and the needs-meeting social institutions in a society. It flows logically that where such interaction and exchanges are delimited by personal characteristics (race, age, religion, gender, disability), affected individuals are likely to have an increased risk of unmet primary needs; altered self-esteem, group identity, and motivation; and higher probabilities of social problems and dependency. These risk factors tend to bring such individuals into contact with social agencies. In some instances, these social agencies focus their services on the individuals, whereas in other instances the plea is made for agency resources to be directed toward societal causes (Williams, 1993).

Based on the connection among social justice, social policy, and social work as discussed here, the following definition is proffered as a point of departure from which to ground the concept in social work education: Social justice is a basic value and desired goal in democratic societies and includes equitable and fair access to all social institutions, laws, resources, opportunities, rights, goods, and services for all groups and individuals without arbitrary limitations or barriers based on observations or interpretations of the value of differences in age, color, culture, physical or mental disability, education, gender, income, language, national origin, race, religion, or sexual orientation.

When this definition of social justice is used as the operating framework, principle, or concept in the curriculum, it means that social work education is committed to building and implementing the curriculum and all other processes of its education efforts around this basic value. What is further implied is that a school's faculty is also committing themselves—as articulated in the National Association of Social Workers (1996) *Code of Ethics*—to actions to help achieve social justice beyond intellectual abstractions. Social justice operationally means the following in social work education:

- commitment to the goal of social justice by social work faculty and administration as well as participation in efforts to ensure its achievement;

- inclusion of social justice as a key value in the mission, vision, or educational goals of social work education programs;

- inclusion of social justice values across all elements or components of the curriculum (formal and informal) course content, teaching, readings, research, and field practice; schools select what design (infusion or single course) they believe will achieve this goal;

- inclusion of social justice values in the conduct of university, school, community, and professional service activities;

- inclusion of social justice values across all educational programs or levels of education: BSW, MSW, PhD, and continuing education, as well as across all specialty or concentration areas and across all courses;

- inclusion of social justice values in processes associated with recruitment, hiring, evaluation, and promotion and retention of faculty;

- inclusion of social justice values in the recruitment, admission, advising, and graduation of students;

- the presence of social justice values in licensure and the ethical base of social work practice and in ongoing accreditation and reaffirmation of social work education programs

The Nexus Between Clinical and Social Reform Efforts

The final two issues to be addressed are to identify the linkages between clinical and social reform methods and the curriculum implications of social policy studies for social work education. The long-term struggle by diverse groups of color in the United States has been and remains an intense struggle by American citizens to obtain the benefits of equitable and fair social policies. Signs and symptoms of this social policy struggle for people of color are found in the previous chapters in this book that focus on disparities in wealth, health, employment, housing, education, and life span. In addition, there have been the not-so-inconsequential racial divisions, conflicts, and violence directed toward these American citizens in their quest for "just" policies. In the perspective of people of color, the content and application of former and prevailing social policies curtail their ability to participate safely and profitably in almost all phases of American life. When policies that cover economics, politics, education, immigration, and health are included, the magnitude of the challenge these groups confront becomes clearer. We must also recognize that the rudiments of these social policies and their goals were established long before people of color were considered citizens by the states or in possession of rights by the courts. Thus, their initial efforts to be included in the social policy process were viewed by the established power structure as unwanted, illegal, un-American, or Communist, and met with resistance supported by the courts and federal law enforcement agencies.

Historically, people of color have applied a number of direct challenges, with varying success, to alter inimical social policies across America: individual lawsuits, class action suits, work stoppages, boycotts, sit-ins, marches, international appeals, and sustained protest. However, less frequently have these groups challenged policy in the social work literature (Schiele, 1997). The social policy responses and reactions to these efforts, although considerable, can be described as "painfully" incremental and resisted. Substantive changes in numerous social policy areas did occur in response to sustained protest over a 100-year span, but were not consistent, nor without substantial expenditures of energy and loss of human life. At the start of the 21st century, major disparities in almost all social indicators remain, although they have been reduced substantially from the figures noted between 1790 and 1900 (U.S. Department of Commerce, 1978; U.S. Census Bureau, 2000, 2002).

Although a constant intellectual, emotional, and political debate about theory remains, it is difficult to give any credence to a view that ascribes the causation of America's long-term social ills to the supposed lower motivation, intelligence, or morals on the part of those persons who live on the precipice of starvation and premature death. It is equally difficult to give stock to the idea that social class, race, gender, language, or religion are now somehow inconsequential variables in understanding the perpetuation of poverty in the United States. Poverty and its attendant conditions are too ubiquitous worldwide, and found too frequently across racial lines, to propose that there is a semi-voluntary selection of these conditions by people of color who reflect them disproportionately. Under these circumstances, it seems incongruent for social work to pursue a singular methodological path or to allow the long-held division and imbalance in the number of students who select one method over another to continue.

The roots of social problems of the magnitude witnessed in the past century remain the complex interplay of public policies, materialistic values, and monopoly of power that have so restricted the economic opportunities of lower socioeconomic groups, resulting in long-term economic and social dislocation. Concomitantly, it is not unrealistic to conclude that these primary conditions would be accompanied by a host of social, economic, and psychological problems. In fact, over time the depth of despair, hopelessness, and psychoeconomic depression could easily become intervening variables that help sustain or cause these conditions anew. Nevertheless, it is important not to conclude that these populations are "damaged" and thus only in need of "treatment" but rather that the policies themselves are damaging and in need of social work intervention and reform.

The long-term struggle by people of color has focused primarily on bringing about changes in the full spectrum of American public policies, the policy formulation process, and the cumulative effects on individuals. This focus suggests that the division between clinical and community approaches in social work practice is a false dichotomy as far as the needs of communities and people of color are concerned. It also implies that a shift in priority toward administration of social services agencies or traditional community planning is of far less consequence and value to communities of color with such a long history of economic and political oppression. It seems clear that the nexus needed between clinical social work and community approaches is social policy and a combination of complex skills and methods based on a vision of a "just" society. Communities of color need a social work discipline that is far more focused on its vision and goals than the exclusivity of one method or theory over another. Whenever a combination of social work methods can be applied to this vision, the effect is likely to be greater than when applied alone.

The historical unjust conditions faced by social workers and their clients underscore the need for social reform efforts, major social change, legal challenges to the federal and state constitutions, and marked changes in the content and implementation of other public policies, particularly at the state level. These challenges should not exclude the possibility of financial reparations for damages and losses experienced by these groups. Many people of color need social workers willing to help them challenge the status quo that denied them legal and civil rights. These groups also needed social workers that will advocate for an integrated and open society and an end to segregation, discrimination, and bias. Additionally, there is a need for ongoing culturally competent treatment and prevention services of all kinds, combined with a policy focus. For many groups of color, it was not a matter of "settling in " or "adjusting to" a new society as a voluntary immigrant. For these clients, settlement could never occur without drastic changes in the status of American social policy that denied them citizenship and human rights. Policy practice, advocacy, and social change efforts were instrumental in changing the shared status of social workers and their clients. By selecting theory and methods or practitioners that placed limited attention on change in public policy, social work risked distancing itself from people of color, the reality of their circumstances, and the role of structural economic factors, as opposed to personal factors, as causes of poverty and oppression.

The status of women, social work, and people of color at the start of the 21st century seems to provide adequate justification for a renewed emphasis on social policy in social work education. Recent changes in managed health care, managed child welfare, welfare reform, Social Security, immigration, and related social policies all point clearly to the role that social policy plays in social work. It seems as though social work cannot afford to allow a *laissez-faire* approach to recruitment or a continued fixation on methodological purity to drive its future practitioners toward clinical practice alone—the direction in which it seems to be headed. The primary reason is the constancy of policy as the key variable not only in charting the destiny of the poor but of social work as well. History shows that clearly.

The chapters in this book suggest that social work must adopt a set of strategic thoughts and plans that will stimulate its schools to venture forward toward greater exploration and creativity in social policy. This can and must include a cross-pollination of methods, theory, research, field placements, and action. Social work schools need to consider expanding courses in some of the areas shown in Chart 1.

Full implementation of the curriculum and program development opportunities that seem to be built into the *Educational Policy and Accreditation Standards* may offer social work the opportunity to build a conceptual bridge between its major and minor methods in such a way as to give social work a heightened sense of identity, a goal that so far seems to have eluded the field for most of the 20th century (CSWE, 2001). The 21st century is a period of unbridled opportunity for social work to deepen its social policy well. These efforts must include developing opportunities for social workers in greater numbers to hold public office at every level, lobbying for new directions in public policy, and participating actively in every phase of policy development. If history shows anything, it shows that there is a relationship between what policies dot the landscape and the level of activity by those who are benefiting from or targets of those policies.

References

Abramovitz, M. (1991). Putting an end to doublespeak about race, gender, and poverty: An annotated glossary for social workers. *Social Work, 36*, 380–384.

Austin, D. M. (1997). The institutional development of social work education: The first 100 years and beyond. *Journal of Social Work Education, 33*, 599–611.

Barker, R. L. (1987). *Social work dictionary.* Silver Spring, MD: NASW Press.

Beverly, D., & McSweeney, E. A. (1987). *Social welfare and social justice.* Englewood Cliffs, NJ: Prentice Hall.

Council on Social Work Education. (1989). *Bylaws.* Alexandria, VA: Author.

Chart 1. Suggested Courses to Promote Social Change

Community Development	Economic Justice	Nonprofit Management	Social Policy	Mixed Change Strategies
Advocacy and leadership	Asset development	Board and volunteer development	Applied social policy	Alliance building
Community analysis/ demographic change	Economic development	Developing non-profits	Legislative formulation processes	Integrative seminar
Community development and planning	Economic justice	Fiscal management and finance	Models of analysis	Mixed social/ economic change methods
Community organizing	Investment strategies	Fundraising methods	Outcome evaluation	Social action methods
Empowerment strategies	Macro-economics	Grant writing	Policy change methods	Successful program design
Housing development	Social marketing	Nonprofit management	Policy theory	Urban versus rural strategies

Council on Social Work Education (2001). *Educational policy and accreditation standards.* Alexandria, VA: Author.

Day, P. J. (1989). *A new history of social welfare.* Englewood Cliffs, NJ: Prentice Hall.

Figueira-McDonough, J. (1993). Policy practice: The neglected side of social work intervention. *Social Work, 38,* 179–188.

Gibelman, M., & Schervish, P. H. (1993). *The social work labor force as reflected in the NASW membership.* Washington, DC: National Association of Social Workers.

Gil, D. (1970). A systematic approach to policy analysis. *Social Service Review, 44,* 411–426.

Gil, D. (1990). Implications of conservative tendencies for practice and education in social welfare. *Journal of Sociology and Social Welfare, XVIII,* 5–28.

Glazer. N. (1988). *The limits of social policy.* Cambridge, MA: Harvard University Press.

Grace, A. B. (2002). *Does Trent Lott speak for the South?* Retrieved February 10, 2004, from http://www.alternet.org/print.html?StoryID=14737

Hamblin, K. (1996). *Pick a better country.* New York: Simon & Schuster.

Hospers, J. (1992). The libertarian manifesto. In J. P. Sterba (Ed.), *Justice: Alternative political perspectives* (pp. 41–53). Belmont, CA: Wadsworth.

Infoplease. (2001). *United States Supreme Court Membership.* Retrieved January 15, 2004, from http://www.infoplease.com/ce6/historya0861367

Klein, P. (1971). *From philanthropy to social welfare: An American cultural perspective.* San Francisco: Jossey-Bass.

McMahon, A., & Allen-Meares, P. (1992). Is social work racist? A content analysis of recent literature. *Social Work, 37,* 533–539.

National Association of Social Workers. (1996). *Code of ethics.* Washington, DC: Author.

Naturalization Act, ch. 13, 1 stat. 103, 104 (1790).

Pinderhughes, E. (1989). *Understanding race, ethnicity, and power: The key to efficacy in clinical practice.* New York: Free Press.

Piotrowski, Z. (1971). A basic system of all sciences. In H. Vetter & B. Smith (Eds.), *Personality theory: A source book* (pp. 2–18). New York: Meridith.

Poen, M. M. (1979). *Harry S. Truman versus the medical lobby: The genesis of Medicare.* Columbia: University of Missouri Press.

Rawls, J. (1971). *A theory of justice.* Cambridge, MA: Harvard University.

Reeser, L. C., & Leighninger, L. (1990). Back to our roots: Towards a specialization in social justice. *Journal of Sociology and Social Welfare, XVII,* 69–89.

Ross, E. L. (1978). *Heritage in Black social welfare 1860–1930.* Metuchen, NJ: Scarecrow.

Saleebey, D. (1990). Philosophical disputes in social work: Social justice denied. *Journal of Sociology and Social Welfare, 17,* 29–40.

Sapiro, V. (1986). The gender basis of American social policy. *Political Science Quarterly, 101,* 221–238.

Schiele, J. H. (1997). An Afrocentric perspective on social welfare philosophy and policy. *Journal of Sociology and Social Welfare, 34,* 21–39.

Swenson, C. R. (1998). Clinical social work's contribution to a social justice perspective. *Social Work, 43,* 527–537.

U.S. Census Bureau. (2001). Overview of race and Hispanic origin 2000. Census 2000 Brief. Retrieved November 18, 2003, from http://www.census.gov/prod/2001pubs/c2kbr01-1.pdf

U.S. Department of Commerce. (1978). *The social and economic status of the Black population in the United States: An historical view, 1790–1978* (Series P-23 ed.) (Vol. 80). Washington, DC: Bureau of the Census.

U.S. Senate. (2001a). *Minorities in the Senate.* Retrieved Febraury 4, 2004, from http://www.senate.gov/artandhistory/history/common/briefing/minority_senators.htm

U.S. Senate. (2001b). U.S. Senate statistics: Women in the Senate. Retrieved February 4, 2004, from http://www.senate.gov/artandhistory/history/common/briefing/women_senators.htm

Van Soest, D. (1994). Strange bedfellows: A call for reordering national priorities from three social justice perspectives. *Social Work, 39,* 710–717.

Van Soest, D. (1995). Multiculturalism and social work education: The non-debate about competing perspectives. *Journal of Social Work Education, 31,* 55–66.

Wakefield, J. C. (1988). Psychotherapy, distributive justice and social work. *Social Service Review, 62,* 187–210.

Williams, L. F. (1993). Revisiting the mission of social work at the end of the century. In D. M. Pearson (Ed.), *Perspectives on equity and justice in social work* (pp. 51–66). Alexandria, VA: Council on Social Work Education.

Contributors

Tricia B. Bent-Goodley is associate professor, School of Social Work, Howard University, Washington, DC.

Namkee G. Choi is professor, School of Social Work, University of Texas at Austin.

Llewellyn J. Cornelius is professor, School of Social Work, University of Maryland, Baltimore, MD.

Sandra Edmonds Crewe is associate professor, School of Social Work, Howard University, Washington, DC.

King E. Davis is executive director, Hogg Foundation for Mental Health and Robert Lee Sutherland Chair in Mental Health and Social Policy, University of Texas at Austin.

Meripa T. Godinet is joint associate research faculty with the University of Hawai'i and Adult Mental Health Division, Manoa, HI.

Manuel Gonzalez is assistant professor, Fordham University, Graduate School of Social Service, New York, NY.

Catherine Levandosky is human resources specialist, Department of the Army, South Central Pavilion Personnel Operations, Redstone Arsenal, AL.

Eunjeong Kim is assistant professor, Department of Social Welfare, Keimyung University, Daegu, South Korea.

Yolanda Q. Mayo is associate professor, Hunter College School of Social Work, City University of New York, New York, NY.

Ruth McRoy is associate dean for research and director, Center for Social Work Research at the University of Texas at Austin.

Halaevalu Ofahengaue-Vakalahi is BASW program director, School of Social Work, San Francisco State University.

Larry P. A. Ortiz is associate professor, School of Social Work, University of Maryland, Baltimore, MD.

Ann Pollock is research assistant, School of Social Work, University of Texas at Austin.

Josie Romero is president, National Latino Behavioral Health Care Association, San Jose, CA.

Lonnie Snowden is professor, School of Social Welfare, University of California at Berkeley.

Barbara Solomon is professor, School of Social Work, University of Southern California.

Nkechi Taifa is senior policy analyst, Open Society Institute/Open Society Policy Center, Washington, DC.

Ethleen Iron Cloud-Two Dogs is mental health program director, Wakanyeja Wape Tokeca, Lakota Nation, Porcupine, SD.

Rebecca Weaver is research assistant, School of Social Work, University of Texas at Austin.

About the Editors

King E. Davis, PhD, MSW

King E. Davis is executive director of the Hogg Foundation for Mental Health in Austin, TX. Since January 2000 he has held the Robert Lee Sutherland Chair in Mental Health and Social Policy at the University of Texas at Austin School of Social Work, where he received the Excellence in Teaching Award in February 2001. In February 2002, he received the lifetime achievement award from the Council on Social Work Education. Davis earned a doctorate from the Florence G. Heller School for Social Policy and Management at Brandeis University in 1971. He holds a baccalaureate and a master of social work (concentration in mental health) from California State University, Fresno. Davis served as commissioner of the Virginia Department of Mental Health, Mental Retardation and Substance Abuse Services, under Governor L. Douglas Wilder from 1990 to 1994. He recently served on the U.S. Surgeon General's Workgroup on Mental Health, Culture, Race, and Ethnicity and helped write sections of the president's New Freedom Commission on Mental Health report.

Tricia B. Bent-Goodley, PhD, LICSW-C

Tricia B. Bent-Goodley is an associate professor at Howard University School of Social Work. She has published in social policy, domestic violence, criminal justice, child welfare, and African American social welfare history. She is a member of the Council on Social Work Education (CSWE) Commission on the Role and Status of Women and is policy and research consultant for the National Association of Black Social Workers (NABSW). Bent-Goodley is former chair and chief instructor of the NABSW Academy for African-Centered Social Work; past chair of the NABSW National Public Policy Institute; and prior NABSW National Student Coordinator. Bent-Goodley serves on numerous boards and local planning committees in her specialty areas. She is the editor of *African American Social Workers and Social Policy* (Haworth, 2003) and the co-editor, with King E. Davis, of *Teaching Social Policy in Social Work Education: Model Syllabi* (CSWE, 2003). Bent-Goodley earned her doctorate from Columbia University, her master of social work from the University of Pennsylvania, and her bachelor of arts in sociology from Queens College of the City University of New York. Prior to coming to Howard University, she was the director of several family violence prevention programs in Harlem, New York City, and Jamaica, New York. Bent-Goodley is proudest of being a wife and mother.

Index